HANDBOOK for CONGREGATIONAL STUDIES

Edited by
Jackson W. Carroll,
Carl S. Dudley,
and William McKinney

Contributors:

Jackson W. Carroll
Carl S. Dudley
C. Kirk Hadaway
James F. Hopewell
Speed B. Leas
William McKinney
Mary C. Mattis
Wade Clark Roof

Abingdon Press
Nashville

For James F. Hopewell

All mankind is of one Author, and is one volume; when one man dies, one chapter is not torne out of the book, but translated into a better language; and every chapter must be so translated; God employs several translators; some pieces are translated by age, some by sickness, some by warr, some by justice; but God's hand is in every translation; and his hand shall bind up all our scattered leaves again, for that Library where every book shall be open to one another.

—John Donne

HANDBOOK FOR CONGREGATIONAL STUDIES

Copyright © 1986 by Abingdon Press

Third Printing 1987

This book is printed on acid-free paper.

Library of Congress Cataloging in Publication Data

Main entry under title:

Handbook for congregational studies.

Includes bibliographies and index.
1. Parishes—Handbooks, manuals, etc. 2. Church management—Handbooks, manuals, etc. 3. Sociology, Christian—Handbooks, manuals, etc. I. Carroll, Jackson W. II. Dudley, Carl S., 1932-
III. McKinney, William, 1946—

| BV700.H36 | 1986 | 254 | 85-22831 |

ISBN 0-687-16562-8 (soft: alk. paper)

Specified excerpts *passim*, totaling approximately 800 words, from BUILDING EFFECTIVE MINISTRY: THEORY AND PRACTICE IN THE LOCAL CHURCH, edited by Carl S. Dudley. © 1983 by Carl S. Dudley. Reprinted by permission of Harper & Row.

MANUFACTURED BY THE PARTHENON PRESS AT NASHVILLE, TENNESSEE, UNITED STATES OF AMERICA

PREFACE

This handbook grows out of the life of the Project Team for Congregational Studies, an informal partnership of representatives from the Alban Institute, Auburn Theological Seminary, Candler School of Theology, Hartford Seminary, McCormick Theological Seminary, and the research offices of the Presbyterian Church (U.S.A.) and the United Church Board for Homeland Ministries.

In the past several years the Project Team for Congregational Studies has initiated a variety of activities aimed at directing new attention to the study of the local church. It sponsored, in 1982, a national conference on understanding the local church, out of which emerged the book *Building Effective Ministry: Theory and Practice in the Local Church.*[1] The team has also published two editions of a directory of researchers engaged in the study of the local church,[2] and *The Whole Church Catalog,* a collection describing tools and instruments for congregational studies.[3] In 1984 it sponsored a Congregational Studies Institute at Auburn Theological Seminary in New York City. In addition, the team is giving concerted attention in 1985 and 1986 to the role of the congregation in public life and to the relationship of the congregation to theological education. The team has been supported by the participating institutions with supplementary support from the Lilly Endowment, Inc.

In the course of its various activities the team has become aware of the volume and quality of the work being done across the United States and internationally to enhance congregational self-understanding. The team has also been impressed by the need for more effective sharing of that work across denominational and disciplinary lines. This handbook is one attempt to address that need. It draws on the work of hundreds of persons whose personal and professional commitments are to the strength and mission of the local church. At the same time, the handbook aspires to be more than a compendium of techniques for congregational study: it also offers a framework for an enriched understanding of the nature of the congregation.

The handbook emerges out of the team's effort to place the congregation itself rather than individual scholarly disciplines at the center. In this sense it is quite different from the team's earlier book, which proceeded from the disciplines to the congregation. Here the focus is on the congregation in its complexity and only secondarily on how particular approaches to congregational study can be useful in its life.

This approach required considerable consultation among the authors, the editors, and the project team. Thus the book is the product of group effort and the individual chapters are unsigned. It is appropriate, however, to identify the persons who worked to organize each of the following chapters. Chapter 1 is an invitation to congregational studies. It outlines the team's commitment to the congregation and offers a framework for understanding the congregation. The organization of the chapters is informed by that framework. Jackson W. Carroll is the primary author of chapter 1, drawing on contributions of the entire project team. Chapter 2 deals with congregational identity; its authors are Jackson W. Carroll and James F. Hopewell. Chapter 3 focuses on the congregation's context; it was prepared by William McKinney and Wade Clark Roof. Chapter 4 turns to congregational processes; its authors are Speed B. Leas and Carl S. Dudley. Chapter 5 deals with congregational program; its author is Mary C. Mattis. Chapter 6 provides an overview and introduction to some of the social scientific methods used throughout the book; its author is C. Kirk Hadaway. William McKinney is the primary author of chapter 7, the afterword.

Of the many others who made contributions to this handbook, several need to be singled out. Barbara G. Wheeler read each chapter and passed along numerous substantive and editorial comments to the editors. Loren B. Mead, H. Newton Malony and the sixty participants in the 1984 Congregational Studies Institute have assisted the project in diverse and important ways. Our respective institutions have provided encouragement and support both for this handbook and for the larger congregational studies enterprise.

We owe special thanks to the Trinity Grants Board,

Parish of Trinity Church in the city of New York, which made a generous contribution in support of this handbook and *The Whole Church Catalog*. We are grateful for the support of the Grants Board and the insightful assistance of the Rev. James F. Callaway, Jr., and Mrs. Pamela Stebbins.

Jackson W. Carroll
Carl S. Dudley
William McKinney

for the Project Team for Congregational Studies:

Jackson W. Carroll
Carl S. Dudley
Mary C. Mattis
William McKinney
Loren B. Mead
Barbara G. Wheeler

The book is dedicated to James F. Hopewell, who died just before it was completed. Jim Hopewell was a founder of the project team and a stalwart member. He was a friend, and we celebrate and miss his presence among us.

NOTES _____

1. Carl S. Dudley, ed. (San Francisco: Harper & Row, 1983).
2. Available from the Rollins Center for Church Ministries, Candler School of Theology, Atlanta, GA 30322.
3. James F. Hopewell, ed. (Washington, D.C.: Alban Institute, 1984).

CONTENTS

CONTRIBUTORS... 1

PREFACE.. 3

Chapter 1 INTRODUCTION: AN INVITATION
           TO CONGREGATIONAL STUDIES........... 7

1.1 Invitation to Congregational Studies.......... 8
1.2 A Perspective for Analyzing
     Congregations...................................... 9
1.3 Relationships Among the Four
     Dimensions... 14
1.4 Getting Started................................... 15
1.5 Theology and the Study of the
     Congregation...................................... 18
     Notes... 20

Chapter 2 IDENTITY...................................... 21

2.1 Situations... 21
2.2 Elements of Identity............................. 22
2.3 History.. 24
2.4 Heritage... 25
2.5 World View.. 32
2.6 Symbols.. 35
2.7 Ritual.. 37
2.8 Demographic Picture............................. 41
2.9 Character.. 43
2.10 Summing It Up in Story......................... 45
     Notes... 46
     For Further Reading on Identity.............. 47

Chapter 3 CONTEXT....................................... 48

3.1 Introduction...................................... 48
3.2 Getting in Touch with the Community..... 50
3.3 Demographic Data in Congregational
     Analysis... 55
3.4 Social Interaction................................ 69
3.5 The Church in the Context.................... 74
     Notes... 79
     For Further Reading on Context............. 80

Chapter 4 PROCESS....................................... 81

4.1 Introduction...................................... 81
4.2 When to Address Process Concerns........ 82
4.3 Gathering Information........................... 83

4.4 Organizational Processes........................ 86
     Notes... 107
     For Further Reading on Process............. 107
     Appendixes for Chapter 4...................... 109

Chapter 5 PROGRAM...................................... 120

5.1 Introduction...................................... 120
5.2 Getting Started with a Program Study:
     Basic Decisions................................... 121
5.3 Program Research Strategies:
     Needs Assessment............................... 123
5.4 Program Evaluation: Research Strategies.. 131
     Notes... 138
     For Further Reading on Program........... 138
     Appendixes for Chapter 5..................... 140

Chapter 6 METHODS FOR CONGREGATIONAL
           STUDIES.. 153

6.1 The Cyclical Research Process............... 153
6.2 Key Concepts..................................... 155
6.3 Designing a Research Project................. 157
6.4 Needs Analysis: The Simplest Design..... 158
6.5 The Case Study: Magnifying an
     Example.. 160
6.6 Experimental Designs:
     Tests, Comparisons, and Evaluation.... 163
6.7 Correlational Designs........................... 168
     Notes... 177
     For Further Reading on
     Methods for Congregational Studies.... 178

Chapter 7 AFTERWORD:
           THE DOUBLE CHALLENGE.................. 179

7.1 Dealing with "Messes".......................... 179
7.2 Beyond Problem Solving....................... 179
7.3 Putting It Together in the Congregation:
     The Unwritten Section......................... 179
7.4 A Second Invitation............................. 180
     Notes... 180

GENERAL APPENDIX:
           Parish Profile Inventory..................... 181

INDEX.. 191

CHAPTER I

Introduction: An Invitation to Congregational Studies

It is no small pity, and should cause us no little shame, that through our own fault, we do not understand ourselves, or know who we are—as to what good qualities there may be in our souls, or who dwells within them, or how precious they are—those are things which we seldom consider and so we trouble little about preserving the soul's beauty.

—Teresa of Avila

For congregations of the people of God, as for the individual soul whose welfare St. Teresa invokes, the good qualities within them and their relation to the world about them have all-too-often been taken for granted. Congregations have frequently been urged into action as agents of evangelization and social transformation and then written off as irrelevant because they failed to perform as desired. But the initial failure may lie not with the congregation but with those who have urged the congregation on without a sensitive understanding of its inner life and resources or of the possibilities as well as the limits placed on the congregation by the context in which God has called it into being.

This is a book which attempts to take congregations seriously in their givenness as earthen vessels through which the transcendent power of God is at work and made known (II Cor. 4:7) and through which God's purposes in the world may be realized. We seek to provide both a framework within which this givenness can be understood in a disciplined way and practical tools to facilitate such understanding. This does not mean that we are not also concerned with transformation, whether of congregations themselves or with their role as agents of transformation for individuals and society; however, we believe that this is best accomplished when we take seriously and appreciatively, through disciplined understanding, their present *being*—the good and precious qualities that are within them—as means of grace themselves that enable the transformation of congregations into what it is possible for them to *become*. Thus we begin this book with an affirmation of the centrality of congregations as vehicles for the knowledge and service of God and thus of the imperative for understanding them in their present being and their possibilities for becoming.

Congregations are embedded in the history, landscape, and mindset of North American culture. Acknowledging pressures that are brought to bear on them as they experience the tensions of living between tradition and modernity, historian Martin Marty speaks of the continuing significance of congregational ex-

pressions of Christian existence: "While efforts to establish an essential form of communal life for Christians everywhere may be futile and may limit imagination, *something like* the local assembly will remain fundamental. . . . [C]ongregations will take on varied colorings in different times or cultures, but in every case they serve to perpetuate embodiment, which is essential in the whole church."[1]

For most people in North America, congregations are the primary expressions of religion. The *Yearbook of American and Canadian Churches* for 1984 lists the existence of some 341,000 local churches in the United States alone, with almost 135 million members and an average weekly attendance in excess of 65 million adults. More individuals belong to congregations than to any other voluntary association, and they provide as much financial support for the work of the churches as is given to all other philanthropic causes combined.

Congregations influence in varied ways both the individuals who belong to them and the communities in which they are present. By the presence of their buildings, their steeples and stained glass, and in the regular gatherings of members for public worship, congregations provide symbols and occasions for trancendence of everyday life and for grounding that life in faith and hope. In services and gatherings for fellowship, congregations draw community residents out of their isolation and differences and into relationship with one another in communities of friendship and mutual support. Through their educational programs, congregations not only transmit knowledge of the faith tradition and its meaning for contemporary life but also transmit values that promote community solidarity and continuity. Historically congregations have socialized youth and newcomers, sustained persons in need, and provided various rites of passage which mark significant transitions of life: birth, puberty, marriage, and death. They have often supported community values and institutions, but at times they have challenged these values and institutions in an effort to reform or transform them in light of the congregation's convictions. Thus congregations have significance not only for the individuals who belong to them but also for the society beyond their membership.

Believing strongly in the importance of congregations for Christian existence, we aim in this book to provide ways to understand them better and to help leaders and members make faithful decisions about their ministry and mission. So we come back to St. Teresa's hopes for the individual soul and apply them to congregations. We hope to enable the discovery of what good qualities there may be in the congregation, who dwells there, and how precious it may be. We also hope to enable discovery of those opportunities for ministry open to it in the place in which God has called it into being. In these discoveries lie the hope of preserving beauty, goodness, truth, and faithful witness in congregational life and mission.

1.1 Invitation to Congregational Studies

In the broadest sense, everyone does "research." That is, everyone gathers information, tests it against experience, and acts in a way which seems appropriate to the information gathered. In the church, pastors gather impressions and insights from the people with whom they talk and the materials they read, from their observations of group activities, and from observing patterns of participation and community trends. Church members are constantly "studying the church" from a casual recognition of the church building to intimate experiences of personal care or communal celebration. In an inclusive sense, we cannot escape the constant experience of gathering and sorting out information as a basis for acting in the church as is the case elsewhere. This kind of "research" is so frequent and natural that it is a part of our taken-for-granted routines.

But there come times when this routine information processing is inadequate. Turning points come into the life of every congregation: expected patterns break down, old assumptions no longer seem to hold, the information we possess no longer seems to be a sure guide to action. In the congregation, these turning points may occur when we encounter a challenge—perhaps a prompting of the Spirit—to address a new and different occasion for ministry. Or it may be the failure of an existing program, a stewardship campaign for example, to achieve its goals. It may be a pastoral change which is the occasion for the need for more than routine understanding of the congregation. Or it may be a sense of apathy and drift, of going nowhere, that calls forth a need to take a new and more disciplined look at the congregation's life and ministry. In such

times, we become self-conscious and disciplined in the ways we gather information, test it against experience, and determine how we will act. This handbook addresses these occasions. It is an invitation to the disciplined study of the congregation. In what follows, we use the phrase "congregational study" to refer to this disciplined form of study.

Congregational study is essentially different from intuitive awareness or random investigation. The methods included in this handbook vary greatly, but all have rules which dictate the role and range of permissible activities, techniques for gathering and analyzing data, protocols for keeping records, and the like. While acknowledging that congregational leaders and members daily learn much of value about their congregation by highly informal means, this handbook strongly advocates that elements of congregational study be observed as congregations reach for self-understanding, especially in times when taken-for-granted routines are called into question. Careful, thoughtful study can, we believe, make several critical contributions.

Congregational study can confer a *balance and sense of proportion* often absent from the spontaneous self-descriptions of congregations. The extreme actions of a church's severest critics and most enthusiastic promoters, and especially the colorful language such persons are wont to use, are far more noticeable and memorable than the regular patterns of behavior and moderate opinions of the majority of members. Small groups with strong views can, of course, be powerfully influential in a congregation; but a carefully conducted study can give less vocal members their legitimate voice in making a decision or in some other important congregational negotiations.

Congregational study can also help congregations with multiple, seemingly unrelated, problems by uncovering *structures or patterns* in the apparent confusion. Identifying a pattern that links a series of problems does not automatically suggest a way to solve the problems. But it can alleviate the crushing sense that the congregation is the victim of an arbitrary series of plagues and afflictions and confer the hope that its multiple difficulties, because they are comprehensible, may be manageable as well. The tracing of patterns can also benefit churches that are not in trouble but that face the happy albeit confusing prospect of having to choose among opportunities for program and service. The systematic review of a congregation's past successes and failures, the illumination of its values, and the mapping of the styles of behavior that hold it together may help it to make decisions consistent with its proven strengths and real priorities.

A third contribution of congregational study, not

always welcomed but helpful in the long run, is the way in which such study sometimes reveals what a congregation does not want to see. For example, an analysis of the social class or racial/ethnic profile of congregational members, when compared with that of the local community surrounding the church, may reveal that the congregation's pattern of bonding is along class or racial lines, contradicting the members' professions of inclusiveness. An analysis of decision-making patterns may reveal considerable frustration with the essentially authoritarian and "top-down" style of the pastor or key lay officials. While such revelations may be painful, seeing the patterns enables the congregation to deal with them in a constructive fashion. It is much easier to change or accept that which we can see and identify than to deal with what is obscure and unacknowledged.

A fourth contribution of study of a congregation's life may be by far the most exciting. The informal, intuitive, and usually unsystematic ways of finding out about a congregation are almost always private and personal exercises. At most these are collections of individual responses, or perhaps more typically, an informal gathering around the kitchen table where impressions are shared of a contentious meeting or highly-charged incident. By contrast, *congregational studies open the quest for congregational self-understanding to corporate participation.* Because such studies are regulated by an established order of inquiry, a discipline for gathering information, and a set of rules for organizing and interpreting evidence, both their methods of procedure and the validity of their conclusions are available for public scrutiny. Certain kinds of studies in which the congregation investigates itself invite an especially high degree of participation and corporate effort. But even those study projects which are assigned entirely to an outside researcher or consultant potentially involve the whole congregation. Any interested member can review the data and audit the process by which conclusions were drawn and judgments rendered. Thus, through methodical study, the congregation has access to a procedure conducted in broad daylight; whatever such study reveals is the shared property of the community itself. In the broadest sense then, one can conceive disciplined congregational study as a way to confess corporately what God has done in the congregation's midst and how the congregation has (or has not) responded to God's gifts.

The methods and resources which we suggest in the following pages provide, therefore, a more disciplined and thorough process of accomplishing, at turning points in the congregation's life, what may be natural but more casual in other circumstances. The data gathered, interpreted, and reflected on provide the basis for affirming old or determining new directions of the congregation's ministry and mission.

1.2 A Perspective for Analyzing Congregations

Our advocacy of congregational studies not only implies methods and resources appropriate to the task (about which much more will be said below) but also suggests the necessity for a framework or perspective on congregations that itself disciplines or guides how we approach our task. In an earlier book involving several of the persons who have contributed to this handbook, academic disciplines were used to provide the framework.[2] Thus, for example, anthropology, social psychology, sociology, theology, and organizational development provided different perspectives for approaching congregational analysis. We suggest another way of organizing the analysis in this handbook. Academic disciplines are not the categories that members of congregations and those who work in and with them use to organize their congregational experiences. It became clear that a more natural and holistic approach was desirable to provide a way of organizing both the handbook and congregational studies. We can best introduce the perspective that we have adopted by presenting four brief cases of congregations whose experiences will be referred to at a number of points in subsequent chapters.

Case 1: Heritage United Methodist Church. Heritage United Methodist Church has slowed down in the last decade. Located in an ethnically changing community of a city in Iowa, its traditional constituency of middle-class descendants of German immigrants is aging. Hispanic and Asian families now crowd into the community, which was already packed by previous waves of southern blacks and Appalachian whites.

The Reverend Ms. Deborah Jones was appointed minister of the church a year ago. In sending her, the bishop had both warned and challenged her: "The community is vibrant, but the church is dying. Here is your opportunity for both ministry and mission." When she arrived, Ms. Jones found a congregation with barely enough volunteers to staff the varied social service programs of the church.

She launched a study of church membership which dramatically showed that more than half of the members were over sixty years of age, and many lived in deteriorating housing near the church. She also discovered that there were many other aging community residents in the same predicament. Armed with these facts, she convinced the church's administrative board to convene a committee to consider sponsoring a housing project for the elderly. The bishop and a local bank promised some financial backing, and the committee found an abandoned public school near the church that was available for redevelopment into apartments. The church would invest some of its unrestricted capital funds, along with the energy and enthusiasm of its members and staff.

At the board meeting called to make the go-ahead decision, one board member opened the discussion by calling for the church "to establish priorities we can all live with." Noting a steady decline in church membership and budget, he argued that "we should begin with our church school and hold off on the housing project." Others joined the chorus: "Volunteers would be distracted from existing programs by the housing project"; "too many of the church's resources are already going 'outside' the church, and not enough is available to nourish the congregation's faith and worship." "We are overinvolved and underfed," said one longtime member. "We need strong youth and evangelism programs," said another.

Ms. Jones pointed to the church's own history as a mission for immigrants and to the United Methodist tradition of caring and service. She pointed out that the project would benefit members as well as nonmembers. In the end, only the committee chairperson and one board member voted to sponsor the project. The pastor was perplexed. It seemed to her that Heritage had just passed up its first opportunity in a long time for new purpose and renewal.

Case 2: High Ridge Presbyterian Church. A large and growing congregation of the Presbyterian Church in America had reestablished its significant place in its affluent California community of High Ridge after an agonizing period of withdrawal from the United Presbyterian Church five years before. The new building was complete and the future looked bright: a media ministry led by the articulate and popular pastor was planned; worship services, featuring contemporary music and dramatized life situation vignettes, were drawing large crowds. Programs of child care, family counseling, and home study prospered. It appeared that even the huge mortgage on the new building would be paid off early through the herculean fund-raising efforts of some lay members.

Abruptly, in a session meeting, an elder made an explosive remark. "I think," he announced, "that it is immoral to have alcohol at the church." In his ensuing elaboration of this remark, it emerged that a leading trustee and member of the session had reserved the church's sanctuary and social hall for his daughter's wedding and reception. He intended to serve champagne. Somehow the pastor had not been informed,

though others on the church staff and in the congregation had been told.

The unscheduled debate was acrimonious. The wedding feast at Cana, described in the Gospel of John, was thrown against Paul's admonition in Romans to give up wine. Claims that the church should maintain purity were met with charges of hypocrisy in the behavior of members. In the end, the vote was nine for allowing the reception to proceed and ten opposed. The father of the bride, one of the church's most influential members and successful fund raisers, was irate. He shouted at the session that he had broken no rule of the church or law of the Gospel, and that he would quit the church and consider suing if the wedding were cancelled. In the heated exchange, two of the majority stated that they could not continue to belong to the church if alcoholic beverages were served on the premises.

"How can Christians fight this way?" the pastor asked his closest colleague in the ministry the next morning. "What do you think I should do now?"

Case 3: Hope United Church of Christ. Hope United Church of Christ had become one of those revolving door congregations: Three times in the last ten years a committee had been through the arduous process of filling out statistical forms with "all the facts" about the church and the community as required by the denomination in a search for a new pastor. "Why not simply change the date on the last set of forms," suggested one committee member, "and save ourselves the trouble?"

The area denominational executive, the conference minister, tried to be gently encouraging. "It's a valuable exercise," he said. "It will help you find out who you are."

The Hope United Church committee thought it knew who it was. The church was proud of its picturesque, beautifully maintained building in the relatively prosperous community of Pleasantville. On the whole, the members were warm and caring, with no more difficult or eccentric members than most churches. Yet, with all three of the latest pastors, there had been tensions from the start, resulting in each case in an early departure. Most of the tensions centered around the church's programs, which had been limited successes at best. The committee and the congregation blamed the pastors for these persistent problems. With so much going for the congregation, they believed the blame must be placed on inadequate pastoral leadership. The conference minister wanted the committee members to analyze, first among themselves and then with him, the histories of these brief pastorates and the tensions that existed. But the committee resisted. Reviewing these matters was more painful even than filling out the forms. Besides, they believed that sharing the stories of their difficulties was likely to hurt their chances of getting the right kind of pastor who would finally provide the kind of leadership they needed. In the face of this persisting problem and the resistance of the committee to confront it, the denominational executive wondered what was really going on in the congregation. What could he do to help the situation?

Case 4: St. Augustine's Church. St. Augustine's, a mostly black Episcopal church, had managed to attract a diverse congregation of both Caribbean and U.S.-born blacks during the 1970s. The Anglican liturgical tradition seemed to serve as a binding force among people of greatly different backgrounds.

With the support of the rector, Father Noah Cummings, a group of the parish's young people volunteered to augment the regular choir with gospel music at Sunday worship services. Some members found the music "spiritually stimulating" but others objected that the music and the movements reminded them of country revivals and bawdy night clubs. The vestry voted to use the Gospel Chorus on "fifth Sundays and special occasions," but Father Cummings continued to encourage the group by taking them with him when he was invited to preach in other churches.

On a recent Sunday, however, the controversy erupted again. During worship, the rector invited a report from a group of younger members who had attended a conference on the black religious heritage. Those making the report concluded by inviting the congregation "to join in singing a genuine Black liberation spiritual."

Remembering the vestry action, Father Cummings tried to stop the procedure, but the moment was contagious, and several members protested his intervention. In frustration he found himself saying, "There is some confusion among us about who is in charge of this service. I am asking my associate to conclude with a hymn while I retire to my study to pray."

As he left the sanctuary, Father Cummings could feel the strains of diversity within the congregation. Which tradition, he wondered, had the strongest claim on this church?

On the surface, these four congregations share little in common save for the fact that each is facing what we earlier called a turning point in which old patterns or assumptions seem to be breaking down. Yet, upon reflection, several common features of the cases provide entry points for analysis and understanding. Two that seem immediately evident are *program* and *process* aspects in the situation of each of the churches. In fact, we suspect that most issues facing congrega-

tions first come to light in one or the other of these areas, or sometimes simultaneously in both.

Consider first *program.* In each of the four cases, problems were encountered first as dimensions of program: *those organizational structures, plans and activities through which a congregation expresses its mission and ministry both to its own members and those outside the membership.* The failure of Heritage's administrative board to approve the housing project was interpreted by the pastor as a program failure—a failure in the church's mission. The members of the pastoral search committee and the congregation of Hope United Church blamed their rapid turnover in pastoral leadership for their lack of success in the programs of the church. The issue for St. Augustine's rector, Father Cummings, was one of lack of appreciation and perhaps also understanding of two approaches to the worship of the church—a more staid Anglican liturgy, on the one hand, versus the spontaneity of the black spirituals on the other. Even the High Ridge Presbyterian Church session's problem had to do with the rules and procedures involving a program—whether or not to allow alcohol to be served at a function in the church. Thus, each congregation reflects, in one or another way, concerns arising around program. Efforts to study any of these congregations in a disciplined and comprehensive way would include analysis of these program issues—for example, study of the relationship of a program to the needs, actual or perceived, of the various members and leaders of the congregation. Attempts might also be made to evaluate the effectiveness of the congregation's programs in terms of various criteria.

But even cursory reflection on the cases suggests that, for each, there are other factors at work in addition to a concern with program. Almost equally obvious are *process* dimensions. While programs point to the *what* of a congregation's life, processes reflect the *how* of members' relationships with one another. Processes have to do with *the underlying flow and dynamics of a congregation that knit it together in its common life and affect its morale and climate.* How leadership is exercised and shared, how decisions are made, how communication occurs, how problems are solved and conflicts managed—these are some of the processes that are critical for congregational life, and they underlie the manifest program issues of the various cases. A person wanting to understand the decision by Heritage's administrative board not to engage in the housing program would need to gather data about who was involved in the initial decision to explore the housing issue, how the plans were developed and communicated to the administrative board and congregation, and undertake an assessment of the congregation's morale—all aspects of process. The High Ridge Presbyterian Church conflict over the wedding champagne raises clear issues around process, especially concerning the norms governing church life which often remain unspoken until surfaced by an issue such as this one. Power issues and the management of conflict in the congregation are also areas where congregational research may prove helpful. Likewise, at Hope United Church, some of the too-painful-to-analyze experiences of past pastoral conflicts reflect failures of process as well as of program, and if the conference minister is to be of help to the congregation, he will need to help them analyze, among other things, how they have been functioning in relation to their pastors, what their mutual role expectations have been, and whether or not there has been a failure in communicating them. Finally, too, the issue of St. Augustine's is not only one of what constitutes appropriate music for worship but also of conflicting expectations for the church that have not been adequately communicated or resolved, and of a failure of communication between the youths and Father Cummings prior to the service. And Father Cummings' concluding comment also reflects the process dimension, that of the exercise of authority in the congregation.

Program and process, therefore, are two quite important dimensions of congregational life around which concerns arise leading to the need for congregational study. Given the prominence in church circles in recent years of both program planning and evaluation strategies as well as organizational development emphases, there is a temptation to conclude that program and process exhaust the dimensions of congregational life where research may be of help. This, we maintain, reflects a serious shortcoming. As important as program and process dimensions are, they are in fact almost always closely connected to two other aspects of congregational life: the *social context* of the congregation and the congregation's *identity*.

By *social context* we refer to *the setting, local and global, in which a congregation finds itself and to which it responds.* Included in the context are people—their culture and characteristics, institutions and social groups, and the various social, political, and economic forces operative in the setting. For each of the four congregations, a probing of its perplexities points to dimensions of its social context that are also operative in addition to program and process. Context factors are most obvious in the case of Heritage United Methodist Church. It was the analysis by the pastor and her committee of the social context of the congregation that led to her program proposal. Though the program was voted down, perhaps from faulty process as suggested above, the kind of analysis that was done was essential to the development of the proposal. Less obvious but no less important is the power of the social context in the other congregations. The problem faced by the High Ridge Church session has much of its rootage in a conflict between symbols of otherworldly purity, important to some members, and the values and life-styles which other members bring to the congregation from their participation in what we call, in chapter 3, "social worlds." At High Ridge it is the social worlds of affluent Californians. And if we were to probe the concern of Hope United Church's leaders over the lack of program success, we might find them tied in part to issues in the surrounding context: for instance, it may be that its programs falter because the congregation is heavily stocked with the families of corporate managers who change jobs often and move before they can carry out the plans they have made. This is a factor in the social context of the church rather than a flaw in the design of its programs which can be blamed on the pastor. Likewise, analysis of the tensions surrounding worship in St. Augustine's would likely reveal that they cannot be separated from the different social worlds inhabited by older and younger members of the congregation, including the social worlds brought by those with Caribbean origins and those whose roots are in Black America.

Finally, there is the dimension of congregational *identity*, which is perhaps even more often overlooked than its context as we seek to make sense of congregations. It is sometimes overlooked because we are not accustomed to thinking about the identity of a congregation. By *identity*, we mean *that persistent set of beliefs, values, patterns, symbols, stories and style that make a congregation distinctively itself.* The convictions about itself that constitute a congregation's identity are rarely stated, even by members to each other. Like the submerged bulk of an iceberg, they often remain below the surface. Their discovery and analysis are central to the understanding of congregational dynamics, as yet another look at the four congregational cases makes clear. A probe of Heritage Church's failure to accept the housing proposal—or better still, as part of the congregational study that preceded the development of the proposal—might include analysis of what the proposed changes would mean to those who currently carry the congregation's identity. The stubborn resistance encountered by the proposal was more than a failure of communication; it can also be understood as an effort to protect the members' already precarious sense of identity. For those session members in the High Ridge Presbyterian Church, there was also a sense of precarious identity. Having recently changed affiliation from a liberal to a more conservative denomination, they resisted a practice that they thought might compromise the congregation's character symbolized by that change. Probing the identity issues around that change and the church's emerging self-image might be one helpful response which the pastor and others could make in dealing with the conflict. Perhaps, too, Hope United Church's pastoral search would be more successful if members and the denominational executive working with them were helped to bring to the surface the strong convictions that they harbor about who this congregation *is*, about its view of the world, its beliefs and values, and the particular moments of its history that are most important. It may be that the congregation is playing hide-and-seek with its succession of pastors: "Find us in our hiding place, or you're out of the game." Finally, congregational identity is particularly crucial for understanding the dynamics of St. Augustine. In the past, the congregation's identity was centered in large part around a single liturgy that had the power to unite people from diverse social worlds. But now, based on a new source of religious and cultural identity—the Black religious experience—younger leaders began to challenge not only the older identity but also the established authority figure. It is not fully possible to grasp what is happening in this congregation—as is also true for the other three—without insight into issues of identity (or clash of identities).

These four aspects of a congregation—program, process, context and identity—form the organizing scheme of this handbook. They are constructs which we believe are useful for congregational study. We chose the four, not because they constitute a comprehensive model of the congregation that defines all that it is and encompasses every possible way of looking at it, but because they are dimensions of congregational life which are recognizable to people who invest their energies in churches. In fact, to a greater or lesser extent, the categories are in use in the everyday quest of church leaders and members to find sense and meaning in their common life.

As already noted, *program* is the "face" most often visible both in the official self-representation of congregations and to the outside world. In annual reports and articles on the religion page of the newspaper, congregations emphasize the program of the church, both its organizational arrangements (fellowship groups, committees) and the actual products—the annual bazaar, a food pantry, revival speakers, the youth group retreat. When churches are enmeshed in controversy, it is most often program issues they debate, such as repairing the organ or supporting fair housing. Denominational staff, seeking to be helpful, most often produce materials directed at developing particular programs of evangelism, education, steward-

ship, social witness or spiritual growth. Program, then, constitutes one important dimension of a congregation's life. In terms of our interest in congregational studies, program is most often addressed in terms of strategies of needs assessment and program evaluation, keeping in focus not only the desires and assessments of members but also the calling to be faithful to the gospel.

The *process* dimension of church life is also very much in evidence. As we have noted, it is evident in a congregation's characteristic patterns of behavior, in the ways its members treat each other, in the agreements they make to maintain the coherence of the body and to nurture its growth. A newly-arrived minister may propose an open congregational meeting to debate some controversial issue in the congregation. "No," she may be told by a long-time lay leader. "That's not the way we fight in this church. Our way is to let things settle out and resolve themselves slowly." "Our way" is a characteristic of that congregation's process. Unlike programs that have a more recognizable content, process is frequently more hidden from view and can often only be inferred from other observations or descriptions by knowledgeable members of the congregation.

Social context, though a persistent condition of the church's existence, is an aspect often obscured by the public bustle of programs or attention given to improving process. If the youth program falls on hard times, some churches have been known to endure a long series of program evaluations and attempts at new program strategies before they have taken a hard look at the demography of their neighborhoods or seen whether there *is* a significant cohort of young people to be attracted by any program whatever. (Of course, the opposite can be true. Some congregations may blame the context, when the problem may be better understood as a failure of process.) What this discussion of the context illustrates well is that congregations can helpfully be thought of as "open systems," implying not only systemic interaction between the various dimensions—a point to which we will return below—but also the interaction of congregations with their environments. Congregations have the potential to affect their contexts as they engage in mission, and they are also shaped by their environments (even when they set themselves in opposition to the values or demands of the context). While its social context does not *determine* the commitments of a congregation, it does provide the setting within which the congregation must make its decisions. Furthermore, the context is not only "outside" the church; it also permeates the values and challenges the commitments of members, as we saw in several of the cases. We would note also that the congregation's social context extends far beyond its immediate neighborhood and is global in scope. Both the universalism of the Christian faith and the interdependence of the global village in which we live make it difficult if not impossible for congregations to ignore the challenges and opportunities of this larger setting.

Like context, *identity* is also a powerful shaping element of congregational life. But it is more often a hidden face of the congregation, publicly articulated and advertised only infrequently. Lodged in gossip, in unwritten rules, and in a myriad of tacit signs, the components of identity are more often stumbled upon than codified. In an interview with one of the contributors to the handbook, a pastor described a recent incident:

Our committees in this parish . . . proposed some very interesting revisions of our worship space. Over a three-year period of study, a representative cross section of people . . . proposed these things, and the church board received the proposals and the architect's drawings and adopted it and said here's what we're going to do. There was a storm—a torrent of protest unlike anything I ever experienced anyplace, and we have spent the last year trying to sort out what that means. . . .

It's the damndest thing. I preach unorthodox, even heretical sermons fairly often, and three years ago the church board took the results of the sale of property [over a million dollars] and set it aside for the meeting of human need in [this city]. There's never a peep about the dramatic action on the part of the board. But when we said we wanted to move the pulpit a couple of meters to the left and the lectern just a couple to the right—I mean there was—a storm is not too strong a term.[3]

The inexperienced pastor, and many currently popular books on church leadership, would seek the source of the storm over moving the pulpit in the process used to make the decision. What procedures should be changed? How could those who protested the decision have been included at an earlier time so that they could have had "ownership" in the proposal? While these are not unimportant issues, this veteran pastor realized that the deeper issue here lies less in the process than in the function of the pulpit—and probably the whole configuration of furniture, space, and decoration—as a powerful symbol of the congregation's identity.

1.3 Relationships Among the Four Dimensions

Up to this point, we have emphasized the distinctions among the four dimensions used to organize the handbook. But the connections among these facets are equally important. Three implications of the relationships among them deserve special emphasis.

First, the four dimensions are not neat divisions or discreet categories. Each is a topic that suggests what kinds of data to gather and then helps to organize that data into coherent patterns. But much of the data may be relevant to more than one dimension. To use the most recent example: information gathered about the pulpit furor may reveal important insights about both process and identity and have relevance for programs of worship. Further, as our discussions of the cases indicated, the four categories are complex, and thus the lines of definition between them are difficult to draw. Program and process, for example, are very difficult to separate, both in abstract analysis and in studies of real life congregations.

Second, the dimensions not only overlap, but there is also a constant interaction among them, reflecting the systemic character of a congregation to which we called attention previously. One way to illustrate this is to think of the congregation as a house. Its foundations, supports, walls, doors for entering and leaving, insulation from the world, and windows on the world are made from materials drawn from diverse sources of supply in its context. Some of these materials are close at hand—values, attitudes, and stories that the members contribute from their personal storehouses to the project of building the congregation. Others are drawn from the surrounding neighborhood—social conditions, local customs, and zoning regulations which influence the shape of the project. Still other elements are more exotic—traditions, symbols, and, again, values imported from the ancient and modern history of Christian churches everywhere, from national and Western culture, and from the global social and political realities that shape all of modern life. The house which emerges is finally a unique and new creation with an identity that is its own, a configuration of God's work in the world which is both more than and different from the sum or product of its building materials. But it has also, as just described, been inescapably shaped and formed by the materials of its context. And its identity—the way that the house takes its peculiar shape in interaction with the context—further affects *what* transpires within the various rooms of the house (its program) and *how* it takes place (its processes). Nor does the relationship between the house—with its distinctive identity, program and process—and its context by any means flow in only one direction. The congregation, the handiwork of God, acts on and changes the world that contributed to its construction. The new house changes the character of the neighborhood, and any single house's impact on its context is carried even further as the neighborhood adds to and deepens the rich resources of the whole created world.

Third, and critically important for the users of this

handbook, anyone who embarks on the study of a local church must recognize that each of the four dimensions is only one facet of a social, cultural and religious reality—the congregation—that has an essential integrity. To concentrate all investigatory attention on any one dimension reduces the rich, full-bodied interplay of human and divine activity in a congregation to a flat abstraction. Certain fads in the study of the congregation have had this effect. Earlier in this century, the primary emphasis in the study of congregations was given to context and program. Demography was practically destiny as far as congregations were concerned. Community religious censuses were taken, population pyramids were drawn of both the local community and the congregation, and programs were assessed in relation to community characteristics. Then, during the 1960s and 1970s, organizational development was "discovered" by the churches. Context was swiftly forgotten as we moved "beyond the population pyramid" and focused on the internal dynamics of the church. Program planning and evaluation, decision-making, communication, conflict management, and the "climate" or psychological well-being of the congregation came to be the dominant emphases. The study of congregational identity has yet to become a fad, though its day seems likely to come as increasing numbers of church leaders become aware of its importance and learn ethnographic techniques for its study. The point is that each of the four dimensions has become, or has the potential of becoming, the *exclusive* focus of study, and as such leads to an unfortunate and distorting reductionism. The part comes to stand for, even to define, the whole. Each of these four dimensions is important for understanding a congregation, and studies of the congregation need to take a multi-dimensional approach. Yet, even when this is done, it is important to recognize that no one dimension, nor all of them together, can replace the integrity and God-given particularity of that congregation.

1.4 Getting Started

We have emphasized the importance of congregational studies, especially at those turning points in congregational life when new opportunities present themselves or old ways of doing things seem not to be working. Further, we have presented a perspective for thinking about congregations as one prepares to engage in congregational study. In the chapters that follow, we will look in some depth at each of the four dimensions and suggest methods and techniques for studying them. Before we turn to these more detailed discussions, several general methodological comments may

be helpful for getting started with the process of disciplined study. Although there is something of a temporal sequence implied in the following steps, it is by no means invariant.

First, there is a need to *clarify and limit the task at hand*. This is easier said than done. On the occasions when the need for congregational study arises, it is often difficult to be entirely clear about what the precise problem is, as the four cases illustrate. Some situations are simply "messes." The following quotation from a management specialist makes this point quite well and is applicable to many church situations:

> Managers are not confronted with problems that are independent of each other, but with dynamic situations that consist of complex systems of changing problems that interact with each other. I call such situations *messes*. Problems are abstractions extracted from messes by analysis. . . . Managers do not solve problems: they manage messes.[4]

The denominational official working with the search committee at Hope United Church, for instance, has little idea what is at the heart of Hope's problem which has created the revolving door for its pastors. He might therefore encourage the leaders of the congregation to do more than fill out a new set of vacancy forms. Instead (or in addition) he might assist them in employing various studies as means of clarifying and defining their problem.

The four dimensions of congregations—program, process, context and identity—offer one way of beginning to clarify and define the problems underlying the "mess" a congregation may be experiencing. Using the four categories as a sort of map or guidebook points to different areas of congregational life that need to be explored in clarifying what the focus of the disciplined study will be. It may be that all four dimensions will be found relevant; or, one in particular may be the focus of the problem. In addition, some of the techniques described in the following chapters can be useful as exploratory devices oriented to problem definition rather than problem solution, and they may be useful gaining clarity about problems that lurk in the "mess" that the congregation experiences.

However one proceeds to problem definition, it is essential that as much clarity as possible be gained so that the task for study can be defined and limited. The key question, "Why do we want this study?" needs to be answered as clearly as possible, and it needs to be asked continually throughout all the steps in the study process.

A second step is *determining who will be involved in the study process*. There is no set answer to this question. In some cases, it will be the pastor and lay leadership of the congregation who will take the initiative not only in calling for the study but in carrying it out. Whether directing the study process is undertaken by the pastor or by a lay leader(s), two guidelines are important. First, the group undertaking the study needs authorization by the congregation's governing body to do so. Without such authorization, it will be difficult to secure the needed information; equally as important, it is unlikely that the results of the study will be taken seriously. Second, and somewhat related, it is important to build ownership across the congregation for the study. Where possible, the study group should include representatives from various formal and informal interest groups within the congregation, and the congregation should be kept informed of the progress of the study, and especially of the results. It is to such a study group or team that the methods and techniques of the following chapters are directed.

There are times, however, when outside assistance is important. One such situation is where the level of conflict within the congregation has escalated to the point that no person within the congregation is trusted to represent adequately the concerns of all groups that have an interest in the outcome. Outside assistance is also desirable when the study needed is more complex than congregational leaders are able to manage, either through lack of needed expertise or time. There are those who believe that outside assistance is *generally* advisable, not only because of the difficulty of the task of congregational study, but also because of the ability of an outsider to see things that congregational members cannot see because of their very familiarity with the situation.[5] We recognize the merits of this view while believing that it is also possible, and sometimes necessary, for a congregation to engage in a *self*-study.

If a consultant is invited to assist the congregation in the study process, it is important that her or his credentials are checked in advance, preferably through people who have used the consultant's services in the past. Does she or he have the skills necessary for assisting in congregational study, ranging from assisting in problem definition to the ability to gather, analyze, and interpret data and assist the congregation in its use? Some consultants may be skilled in process or program consultation but not equipped to assist in doing congregational study. Others may be skilled in research methods but lack the capacity to assist the congregation in interpreting and using the information in a helpful way. What is needed is someone who can assist with both tasks or a division of labor among several consultants. Also, it is important that the consultant not be tied to a single approach but be flexible enough to help the congregation gather and use whatever information is needed. In contracting with

the consultant, clarity should be developed concerning the consultant's role, access to members and to information, accountability, schedule, and cost.

Third, *a design for the study and a plan of work must be developed*. There are a number of issues involved, some of which will be touched on in greater detail in subsequent chapters, especially in chapter 6, where a number of more technical aspects of research methods will be discussed.

An important consideration of study design is deciding *what kind of information will be relevant and useful to address the task or problem that has been defined* (step 1 above). If the problem is primarily one of process, then program statistics or census data will probably be of limited relevance; however, a transcript of or a visit to a committee meeting will likely be of great value. Usefulness of the data is also a crucial consideration. What is sometimes of interest and importance to an academic researcher in testing or expanding theoretical understanding may be of limited usefulness to a congregation in dealing with its particular issues. "Why do we want this information?" and "What will we do with it?" are important questions to be considered as one is deciding what information will be gathered in the study process. Finally, the credibility of the information to the audience who will use it must also be considered. The audience needs to be able to believe that the methods employed in the study process and the individuals who conducted the process are trustworthy. A study team will save itself considerable grief in later stages of the process if it does a careful job of asking these questions of the relevance of the information to understanding the problem that has been identified, its usefulness for decision making and problem resolution, and its credibility.

Some information that meets these criteria will be relatively accessible. It already exists, for example, in annual reports, membership records, or Census documents. But new information will often also be needed to address the congregation's issue(s). Here, too, there are levels of ease of accessibility. It is relatively easy to develop and administer a simple pencil and paper questionnaire to ascertain member evaluations of particular programs; however, it is much more difficult to gain insight into more elusive aspects of a congregation's life, its identity, for example, or members' social worlds. These areas should not be avoided because of their elusiveness. Sometimes, like Jacob, one can only gain the "blessing" of insight into the congregation's dynamics if one is willing to engage in a "wrestling match" with these tough "angels." We do not mean to suggest that the often unknown and unconscious dimensions of a congregation are more powerful than more manifest ones in the decision making of a congregation; however, unless the study team is willing to wrestle through to an understanding of them, they can haunt a congregation and make resolution of the issues impossible.

A closely-related issue is *how* the information will be gathered. Some areas of congregational life lend themselves more easily to quantifiable data (whether easy or difficult to gather). Demographic characteristics of church members and community residents, rates of giving or attendance, and the strength with which beliefs, values, attitudes, or opinions about various aspects of congregational life are held can be obtained through structured interviews, questionnaires, or in some instances from existing records. Other areas of church life, as we have already noted, can only be studied by more qualitative methods involving a considerable degree of empathetic involvement on the part of the one gathering the information. Elements of a congregation's culture, expressed in its language, symbols, and rituals, or dimensions of congregational process can often only be studied through these more qualitative approaches. Various ethnographic techniques such as participant observation and open-ended interviews are best used in these situations. There is a temptation to set more quantitative methods over against more qualitative ones that involve greater subjectivity and empathy, and to say that one or the other is inappropriate for the study of congregations. A recent, very helpful book on congregational analysis by Christian educator Denham Grierson argues strongly *for* participant observation as *the* appropriate way to understand congregations and *against* more quantitative approaches.[6] Though we appreciate Grierson's position, we are much more eclectic in our approach. Each of us involved in producing this handbook probably leans in one direction or the other in preferred methodology and techniques; however, we believe that there are circumstances and issues for which more objective, quantifiable approaches are most helpful, and the same is true for the more subjective, qualitative and descriptive approaches. Often one will find her or himself using first one and then the other in the same situation.

The *how* of gathering needed information will also necessitate other decisions, such as *from whom it will be gathered and when.* Will a questionnaire be administered or interviews conducted with the total congregation or a representative sample of members? How can first impressions and gossip (which are valuable resources for descriptive studies) be validated? What range of activities or aspects of church life will need to be observed in order to form reliable impressions? How will such observations or responses to unstructured interviews be recorded? How will the information gathered, whether quantitative or qualitative, be analyzed, summarized, and reported so as to be maximally helpful for addressing the congregation's needs? These are critical questions for any congregational analysis and are treated at length in this book.

The final step in the process of congregational study is that of *planning for the use of the information to address the issue(s) that the congregation is facing.* While it may seem gratuitous to include this—"After all, isn't that why the congregation undertook the process in the first place?"—there are many studies that have gathered dust upon completion because of inadequate attention to how they would be used. This is why we have insisted, in discussing several of the steps in the process, that attention be given to the ultimate use of the information: in the efforts to identify what the issue to be studied actually is; in being sure that the study team has authorization to proceed and therefore has some official status which warrants attention to their findings; in the process of selecting and contracting with a consultant; in the types of information one chooses to collect, making sure of its relevance to the issue and its usefulness in pointing to possible solutions; and in the techniques for gathering, analyzing, and presenting the information. Even when all of this has been carefully done, there will be work remaining in deciding what, if anything, is implied by the data for responding to the issue, what those responses will entail, who will make them, when, and how. Such steps, which take us beyond the congregational study process into decision making and planning, are also beyond the scope of this handbook; nevertheless, they are a critical part of the flow that begins with recognition that the congregation has reached a turning point in its life and proceeds through congregational study to an informed response to the congregation's situation.

Since this list of the steps in the process may seem rather daunting, it is worth recalling, as we conclude this section, why such studies are important. First, for troubled congregations, they will yield studies that bring clarity, intelligibility, and possibly improvements and solutions to many vexing issues in congregational life. For strong congregations, full of energy and hope, they will help identify directions for even greater mission and service. And for all kinds of congregations, the guidelines recounted here offer an order that makes it possible for a whole community—because it has entered into a common agreement on how to proceed—to participate in the enrichment and deepening of its self-understanding. It is on the basis of such self-understanding that God's work in and with local communities of believers becomes manifest, that love deepens and expands, and that the redemption of the whole created world finally depends.

1.5 Theology and the Study of the Congregation

This affirmation of what we believe to be a core purpose of congregational studies brings us finally to identify several theological concerns which are at least implicit if not always explicit in our approach to the study of the congregation. While as authors of this handbook we differ among ourselves at a number of points concerning the relation of congregational studies and theology, there are several areas in which we share general agreement and which we believe should be stated, albeit briefly.

We begin with the acknowledgment that we are neither neutral nor value free in our approach to congregations. We all come with a variety of values— some theologically grounded, some from the disciplines of study that we represent, and some from interests that we bring. In the case of theological assumptions, for example, what one believes about God's purposes for the church will shape the agenda for what will be addressed in congregational study. Thus those who believe that it is God's intention for the church to grow will be led to study the congregation and its context in ways quite different from those who are more in sympathy with liberation theology and who assume that God has a preferential concern for the poor. We too have our own convictions about the church and God's purposes for it which we will indicate below. But before doing so, we wish to consider further how such convictions affect what we study and the conclusions we draw.

Does acknowledging that we are not neutral or totally objective in our approach to congregations constitute a fatal flaw in our efforts at understanding? We think not; although, some who argue for the strict objectivity of a scientific approach would doubtless say yes. While one's values and beliefs, as we acknowledge, do influence what one looks for and is able to see in studying a congregation, they need not prevent one from taking an approach that is disciplined and rigorous, that follows rules and procedures that are open to the inspection of others. Nor does it imply that honesty in gathering data and drawing inferences about the data is impossible.

The importance of discipline, rigor, openness, and honesty in studying congregations cannot be overemphasized. Because of deeply held values and commitments, often unstated and even unrecognized by us, there is a danger that we will see only what agrees with what we already believe and value and deny that which we do not believe or value. There is an old story about certain theologians who refused to look into Galileo's telescope when invited, because they were afraid of seeing something that they could not believe. We believe, however, that the approach and methods advocated in this handbook work against refusing to see what we do not wish to see by stressing a discipline of study with rules for proceeding and sharing findings that are public and communal, not private. While these things do not guarantee honesty nor totally rule out the possibility of avoidance or denial, they make them much more difficult.

However, the fact that we bring our theological assumptions and values to congregational study can also have a positive effect. Not only do our assumptions direct our efforts at defining what we want to know, but they also help us in raising the questions that we want to put to the data we collect. Furthermore, it is easy to get "taken in" or seduced by the appearance of the objectivity and "hardness" of one's findings. Rather than not believing what we see, sometimes the opposite temptation is there: to believe *only what we see* and to see no possibilities in and beyond the apparent givenness of what is. If, for example, what we see is a negative or very difficult situation facing the congregation—for example, a deteriorating neighborhood or a serious financial shortfall—there is the temptation to accept the situation as a given that has no possibilities for a creative and faithful response. But congregational study that is rooted in a belief that God is at work for good in all things can inform a lively and playful imagination that leads us to push beyond a deterministic acceptance of the apparent givenness of the situation. In the interplay between the congregation's present being and envisioned possibilities for its becoming, new openings for ministry and mission in and through its present circumstances may be discovered. By so informing our imaginations, our beliefs and convictions play an important positive role in the process of congregational studies.

Having said this, what are our convictions about congregations that we as authors of this handbook bring to the study process? Our affirmation of the significance and centrality of the congregation with which we began this chapter grows out of a twofold conviction that local congregations are major carriers and shapers of the faith tradition of the church, and that God is at work powerfully in and through them. To be sure, there are other carriers and shapers of the church's heritage and interpreters of God's activity in the world, such as Scripture, creeds, ecclesiastical councils, denominational agencies, or theological seminaries. There has been a tendency to think of these sources as primary bearers of the tradition and interpreters of the activity of God in the world, and to consider local congregations essentially as consumers of truth generated from other sources. We disagree. As important for the life and mission of the church as these other interpreters of God's activity are—and we would add to the list prophetic voices standing outside the church—they are not the reservoirs of truth from which dependent local churches are simply to be spoon-fed. God is alive and active in the local church at least as much as in the theological centers or church hierarchies. Thus, we bring to the study of congregations an expectation that we will find evidences of God's activity in and through these local bodies and through the efforts of their members to live out their faith.

We are not so naïve as to believe that all that is said and done by local congregations and their members is faithful to the gospel. There is more often than not a tension, if not a conflict, between faithfulness to the gospel that is confessed in a local congregation and the actual living out of that gospel in the behavior of the congregation as a corporate body or in the lives of its members. Congregational study is an important means of holding up these behaviors for examination in the light of the faith a congregation espouses. In the chapter on congregational identity, we will consider further ways of examining possible tensions that may exist between the broader Christian tradition (what we call the great tradition) and the distinctive traditions of local congregations (the little tradition). We might add, however, that we believe that other bearers and shapers of the faith tradition are also subject to tension between the understanding of the faith they convey and what it is that God is calling churches to be and do in new and different situations. Being anchored in interpretations of the faith in the tradition that seem anachronistic in light of present realities—as, for example, theological assumptions based on the pre-Copernican view of the earth as the center of the universe—is no better than the failures of local congregations to practice what they preach. Congregational study is also helpful in these situations by assisting congregations (and other bearers of the tradition) to examine traditions in light of present realities as a part of their efforts to respond to the leading of the Spirit.

In our belief that congregations are key bearers and shapers of the faith tradition and that God is at work in and through them, we are affirming an essentially incarnational view of the church. It is our conviction that God's presence to the world in the ministry and mission of Jesus is continued in and through the life and ministry of local congregations as well as other expressions of the church. Much of what the world sees and knows of the Gospel and its meaning for life; much of what it sees and knows of God's concern for the poor, the suffering and alienated; much of what it knows of God's concern for reconciliation and peacemaking; it sees and knows through the life and activities of congregations and their members at the local level. It is through these often frail, earthen vessels that the Word becomes flesh in different times and places and under changing circumstances.

In the Incarnation, God became present to the world in human form, in a particular place, at a particular historical moment, in a particular society and culture. While, in effect, this limited who could hear the Word and how they would hear it through available language and cultural forms, this very particularity made the Word hearable and seeable. And while the Resurrection was, in one sense, a freeing of the Word from those particularities so that it could become fully universal, it was, in another sense, a freeing of the Word so that it could become particular again and again, in different times and places, under different social and cultural forms, and be given voice in a multitude of languages. It is our conviction that local congregations are one of those instances through which the Word continues to become flesh.

But if this is true, then congregations need to be helped to discern the intention and tendency of Jesus' ministry in which they are called to participate, to examine their present life in terms of that intention, and also to find ways of becoming truly indigenous in the social and cultural setting which they find themselves called to serve. We believe that congregational study can assist in this process by holding congregational life up for such critical inspection: considering its programs and processes, its relation to its social and cultural context, and its identity. To what extent is a particular congregation captive to past expressions of faith and practice that are unfaithful to God's calling in the present? Or conversely, to what extent is the congregation—open system that it is—so captive to its context that it has lost its critical edge? What opportunities exist for it to become more faithful and authentic in its particular place and circumstances at this time in its life? A commentator on an early draft of the handbook illustrates the potential of such questioning from the perspective of liberation theology, and provides a helpful conclusion to this introductory chapter:

The real promise of Congregational Studies in the context of the American church is that it may become a means of indigenizing our theological heritage in the first world in the way that base communities are doing in the third world. As such it could be the salvation of liberation theology which now admires the application of the gospel abroad but cannot imagine what shape the church should take at home. In its anxiety to be prophetic, liberation theology tends to project scenarios for the American church that fly by the reality of congregational life as it is.[7]

The comment sums up well our conviction about the contribution that congregational studies can make to congregations as they seek to be faithful in continuing the ministry of Jesus in their particular time and place.

NOTES ────────────────────────────────

1. Martin E. Marty, *The Public Church* (New York: Crossroad, 1981), p. 45.
2. *Building Effective Ministry, Theory and Practice in the Local Church.* Carl S. Dudley, ed. (New York: Harper & Row, 1983).
3. From an interview later recorded in "The Educational Preferences and Practices of Talented Ministers: Report on an Exploratory Study," an unpublished study by Barbara G. Wheeler (November, 1984). Distributed by Auburn Theological Seminary.
4. Russell Ackoff, "The Future of Operational Research is Past," *Journal of Operational Research Society;* 30, 2 (Pergammon Press, 1979) pp. 90-100. Cited in Donald A. Schön, *The Reflective Practitioner* (New York: Basic Books, 1982), p. 16.
5. See Lyle E. Schaller, "A Practitioner's Perspective," in Dudley, ed., *Building Effective Ministry,* 160-62. Also, see Loren B. Mead, "Seeking Significant Intervention," ibid., pp. 155-59.
6. Denham Grierson, *Transforming a People of God* (Melbourne: The Joint Board of Christian Education of Australia and New Zealand, 1984), pp. 39-49.
7. Neill Q. Hamilton, "Friday Morning Comments on the Handbook," correspondence to the authors.

CHAPTER 2

Identity

To speak of the identity of a congregation is a way of talking about the "we" that persists through shifting styles and circumstances. No matter how drastically changes affect a congregation, it remains "us," recognizable in many ways both to members and to other observers. Another way of putting it, as we did in chapter 1, is that the identity of a congregation is the persistent set of beliefs, values, patterns, symbols, stories, and style that makes a congregation distinctive. A congregation's identity is a result of the elaborate communication among its members through which they share perceptions of themselves, their church, and the world—communication in which they develop and follow common values and by which they engage in corporate recollection, action, and anticipation. Identity itself changes over time, but it mirrors a congregation's enduring culture.

Context, the subject of the next chapter, focuses on how environment conditions the life of a local church; however, identity explores the individuality of a congregation that distinguishes it from its conditioning environment. The larger context gives a church, say, its suburban, white, middle-class, Lutheran, Texan, late twentieth century attributes; but the manner in which the congregation incorporates these factors within its own culture differentiates its identity from all the forms the same environing factors elsewhere take. Likewise, a congregation's program and process, the subject of chapters 4 and 5, can be studied in their own right as the structures and activities (program) and the underlying dynamics (process) through which the congregation gives expression to its ministry and mission. And, while a congregation's programs and processes—for example, its church school or its style of planning—will share much in common with those of other congregations, they will also manifest distinctive characteristics, peculiar to that congregation, as they are shaped by the congregation's singular identity.

Christian congregations proclaim their identity to be summed up and ascribed in Jesus Christ. The methods of empirical analysis employed in the description of a congregation's identity, a number of which we will describe, do not qualify or deny the theological understandings of a local church as the body of Christ or the household of God, but rather they help one understand something of the manner in which a congregation perceives its unique historical life and expression within the gospel promise. As individuals may simultaneously identify themselves to be Christians and yet to have unique personalities, so a congregation can, without compromising its Christian attributes, claim a singular corporate character.

2.1 Situations

Although as susceptible of analysis as the context, program, or process of a congregation, identity is often its less examined aspect. Consider how the issue of identity lurks below the surface of the church situations described in chapter 1.

Case 1: The graying Methodist church that hesitates to house the elderly. Ostensibly the issue presents a conflict between the pastor and her board, and requires program and process skills for its resolution, as well as an understanding of the dynamics of the context. But note how both the pastor's initiative and the board's resistance draw their definition from aspects of identity. Contributing to the tension are *symbols* of what the church represents to its members ("the classic beauty of its sanctuary") and understandings of Heritage's *heritage* (its traditions of social service; its long life of Christian action and challenge). We learn that Heritage's problem also springs from its *demographic profile:* an aging membership with a "dying" image in a lively neighborhood. In its attempt to establish priorities, the Heritage board searches to express its authentic *character.* Symbols, heritage, demographic profile, and character are all elements of a church's identity that will be examined later in this chapter.

21

Case 2: The breakaway congregation threatened by wine at a wedding party. Here is a church that has recently paid unusual attention to its identity, finding its beliefs and values sufficiently at odds with those of its founding denomination to sever its connection. Its own *world view* has been projected by a popular pastor and media ministry. Its contemporary *ritual* gives it further distinction. In the wedding wine incident, moreover, it faces a test of *character*. What, members now ask, constitutes the faithful nature of the congregation? Like the element of character, those of congregational world view and ritual form other features of identity that this chapter examines.

Case 3: The pretty white church that blames its pastors. The conference minister presses the congregation to explore its identity more fully. He wants members to move beyond the mere facts of their policies and program in order to explore their painful *history*. Pulpit ghosts, fights and funny situations, saints and grief—all crowd the collective past of the congregation, seemingly too hurtful for them to examine formally. This chapter therefore descibes ways to examine the local church's history as an element essential to its identity.

Case 4: The black Episcopal church seeking an authentic heritage. The struggle of St. Augustine's Church to sing its Lord's song so illustrates the many dimensions of identity that the story forms the backdrop of the next section.

2.2 Elements of Identity

In psychological terms, identity is the singular sense of who one is. The concept of identity becomes more complex when it describes a quality possessed by a group such as St. Augustine's Church. Here identity again refers to a reflexive awareness, but now meanings are communicated not merely within a single person but within a group, now by what Clifford Geertz, following Max Weber, calls "webs of significance."[1] The web of meanings—the network of natural awarenesses, beliefs, values, goals—is a way of speaking about the culture of a local church. *The identity of a congregation is the perception of its culture by either an observer or the congregation itself.* The function of observers is important because they often contribute to the meaning that a group comes over time to attach to itself.

The struggle for an authentic heritage in St. Augustine's provides an instructive example of collective identity. In spite of deliberate and prolonged attempts

in slaveholding days to destroy an Afro-American understanding of roots, solidarity, and religion, and in spite of present-day oppressions that erode a sense of cultural worth and purpose, members of St. Augustine's are struggling, not without conflict, to meld and enrich an identity that honors their Anglican heritage and their black religious experience. The tension over the music marks part of their quest for their unique identity.

St. Augustine's experience offers a lesson to church analysts in what to expect in congregational identity:

1. Identity often opposes despair. Without the meaning and self-awareness that a positively valued identity gives, this and any congregation is likely to drift without direction. Both aspects of St. Augustine's identity—Anglican and black—were positively valued, and the conflict that ensued over them, though frustrating to Father Cummings, signals an essentially healthy situation. Both aspects of this congregation's identity enabled it to discover and affirm its particularity, and prevented it from drifting without definition, taking cues from whatever might come along. Without a positively valued, collective identity—even a divided one seeking reconciliation—the congregation could be without hope, having little sense of present character and thus small expectation for themselves in the future. A despondent group is often dissociated from the web of meanings that forms its identity and gives coherence to its experience; its identity is out of touch with its present circumstances.

Congregations that give all of their attention to programs, process, and context and no attention to the relationship of these dimensions to identity are in danger of despair. Any local church can become so occupied with the dynamics of its programs, the resolutions of its process, and its transactions with its environment that its sense of intrinsic identity becomes diffuse and disregarded. The church may so focus its activities and adaptations that it forgets to comprehend who it is and why it invests in such behavior.

2. St. Augustine's identity has a number of dimensions open to analysis:

a. Cognizance of the struggle of the group through its *history*. Not only does a church acknowledge a heritage that in part transcends its own experience; it also recalls its own particular story that traces its life to the present and into the future.

b. An appreciation of the traditions that constitute the congregation's *heritage*. Heritage gives a continuity and legitimation to a group's outlook and ideals.

c. Perceptions of the way things are: a *world view*

that gives a particular significance to human lives and larger happenings.

d. The use of *symbols*. Certain signs that convey powerful meaning also express and reinforce the identity of a church.

e. A practice of group *ritual*. Repetitive actions that have more than utilitarian significance, such as ways of greeting, celebration, negotiation, intimacy, and grief, are another dimension of collective identity.

f. An understanding of the group's *demographic picture*. Groups have an image of their more measurable characteristics and possessions such as age, sex, race, class location, education, property, and power.

g. A grasp of group *character*. Churches exhibit and recognize in themselves a particular configuration of values and dispositions that frame that group's ethos.

3. An analysis of St. Augustine's identity must bear in mind both identity's integrative function of *being* in the present and its transformative function of *becoming* as it moves into the future. Some students of identity restrict their definition of identity to the former function, but our observation of St. Augustine's suggests that a group's perception of itself involves both what it finds itself to be and what it determines to become. Gaining appreciation of heritage is not merely to enhance the sense of its present state of being; it is also, as Erik Erikson says of identity in general, an "accrued confidence,"[2] a dimension that enables members to transform even their own nature in future liberation. St. Augustine's has not only a unique heritage of an Anglican tradition but is also adjusting to a different future. A similar sense of both being and becoming accompanies any congregation's apprehension of its identity. In fact, so consciously occupied are some present-day American congregations with what they might become, spiritually and socially, that they may overlook their being—who they now are.

To emphasize only *being* reduces the elements of identity to traits that freeze corporate life in a museum-like preservation. To emphasize only the phenomena of *becoming*, on the other hand, diminishes church identity to wraithlike transience. Strategies that seek a homogeneous congregation with members of similar outlooks and backgrounds tend to get trapped in the first mistake: seeing identity solely in terms of being. When we feel the attraction of "our kind of folks" we are responding to a given set of identity traits, a sameness that assures us that our character would not

be lost in adaptation. Strategies, however, that seek new liberationist structures for congregations tend to fall into the second snare that sees identity only in terms of becoming. In our quest for social change we may think our church can leave behind its present culture and enter another context without loss of identity. Neither strategy usually works; neither provides the "accrued confidence" that finds in congregational identity both its reliance upon being and its capacity to become.

A full exposition of congregational identity juxtaposes functions of being and of becoming. Specifically that means that in the analysis of the various aspects of a congregation's identity, one should look for both of these functions, to wit:

History:	both its representation of the past and its expectation of the future;
Heritage:	both the integrative and transformative forces of tradition;
World View:	perceptions of both order and of crises that counter it;
Symbols:	both their cohesive focus and also their "multivocality" that changes life;
Ritual:	both repetitive action and its access to "liminality" in which the group discards normal corporate structure;
Demography:	both the naturally given attributes of members and their desire to change their demography by assimilating different member types;
Character:	both its characteristic traits and also the sense of "having character" that chooses the way of difficult adaptation.

The parables of Jesus were an early portrayal of the identity of people. On the one hand the stories deal with familiar, integrative aspects of being, such as shepherding, lost coins, and worship in terms of which hearers could identify and locate themselves. On the other hand, they conclude with stranger, transformative events of becoming such as the justified sinner and the welcomed uninvited. A similarly parabolic outlook is needed to understand the full identity of a present-day religious community. Identity reflects both being and becoming. Expressing neither just fashion nor just unconvention, identity binds both these modalities in representing congregations that Paul calls households of God—a designation that, like identity, juxtaposes the familiar and the strange.

In the following sections we consider each of the aspects of identity with suggestions for gathering and analyzing information about a congregation's identity. There is a certain eclecticism about the elements we consider; they are like multiple facets of a precious stone, each of which reveals something distinctive about the stone. There are, however, obvious overlaps between the aspects that should not be ignored. No one congregational study team will likely find it necessary to explore all of the elements we treat, but we recommend analysis of several elements as essential for discovering the richness of the congregation's identity.

2.3 History

2.3.1 *History and Identity*

When somebody is genuinely interested in who we are, we soon start recounting to them incidents in our past that reveal additional aspects of our nature. As Denham Grierson has written, "The act of remembering is essential for the creation of identity and corporate integrity in any community. A community is by definition a sharing together of significant happenings, the substance of which comes largely from remembering."[3] But as Grierson implies, not everything that has happened to us is of equal significance. We could easily bore our friend with accounts of how we tied our shoes or bought groceries. Thousands of events happen to us each week; relatively few are worth remembering for their disclosure of who we are, either to ourselves or to someone else. To distinguish the one type of happening from the other, Norman Perrin speaks of both "history" and the "historic."[4] History could conceivably acknowledge any sort of incident; a focus on the historic restricts apprehension to those occurrences that distinguish their subject's identity. Were we to be musing about a present-day congregation a half century from now, the historic elements in that church's history would be the stories, large and small, that would most helpfully characterize the present group for us.

Many attempts to articulate parish history get trapped in describing the less telling regularities of the past and have little to say about a congregation's more historic activity, such as its founding, significant experiences in its past, critical turning points, important people or "heroes" past and present. Annual reports, for example, may concentrate only upon statistics and programs. Parish profiles prepared to guide the selection of a new pastor or adoption of a new strategy tend to get locked in cross sections of opinion without exploring their historic antecedents. Amateur histories of local churches are sometimes little more than genealogies, or chronicles of predictable changes in leadership, property or program.

Suggested below are two ways of gaining a deeper

appreciation of the historic "plot" in which congregational identity develops.[5]

2.3.2 *Gathering Oral History*

Pastors may already encourage the older members of the congregation to reminisce merely for therapeutic reasons, but the activity also provides an opportunity that could strengthen the congregation's understanding of its story. Long-term members are a primary source for oral history. Other members besides the pastor, of course, can be the investigators, and the project can be carried forth to several different conclusions that would enrich the identity of the congregation.

Critical to the process are guided interviews. Questions like the following would be asked members who have been intimately associated with the church for shorter and longer times:

What's the news around the church now?

Tell me about your association with the church.

What changes have you noticed about the church during the time you have been associated with it?

What has happened that you would like not to have occurred?

What has happened that you would like to have been followed up in a different way?

More specific questions would follow such general inquiries. Informants might also contribute documents and other artifacts to a project, but the purpose would not be primarily the accumulation of archives. More important to a congregation's "becoming" would be its development of a recognized plot played out in its actions, sermons, administrative deliberations, entertainment, and education.

2.3.3 *Time Line*

Another way of gaining a firmer understanding of the historic is to gather a group of parishioners for an evening of disciplined recollection. Tape up on a wall a long sheet of wide, light paper, and mark a longitudinal line from one end to the other, a third of the way from the paper's top. Put the founding date of the congregation at the left end of the line, the present date at its right end. Mark off in suitable time intervals the intervening period: decades, single years, and so forth.

1. Encourage members to recall important events in the church's past. Title these and note them on the paper near their date, but below the line.
2. In the section above the line describe at their appropriate date significant events of the neighborhood, region, nation, and world.

3. Encourage participants in their attempts to connect and elaborate the events noted.
4. Leave the paper up so that participants may later supplement their findings.
5. Record and transcribe the session for multiple uses, including more comprehensive inquiries into the history of the congregation. The time line may be an item for general distribution to the membership.

Figure 2–A provides an example of a brief segment of a congregation's time line.

Figure 2–A

A "Slice" of a Time Line

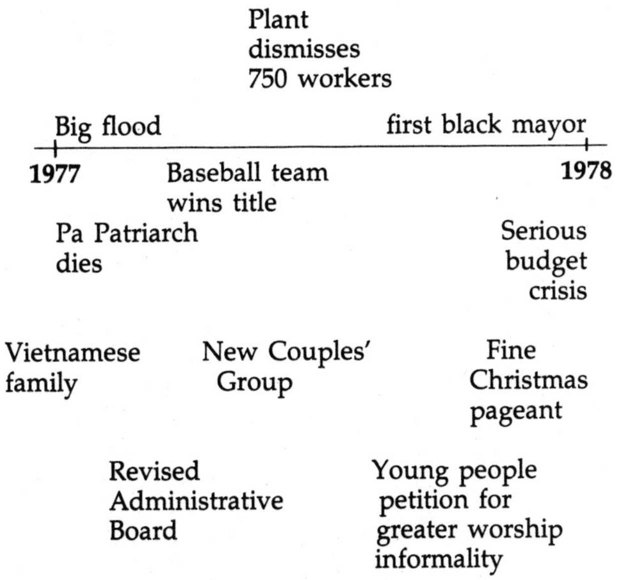

```
                    Plant
                    dismisses
                    750 workers

Big flood                        first black mayor
+---------------------------------------+
1977         Baseball team              1978
             wins title
Pa Patriarch                     Serious
dies                             budget
                                 crisis

Vietnamese   New Couples'        Fine
family       Group               Christmas
                                 pageant

      Revised              Young people
      Administrative       petition for
      Board                greater worship
                           informality
```

2.3.4 Analysis

Perhaps nowhere in the study of a congregation's identity are its dual aspects of "being" and "becoming" more patent than in writing a parish history. In its history, that which a congregation *be* is glimpsed in the changes that compose what it *becomes*. One way to reflect upon the nature of transformation in congregational history is to characterize the dominant functions of successive historical events in a congregation and to note how one function seems achieved at the expense of another.

Were we to treat history as a story, we could delineate four different functions that events may assume in its plot. We use the slang of narrative analysis to identify the functions.

1. Plots *link*. Within the cascade of events that constitute the total past of a congregation, a plot (or history) *connects* relatively few incidents and aligns them as a sequence significant to understanding the character of the parish. The Greeks called this function *anamnesis*.

2. Plots *thicken*. They complicate a single story line by also involving other unintegrated factors in parish life. Thickening is an action of acknowledging disparate elements in congregational life.

3. Plots *unfold*. They show cause and effect. Certain events are historic primarily because they seem to be the instruments of subsequent happenings, not because they identify the congregation or thicken its plot. In unfolding, plot gives reason for the course of events.

4. Plots *twist*. They are not predictable; a parish history is not, therefore, a rigid formula by which the future is projected. Plots rather manifest the uncertain. They do not just unfold; they move in surprising directions that especially reflect the "becoming" aspect of parish identity.

An analysis of parish history might include the following exercise:

1. Develop a comprehensive account of the congregation's last decade. Note what seem to be the somewhat distinct events within the history.

2. Ask which of the four functions seems most active in each event: linking, thickening, unfolding, twisting. All functions accompany each event, but one will probably seem to dominate the manner in which it has been related.

3. Ask which of the four functions seems most suppressed in any single event. There is evidence that in undertaking a certain action a congregation diminishes its attention to other functions.

4. Ponder the sequence of functional emphases and suppressions. Does the pattern itself suggest anything about the character of the congregation?

2.4 Heritage

2.4.1 Heritage and Identity

The heritage of a congregation is that which comes to it out of its past by inheritance. At first glance, heritage and history might seem to refer to the same matter; however, we do not use them synonymously here. Heritage represents what a congregation considers to be its sacred deposit from its total past, while history tells the congregation's own particular story. By heritage, then, we will mean *a congregation's acknowledgement of the inheritance of beliefs and practices about the Christian faith and life and the purpose of the church that it has by virtue of being a Christian church and standing in that particular historical stream.* These beliefs and practices— the Christian heritage—are contained not only in the Scriptures, but in the creeds and confessions, the councils of the church, the writings, liturgies, hymns, and stories of the church through the ages in its variety of denominational expressions. They are mediated to an individual congregation, not only through the denominational stream of which it is a part, but also through the peculiar experiences of the congregation itself, both in its past and present.

We shall come back to this dual character of a congregation's heritage. First, however, what is the relation of heritage to identity? The heritage, as we have restricted its use here, contributes a singularly important element to the web of meanings that constitutes a congregation's identity: its identity as a *Christian* community rather than a Jewish synagogue or Buddhist temple, a service club, a corporation or a university. To be sure, a congregation's web of meanings may include elements that are similar to these other collectivities— sometimes, some would say, to the point of obscuring its identity as a Christian congregation; however, it is its *Christian* heritage that contributes a distinctive element to a congregation's identity and sets it off from other communities. Thus heritage is especially important in defining the boundaries of a congregation's identity.

The two-sided character of the heritage of a congregation that we noted previously—its inheritance as a part of the Church Universal (mediated through its denomination) and that which comes to it through its particular local history as a congregation—is an important distinction for consideration of the relation between heritage and congregational identity. As they have studied religious life in various societies, anthropologists and others have sometimes used a distinction between two types of traditions that exist simultaneously within the same religion. Although the distinction has been given various names, we will refer to it, following Robert Redfield, as the "great tradition" and the "little tradition."[6] By the great tradition, we refer to the classic expression of a particular religion. It is the official or orthodox tradition (although we know that within Christianity there have been numerous "orthodoxies" reflecting the various denominational streams). Some Protestant groups have wanted to restrict the great tradition to the Bible—*sola scriptura;* however, they have frequently developed creedal or confessional statements in addition to the Bible, and they also have stories about and writings of various Christian luminaries and denominational founders—St. Augustine, St. Francis, St. Teresa, Luther, Calvin, or Wesley, for example. These also come to have a place in the great tradition. Scholars in theological seminaries and ecclesiastical councils as well as the official leaders of a congregation often feel a special responsibility for exemplifying and perpetuating the great tradition.

At the same time, however, there is the little, or local, tradition of a congregation. It is that particular distillation of beliefs and practices from out of the great tradition, mixed with elements of the peculiar history and experiences of the congregation. Of course, we should not forget that the great tradition also reflects the experiences and peculiar histories of individuals and congregations in the past that have now been incorporated into the stream of the great tradition.[7] Nevertheless, each congregation has its own little tradition, its peculiar interpretation of Christian faith and practice, which may be commensurate with the great tradition or at odds with it at one or several points. The conflicts that have developed in many white congregations over the inclusion of blacks in the membership point to the tension that exists between the universalism of the great tradition and the particularism of some little traditions. Within the great tradition, an inclusive church is the norm; within the little tradition of First Church, Centerville, the congregation's wisdom about how to handle such things as racial, ethnic, or social class differences has taken on sacred status which the congregation aims to maintain. The little tradition of a congregation is perpetuated informally by a larger number of church members than those charged with maintaining the great tradition.

The tension that often exists in congregations between its great and little traditions is an important dynamic to be considered in congregational analysis, and a potentially important ingredient in the kind of reflection in a congregation that can lead to renewal. A congregation's heritage (drawn from the great and little traditions) forms part of its present identity—its *being*. And there are expressions of that heritage, currently neglected, that can shape its potential identity—its *becoming*. In one of the analyses of the congregation which formed the focus of the book, *Building Effective Ministry*, the current theological identity (called there the "operational theology") of the congregation—an upper middle class congregation in an affluent suburb—was described as follows:

The "operational" beliefs of the congregation . . . are centered in belief in a God who loves individuals, calls them to fulfill their potential as individuals, forgives and supports them when they fall short and are hurt, and blesses them with the good life. There is an especially strong belief that individuals are called to fulfill their potential and must refuse to give up or to sell themselves short.

This operational belief system also seems to carry over into the belief that the congregation itself must refuse to sell itself short or to be less than "the best show in town.". . . Additionally, the theme, repeated several times by leaders, that the congregation must be a "hospital" to bind up those hurt by the stresses and strains of life seems also to be a part of the operational belief structure and parallels the individual's belief in a loving, forgiving, supporting God.[8]

These beliefs reflect the peculiar refraction of parts of the great tradition through the congregation's little tradition. While the beliefs are in tension with important themes of the great tradition, the congregation nevertheless stands in that tradition. The Christian heritage is a part of its identity, and the broader elements of that heritage are available to members as a resource for critiquing and challenging elements of their current identity. As a theologian analyzing the same congregation pointed out,

It is true that this congregation falls far short of the biblical promises of what the congregation can be, but for all of that, we must remember that it is a community of the people of God. That is the audacious claim they can make and that claim is an expression of hope in God. . . . [T]his church is the body of Christ. That statement is one of belief in God's promise to be with Wiltshire Church and to be for Wiltshire Church. It is an expression of my expectation that community is, has been, and will be justified by God in her gracious and steadfast love.[9]

2.4.2 Exploring a Congregation's Heritage

There are a number of ways—more than can be described here—for exploring a congregation's heritage as it contributes to its identity. We will note several that we believe are especially helpful for a congregation that would explore both its great and little traditions and the relationship that exists between them. First, however, let us describe essentially what is at stake in any such exploration.

On the one hand, there is the need to understand the current being of the congregation with respect to its heritage—its present theological identity. This involves study of what Joseph Hough[10] calls the " 'documents' of a congregation, living and written." These documents, Hough continues, "must be examined in order to determine the present, concrete working understanding that the congregation has of itself. This analysis should make transparent the purpose of the congregation as it is articulated and understood by the members." Among such "documents" available for analysis are:

—the beliefs held by congregational members
—themes and dominant theological images communicated in sermons, liturgies (to be explored further in the section on ritual), symbols (to be explored further in the section on symbols), teaching, and written statements of the congregation's purpose
—and behavioral expressions of the congregation's theological identity in its organizational life, both internal and external

On the other hand, there is a need to examine the congregation's present theological identity in light of elements of the great tradition. To quote Hough further:

Utilizing an explicit understanding of the nature of the congregation based on interaction with the biblical and theological sources, the analyst [of the relation of identity and heritage] becomes an external critic, raising questions about the adequacy of the congregation's self-understanding in light of the universal theological dialogue in the church about the mission and ministry of the church as the body of Christ in the world. Theological analysis has this normative function. It calls the church into account to be faithful to its covenant with God and to respond creatively to the promises of God for the church and the world.[11]

How does one put together these two foci of the analysis of a congregation's theological identity? Analysis of the theological themes present in the "documents" of the congregation may follow several different strategies.

One may proceed in an inductive fashion, listening attentively for themes, images and metaphors that are present in the various kinds of documents referred to above. Participant observation, unstructured interviews, and content analysis of written materials (such as sermons, church school literature, annual reports and meeting minutes) are useful techniques for inductive exploration. (See chapter 6 for a discussion of many of these techniques.) As one observes the congregation in action, questions its members and leaders, explores the content of sermons and other written materials, certain theological themes and metaphors will begin to emerge with considerable frequency and usually they will begin to take on some degree of coherence as expressive of core elements of the congregation's identity. This is essentially the strategy used to discern what were called the "operational beliefs" of the congregation described previously. Denham Grierson notes how these themes or metaphors function to "select, emphasize, suppress, focus, and organize features of the common life of the people. 'We are the soldiers of Christ.' 'The church is God's missional arm.' " The total configuration of such themes, he argues, embodies a congregation's fundamental vision.[12]

One may also proceed in a more structured fashion by using various predefined theological categories to describe a congregation's identity. It is particularly useful when one wishes to compare two or more congregations and therefore needs common categories by which to compare them. But predefined categories can also be helpful in analyzing a single congregation when one wishes to describe the degree of theological diversity or homogeneity that exists in the congregation and needs some common categories for comparison of individual member's beliefs. Obviously there are a variety of categories and techniques which one can use. We cite two examples of measures of theological orientation. Additionally, the Parish Profile Inventory (see General Appendix) provides additional examples of measures of religious beliefs.[13]

Before proceeding to these examples, we simply note here the difficulty of writing belief statements that represent the options appropriate to a particular congregation or group of potential respondents. If the study team is not satisfied with those given in the examples, it is encouraged to write more satisfactory statements. In undertaking this, the team will find it helpful to consult one of the many guides to questionnaire construction[14] as well as to the references cited in the preceding note.

In the two examples which follow, each provides a way of studying important but different aspects of a congregation's theological identity.

The first includes several questions having to do with basic Christian beliefs. Carefully developed by a group of social scientists and theologians, with the support of the Lutheran Church in America, the questions were designed originally to provide a profile of the religious beliefs and religious experiences of Lutheran laity and clergy.[15] The questions are, however, quite appropriate for use in other denominational traditions and for developing a profile of the religious beliefs of members of a particular congregation. Each provides a question stem with several response categories representing different possibilities for holding the belief in question. We have included, with minor alterations, only a few of the many questions that were developed for the larger study. A congregational study team may wish to consult that study for additional questions or use the examples here as guides to constructing additional belief questions for use in its analysis of its congregation's heritage. Representative questions include:

1. "Faith" has meant many different things to people. Which one of the following statements *comes closest* to describing your own view of faith? (Circle one response only.)
   a. a life of commitment to God that I demonstrate by trying to do what is right.
   b. My decision to accept Christ instead of going on in my own sinful ways.
   c. My trust in God's grace.
   d. My belief in all that the Bible says.
   e. In my view, as long as people are truly sincere in their beliefs, they show faith.
   f. I am not sure what "faith" means, although I am convinced that it is important.
   g. To be honest about it, the idea of faith doesn't seem very meaningful to me.
   h. None of these; what faith means to me is ____.

2. Which one of the following comes closest to your view of the way in which God influences the things that happen in the world? (Circle only one response.)
   a. God sets history in motion but really doesn't interfere with it anymore.
   b. God influences individuals, who then shape events.
   c. God influences individuals, but also shapes events directly through nations and social affairs.
   d. I don't think of God as "influencing" the things that happen.
   e. Not sure because I haven't thought about it much before.
   f. None of these; my view is _____.

3. People often wonder how a merciful God can allow terrible things to happen, such as the killing of six million Jews during World War II. Which statement *comes closest* to your view of why God lets these things happen? (Circle only one response.)
   a. God allows terrible things to happen in order to punish people for their sins.
   b. We don't know why these things happen, but we know that God is able to use them for good.
   c. God doesn't have anything to do with these things; the devil causes them.
   d. People cause these things to happen, not God.
   e. Frankly, I don't know how God can allow these things to happen; it doesn't seem right to me.
   f. I don't have a view on this topic.
   g. None of the above; my view is _____.

4. Which one of the following statements comes closest to expressing your view of life after death? (Circle only one.)
   a. I don't believe that there is life after death.
   b. I am unsure whether or not there is life after death.
   c. I believe that there must be something beyond death, but I have no idea what it may be like.
   d. There is life after death, but no punishment.
   e. There is life after death, with rewards for some people and punishment for others.
   f. The notion of reincarnation expresses my view of what happens to people when they die.
   g. None of these expresses my view. What I think about life after death is _____.

5. Which of these statements comes closest to describing your feelings about the Bible? (Circle only one.)
   a. The Bible is the actual word of God and is to be taken literally, word for word.
   b. The Bible is the inspired word of God but not everything in it should be taken literally, word for word.
   c. The Bible is an ancient book of fables, legends, history, and moral precepts recorded by men.
   d. None of these; my view is _____.
   e. Can't say.

6. Which of the following comes closest to your attitude toward people in other countries who have never heard about Christ? (Circle only one.)

a. A desire to share the love of Christ with them.

b. A feeling that if we do not preach Christ to them, they will be damned forever.

c. A feeling that we shouldn't worry about them because there are so many people in this country who haven't heard about Christ.

d. A feeling that we should respect their religions and stop trying to impose Christianity on them.

e. Frankly, I haven't thought about it.

f. Can't choose.

7. Christians sometimes describe God as a "God of justice" or a God who commands us to bring about justice. Which *one* of these statements comes closest to your own ideas about what this means?

a. It means that the church should work for justice and support groups that are working to end inequality and oppression.

b. I think of it at a more personal level. It means I should try to be just and fair in all my dealings.

c. I think this is actually a spiritual term that refers to God punishing evil, rather than activities of the church or individuals.

d. Frankly, the concept of God's justice doesn't have any particular meaning to me.

e. I'm not really sure what it refers to.

f. None of these; its meaning to me is _____ .

The use of these questions, or ones like them, can be important not only for comparing the profile of one congregation's beliefs to another, but for understanding the distribution of beliefs within one's own congregation. Furthermore, it is possible, especially if one has access to a computer to aid in the analysis, to compare the responses of significant groups within the congregation—for example, leaders versus nonleaders; actives versus inactives; new members versus old-timers; various age groups within the congregation; and so forth.

The profile (or subgroup profiles) that emerges gives insights into a congregation's identity in several ways. First, the profile enables the study team to get a sense of the typical or modal pattern of belief within a congregation, ranging from highly orthodox to unorthodox or agnostic. Where there is considerable agreement on beliefs, one may infer a rather clear theological identity; where there is considerable spread in the response pattern, the theological identity is much less clear, which, in itself is an important datum about the congregation's identity. In either case, the analysis provides some clues into the interaction between the little and great traditions within that congregation. Second, assuming that what a person or group believes has some consequences for behavior—a point we will discuss further under the heading of character—the belief profile that emerges can stimulate fruitful discussion about the degree to which a congregation's behavior, reflected in its programs, processes, and relationship to the world about it—is consistent with its fundamental beliefs about God and God's purposes in the world. Additionally, leaders of the congregation, who are typically concerned with bringing the congregation's little tradition more into harmony with the great tradition, may find helpful insights into areas of needed emphasis in the programs of the church. Finally, the responses to several of the belief items listed above can be useful in the analysis of a congregation's world view, which will be considered in the subsequent section.

A second structured way of characterizing the current identity of a congregation with respect to its heritage is in terms of the congregation's orientation to mission—how its members understand and act in relation to issues in society. As is well known, many conflicts have occurred in congregations over such issues. In a study of congregational orientations to mission, Roozen, McKinney, and Carroll[16] developed a set of questions that enables a congregation to characterize itself in terms of four different orientations to mission. Most congregations are a mixture of the four, but typically one of them is dominant. The first two orientations are "this-worldly" in focus; the latter two are more "otherworldly." The orientations are as follows:

Activist   This world is the arena of God's redemptive activity and also, therefore, the arena in which God calls the *congregation* to speak out on issues and engage in corporate action, working for social change and transformation towards a more just and loving society. The activist orientation includes a critical stance towards existing social and economic structures and does not shy away from controversy in the interest of maintaining harmony.

Civic   This world, as for the Activist, is the arena in which God calls Christians to act and to take responsibility for public life; however, the civic orientation is more comfortable with the existing social and economic institutions. It is more concerned with making them work well than with challenging them. Furthermore, the congregation itself resists acting as a corporate body in public; rather it provides a forum in which social issues can be discussed and debated in a way that enables *individual* members to act responsibly as Christians, though not as representatives of the congregation.

Evangelistic   This world is devalued in favor of the world to come. To call persons to salvation and the promise of eternal life in the world to come, members are encouraged to witness to their faith, sharing the message of salvation with those outside the fellowship and leading them to membership in the church. The spirit of the Great Commission is at the center of congregational life, and the power of the redeemed life is sufficient to overcome members' hesitancy to proselytize among members of other religious traditions as well as among the unchurched.

Sanctuary   Also otherworldly in emphasis, this orientation encourages the view that church exists mainly to provide persons with opportunities to withdraw, in varying degrees, from the trials and vicissitudes of daily life into the company of committed fellow believers. A sharp distinction is made between the sacred and secular, between the spiritual and temporal realms. The temporal realm is sinful, but nevertheless God-given and necessary to human existence. Thus Christians are expected to live in the world, accepting it as it is, and to uphold its laws; but they are to be "not of this world" in their deepest loyalty which belongs only to God.

We repeat: each of these orientations may be found in a single congregation. Some members may understand the church more in terms of one than another of the orientations; however, there is typically a modal or dominant orientation. It can be discerned, not only in verbal statements such as descriptions of the church's purpose or in sermons, but also in church programs—in those things that a congregation emphasizes or does not emphasize in its programs. As the dominant orientation, it is very much an element in the congregation's identity.

The four statements above can be used as is, for example, as guides to participant observation in the congregation. In the book from which they are drawn, there are case studies of ten congregations based on participant observation. Observers participated in worship services and educational programs, talked with members, attended board and committee meetings, examined annual reports, budgets and minutes. They listened and watched for significant themes, images, and metaphors which would help them understand the congregation's orientation to mission. From this, it was usually possible to identify one theme that was dominant in the way the congregation understood its mission.[17]

As an alternative, one might give the statements to members or leaders as a paper and pencil exercise, asking them to rank the orientations in terms of how each is (or should be) reflected in the mission of the congregation. Such an exercise is a helpful way to initiate a discussion on the congregation's identity.

Yet another alternative is to use a questionnaire with the following statements which have been found to measure the four orientations.[18] The statements can be preceded by a question such as: "Listed below are several descriptive statements regarding activities in which a congregation might engage. How likely would your congregation be to engage in each one?" Four response categories can be given for each: (1) Very Likely, (2) Somewhat Likely, (3) Somewhat Unlikely, (4) Very Unlikely. We have grouped the statements under the four orientations; however, in a questionnaire, the theme names should not be used, and the statements should appear in random order.

Activist
1. Sponsor organized social action groups within the congregation.
2. Promote social change through organized, collective influence.
3. Encourage the pastor to speak out on social and political issues.
4. Provide financial support for social action activities.
5. Support corporate congregational participation in social and political issues.

Civic
1. Cooperate with other religious groups for community improvements.
2. Provide aid and services to people in need.
3. Help persons understand themselves as agents of God's love and hope.
4. Encourage members, as individuals, to be involved in social issues.
5. Encourage members to reach their own decisions on matters of faith and morals.

Evangelistic

1. Maintain an active evangelism program, inviting the unchurched to participate.
2. Encourage members to make explicit faith declarations to friends and neighbors.
3. Reach out to members of other religious groups with the message of true salvation.
4. Protect members from the false teachings of other religious groups.
*5. Prepare members for a world to come in which the cares of this world are absent.

Sanctuary

1. Resist the temptation of contemporary "pleasures" and lifestyles.
*2. Prepare members for a world to come in which the cares of this world are absent.
3. Accept one's condition and status as controlled and determined by God.
4. Encourage obedience to civil laws as a religious duty.
5. Foster a sense of patriotism as a religious duty.

*NOTE: This item is included in both the Evangelistic and Sanctuary orientations because of its importance for each.

The pattern of response for each of the statements can be summarized for the congregation as a whole, using either percentages or an average score. (For computing the average scores, a "Very Likely" response should be scored as 1; a "Somewhat Likely" as 2, and so forth.) Additionally, a score for each orientation can be computed for each person responding to the questionnaire by summing the responses to each question reflecting the orientation. From this, an aggregate score for the congregation can be computed for each orientation by summing the orientation score for each individual and dividing by the total number responding. For example, this method of scoring might reveal that a congregation has aggregate scores of 1.2 for Activist, 4.3 for Civic, 5.2 for Evangelistic, and 3.2 for Sanctuary. In this case, its orientation to mission would reflect a somewhat otherworldly focus, with considerable emphasis on evangelistic outreach but little on work for social change. The responses of types of members within a congregation—leaders and nonleaders, actives and inactives, and so forth—can also be compared to examine areas of agreement/disagreement. Any one of these methods for scoring or summarizing the responses can become the basis for a lively discussion of a congregation's identity as expressed in its orientation to mission.

The various techniques we have described thus far are ways primarily of describing the current theological identity of a congregation—its *being*. But we said that the current identity, which generally reflects a congregation's little tradition, needs to be examined in light of the great tradition. Such an examination is necessary both as a critique of the congregation's current identity and as a way of helping it to explore its identity as *becoming*. In general, such reflection as this follows the pattern suggested by Joseph Hough in the passages cited previously. It is a task of biblical and theological reflection. There are many differing methods for doing such reflection; however, let us simply cite two that we believe are especially helpful. Because they are described in considerable detail elsewhere, including helpful illustrations and guides to their use, we will be quite brief.

For the study of biblical passages and themes in their relation to a congregation's being, the method developed by Walter Wink and described in his book, *Transforming Bible Study*[19] is useful. The method not only takes the text in its literary and historical context seriously, but also through a method of questioning, it enables participants in the study to "live into" the text so that it becomes vivid for them. Most importantly, it leads them to apply it to themselves and their situation in a way that can be deeply transformative. In studying a congregation's identity, biblical passages on the church and its mission are especially appropriate.

Somewhat similar to Wink's method, but drawing on other elements of the great tradition as well, is a method of theological reflection developed by James D. Whitehead and Evelyn Eaton Whitehead and described, with examples and exercises, in their book, *Method in Ministry*.[20] The method involves bringing to bear three sources of information in reflecting on issues in the ministry of the church: the Christian tradition (what we have called the great tradition); personal experience (including the experience of a congregation—its little tradition); and cultural information. Through reflection on this mix of information, a congregation can find resources to critique its being and be opened to new possibilities for its becoming.

In addition to these two methods for bringing images and themes from the great tradition to bear transformatively on a congregation's current identity, a number of other methods of exploration exist, including study and discussion of such books as *Christ and Culture*, by H. Richard Niebuhr, or Avery Dulles' *Models of the Church*,[21] both of which lay out clear models, drawn from the great tradition, for thinking about a congregation's identity.

2.5 World View

2.5.1 What Is a World View?

Closely akin to heritage is world view, and though they are related, they are also helpfully distinguished. Our world view is the perspective we use to make sense of our total life. That life touches not only our personal selves but also the various societies in which we participate, as well as nature and what we find sacred. World view gives powerful shape to what we experience; it combines into images the raw data we receive through our five senses, gives the images universal significance, and evokes in us deep emotions about their reality. Our world view is the scene we see in which our lives gain ordered significance.

World views differ. What one person or group finds to be valid, real, feared, or suspected about life is often distinguishable from that which another person or group sees. When speaking about variation in world views we generally differentiate the variety according to a liberal-conservative spectrum of beliefs. That distinction, based upon two categories of world view, is too simple to guide an inquiry that attempts to understand the complex but fragile shaping a person or congregation gives to their experience. In the analyses that follow we shall therefore suggest a somewhat larger set of categories by which we might tune in more finely to a congregation's particular expression of world view.

While world views differ, they do not occur indiscriminately in human groups. One of the major forces that binds a congregation, and thus effects its identity, is the roughly common pattern of members' world views. Individuals may both select a local church that possesses a world view congenial to their own, and also, once a part of that fellowship, align their own perspective more closely to the dominant interpretation of life shared by other members. World views are negotiations; members work to align various options in explaining the events of their lives. A congregation's struggle to make coherent sense of an uncertain world is a wondrous transaction that we are privileged to uncover, if only slightly, in this exercise.

2.5.2 Setting the Scene

Consider a church building made largely of windows that permit the building's occupants to look out four sides to a continuous horizon. Now picture that horizon to be a gigantic circle of western literature, with its many books arranged according to a pattern in which books placed closest to each other have the greatest similarity of motif, and those whose outlooks differ the most from each other are separated by half the horizon.

The literary critic Northrop Frye has laid out literature in such a cosmic circle, and has delineated it much as one might box a compass.[22] As a compass in its 360-degree swing passes four cardinal points, so Frye's depiction of literature acknowledges four basic narrative categories, each joined to the next in a total turn. The cardinal categories, which we, following Frye, have used in a technical way, are comedy, romance, tragedy, and irony.

One reason that Frye gives writing such a spatial orientation is to enrich its meaning. It is toward the promising eastern dawn that he orients comic literature. Towards an adventurous southern noonday he marshalls romantic works. He places tragic literature in the declining western sunset, and consigns ironic writing to the northern night. Viewed as a whole (which a human can never do) the entire collection forms one gigantic repetitive story that moves from cosmic security through romantic quest to tragic defeat and then to ironic death, but then beyond through resurrection again to comedy, there to begin the round again. Any single writing is a manageable bit of this gigantic myth.

Were members of a congregation to stand in our transparent building in such a way that they could react to the messages of the literary horizon, they would probably cluster themselves closer to one side than another. They might prefer a tragic interpretation rather than a comic one. Other congregations would seek different orientations, reinforcing their own ideas in relation to a particular sector of literary understanding.

Like the directions marked on a compass, one could be pointed to many gradations between literature (and we between congregational world views) that are, for example, comic ironies and those that are ironic comedies, depending upon which primary category they most resemble. What is at least uncommon and logically difficult is for a book or congregational world view to be simultaneously pointed towards the opposite points of the circle: comic and tragic, or ironic and romantic.

We will first give a brief, more literary definition of the four categories and then look at ways in which each is expressed in congregational world view.

1. *Comedy* is basically concerned with the development of harmony. It is not necessarily humorous. The complications of life are found to be illusory when actors find the true nature of reality and join in its accord. The opposite of tragedy, comic development moves from a supposed subordination beneath power to union with it.

2. *Romance* involves a quest. The complications of life are the real consequences of embarking upon an

adventure that pits protagonist against antagonist. Such struggle results in a priceless reward: a great love, a holy object, a boon for the world. The opposite of irony, romance requires a hero or heroine to move from a domestic uniformity into outlying uncertainties and uncommon blessings.

3. *Tragedy*, like romance, involves a hero or heroine but one whose vicissitudes force his or her decline. The opposite of comedy, tragic development moves from a mistaken union of the hero and power to his or her subordination, and often death, beneath power. One's tragedy is resolved not by gaining better status but by accepting the pattern which restricts and diminishes one's autonomy.

4. *Irony* has no heroes and heroines; supposedly heroic situations and their actors are found to be all too human. In this motif, the opposite of romance, life moves from strange uncertainties and uncommon blessings toward uniform, natural explanation. Irony is resolved in empirical understanding and in the camaraderie of persons who recognize their equally human, nonsupernatural equality.

2.5.3 Congregational Language

World views that reflect images like the above do not seep imperceptibly among members of a group; views are conveyed by recognizable signs and codes by which people communicate with each other. That common language is primarily verbal and written, but it also includes, especially in groups like congregations, a large number of gestures, marks, physical signs, and symbolic activities that themselves transmit the nuances of a world view. By this varied but common language members exchange information about their world. We can overhear much of what they say.

In congregational communication that conveys a *comic* interpretation of the world, we can recognize varied degrees of a gnostic drama that intuits a hidden unfolding of meaning in the world. Through their deepening consciousness, seekers unite with that meaning and thus gain an ultimate peace and perpetuation.

Phrases and signs that tend to convey a comic sense of the world include:

—"It all adds up"; "It will all work out"
—"Let go and let God"
—"Possibility thinking"
—"Go with the flow"
—Acknowledgments of a cosmic force
—Acts of meditation
—Consciously symbolic gestures and artifacts that beckon deeper contemplation
—Holistic healing practices

Communication within a congregation that pursues a *romantic* world view is more heroic than that pursuing the comic interpretation. But romance occupies a position adjacent to comedy on the horizon, and congregations can partake of varying degrees of both orientations. A critical difference in the romantic view is its charismatic understanding of a supernatural spirit that encounters and transforms seekers but does not merge with them into one being. The indomitable love and power of a transcendent God rather meets those who undertake the adventure away from routine existence.

Phrases and signs that tend to convey a romantic sense of the world include:

—"Expect a miracle"
—"I want Jesus to be my Lord and not just my Savior:
—"God told me . . ."; "God wanted me to . . ."
—"We met Christ"
—Experiences of God's felt presence
—Manifestations of a Spirit baptism, including glossolalia
—Healing requiring touch and prayer
—Visions

In *tragic* communication a congregation speaks more in terms of obedience than adventure. Although a heroic situation characterizes both the realms of romance and tragedy, the romantic hero meets God in personal encounter, while the tragic hero confronts God's word and will. A congregation may orient its perceptions somewhere between these adjacent positions, relying in part upon a direct experience with God and in part upon a mediating canon such as Scripture or an authoritative church. But members seldom reflect the opposing views of comedy and tragedy. The tragic perspective opposes gnostic aspects of comedy that find life's contradictions solved by a consciousness of cosmic harmony. Instead, the tragic orientation of a congregation is canonic; it decrees that life submit to, but not merge into, a transcendent canon given by God. Fundamentalists offer a highly tragic interpretation of the world when they speak of an infallible biblical pattern that orders human knowledge and world history.

Phrases and signs that convey a tragic sense of the world include:

—"The way of the cross"
—"Bible-centered, Bible-believing churches"
—"Get right with God"
—"Dying to self"
—References to moral decay and damnation
—Acts of allegiance and submission to God

—Acceptance of illness and catastrophe as part of
  God's plan
—Traditional missionary activities

Other congregations convey more of an *ironic* world
view. Relying upon an empiric understanding of
phenomena that questions the validity of gnostic
intuitions, charismatic blessings or canonic patterns in
life, an ironic congregation instead expresses belief in
the integrity of simple human experience. Such an
orientation is not irreligious; it also gives faith to a world
view, but one in which supernatural explanations are
suspect. Especially troublesome to an ironically
oriented congregation are the charismatic claims of a
romantic church. Both focus upon love, but for the
ironists that love is a horizontal power among fellow
humans, not a vertical power that singularly blesses
certain events and persons. Ironists regularize but
celebrate humanity. Congregations may combine this
perception with either of the adjacent views, giving a
tragic or comic edge to their perspective.

Phrases and signs that convey an ironic sense of the
world include:

—"Not holier than thou"
—"Being honest and realistic"
—"Relevance to everyday life"
—"Fulfilling human potential"
—Attention to issues of justice
—Acceptance of illness or catastrophe as a fact of life
—Emphasis upon fellowship
—Symbols used for their ethical implications

2.5.4 Hearing the Language

World view is communicated within a congregation
by its language of phrases, signs, and stories like those
described in the previous section. The components can
function as *indicative* aspects of that language; they thus
describe life as the congregation experiences it, giving it
specific shape and meaning. As a congregation's
language also performs *subjunctive* functions that
valuate life and *imperative* actions that actuate it, we
have to use an analytical method that helps to
distinguish its indicative aspect.

Several methods such as participant observation and
documentary analysis are useful, but here we suggest
uses of a guided interview technique as particularly
well-suited to the task. Not only can a guided interview
of this sort help disclose the indicative nature of a
congregation's expression of "being"; it can also work
to nuance the indicative dimension of the group's
"becoming." The suggested interview questions concern crises. Crises challenge the very world view

advanced in their answer. In participating in conversations built on crises, we are privileged not only to learn
something about the informants' constructions of
reality, but their responses to threats to their world
views. While there may be some initial anxiety or
uneasiness on the part of respondents before the
interview, most, however, soon sense the open spirit of
the conversation—that they are not being tested and
that their answers are in fact useful and interesting—
and many become enthusiastic about the process.
Pastors who have used this method report that some
interviews are among the more satisfying of their
pastoral calls, opening unprecedented communication
between pastor and parishioner.

In the interview, the interviewer asks a person to
recall his or her thoughts about different sorts of limit
situations. When informants in a friendly atmosphere
can nonetheless address threatening topics, they often
explore aloud the "being" and "becoming" of their own
stories. At some point in the interview three questions
are asked that portray crises related to one's person and
group:

—Think of the death of a friend or relative. What do
  you suppose was going on?
—Tell me about the way your faith has changed
  throughout the years.
—What is happening with someone who is senile?

Although these questions may be asked at any
appropriate moment in the interview, it has proved
generally helpful to begin with the instance of death.
The question often releases an extraordinary number of
ideas and suspicions that the informant has seldom
shared, and the exchange sets the tone for the rest of the
conversation.

To understand other aspects of the world that the
informant expresses, further questions are asked about
crises in larger contexts:

—Remember a time where life in your family seemed
  out of control. What was really happening?
—What is God doing with our nation?
—What would a new pastor do to the life of your
  church?

And some questions that deal with the supernatural:

—Has God ever spoken to you? Given you a sign?
—Have you felt God's presence?
—How do you get in touch with God?

Write down as much as possible of the informant's
answer as it is spoken, and later fill in the gaps. The

interview may be tape-recorded, but note-taking is recommended. Use five-by-eight-inch cards; they permit the easier comparison and rearrangement of notes. Mark the source and sequence of each card.

About half of the persons interviewed should be those who give formal and informal leadership to the congregation. The other half should be a sample of membership varied according to sex, age, education, and intensity or participation. Interview people individually, not as couples or groups.

2.5.5 Analysis

1. Read your notes as if they were spoken by inhabitants of a recently discovered village. Your task is to find out, with as little preconception as possible, how your informants describe what is going on in life, where it seems headed and why. Explore how they perceive themselves as persons, how they typify their church, their world, and their God.

2. Underline phrases that characterize the nature of things and events.

3. Note recurrent themes: images that organize the ideas of several informants, similar phrases, common solutions, reiterated stories, repeated symbols. Put each theme on a separate card.

4. Arrange the cards in a spatial pattern that suggests the affinity of each of the four world view categories, the closer the card to the cardinal point the greater the consonance between its language and the world view type, as illustrated in figure 2–B.

Figure 2-B

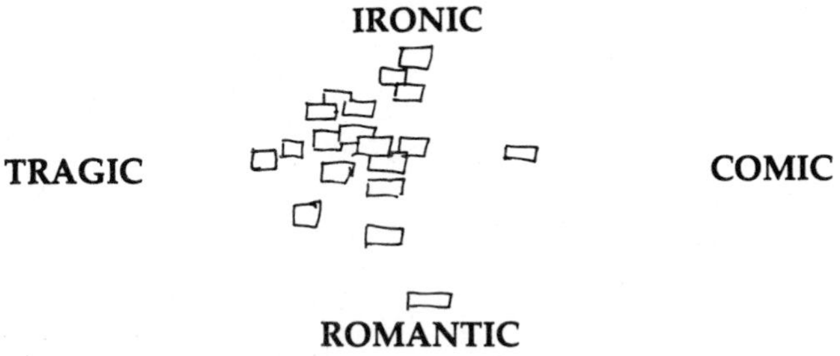

IRONIC

TRAGIC   **COMIC**

ROMANTIC

5. Against that background write down a composite depiction of life viewed from the perspective of the local church.

From this base further inquiries could:

—*thicken* the description by a second round of interviews (some with the same informants) and by participant observation and analysis of documents written by members of the congregation

—*test* the picture by a survey instrument that asked similar questions, and/or by the objective assessments of members of the congregation

—*determine* whether the picture is more characteristic of nuclear than marginal members

—*compare* the view with that of another congregation. In that much of a congregation's expression is already familiar to its church-going observer, the contrast between the pattern of two churches would bring a deeper appreciation of the variables in world view that each employs

A clearer understanding of a congregation's world view enables one to perceive with greater accuracy what is communicated in preaching, prayer, and counseling. Differences in world view often play a part in conflicts among members, and may distinguish various adult groups and church school classes. Caring for a person requires that a minister comprehend that person's world view.

2.6 Symbols

A symbol stands for something else. Virtually everything said and done in a parish is, therefore, symbolic, representing matters different from the actual sounds, sights, and movements that convey their meaning. We participate in congregational life not merely to experience the direct effect of its words and actions but also to represent symbolically our association with a reality beyond the specific event we ourselves make. Bowing one's head is symbolic insofar as it suggests a disposition other than physically inclining one's neck. Not only, however, are singular parish gestures like bowing symbolic; all words uttered are themselves symbols, for they stand for things other than their actual sounds. Built largely on words, gestures, and their combinations, a congregation is in one sense constituted by a highly complex system of symbols.

To distinguish, however, those relatively few symbols within its whole system that appear critical to a congregation's identity, we shall make a somewhat arbitrary distinction between signs and symbols. Both signs and symbols stand for something else, but signs can be said to make their points with low emotional stimulus but with high specificity about their referents. Most signals in a congregation's communication system are by this definition signs. Everything from the "office" marking on a door to the report of the building and grounds committee are signs insofar as they convey information dispassionately and clearly. If we designate most of a congregation's language to be signs, we may permit ourselves a more restricted definition of symbol. A symbol thus stands for something else, but with high emotional stimulus and low specificity about what that something is.

Frequently a congregation uses the cross as its primary symbol. While members express a relatively high degree of emotion in their associations with the cross, they have difficulty pinning down precisely what the cross signifies, in comparison to the precision by which they could state what "office" means. Symbols, in Victor Turner's term, are multivocal; they evoke a mysterious complexity of meaning and do so in a way that one's identity is itself caught up in their enactment.[23]

The symbols of a congregation often have no patently Christian association. The building and grounds of the group symbolize many qualities implied in "turf." A graceful chandelier in the sanctuary may convey senses of illumination, beauty, and property important to a congregation's identity but may imply no distinctly Christian quality. Symbols, moreover, are often unconsciously presented. While some objects such as a banner may be deliberately displayed as a symbol, many others, such as furniture arrangements and financial disclosures, function less obviously in the symbolic realm but nevertheless represent aspects critical to a congregation's identity.

2.6.1 Methods of Exploration

A helpful way of examining the symbology of a congregation is to look at the parish as if it occurred in the distant past and to ask of its artifacts that do not have an obviously instrumental explanation, "What did this mean to its members?" The point is to take no part of parish life for granted, to ponder not only what things and behaviors do but also what they signify to their participants. As one finds certain items, such as a particular joke, or a type of literature in the church foyer, that seem especially linked to identity, one asks members about them:

—How come the pictures in the hall show no women?
—Tell me the story about the unused parlor.
—What does this altar rail mean to you?

A church frequently holds, moreover, one or more areas that members sense to be "warm" or perhaps "holy," indicating space that is highly charged with symbolic meaning. Warmth may manifest itself in different places in different churches: at thresholds, Bible classes, altar, around the coffee urn, in the pastor's study. Holiness frequently accompanies the area in which unambiguously Christian symbols, like sermon and sacrament, are presented. In analyzing the

meaning of such areas, one would both observe the styles of behavior (see also the following section on ritual) that occur there and also encourage participants to express their understanding of what the place and their actions signify.

People as well as objects and actions function as symbols in a congregation. The person in the congregation most often perceived to represent something beyond himself or herself is the ordained person, especially the congregation's chief pastor. As Urban Holmes would point out, the pastor acts as a bridge by which a community links its formal and empirical comprehension with its intuited sense of myth and metaphor.[24] Characters other than the pastor in the congregational drama serve a similarly symbolic function, and the analyst of parish identity would seek their significance as well.

2.6.2 Analysis

Their diffuse meanings notwithstanding, congregational symbols seem specific enough to be differentiated according to several categories. We use these categories to explore more precisely the symbols of congregational identity.

1. Certain symbols seem employed primarily to indicate the link between the congregation and *transcendence*. They are often found in the precincts of the sanctuary, and they employ the more recognizably Christian representations of God's salvation: Bible, cross, sacrament, biblical figures in stained glass, and so forth. Such symbols communicate the congregation's participation in the great tradition and intimate the ultimate worth of the identity provided a congregation.

2. Other symbols indicate the intertwining of a congregation's identity and *love*. Food is a primary symbol employed by the parish in this category. Except in the case of meals for the destitute, where plain nutrition is more the object, food in the congregation usually is a way of signifying love; it is a sign of fellowship. When we want to indicate the solidarity with others our corporate identity provides, we may show it in symbols like coffee, doughnuts and parish suppers.

3. Other symbols express the association of a congregation's identity with *power*. Here neither ultimacy nor intimacy are so much at stake as an assurance of consequence in what the group does. Some symbols such as money are used by the parish to signal its capacity to achieve or miss its goals. Money—its pledging, offering, display, and accounting—is a primary symbol by which a congregation shows to itself its authority. A seemingly drab financial report of the

parish may in fact signify the identity of the church with accomplishment or failure.

4. Still other symbols may represent a congregation's sense of *justice*. While the signals in a parish may not be as radical as symbols used by a social action group, they nevertheless exhibit the congregation's identification with ideals of fairness and human rights. Posters, donations, and social programs may not only have an instrumental effect but also express a symbolic commitment of the church to principles of justice.

The variety of roles expected of the congregation's pastor reflect such different symbolic referents. For example, in classical distinctions among the "offices" of ministry, we can examine the representations of transcendence that are primarily associated with a priestly role, or the symbols of love generally associated with a pastoral role. The images of power and justice are largely allied, respectively, with the kingly and prophetic offices. As pastors move through their day's diverse activities, they not only do things, they also represent qualities of the Christian life such as the four suggested here. To analyze the particular symbolic pattern of an individual pastor, one might begin by asking how the pastor's person and actions portray ultimacy, love, authority and justice.

Other people in the congregation, of course, also stand for these qualities. The equivalent of "Mr. Methodist" in the parish, or the family that always sits up front, seems often to symbolize a congregation's sense of transcendence, while "Ma Smith" in the kitchen represents love. "Old Man Bigbucks" typifies its power, and teenagers may embody the church's hopes for justice. Members should be examined both for what they do for a congregation and for what they mean to it.

2.6.3 Becoming

Symbols are seen primarily as assurances of being, but they are also instrumental in representing changes in congregational identity. Frequently this change seems to occur in a deliberate shift in a symbol's referent. When an image such as the cross is conscientiously related to negotiations usually symbolized by references to money, or when Old Man Bigbucks identifies himself with an issue of social justice, we witness what could become a paradigm shift, a basic transformation in the way a congregation views and values itself.

2.7 Ritual

2.7.1 Ritual and Identity

Ritual, as we defined it earlier, is repetitive action that has more than utilitarian significance. It is a form of nondiscursive, gestural language through which a group acts out meanings and relationships that are of enduring significance to its life. All ongoing groups develop rituals through which they communicate that which is central to their existence; here, however, we are especially concerned with rituals in congregations and their relationship to identity.

Rituals function analogously to various creedal statements and symbols. They communicate meanings and relationships that express a congregation's identity—either what its identity actually is (or once was), or what its identity is becoming. Thus a congregation says something about itself as a community by the sincerity of the ritual greeting one receives at the door of the church. And it says something also about its identity as the Body of Christ as members share the cup and bread of the Lord's Supper. The congregation is not simply saying something in these rituals that could as equally well be said verbally. Anna Pavlova is said to have responded when a questioner asked "What do you say when you dance?": "If I could tell you, I wouldn't dance." Orrin Klapp refers to this quality of communication through ritual action as "mystique." It is "the whole meaning that a person gets, usually without being able to fully describe it."[25] This is why a congregation cannot rely solely on verbal statements to communicate its identity. Ritual and symbols are needed as well; although, to be sure, ritual events are important for reasons other than communicating a congregation's identity. In exploring ways rituals function as communication about a congregation's identity, two distinctions are helpful.

First there is the distinction made earlier between the great and little traditions. There are rituals that communicate about identity related to each of the two traditions. The former express meanings about the congregation's identity as standing within the broad sweep of the universal church; the latter communicate the identity of a particular congregation, its appropriation of the great tradition as that tradition is refracted through the congregation's peculiar historical experience.

The second distinction reflects the difference between rituals that are "rites of passage" and those that are "rites of intensification." The former were first so designated by Arnold van Gennep and refer to rituals that have developed in every known society around particular times of transition in individual life: birth, puberty, marriage, and death.[26] The recent emphasis on various life stages has made us aware of the importance of a variety of other life cycle transitions as well. Transition periods are not only potentially disruptive to the individual involved, but also to the society or group of which he or she is a member. Rites of passage, van Gennep pointed out, involve a period of separation from a previous status, a transitional or liminal (threshold) stage; and a stage of incorporation into a new status. The rites enable both the individual and group to deal with and accept the transition. In the process, especially during the liminal or threshold period, the individual moves from one state of being (a previous identity), through a period of becoming, to a new being (a new identity). He or she is now an adult rather than a child, or a spouse rather than a single person, or a member of the congregation rather than a non-member, or a loved one who is now with God in eternal life rather than present with her or his human family or community. In the process, too, the rituals enable the group to rehearse and reaffirm its identity in relation to the changed individual—the "new being" that is in their midst, or now physically absent in the case of a death.

Other anthropologists have called attention to a second type of ritual: those rites aimed at intensifying a group's commitment to its shared beliefs and meanings.[27] Rites of intensification include a variety of occasions—for example, Thanksgiving, Christmas, Easter, Memorial Day, Fourth of July—in which core meanings of a group, be it church or nation, are lifted up and celebrated. They too can involve a kind of liminal or threshold experience through which one passes from "everyday life" to a rehearsal of core aspects of the community's life and back to "everyday life" as a renewed individual or community.

Without trying to be exhaustive, let us consider several rites of passage and rites of intensification that reflect either or both the great and little traditions:

1. *Rites of passage.* Such rituals as baptism, confirmation, receiving new members, funerals, ordaining/installing a new pastor, and even greeting newcomers at the church door reflect transition events not only for the individuals involved, but also for the congregation. They are occasions for rehearsing aspects of a congregation's identity in relation both to the great tradition (the church universal) and the little tradition (the congregation's unique heritage). In greeting newcomers, or baptism, or confirmation, or receiving new members, what is the congregation communicating to itself and others about its identity? A warm and open family as part of the "family of God" or one that newcomers will have difficulty joining? A body of Christians who take their commitments seriously, or one that demands little by way of belief or participation? (One congregation of our acquaintance asks new members only, "Do you believe in Jesus Christ, whatever that means to you?")

Increasingly, too, the entire period surrounding the change of pastors is seen as a transitional stage of great significance for examining a congregation's present identity (its being) and asking what it would like to become. In this, both the great and little traditions come into play, especially as the time is used for self-study and determining the type of pastoral leadership that is needed. For Hope United Church of Christ, the congregation introduced in chapter 1, participation in the rite of passage around pastoral change was painful because, in part at least, members resisted confronting honestly aspects of their identity which the transition period requires in the process of moving from "being" to "becoming."

How congregation members act at the time of a death of one of its members provides additional significant opportunities for observing a major rite of passage and discerning aspects of congregational identity. While every death is a disruptive experience, this is especially true for a congregation when it is the death of a core member or when the death has occurred unexpectedly, prematurely, or as the result of an accident. Of importance is not only the actual funeral rite itself—the place it is held, the words, symbols, gestures, liturgical pattern, presence of the body during the service, whether the casket is open or not, the behavior of those present, and so forth—but also the patterns of the members in coming to the support of families before and after the funeral—bringing food, attending wakes, ways of expressing condolences. These behaviors are not random; rather every congregation (and community) develops patterned ways—rituals—for dealing with them. And these various behaviors and symbols are clearly significant clues to a congregation's attitudes towards death, their relation to the great tradition and especially, their little tradition. They also are important clues to their world view. When a young member is killed in an automobile accident, the patterns of behavior of a congregation with a *comic* interpretation of the world will respond quite differently from one with a *tragic* perspective.

2. *Rites of intensification.* Some rites of intensification in congregations are especially significant in renewing and intensifying commitment to the great tradition: the various seasons and special days of the Christian year as a whole; the celebration of the Lord's Supper; and, in general, the "shape" or order of the regular Sunday worship, with its movement from adoration to confession, to assurance of forgiveness, to thanksgiving, to reflection of the meaning of God's Word, to offering and rededication. This order in effect rehearses the story of the congregation's life. In addition, some rites of intensification are especially important for communicating those aspects of congregational iden-

tity related to the little tradition: homecoming celebrations; an annual strawberry festival or church fair; coffee hours and potluck suppers; and annual meetings of the congregation which not only conduct church business but rehearse the events of the past year. What happens in such rites, both those reflecting the great and little traditions? Not only do they provide occasions for remembering the congregation's history—one in which they share by being members of the congregation—but also their history as a part of the Church Universal. They also help disparate groups within the congregation experience their oneness as a particular people and as members of the Body of Christ. Then, too, they provide occasions for young and old alike to learn about the heritage of the congregation—its particular heritage and its heritage as a Christian community. Without such ways for transmitting its heritage, the congregation's identity would not likely be maintained.[28]

Rites of passage and intensification do not exhaust the ritual expressions of a congregation. Without trying to be exhaustive, we will mention several other rituals important to identity.

1. *Spatial arrangements and seating patterns.* Ritual and symbol come together in expressing clues to congregational identity in the arrangement of sacred space in the sanctuary or meeting room and in the patterned ways that individual members or types of members are seated. As is well known, some members have great difficulty emotionally if "their" seat in the sanctuary is preempted by a visitor or other member. Rather than ignoring or dismissing such behavior as irrational, one might begin to explore what the pattern is in a particular congregation and what it means, both to the individuals involved and also as expressive of the identity of the congregation itself. What is it about their particular spaces that have become sacred to the members?[29] What do the observed patterns say of the congregation as a whole? Is having a special seat or pew more typical of older members than younger? Long-time members than newer ones? "Pillars" of the congregation than "rank and file" members? Higher status than lower status members? Is it possible to get any clues to the "power structure" of a congregation by these seating patterns? Here is how anthropologist Melvin Williams describes the situation in a black Pentecostal congregation that he studied:

Physical setting in the sanctuary of Zion Holiness Church provides a critical index to the power and importance of particular persons. Although all of the sanctuary is sacred, some places have accumulated more status than others. Not only do the chorus and choir have their designated places, but the missionaries, church officers, and pastor's wife, as well as the pastor, have their places within the inner sacred space of the liturgical event every Sunday. Within this inner sacred space, the offering is received, preaching is lifted up, Communion passed out. The closer to the inner space, the more powerful a person is perceived to be. One's seat in Zion is more than a place to sit; it is an expression of one's status.[30]

This pattern is considerably different from that in congregations with different identities—for example, one made up of highly mobile, upper middle class individuals for whom the church is but one of the many associations to which they belong. Thus seating arrangements (as well as church membership itself) are less likely to be an important means for expressing status or power as for those for whom the congregation is a central focus of their lives. These differences are clear in the contrast which Williams draws between Zion Church and Wiltshire Church, a white, upper middle class, United Methodist congregation.

2. *Typical patterns of dealing with crises and conflicts.* More will be said about how congregations deal with differences in the chapter on process (chapter 4). Here, let us simply note that congregational identity is often expressed in the typical patterns for responding to crises and conflicts in the congregation that have developed over the years. The style of dealing with conflicts in the past will likely carry over into the present. It is not incorrect, we believe, to refer to these typical patterns as a form of congregational ritual through which it enacts an aspect of its identity. Its ritualized ways of facing crises and conflicts may include patterns of avoidance, denial, confrontation, working for amicable resolution, or a variety of other patterns. There is likely also to be a relation between these patterns and the theological assumptions and world view operative with the congregation.

3. *The underlife of the congregation.* Erving Goffman[31] has used the concept of the "underlife" of an institution to describe the way that individuals make adjustments to the demands that an institution places on them. There are in congregations explicit or implicit expectations ("demands" is probably too strong a word) for proper behavior of members. Such expectations, which are explored in more detail in the discussion of norms in chapter 4, grow out of the congregation's sense of identity. They can range from appropriate attitudes to be expressed in worship to appropriate dress for different occasions or for persons engaged in specific roles, or to appropriate behavior for members in their daily lives (e.g., members of this congregation don't drink alcoholic beverages, or members of this congregation are committed to social justice). The conflict over wine for the wedding at High Ridge Presbyterian Church reflects such an expectation for proper behavior by its members. Dean Kelley has noted that conservative churches typically have more explicit and stringent

expectations for their members than their more liberal counterparts.[32] Such expectations grow out of a congregation's identity, its sense of who it is. But, as Goffman noted, participants sometimes develop ways of seeming to honor these expectations while, at the same time, pursuing goals important to them that may run counter to the formal expectations. He calls these "secondary adjustments" and refers to them as making up the "underlife" of the institution. In such ways individuals acknowledge the congregation's identity but find ways of expressing their own goals where these come into some conflict. Some examples include:

—the teenaged couple who attend worship as they are expected to do but sit on the back row of the congregation so that they can carry on their courtship during the service
—the deacon who takes the morning offering to the bank for deposit allowing him to miss the remainder of the service while having nevertheless made an appearance
—the men who, in some rural churches, stay outside during the first hymn (the "cigarette hymn") to smoke and talk, which may be both a way to socialize but also to express, implicitly, the attitude that participation in the service is more important for women and children than for men
—members who like the pastor and rationalize her sermons on controversial subjects with which they disagree as being ones "the denomination required her to preach."

Sociologist Larry Ingram[33] has described a number of these "underlife" patterns in a Southern Baptist congregation. They too can be thought of as rituals or patterned behavior. Attention to them can give important clues to the norms of a congregation that express its identity as individual members honor them "in the breach."

2.7.2 Methods of Exploration and Interpretation

As with other aspects of identity, the method of participant observation is likely to be the most helpful for the study team in studying the rituals present within a congregation's life. Let us, nevertheless, suggest some explicit guidelines for observing ritual.

1. Make a list of all the ritual events that take place within the life of the congregation, from the seemingly peripheral ones (for example, the greetings at the door) to the central ones (for example, the Lord's Supper). Do not ignore the patterned behaviors that are not typically considered to be rituals, such as seating arrangements, responses to crises or aspects of the congregation's

"underlife." Enlist the aid of members in doing so.

2. Note the times of observance for each of the rituals listed. When are they carried out? Are they recurring throughout the year? Seasonal? Annual? Irregular, reflecting particular occurrences such as a birth or death or a specific congregational crisis?

3. Where do the rituals occur? In what space? As with the analysis of symbols, are some places where particular rituals occur more "warm" or "holy" than others?

4. Who is involved in the rituals? What are the roles of the various actors? Are the roles of some persons more important than others in the rituals? What are the characteristics of these people (e.g., their age, sex, position in the congregation, socioeconomic status)?

5. What are the attitudes and emotions displayed by the actors as they engage in the ritual? Awe? Respect? Seriousness? Sorrow? Happiness? Humor? Closeness with others? Distance from others?

6. What are the symbols used in the rituals? Would members object if they were changed?

7. What is the sequence of events in the rituals? Is the sequence generally invariant, or does it not seem to matter?

8. How do the congregation's members interpret the purpose of the ritual?

9. In analyzing the seating patterns of a congregation, it may be helpful to draw sociograms: diagrams drawn over several Sundays (if the morning worship service is what is being studied) or following several meetings of the official board, which note where people sit. Sociograms facilitate reflection on whether there is a pattern to the seating arrangements and whether this pattern reveals anything about a congregation's identity.

When questions like those above have been asked of the ritual, it will likely be the case that one will already have begun to discern clues to the congregation's identity. However, several further steps of analysis may also prove helpful.

1. Try to classify the various rituals in terms of the distinctions between rites of passage and rites of intensification or other forms of ritual. This will give clues as to the functons of the rituals. From observing the various rituals and from answers given to the questions above, one should begin to be able to say what it is that is being communicated to or about the congregation at particular transition points that have the potential of being disruptive to its life, or what meanings are being rehearsed in the various recurring sites of intensification. Or what is being said about the power structure of the congregation or tensions between congregational norms and those of individual members?

2. The distinction between the great and little traditions should also be useful in making sense out of the meanings being communicated. What aspects of the catholic tradition are being communicated about this congregation's identity? What aspects of its own peculiar heritage are being communicated? How does the latter affect the former and vice versa? Are there tensions between them that are potentially transformative and that may signal the congregation's "becoming?"

3. The discussion of the relation of symbols to transcendence, love, power, and justice in section 2.6.2 is equally appropriate to the analysis of a congregation's ritual, and it can be applied to the responses given to the questions in 1 and 2 above.

4. Are there common themes that begin to emerge out of the analysis of the various rituals? Are they recurring themes? Do they make sense when we think of them in relation to other aspects of the congregation's identity that we are studying? Do they make sense when we consider the congregation's program and the social and cultural context in which it is set? If the answer to these questions is generally affirmative, then we can be reasonably certain that we have heard what it is that the congregation is communicating through its rituals, whether explicitly or tacitly, about its identity.

2.8 Demographic Picture

2.8.1 Demography and Identity

Demography involves the careful description of groups of people, typically using statistics. In the following chapter on the congregation's context, demographic analysis is used as a way of understanding the context. Here it is employed to understand the congregation's identity, both its perceptions of itself and the identity it presents to outsiders. When we describe the age, gender, marital status, race, ethnicity, or socioeconomic characteristics of a congregation, we are presenting the congregation's demographic picture. How is this related to identity? In the case of an individual, personal characteristics (age, sex, marital status, race, ethnicity, and so forth) contribute to her "singular sense of who she is," as we defined identity earlier in psychological terms. And this sense of who she is is not only an identity of her own making, but is partly derived from the culturally defined meanings which others attribute to her in light of her demographic characteristics. Consider, for example, a thirty-year-old single woman, the daughter of Italian immigrants, with a college education and a middle management job in an insurance company. These characteristics by no means exhaust her identity, but they

constitute important ingredients of the meanings that both she and others attach to her and from which she derives a sense of who she is. To ignore them would be a mistake if our interest is to discover who she is or help her in self-discovery.

If this is true for individuals, it is also true for groups and, in particular, for congregations. Here our concern is not with the individual identities of the congregation's members, but of the demographic picture that the members constitute in the aggregate. And they involve the same kinds of characteristics we took note of for the individual. What we are interested in are both the distribution of the various demographic characteristics across the congregation—how homogeneous or heterogeneous the congregation is—and a picture of the typical or average member, if there is such. Both are important ingredients of a congregation's identity, especially what we earlier called its "being" or given character; but both also can be ingredients in its "becoming." Consider the following example, which illustrates the importance of these aspects of the demographic picture and their interaction with both context and program, which are discussed in subsequent chapters.

A congregation has for years prided itself on being a "family church." In the 1950s and 1960s, in particular, this image of its identity was accurate, based on its demographic picture, and it was reflected in its program. The congregation was quite homogeneous—white, upper middle class, mostly married with children of school age. These were its typical members. This "family church" identity persisted into the 1970s; however, the number of members began to decline sharply, and the families in the church increasingly were represented only by the mother and father. Few children and teenagers were present or active. The demographic picture of the typical congregation had changed; both the distribution of member characteristics and the typical member were no longer the same as before. Furthermore, the congregation was having difficulty reaching out to newcomers in the high rise apartments that were being built in the surrounding neighborhood. These persons were much more likely to be young singles, divorced persons, widows and widowers, or couples with no children. In short, although "family church" identity, reflecting an earlier demographic picture, was still dominant in the culture and program of the church, it had become dysfunctional both for its current members and for outreach to new residents in the neighborhood. Its identity and program were incompatible with its context. Analysis of their current demographic picture led congregational members to an awareness of who they presently were and how they had changed; and it led them to reflect on who they would like to become and what was necessary to bring about the change.

Another important way that analysis of the congregation's demographic picture gives insight into its identity is in the area of social class. This concept is difficult to define, and there is considerable debate among social theorists about its precise meaning, though not about its importance.[34] Generally (and begging the question of the distinction often made between class and status), we understand class to refer to those who share similar positions in society related to their education, income and occupation. As a consequence of being in a similar position on these attributes, they also tend to have similar social and political attitudes, economic interests, life-style, and life chances (access to such necessities as food, clothing, shelter, and health care). Although, in American society there are not the kinds of self-conscious classes that Karl Marx believed would always arise as a result of varying relationships to the means of production, it is not difficult to see the effects of class position in these various ways. Especially important are the class-related inequalities that exist. Various aspects of religious life itself are also affected by class. Thus, an important component of the identity of congregations—especially because people have considerable choice among the congregations they join—is the typical or dominant social class of its members. Preferred styles of worship (for example, informal and spontaneous vs. formal and structured) are related to class preferences, as are also differences in theological orientation, world views and beliefs about the mission of the church and of individual Christians in society.[35] The sharp debates between the "new Christian right" and socially liberal Christians over various social issues are in part reflections of different class interests as they interact with and influence theological and ethical orientations.[36] Thus, class analysis provides important clues to congregational identity and to a variety of aspects of congregational life and mission.

Other examples of the importance of understanding a congregation's demographic picture include the predominantly white congregation that wishes to reach out to blacks who are moving into the community, or the judicatory official who encounters resistance in trying to bring about the merger or clustering of congregations with differing demographic pictures.

2.8.2 Methods of Exploration

Of all the elements of identity that we discuss, the demographic picture is perhaps the easiest for which to gather the necessary data. There are two ways of going about it.

One way is to gather together a small number of people who are considerably knowledgeable about the membership. They pool their knowledge to come up with estimates of the percentage of members in different age, sex, racial/ethnic, marital status, educational, or occupational groups in the congregation. In a congregation with no more than three to four hundred members, this method generally works quite well. The percentages need only to be reasonably accurate to be helpful in describing the congregation.

The other method, especially necessary in larger congregations, is the use of a questionnaire, or inventory, filled out by the members themselves. The Parish Profile Inventory (General Appendix) includes a section of questions that can be used by a study team to develop a demographic profile. Such records can be updated periodically to provide insight into the changing demographic picture.

Using either method, the goal is to be able to describe the demographic picture quantitatively so that one can consider both the distribution of the various member attributes and give a profile of the typical member. Furthermore, because it is often important to be able to compare the demographic picture of the congregation's members with the profile of residents in the church's context, the study team should use categories comparable to those of the U.S. Census of Population (available in public libraries). These categories can be found in demographic questions used in the Parish Profile Inventory and in the discussion of the use of the Census in chapter 3.

2.8.3 Analysis

In summarizing the distribution of the various demographic characteristics, it is usually most helpful to convert them into percentages which will not only indicate the proportions in each category (thus showing the homogeneity/heterogeneity of the congregation), but will also reveal the typical or modal member (the category with the largest number). Using the median or mean as measures of the average will also provide a picture of the typical member; and the standard deviation (for those statistically inclined) can be computed to indicate the diversity that exists. Constructing an age-sex pyramid[37] is a graphic and often helpful way to represent the age-sex identity of a congregation; while other types of graphs (e.g., bar or line graphs or pie charts) also provide ways of picturing the congregation demographically.

A social class analysis of the congregation can draw on the various data gathering techniques described above to get a profile of the educational, occupational and income distribution of the congregation. But it also requires some imaginative reflection by leaders and members on the ways that their congregation's beliefs, practices, orientations to mission (or those of particular groups of members) are reflective of (not necessarily determined by) their social class position. One way to help this along is to do a comparative analysis of other congregations in the community and probe differences that may be related to the typical social class of members. Another way is to do interviews with nonmembers in the community, especially those from different economic, racial, or ethnic backgrounds, to probe how they view one's congregation. When leaders of one New England congregation asked a group of blacks in the town to tell them how blacks perceived the church, the church was described as "the big white church on the green." The double meaning of "big white church" was clear.

We have already suggested some uses of the demographic picture but let us reiterate them and add several others:

—To provide a profile of the congregation's typical member
—To indicate the degree of diversity that exists in a given congregation
—To compare the congregation's presumed demographic picture with its actual one
—To compare the congregation's demographic picture with that of residents in the community served by the congregation
—To provide important clues for program development for both present and potential members
—To assist a congregation to reflect on its given demographic identity in comparison with that which it would like to become
—To assist judicatory officials in understanding the congregations with whom they work—for example, when there is a pastoral change, when consultation or support is needed, or when clustering or mergers are contemplated.

2.9 Character

When leaders refer to the "personality" of their congregation, they generally have in mind all its traits and dispositions that distinguish it from other churches they have known. Their concept of personality is thus a summary way of talking about a parish's identity. We suggest that the concept of *character* is a more ample way of getting at the same issues. Less tied to connotations of the person than personality, character can better embrace corporate dimensions of outlook (heritage and world view), activity (history and ritual), constitution (demographic picture) and expression (symbol). Thus, in this sense, character is virtually synonymous with identity.

But character also more clearly identifies another aspect of identity not yet fully analyzed. This is the moral dimension of congregational life, its values, its preferred behavioral tone, its ethos, its corporate integrity. Like the other elements of identity, character thus refers both to the congregation's being and to its becoming. On the one hand character brings together the means by which a congregation merely exists in the world: what Clifford Geertz calls its "tendencies, capacities, propensities, skills, habits, liabilities, pronenesses."[38] On the other hand, character refers to the capacity of the congregation to engage also in moral deliberation. A church has the freedom to "have character" as well as to just "be" a collection of characteristic traits. Character, in the understanding of Stanley Hauerwas, "denotes not only what is distinctive but also what is in some measure deliberate, what a man can decide to be opposed to what he is naturally."[39]

It is helpful to contrast what is central in the valuing element of character with world view. While the latter refers to what a congregation perceives, character represents what the group prefers or values. World view treats what people suspect is going on, character what they wish would go on.

2.9.1 Studying Character

Participant Observation and Interviews

To understand some of the constituents of the character of a congregation, one may use the basic methods of ethnographic inquiry already described. Here we look for the themes by which the congregation prefers its life.

1. *Participant observation* is essential to the search. The study team analyzes the characteristics of nuclear members and principal leaders and contrasts these with the attributes of marginal members. Observers record actions and ponder the nature of events, and especially, because values are at stake, those events that show stress. Special attention must also be paid to a congregation's "street wisdom" about how things really get done and what really to avoid. Additionally, the observers note wishes, desires and instances of their fulfillment. Etiquette, style, and stereotypic behavior are watched and described. Throughout the study, the team keeps in mind the underlying questions: What do members show to be the preferable and reliable practice of their congregational household?

2. *Guided interviews* are also important in the study of character. They permit the actors themselves to ponder

their behavior and develop their own ideas about what congregational actions intend. Some of the better interviews may be with marginal members who often bring a more critical interpretation to church behavior. The type of questions to ask of all informants includes:

—Tell me about your own association with this church.
—How is this church most likely to fall apart?
—What sort of talk dampens the spirit of this church?
—What distinguishes this church from (a nearby competitor)?
—What sort of church program or project is frustrating and unproductive here?
—Think of a respected member. Without naming him/her, describe his/her characteristics.
—Think of an embarrassing member. Without naming him/her describe his/her characteristics.
—At what points in church life do you feel closest to God?
—At what points in church life do you feel in danger of losing touch with God?

As in other types of inquiry already described, data from informants contain themes and images that are not idiosyncratic to the individual but rather reflect a corporate pattern of culture. The study team's task in delineating congregational character is to pick out and describe those strands in the pattern that reflect values and disposition.

Corporate Moral Inquiry

Another way of exploring parish character is to assemble ten or twelve representative members of the parish to ponder some knotty moral issue such as abortion or a dimension of business ethics. The point is not so much to help people in their ongoing lives as to learn more clearly what constitutes the premises and range of variance in current parish attitudes. Both initial perceptions of participants and the ways by which they struggle for consensus should be recorded. Writing main points on newsprint would help the group themselves see the shape of their deliberations, but a more detailed record for later perusal should also be written or taped.

When approached as an exercise to discover parish character, the session might encourage deeper moral reflection than a session set up to promote a particular "right" response. Parish discussions of moral issues frequently begin with a formidable challenge such as "What is *the* Christian answer to _____?" A discussion conducted in the light of such an introduction has several handicaps, including an implication

that some people, like the pastor, harbor more profound answers than others. It also gives an opportunity for persons to assume a party line on the issue that does not really expose their personal handling of it.

Rather, the study team should try a discussion that begins in a more adventuresome way: "We all have deep opinions about this issue, and we want to see how they differ but relate to each other." Later on, the discussion leader may sketch some obviously extreme positions that seem to fall outside the opinions expressed. Ponder with the group how their distinctive insights may be related to each other and to interpretations of the Gospel.

2.9.2 *Analysis*

One way of looking at the rich material gathered from participant observation, guided interviews, and group discussions is to ask of it four questions:

—What virtues does the parish characteristically find in *crisis*?
—What qualities are expressed in the dominant *mood* of the congregation?
—What styles reflect its dominant *manner* of behavior?
—What does the congregation *wish to become*?

Congregations develop particular valuations of *crisis* and frequently use the assessment of an especially serious crisis to characterize their present corporate life. Listen for recurrent references to a certain death, perhaps of a prominent member or one that was especially unjustified, and see how its experience and parish responses portray certain deep traits of parish character. The death may also be a real or threatened corporate disintegration, such as a schism, a parish fight, or a difficult change in leadership.

Congregations also exhibit a pervasive *mood*, a distinctive temperament that qualifies and also assesses the way the parish expresses its corporate life. Moods are atmospheres; they may waft an air of innocence or complicity through the church, or perhaps one of fertility or decay.

The *manner* by which congregations feel they get things done is another variable in the configuration of character. Congregations develop particular sets of sharpened skills whose employment form the dominant style of parish life, its dependable behavior.

And parishes also *wish to become* some embodiment of qualities that they now are not. Congregational character includes both a recognition of present traits and the anticipation of their transformation.

How might such a diverse collection of crises, moods,

manners, and desires be summarized so that the "spirit" of a local church may be seen in some holistic, more communicable pattern? Actually, this is a question that extends beyond summing up the character of a congregation, as we are using the term here to express the valuing dimension of identity. It is also an appropriate question with reference to the whole of our concern with a congregation's identity; thus, the following section provides a guide for interpreting the insights from the more focused analysis of a congregation's character, but also as a way of bringing together the varied insights garnered from exercises suggested in the previous sections of this chapter.

2.10 Summing It Up in Story

Early in this chapter, we suggested that a study team probably would not find it useful to explore all of the various methods suggested for understanding a congregation's identity; however, it is strongly recommended that at least several be explored. And while we have suggested methods of analysis and interpretation of the specific "windows" into a congregation's identity, it is also important to attempt to bring together these various findings into a more holistic perspective. What we suggest is a form of "triangulation" where the various angles on identity are combined to provide a more comprehensive view. We would suggest that this may be appropriately done through a conscious effort at storytelling in which the study team attempts to express what it has learned of the congregation's identity in a story.

Throughout many of the guides to analysis of identity there has run a persistent reference to story. Story is the way a community usually views, values, and talks about itself in relation to its world and heritage. Most communications in a congregation are narrative in their nature. The pervasiveness of narrative in congregational life is acknowledged in this handbook's predecessor, which examined a single congregation through the perspectives of many disciplines:

Story is not then just the play of children by which a group interprets its common life. . . . Any ongoing ministry in a church relies upon story in its attempt to interpret its life. It is not just sermons that need illustration; all of corporate life needs imaging for its communication.

Once one begins to sense the power of narrative in congregational life one finds it everywhere. It constitutes the news that members share about their common life. A large part of that news is gossip. In one of the best ethnographies of a congregation Samuel Heilman shows how gossip—that is, stories about other members—is essential for corporate existence. Heilman even demonstrates the presence of four layers of gossip, increasingly private and potent, that enrich

activities and relationships in a congregation. Stories of origin and narrative explanations of behavior also define life together, as do schemes for the future and reports of the past. Introductions, confessions, testimonies, and other accounts further tie individual lives to the group story. Even jokes serve the common narrative pattern, their telling deemed tasteful if they somehow advance the common story. Longer sequences of group behavior such as fights and social events have a dramatic framework that holds actors, plot, props, and setting. Added to all of the above is the more consciously storied nature of divine worship: its liturgical drama, its Scripture, hymns, sermons, and symbols. From its conception to its death the local church exists by the persistent imaginative construction of its members.[40]

In spite of the prevalence of storied communication in the life of a congregation, its leaders and members seldom consider their corporate identity in narrative form. Instead, they talk about their parish in terms of numbers, programs, and environmental circumstances. They thereby avoid the fact of their character, the challenge of who they are, and who in Christ they can become. Necessarily they tell stories about their smaller actions and ideas, but they usually conceal the larger story of who they are and can become.

A study team's investigations into identity, and especially into character, have important implications, therefore, for what James Hillman called "restorying."[41] The use of analytical devices that possess narrative dimensions encourages both study teams and their congregations to find the pregnant stories that bear the church's identity. In telling its own story, in discovering its richness of character and in playing with its plot and weighing its setting, a local church gains a new sense of what has become a largely lost art, that of recounting the big story about its congregation and its world.

Attention to the narrative quality of corporate life seems to promote three closely related features of identity formation. Story first relates an *evocation* "that we are." Instead of considering our congregation as an accidental collection of miscellaneously motivated people, through narrative we build metaphors that show our corporate nature, our body that congregates our group. Second, story reports a *characterization*, our sense of "who we are." We are not a copy of another congregation; we discover our peculiar identity largely through the narrative told of ourselves. In understanding the particular story of a congregation, we more or less consciously contrast it with other stories and thus come to appreciate our unique participation in a world of storied communication.

Third, story tells our *confession*, our account of "what we are" in terms of our ultimate goal. In that it relates past, present, and future, our account of even our past reflects our hopes about our future. The story we live, uniquely our own, is confessed even to ourselves in the larger context of the world's becoming, the story of God's redemption.

Insofar as a story emerges from the deliberations among its members, and insofar as it continues to be told and shaped by members, it constitutes a way by which the congregation may evoke, characterize, and confess its identity. What therefore develops is a storytelling pattern similar to that of a family. Not having lost the art of storytelling as thoroughly as have most congregations, healthy families use and play with the stories to understand their character. Members of the family help each other tell them. "No," says one, "you got it all wrong," and relates her own version of a family event that mirrors its identity. "What if," begins another, and the family recollects its past, represents its embodied present, and projects its future in a sequence of related stories.

When used without regard to the other, either hard data about a congregation or a telling of its story may distort its identity. Data, such as findings distilled from the various exercises of this and other chapters of this handbook, may without their narrative accounting suggest that a congregation is merely a collection of behavioral predictabilities and not a twisting, unfolding human drama. Story, however, unaccompanied by the types of empirical inquiry suggested in these chapters, tends towards self-deceiving fancy that avoids unpleasant features of corporate character. A congregation's identity must reflect both critical inquiry and its story.

Each congregation, each the household of God, has its own identity. By analyses like those suggested in this chapter, the identity of the household may be better understood. As a result, the congregation may evalute its identity positively, or it may discover elements it wishes to change. In either case, such understanding is an essential foundation if the household is to be able to express with integrity who it is through its programs and processes and serve faithfully within its setting. By learning to tell the story of who it is and who, by God's grace, it aims to become, the local church is in its storied identity a token of the greatest story of all, the account of the world's salvation.

NOTES

1. Clifford Geertz, *The Interpretation of Cultures* (New York: Basic Books, 1973), p. 5.
2. Erik H. Erikson, *Childhood and Society* (New York: W. W. Norton & Co., 1950), p. 261.
3. Denham Grierson, *Transforming a People of God* (Melbourne, Australia: The Joint Board of Christian Education of Australia and New Zealand, 1984), p. 55.
4. Norman Perrin, *The New Testament: An Introduction* (New York: Harcourt Brace Jovanovich, 1974), pp. 27-29.
5. For other suggestions about studying a congregation's history, see Grierson, *Transforming a People of God*, pp. 53-55, 97-104.
6. Robert Redfield, *Peasant Society and Culture* (Chicago: University of Chicago Press, 1956), pp. 40-59.
7. Recent scholarship reveals a variety of little traditions in the New Testament itself, each reflecting the peculiar experience of an early Christian congregation. See, for example, Wayne A. Meeks, *The First Urban Christians* (New Haven: Yale University Press, 1983).
8. Jackson W. Carroll, William McKinney, and Wade Clark Roof, "From the Outside In and the Inside Out," in Carl S. Dudley, ed., *Building Effective Ministry*, (New York: Harper & Row, 1983), pp. 102-3.
9. Joseph C. Hough, Jr., "Theologian at Work," in Dudley, ed., *Building Effective Ministry*, p. 119.
10. Ibid., p. 112.
11. Ibid., p. 113.
12. Grierson, *Transforming a People of Goddt*, p. 109.
13. *See also Richard A. Hunt, "Mythological-Symbolic Religious Commitment: The LAM Scales," Journal for the Scientific Study of Religion; 11, 1 (March 1972), pp. 42-52.*
14. For example, Earl R. Babbie, *The Practice of Social Research* (Belmont, Cal: Wadsworth Publishing Company, 1973); or A. N. Oppenheim, *Questionnaire Design and Attitude Measurement* (New York: Basic Books, 1966).
15. The complete questionnaire and chapters discussing the findings are in Roger A. Johnson, ed., *Views from the Pew, Christian Beliefs and Attitudes* (Phildelphia: Fortress Press, 1983), esp. pp. 182-200.
16. *Varieties of Religious Presence, Mission in Public Life* (New York: The Pilgrim Press, 1984).
17. Ibid., chapter 6.
18. Ibid., pp. 83-86.
19. Walter Wink, *Transforming Bible Study* (Nashville: Abingdon Press, 1980).
20. James D. Whitehead and Evelyn Eaton Whitehead, *Method in Ministry.* (New York: The Seabury Press, 1981).
21. H. Richard Niebuhr, *Christ and Culture* (New York: Harper & Bros., 1951); Avery Dulles, *Models of the Church* (Garden City, N.Y.: Doubleday, 1974).
22. Northrop Frye, *The Anatomy of Criticism* (Princeton: Princeton University Press, 1937). See especially the essay, "Theory of Myths," pp. 131-239.
23. Victor Turner, *Drama, Fields and Metaphors* (Ithaca: Cornell University Press, 1974), p. 29. For an extended discussion, see Victor Turner, *The Forest of Symbols* (Ithaca: Cornell University Press, 1967), pp. 19-41.
24. See Urban T. Holmes, III, *The Priest in Community* (New York: The Seabury Press, 1978), p. 56.
25. Orrin Klapp, *Collective Search for Identity* (New York: Holt, Rinehart & Winston, 1969), pp. 119-20.
26. Arnold van Gennep, *The Rites of Passage* (Chicago: University of Chicago Press, 1960 [first published in 1909]).
27. See Eliot D. Chapple and Carleton Coon, *Principles of Anthropology* (New York: Holt, Rinehart & Winston, 1942).
28. For further discussion of the importance of rites of passage and intensification for congregations, see Carl S. Dudley, *Making the Small Church Effective* (Nashville: Abingdon, 1978), pp. 104-20.
29. See Dudley, *Making the Small Church Effective*, pp. 95 ff. for one example.
30. Melvin D. Williams, "Corporate Church and Spiritual Community," *Building Effective Ministry*, Carl S. Dudley, ed., (New York: Harper & Row, 1983), p. 65. See also Williams, *Community in a Black Pentecostal Church* (Pittsburgh: University of Pittsburgh Press, 1974).
31. *Asylums* (Garden City, N.Y.: Doubleday, Anchor Books, 1961).

32. *Why Conservative Churches Are Growing* (New York: Harper & Row, 1977).

33. Larry Ingram, "Underlife in a Baptist Church," *Review of Religious Research*, 24 (December 1982), pp. 138-52.

34. See Robert A. Nisbet, *The Sociological Tradition* (New York: Basic Books, 1966), pp. 174-220, for a discussion of various uses by social theorists of the term *class* and the closely related term *status*.

35. For a discussion of the relation of class and Protestant religious life in America, see N. J. Demerath, III, *Social Class in American Protestantism* (Chicago: Rand McNally & Co., 1965).

36. See Peter L. Berger, "The Class Struggle in American Religion,"

The Christian Century, February 25, 1981, pp. 194-99.

37. For instructions for constructing an age-sex pyramid, see Murray H. Leiffer, *The Effective City Church* (Nashville: Abingdon Press, 1961), pp. 150 ff.

38. *Interpretation of Cultures*, p. 95.

39. Stanley Hauerwas, *Vision and Virtue* (South Bend: University of Notre Dame Press, 1981), p. 52.

40. James F. Hopewell, "The Jovial Church: Narrative in Local Church Life," in *Building Effective Ministry*, Carl S. Dudley, ed., (New York: Harper & Row, 1983), pp. 81-82.

41. James Hillman, "Archetypal Theory," in *Loose Ends* (New York and Zurich: Spring Publications, 1975), p. 4.

For Further Reading on Identity _____

Demerath, N. J., III. *Social Class in American Protestantism.* Chicago: Rand McNally & Co., 1965.

Ducey, Michael H. *Sunday Morning.* New York: Free Press, 1977.

Dudley, Carl S. *Making the Small Church Effective.* Nashville: Abingdon Press, 1978.

Dulles, Avery, S. J. *Models of the Church.* Garden City, N.Y.: Doubleday, 1974.

Frye, Northrop. *The Anatomy of Criticism.* Princeton: Princeton University Press, 1937.

Geertz, Clifford. *The Interpretation of Cultures.* New York: Basic Books, 1973.

van Gennep, Arnold. *The Rites of Passage.* Chicago: University of Chicago Press, 1960. (First published in 1909.)

Grierson, Denham. *Transforming a People of God.* Melbourne, Australia: The Joint Board of Christian Education of Australia and New Zealand, 1984.

Heilman, Samuel C. *Synagogue Life: A Study in Symbolic Interaction.* Chicago: University of Chicago Press, 1976.

Hopewell, James F. "The Jovial Church: Narrative in Local Church Life," in *Building Effective Ministry*, Carl S. Dudley, ed., New York: Harper & Row, 1983, pp. 68-83.

Hopewell, James F., ed., *The Whole Church Catalog.* Washington: The Alban Institute, 1984.

Ingram, Larry, "Underlife in a Baptist Church." *Review of*

Religious Research. Vol. 24, December 1982, pp. 138-52.

Klapp, Orrin. *Collective Search for Identity.* New York: Holt Rinehart & Winston, 1969.

McGaw, Douglas B. *A Tale of Two Congregations.* Hartford: Hartford Seminary Foundation, n.d.

Meeks, Wayne A. *The First Urban Christians.* New Haven: Yale University Press, 1983.

Mol, Hans J. *Identity and the Sacred.* New York: The Free Press, 1976.

_____. *Meaning and Place.* New York: The Pilgrim Press, 1983.

Niebuhr, H. Richard. *Christ and Culture.* New York: Harper & Row, 1951.

Redfield, Robert. *Peasant Society and Culture.* Chicago: University of Chicago Press, 1956.

Roozen, David A., William McKinney, and Jackson W. Carroll. *Varieties of Religious Presence, Mission in Public Life.* New York: The Pilgrim Press, 1984.

Turner, Victor. *The Ritual Process, Structure and Anti-Structure.* Chicago: Aldine Press, 1969.

Williams, Melvin D. *Community in a Black Pentecostal Church.* Pittsburgh: University of Pittsburgh Press, 1974.

_____. "The Conflict of Corporate Church and Spiritual Community," in *Building Effective Ministry.* Carl S. Dudley, ed., New York: Harper & Row, 1983, pp. 55-67.

CHAPTER 3

Context

3.1 Introduction

Congregations are, in Paul's words, "earthen vessels"—human institutions shaped by a myriad of social influences. To describe them in this way does not detract from their religious character. Indeed, their human qualities make them effective in carrying out their mission in all sorts of conditions and circumstances. "The church is a chameleon," observes James Gustafson, as he points to its capacity to adapt to new surroundings, to find colors that fit into various environments.[1]

Because a congregation is an adapting organization, it is important to see it in relation to its social context: *the setting, local and global, in which a congregation finds itself and to which it responds.* This chapter advances a perspective for doing this which focuses on the context and then works "from the outside in" to the life of the congregation.[2] The perspective takes seriously the interrelations of the social and cultural setting and religious organizations; the structures and processes linking the congregation to its environment are regarded as crucially important in understanding the inner workings of the congregation. While the authors do not subscribe to a deterministic viewpoint, they do believe the environment both sets limits on and provides opportunities for a congregation.

In a very basic sense this chapter understands congregations as "open systems." This notion implies permeable boundaries, or flow between the environment and the congregation. H. Paul Douglass and Edmund deS. Brunner, pioneer sociological researchers, emphasized one dimension of the flow:

The quality and changes of this environment are almost inevitably communicated to the church. Differences in human fortunes suffered by the church's immediate constituencies and changes in these fortunes due to changes in the environment largely control the institutional destinies of each particular church. Where the environment is prosperous and progressive the church can scarcely fail to "succeed." Where it is miserable and deteriorating the church can scarcely avoid failure.[3]

Implicit here is a view of the congregation as constantly in a state of flux and adaptation. The sources of change are primarily environmental, forcing the religious institution to adjust to what is going on around it. Even if the environment is not fully determinative of what happens, an institution for its own survival must come to terms with a changing context.

But also, open system implies that the congregation *interacts* with its environment. While the power of the social context is quite persuasive, congregations do respond and can make choices affecting their destiny. The two-way, interactive process can be stated as follows:

A congregation—its theology and ethics, its worship, its style of operation, and what it does or does not do with reference to mission—is profoundly shaped by its social context.

A congregation, by virtue of its relationship to a religious or faith tradition, has the capacity, in a limited but crucial way, to transcend the determinative power of the social context so that it influences the context as it is being influenced by it.

These two propositions suggest the complexity of the interrelationships between congregations and their environments. The first proposition tells us simply that how a congregation expresses its faith—in beliefs, programs, organizations and behavior, is influenced by its social location—the people, politics, economic life, values, and class interests present in its setting. These are consequences of its character as an "earthen vessel." But the second proposition holds out a crucial freedom from determinism. Congregations participate in social and faith traditions that contain within them ideas and inspiration, beliefs and experience, on the basis of which the context may be challenged and at least partly transcended. The more leaders and members are helped to see and understand the power of the context on their congregation's life and their participation in it, the greater the possibility they have of cultivating a more responsible and effective expression of their faith commitments. Also, the more likely they will be to discover ways of influencing this context rather than simply being influenced by it. Open systems have the capacity for self-renewal based on feedback and insight, or at least some power to transform the world around them. An analysis of the context of the congregation will not prescribe to the congregation what it should be or do; but it can provide the congregation with information and insight about itself and its setting that open it to new possibilities for response.

To view congregations as open systems is to risk making a theological statement. To take the congregation's social context seriously is also a statement about the work of God in history and the church's mission in its world. One finds in scripture and in the witness of the Church over time the response of Christians to a God whose concern extends to the whole of life, in which human boundaries between people and nations and rich and poor are overcome, and in which God's intentions for all people are made known afresh in each generation. The local congregation is an agent of God's larger purposes, equipped for its mission both by its participation in God's larger design and by its human character. The authors of this chapter confess special excitement in congregations whose sense of God's vision takes them beyond concern for themselves, who provide social space where social distinctions are overcome, who can see beyond their own problems to the needs and struggles of their immediate neighbors and of suffering brothers and sisters half a world away. While these may be viewed by some as biases, the methods for looking at the congregation's social context presented in this chapter should be useful for those whose perspective may be quite different.[4]

Components of the Congregation's Context

To say that a congregation exists in relation to an environment is an encompassing generalization that begs for greater specificity. The environment, or that which is external to an institution, is *inclusive* as well as *multi-layered*. Let us examine each of these to see what is implied for congregational studies.

By inclusiveness is meant the open-ended character of a congregation's context—extending from the local neighborhood to the global community. A congregation is linked to networks and events on a national and international scale; as a religious and moral community it is called upon to respond to issues that arise from beyond the geographic locale in which it exists.

Examples abound: Wars in Southeast Asia contribute to an influx of immigrants from Vietnam, Cambodia and Laos, while poverty and political oppression in Central America and the Caribbean stimulate immigration from Mexico, El Salvador, Guatemala, Cuba, and Haiti. Worldwide inflation and high interest rates place strain on family budgets which in turn affects giving to local churches. Changes in the national economy provide incentives for industry to relocate to growing areas of the United States or to other countries, making it difficult for local communities and metropolitan areas to maintain their economic viability.

Normally, however, the starting point for the contextual analysis of congregations is the *local community*. For here it is, in the immediate neighborhood or community, that most of the external influences on congregations find expression. In the abstract one can speak of broad cultural trends such as immigration, economic dislocation and changes in family patterns; in the concrete one thinks of the Cruz family down the street who have come here from Mexico to work in the packing plant, or of Mr. D'Amico, who is out of work because the electronics factory has relocated to Taiwan, or of Ruth Hansen's daughter Cheryl, who is living with her boyfriend in Syracuse. In the local community people move in and out, group life takes on a particular style, fads and fashions come and go. Widespread social and cultural changes come to bear on the congregation as an institution rooted in community life.

In the modern world, the local community is no longer a self-contained geographic entity. Often the physical boundaries of neighborhoods and communities are indeterminate, and for many urban dwellers especially, spatial proximity is not a perfect index of social participation. Social networks and patterns of institutional involvement extend beyond the immediate locale. Hence, while this chapter focuses primarily on the local community as the principal context for a congregation, it is important to keep in mind that the *linkages* to the outer world are important in understanding the community and the congregation. Even in the most remote geographical locales, "connections" outside play a big part in determining the pulse of social and religious life.

Multi-layered refers to the fact that the impact of the environment on a congregation, or any institution, occurs at various levels. Social conditioning is sometimes open and visible, sometimes more hidden and subterranean. The web of interrelationships is such that changes at one level can lead to numerous and unexpected consequences at another. The social fabric of any community is a complex web of rules, roles and relationships; alterations in one or another of these can result in social ramifications elsewhere. Shifts in a community's demographic growth rate, changing patterns of social class, emerging new life styles and values—any of these can lead to far-reaching and sometimes unexpected implications for congregational life.

The pages that follow explore several "levels" at which the environment exerts a powerful impact on the congregation: the *"social worlds"* of community residents, the *demographic* character of the local community, and patterns of *socal interaction* within the community itself. The three are interrelated, and the contextual approach to congregational analysis moves freely among them. However, for analytic purposes, it is useful to look at them separately. The final section looks specifically at religion's role in the community.

3.2 Getting in Touch with the Community

Chapter 1 introduced Heritage United Methodist Church, whose leaders sense a need to take a fresh look at mission possibilities in their neighborhood. Some members feel it is time to press on with the church's involvements in elderly housing, while others are concerned about membership declines and feel the need for new programming in evangelism and church growth that will enhance the church's appeal to young families. Heritage Church has an opportunity to reacquaint itself with its neighborhood and to look at new possibilities for mission that community changes have brought about. It approaches the community with some fairly specific questions: What are the needs of our older neighbors? Who are the young families and what might Heritage do to reach out to them?

It is helpful to go a bit beyond the case and make some assumptions about the way the church's research needs might be approached. One constructive step would be for the church board to appoint a "special committee on community ministries" to conduct research on its behalf and to report back its findings within a reasonable period of time. For Heritage, a committee of eight to ten members who are broadly representative of the congregation would probably suffice. The board would do well to include both "experts" and "amateurs" in community studies and a mix of both persons who are advocates of particular program possibilities and others who are more neutral. It might ask Deborah Jones, the pastor, to assist the committee in its work and relieve her of other duties to free time for the special project.

3.2.1 Identifying the Church's Neighborhood

A crucial first step is to identify the neighborhood or community being studied. "Neighborhood" and "community" are defined in many ways—sometimes on the basis of spatial patterns, but often along lines of group interaction as well.

Usually the notion of a neighborhood is grounded in part in the subjective: the context in which an individual is related to a society or through which the individual experiences society—often at a particular period in one's life such as child, teenager, parent, grandparent, retiree. David Morris and Karl Hess put it this way:

When people then say "my neighborhood," it usually means they have found a place to live where they feel some human sense of belonging, some human sense of being *part* of a society, no matter how small, rather than just being *in* a society, no matter how large.[5]

The neighborhood is a crucial link connecting the individual to the larger society, generating a sense of belonging, and giving shape to individual and group life. More than just a geographic locale, a neighborhood or community is a normative system with its own rules, roles and relationships; a shared identity and consciousness; a distinctive social and status order; a common culture and way of life.

How does one "map" the social boundaries of a congregation's neighborhood or community? Many congregations find it helpful to begin with a map of the residences of member families. Using a detailed street map and a list of church members, place a pin on the map for each member household. Churches concerned wih evangelism might use a different color pin for members who have joined the church in the past two or three years. A completed membership map often yields surprises. Some churches discover they are more (or less) a "neighborhood church" than popularly perceived. Others find their membership "skips over" some residential neighborhoods. With increased mobility, historic links between congregations and specific neighborhoods have diminished. Where this is true the church will want to probe the reasons.[6]

Another exercise that is especially helpful for a committee as it begins its work is to provide a large blank street map and have group members mark places that have special meaning in their own lives and in the life of the community (e.g., "our first home" "the street my parents lived on," "the site of the old shoe factory," "the square where Kennedy had his big rally in 1960"). This exercise is a good reminder that the neighborhood has a history, that committee members bring past experiences to their community study, and that the neighborhood itself is a complex of varied meanings and experiences.

At some point Heritage committee will need to specify what it means by "the church's community." Some churches find it helpful to work with two definitions: the "immediate neighborhood" of several blocks surrounding the church building and for which the members feel some special responsibility, and a larger "parish area" from which the church draws members. Others, out of a sense of the congregation's larger social responsibility, may want to look at their own community alongside others in which they are considering new programming. In rural areas the larger "parish" may include several towns or counties.

3.2.2 Some Key Documents

There is an enormous amount of printed information produced by governmental and private groups that can help a church study committee explore its community or neighborhood. It is helpful to have these printed documents available early in the committee's work. A partial list might include the following:

Annual reports of local officials
Local histories
Maps
Land use plans
Analyses of local voting patterns
Reports of social service agencies
Planning documents
Local newspapers
Chamber of Commerce publications
Real estate brochures
Welcome Wagon packets for new residents

Planning agencies are particularly good sources of basic documents and information on local communities and neighborhoods. There are few American communities that do not have at least one person asking questions about their future. The planning may center on economic development, recreation, land use, public health, school needs, transportation or a host of other issues. In some areas planning is a state function; in others it is done by county or local governments or by intergovernmental groups. Some planning agencies work hard to secure public participation in their work; others work behind closed doors.

Government agencies are not alone in developing plans for a community's future. Banks, utility companies, citizen action groups and nonprofit organizations may all share your interest in the community and welcome your requests for information and documentation. Heritage would want to give special attention to groups concerned with aging and needs of young families.

3.2.3 Take a Walk!

One of the most important parts of any community study is also the simplest. It involves setting aside the major portion of a day to walk through your neighborhood or community absorbing its sights, sounds, and aromas. The purpose of such an exercise is to expose you to things you may already know but that have become so familiar you no longer notice them. Who is on the streets at various times of the day or night? Why aren't those teenagers at school? How's business in Mr. Caporale's bakery? When did the O'Brien house get so run down? How is the new mall affecting Jim Smith's carpet business? Who in this town would wear that sexy dress in Mrs. Buttner's dress store window?

In the course of the walk be alert to your own reactions to what you see and hear, but also try to look at things from the perspective of other people and groups. Put yourself into the role of a newcomer to the community. How apparent are the basic services a person would need in locating in town? Where does one find a family doctor, an AA meeting, a laundry, a church, a pizza? How would an older or physically disabled person handle the curbs on the sidewalks? Where would a homeless person spend the night? How does a six-year-old get across a busy intersection on the way to school?

The walk can be modified to meet a particular situation, but avoid the temptation to spend too much time in a car. Get out and stretch your legs! A group can take the walk by assigning teams of two to three persons to cover the same geographic area, each with a different perspective in mind: that of a young family newly arrived in the community, an older person on a fixed income, a drifter, a person who has difficulty with English, a college student.

Save time at the end of your excursion for recording your impressions. A simple list of "What I Saw" and "New Questions Raised" will help organize your thoughts if you're on your own. A discussion of what group members observed is always an educational and enlightening experience.

3.2.4 Exploring "Social Worlds"

To understand a community it is essential to explore the "social worlds" represented in it. By social worlds is meant the perceptions of reality that inform people's daily lives. To speak of a social world is, in a most fundamental way, to acknowledge the human need for meaning and order in personal experience, for making sense out of life. More than this, it is to acknowledge that reality is "socially constructed"—that the social context is crucially important for how individuals create and sustain their symbolic worlds. While some people are aware of how they shape their own worlds, most simply take them for granted. Nevertheless, all human beings, consciously or unconsciously, strive for an integrated and meaningful outlook.

In recent times the study of social worlds has become both more important and more complex. Scholars cite two key reasons: First, traditional ways of viewing the world and attributing meaning to social events and behavior have lost much of their influence. As a result of this increased "pluralization" of social worlds, people discover alternative and competing ways of viewing the world and the need to choose among them. Second, in a process called "privatization," the attribution of meanings has become highly individualistic. Meanings are no longer universally shared throughout the society as a whole, but individuals fashion for themselves systems of meaning that are personally satisfying and fulfilling. Often they reflect the class position of social groups. Sociologist Peter Berger argues that the new situation of religion in the modern world forces upon individuals a "heretical imperative"—the need to make choices among alternative interpretations and select out those elements of a religious tradition that are illuminating for a particular life-situation.[7]

Congregations are directly affected by the processes of pluralization and privatization. As the world has become more fragmented, the "private" and "public" spheres have become more separated from one another. Separation has also meant functional differentiation, to the point that private life is increasingly treasured for its nonpublic character. Boundaries between the two are carefully drawn, with the private realm often held up as a refuge and retreat. The consequences for religion are far-reaching and significant: *church life becomes to a considerable extent captive to the private realm.* With family, friendships and hobbies, church participation becomes part of a world removed from the public. The situation is somewhat paradoxical: as communications technology brings communities closer to events in other parts of the world and in other neighborhoods, increasingly people look to religion to help them secure "private" space removed from that wider world. An increasingly privatized religious world bears a host of implications—for religious belief and psychology, understandings of community mission, and institutional patterns and styles. The case of High Ridge Presbyterian Church, discussed in chapter 1, can be viewed as a struggle between two social worlds present in a single congregation; on the issue of allowing champagne in a congregational setting some members reflect the social worlds of their affluent suburban California community while others hold to

fundamentally different perceptions of what is appropriate behavior in the church.

Methods for studying the social psychology of community life are not as well-developed as demographic and interactional analysis, which will be discussed later in this chapter. Getting "inside" the worlds in which people live and grasping their meanings is difficult. One does get clues from surveys and records, cultural styles, and examinations of community tensions and conflicts. For understanding social worlds and meaning systems, however, careful observation and ethnographic inquiry are essential. The perceptive observer who "takes a walk" in the community will learn a great deal about the way people live and their values simply from observing family and housing styles, "status symbols" such as automobiles and boats, evidence of consumption patterns, specialty shops, types of organizations and hobbies, newspapers and magazines read, the uses of weekend and other "private" time.

The best way to get "inside" the social worlds of neighborhood residents is, of course, to engage in conversation with them. People love to talk, even with strangers.[8] Many churches have used the simple technique of having all members of their study group "interview" a friend or neighbor. Heritage Church might want to have each committee member interview two people: one an elderly resident and the other a young newcomer. The interview focuses on a few broad questions that move from the very general to the fairly personal. Here are some examples that can be modified to meet specific group objectives.

—What are the things that attract people to live here in this neighborhood? Were those the things that attracted you?

—As you think about the time you have lived in this neighborhood, what are the most important changes you've seen? What has caused these changes? Have there been major events or happenings that are especially important—for example, a strike or disaster—that have affected the ways people look at the neighborhood?

—Who are the people that seem to care a lot about what happens in this community, who really want to make it a better place to live?

—How would you describe your neighbors? What kind of people are they? What do you think are the most important things in the lives of people who live here in the neighborhood? Are those the most important things in your life?

—Are there people who don't seem to fit in very well with others who live in the neighborhood? What's different about these people? How do others react to them?

—What do you think keeps people going when times get tough?

—Can you think of times in your own life when you've undergone an important change in the way you looked at the world? When you've had a really clear sense of what counted in your life?

It's important in any conversation to be alert to what the other person is saying—and trying to say. The interviewer should be prepared to share his or her own views where appropriate, but the main purpose is to listen and to learn. Taking notes is fine and will be helpful in summarizing your interview. If taking notes disrupts the flow of the conversation it is better to try to reconstruct the session on paper as soon as possible.

3.2.5 Analysis and Interpretation

There have been a number of attempts to identify the dominant social worlds or meaning systems at large in American communities. One that is especially intriguing is suggested by sociologist Robert Wuthnow and grows out of his research on the *content* of persons' meaning systems in California's Bay Area.[9] Wuthnow suggests four major meaning systems and some of their attributes:

1. The *theistic* is closest to that traditionally associated with major American religious traditions. People look to God as the agent who governs life and the source of purpose and direction for individuals. Bringing one's life into conformity with God's will is the key to personal meaning and happiness. God is the creator of the universe and is active in history. The Bible is God's law and humanity's guide to appropriate living.

2. *Individualism* places the emphasis on human beings as being in control of their own destiny. Success or failure is in the hands of individuals, who set their own course in life and are free to choose their futures. Individualism has deep roots in America and is associated with traditional values of hard work, willpower, determination, thrift, honesty, and the avoidance of such vices as laziness, drunkenness, and deceit. Special emphasis is given to personal willpower as the key to happiness and good fortune.

3. *Social science* is a third meaning system and is similar to individualism in its emphasis on human beings' roles in history. Its emphasis, however, is on the key roles of social forces rather than individuals. Family background, social status, and class, the society a person lives in and its cultural, economic, and political systems combine to shape a persons' position in life. Less control is in the hands of individuals; rather, one is socialized into patterns of thinking and acting. A person's sense of happiness and success varies according to the opportunities the society has provided and not simply to his or her energy and hard work.

4. *Mysticism* is somewhat different. It is suspicious of the ability of the other three meaning systems to understand the meaning of life and account for the forces that govern it. It places special reliance on experience, particularly ecstatic experience, as the source of knowledge about life. The stress is on intuition and feelings. At the same time, Wuthnow stresses that the mystic also has a philosophy of life that places one's own most intense experiences at the center; "In such experiences he can alter time and space. He can experience God. He can escape the social and cultural forces that impinge upon him. He can create reality itself."

Wuthnow's classification of meaning systems is helpful for organizing observations from both formal and casual conversations conducted within the community.[10] While Wuthnow used his classifications to formulate a formal survey questionnaire, they can also be used in a more informal manner to help organize data from neighborhood interviews. Following a series of interviews, the study group can use its interview notes to identify specific comments that reflect the four meaning systems and record the comments for group discussion. The following examples are suggested by interview items used in Wuthnow's California survey instrument:

THEISTIC

I definitely believe in God.
God has been a strong influence in my life.
People suffer because they don't obey God.
God created the first man and woman.
There is life after death, with rewards and punishments.

INDIVIDUALISTIC

People usually bring suffering on themselves.
The poor simply aren't willing to work hard.
If one works hard enough, a person can do anything he or she wants to do.
If someone does not succeed, it's his or her own fault.

SOCIAL SCIENCE

I believe forgotten childhood experiences have an influence on me.

Suffering is caused by social arrangements that make
   people greedy for riches and power.
Man evolved from lower animals.
Beliefs are influenced by income.

MYSTICAL

I have had the feeling that I was in close contact with
   something holy or sacred and it has had a lasting
   impact on my life.
It is good to live in a fantasy world every now and
   then.
New insights about myself have had a strong
   influence on my life.
I have experienced a feeling of harmony with the
   universe, and it has had a lasting influence on my
   life.

When the interview comments have been organized
the group should discuss what members have found.
The group will want to focus on questions like these:
What have our interviews told us about the ways our
neighbors view the neighborhood and the world? Are
there differences between older and younger people we
have visited with? To what extent are they similar to or
different from the message of the gospel and the way
our own members view the world? How can we relate
to those who view the world differently than our
members do?

Another approach to analyzing social worlds focuses
on an individual's *breadth of perspective*. Here the
concern is less with content of meanings systems than
with frames of reference—whether a person is oriented
mainly to the immediate environment or the larger
social world. In many studies throughout America two
major character types have been identfied:

   Locals are very much oriented to neighborhood
and community. They favor voluntary organizations
in which stable, communal relationships are possible; they are deeply immersed in friendships and
social networks. They tend to personalize interpretations of social reality and to hold firmly to
traditional beliefs and moral values.

   Cosmopolitans are more oriented to the larger
world. They tend to prefer professional memberships and specialized voluntary organizations; their
contacts and "significant others" extend beyond the
immediate community. In life-style and ideology
they are more tolerant of diversity and more open to
social change.

This distinction is useful for congregations studying
their communities and has been applied to congrega-

tions.[11] Research suggests that locals are "belongers"
and tend to be deeply involved in church and
synagogue activities. Locals emphasize norms of
participation, sociality, and traditional modes of commitment; they are defenders of conventional beliefs and
practices. Cosmopolitans, in contrast, are less concerned about community (and congregational) norms,
but tend to place a great deal of emphasis on the ethical
and meaning aspects of religion; their belief systems are
less particularistic and more organized around personal
religious quests. The two types differ religiously in
fundamental ways—in beliefs, practices, and styles of
institutional commitment.

In virtually every community or congregation it is
possible to identify the two character types. Some clues
can be obtained from exploring the following:

—What types of organizations and groups do people
   join and take part in? Increasingly, people wear their
   organizational memberships and commitments on
   their chests. A preponderance of T-shirts proclaiming
   membership in Max's Gym or loyalty to Annie's Bar
   & Grill suggests more localistic ties than those
   arguing for an end to nuclear testing or to the killing
   of baby whales.
—What is the breadth of people's concerns? What is
   talked about in the barber shop: the shot Al Maguire's
   kid made at last night's basketball game and the new
   waitress at the donut shop or the prospects for peace
   in the Middle East and enthusiasm for the "Live from
   Lincoln Center" broadcast on public television?
—How strong are social attachments—to the immediate neighborhood and to the larger world? How is the
   turnout at community events? Do people *go* home or
   come home for the holidays?

Answers to these questions can help provide a
"cognitive mapping" of the community and yield
valuable information as to frames of reference and
significant others. Such information is valuable not only
for what it tells you about individuals, but also because
it defines the character of the symbolic worlds in which
religious meanings take on significance and are acted
upon. A study committee will want to reflect on two key
questions as it considers the relationship between social
worlds and congregational life: 1. What can be said
about the social worlds of members of the congregation? How are they similar to those of other community
residents and how are they different? 2. To what extent
does religion inform persons' social worlds? Do people
carry their understandings from their religious and
faith commitments or is their understanding of the
world carried to their congregation membership from
their class position and "secular" involvements?

3.3 Demographic Data in Congregational Analysis

In recent years technological advances have made demographic data available for a range of purposes and applications that could not have been envisioned at the time of the first federal census in 1790. Today, corporations from American Airlines to Xerox will use census data in shaping marketing strategies. Burger King, McDonald's and Wendy's will pore over census data in determining potential sites for new fast-food franchises. Political organizations will run the data through their computers seeking voters and contributors. The federal government will use census data in apportioning revenue sharing funds.

Churches have also become major users of census data. Rare is the denomination which locates a new church without a careful examination of the demographic composition of the proposed site. Some mission agencies target resources toward communities with high need for their services and at least one group conducts careful analyses of respondents to its direct-mail advertising. Census data is also used by congregations. Long-range planning committees, committees planning church extension projects, task groups considering service projects such as day care centers, elderly housing and other types of outreach, and church boards considering stewardship goals or salaries for staff frequently rely on census data in their work.

For analyzing the demographic and social characteristics of the congregation's immediate environment, the census is a key resource. This is especially true for a church like Heritage Methodist, which is looking fairly specifically at needs of particular groups in its neighborhood. Before turning specifically to Heritage a reminder about some key census concepts will be helpful.

Taking the Census: In 1980 the census was undertaken by mail in most of the country. Every census questionnaire contained seven questions about each household member plus twelve questions about housing. About one-fifth of all households received a longer questionnaire with an additional 40 population and housing items. The "short form" took an average of 15 minutes to complete, the "long form" 45 minutes. The questions themselves are the product of a lengthy process involving governmental officials and various interest groups. Some areas such as housing conditions receive considerable attention, while others, including religious affiliation and participation, are not included at all.

In recent years, the Bureau of the Census (which has responsibility for conducting the census) has given special attention to including groups which have traditionally been "undercounted." Their efforts included personal visits in isolated areas and diverse special efforts in minority communities. While the figure of 226,545,805 persons will stand as the "official" count of the U.S. population on April 1, 1980, virtually no one will argue it is complete. Some persons were missed, and members of minority groups, Southerners, persons in the country illegally, and men are disproportionately represented among those not counted. The 1980 Census, while not perfect, is estimated to include 99.4 percent of the "real" population. Users of census data will want to be aware, however, that some people are "missed" by the census itself.

Census Geography: One of the greatest values of the federal census—in comparison, for example, with national opinion polls—is its geographic comprehensiveness. To understand census geography requires a brief outline of its key concepts.

Some of the units of census geography are quite simple. For example, each U. S. household is located in a single state and county or county equivalent (parishes in Louisiana, independent cities in Virginia). Counties are further subdivided into minor civil divisions (MCDs) or census county divisions (CCDs). MCDs are political or administrative subdivisions (commonly townships) in 30 states; they usually have some legal standing. CCDs are statistical areas defined in the 20 states where minor civil divisions are not legally defined, are not well known, or have frequent boundary changes. CCDs are especially common in the Western states.

Census tracts are another type of geographic unit used for census purposes. Tracts are found in urbanized areas known as metropolitan statistical areas (MSAs). They are small, relatively permanent areas averaging 4,000 persons each and are intended to be socially homogeneous (that is, they contain people of similar backgrounds and economic status). They respect natural and human boundaries such as rivers and major highways. Unlike states, counties, MCDs, and CCDs, tracts have little intuitive meaning for people. They require special maps that identify their boundaries.

Incorporated and census-designated places are still another important type of area designation. These are concentrations of people that have legally prescribed boundaries or have a definite residential nucleus but lack legal standing. Unlike the other units, places need not conform to county or state lines and are subject to redefinition over time as population patterns change.[12]

Insert 3–1 illustrates key points in census geography using the state of Iowa as an example. Figure A shows Iowa's counties and metropolitan areas. Counties in the state's seven metropolitan statistical areas are shaded. MSAs can cross state lines.

Figure B is an enlarged view of Linn and Jones counties. Linn County, which includes Cedar Rapids city is classified as metropolitan. Jones county, located to its east, is classified as nonmetropolitan. Figure B shows the county subdivisions (minor civil divisions) for Linn County and both minor civil divisions and places for Jones county. Places have been omitted from Linn county in this illustration.

Figure C looks in greater detail at the four minor civil divisions (in this case townships) that comprise the southwest quadrant of Jones county. Three of the four townships contain places with independent legal standing as Iowa cities (shown in capital letters). One city, Onslow, overlaps two townships (Madison and Wyoming). Figure C is quite typical of census geography patterns in nonmetropolitan areas, although there are regional variations.

Figure D is an enlargement of Cedar Rapids city and illustrates census geography for SMSA counties. For census purposes Cedar Rapids is both a minor civil division and a place. The enlargement shows the city divided into segments of varying size and shape. These are the city's census tracts. They average about 4,000 persons and are socially homogeneous. They can be thought of as small neighborhoods.

Figure E enlarges five census tracts in the southwestern portion of Cedar Rapids. It shows the tract numbers and key boundaries of the tracts. This might be thought of as typical of an urban parish area such as that served by Heritage Methodist church.

3.3.1 Using Census Data: An Example

When the Census Bureau completes its work on a decennial census it releases several sets of tables covering various American communities and neighborhoods. These tables are released first in computer tape form as "Standard Tape Files" and later as printed reports similar to this excerpt from the Cedar Rapids Standard Metropolitan Statistical Area report.[13]

The previous section used the state of Iowa to illustrate census geography. It moved from the state to the county to the county subdivision level and in Linn County (which is classified as metropolitan for census purposes) to the tract level, and identified tracts 10, 11, 23, 24, and 30.01 as the "neighborhood" served by Heritage United Methodist Church. This section introduces the kinds of information available from the Bureau of the Census, covers some key census terms, and suggests, by example, some ways demographic data can inform church mission planning. Persons needing more detailed information on the census itself

or sources of demographic data can turn to the sources listed later in this chapter.

The first three tables look at three changes in this five-tract area between 1970 and 1980. Table 1 looks at population and household change. The neighborhood is growing, but slowly; its 14 percent increase is just a bit higher than the nation's 11 percent growth.[14]

Table 1 also shows change in households. A household, for census purposes, is a person or collection of persons sharing a living unit. In this neighborhood the number of households rose 42 percent in the ten years. Family households (two or more related persons sharing a living unit) grew by 24 percent while the number of nonfamily households (persons living alone or unrelated persons living together) nearly tripled. The number of persons in group quarters (institutional living arrangements such as nursing homes, military barracks, prisons, extended care hospital facilities, etc.) declined. The "typical" household declined from 3.5 to 2.9 persons in the 10 years.

Table 2 turns to racial and ethnic changes. Comparing racial-ethnic data over time can be risky because the Census Bureau has asked these items different ways and of different samples of the population. Between 1970 and 1980 these changes affect totals for the white, Asian and Pacific Islander and Hispanic populations. The 1980 data is much more reliable than data from earlier censuses. While the number of minority group persons has risen in percentage terms, this community remains virtually all white.

Table 3 looks at change in the various age groups within the community. While the total population rose by just over 14 percent, there is great variation in growth of specific groups. The number of young people has declined quite sharply; at the same time other groups are growing. The number of persons in their twenties and thirties has grown significantly, as has the number of older residents. The table gives Heritage Church the useful information that the number of persons age 75 and older (and thus likely to be prime candidates for elderly housing) has risen from 764 in 1970 to 1,046 in 1980 (up 36.9 percent); in addition, the number of persons age 65 to 74 has grown from 949 to 1,360 (up 43.3 percent).

The two population pyramids give further insight into the age structure of the population and recent changes in it. The pyramids are pictorial representations of the community, dividing it by age and sex. In 1970 the pyramid looked like a pyramid; wide at the bottom, it narrows as it moves toward the top. By 1980 the shape is somewhat different. It is narrower at the bottom (reflecting the decline in the number of children and youth), widens toward the middle to reflect the

Insert 3-1

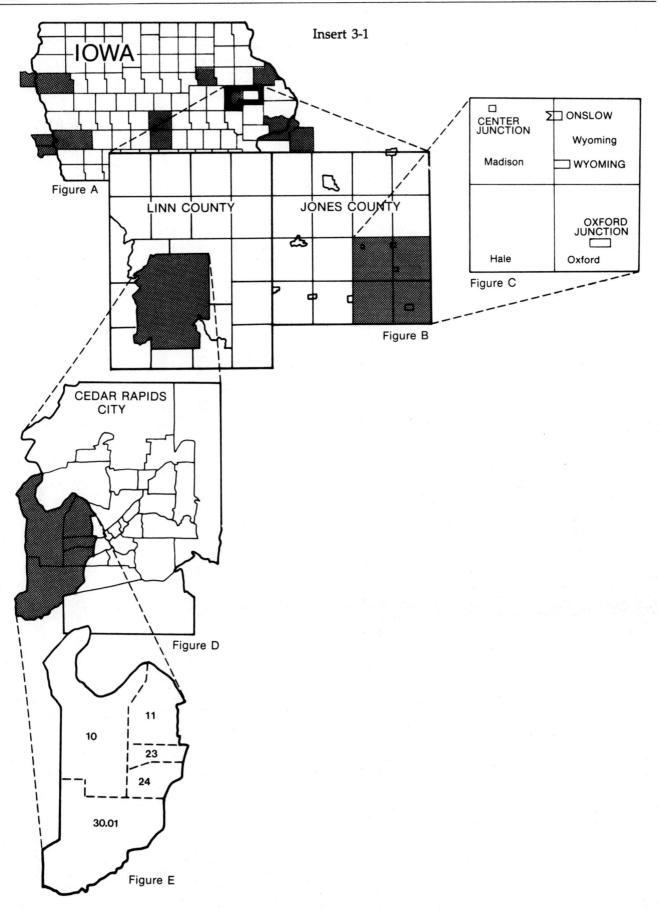

Figure A

LINN COUNTY

JONES COUNTY

Figure C

CENTER JUNCTION

ONSLOW

Wyoming

Madison

WYOMING

OXFORD JUNCTION

Hale

Oxford

Figure B

CEDAR RAPIDS CITY

Figure D

11

10

23

24

30.01

Figure E

General Characteristics of Persons: 1980—Con.

Census Tracts

Cedar Rapids city, Linn County—Con.

	Tract 0009*	Tract 0010*	Tract 0011	Tract 0012	Tract 0013	Tract 0014	Tract 0015*	Tract 0016*	Tract 0017	Tract 0018	Tract 0019	Tract 0020
AGE												
Total persons	7 633	11 620	6 406	3 725	4 216	3 731	2 383	5 819	7 563	3 922	2 362	1 727
Under 5 years	560	953	540	296	281	245	109	331	666	270	150	26
5 to 9 years	643	1 057	511	241	208	228	133	383	553	211	120	6
10 to 14 years	806	1 169	481	272	191	224	169	492	630	208	92	14
15 to 19 years	762	1 196	529	327	372	263	187	509	753	277	197	514
20 to 24 years	614	930	563	396	701	283	211	267	766	446	487	575
25 to 34 years	1 372	2 278	1 506	548	721	649	370	776	1 429	765	445	132
35 to 44 years	1 158	1 637	750	333	301	403	275	763	762	294	141	45
45 to 54 years	985	1 061	538	360	291	393	282	743	604	305	147	56
55 to 64 years	520	705	494	421	434	481	260	812	563	343	146	93
65 to 74 years	159	337	234	323	395	372	220	476	453	371	191	103
75 years and over	54	297	260	208	321	190	167	267	384	432	246	163
3 and 4 years	215	392	215	105	96	94	40	138	243	98	54	5
16 years and over	5 450	8 170	4 751	2 846	3 507	2 982	1 940	4 500	5 570	3 175	1 981	1 675
18 years and over	5 109	7 675	4 533	2 715	3 430	2 864	1 855	4 254	5 248	3 083	1 939	1 654
21 years and over	4 756	7 052	4 271	2 528	2 986	2 725	1 742	4 045	4 803	2 886	1 677	937
60 years and over	397	930	703	736	932	806	498	1 113	1 079	982	510	320
62 years and over	330	802	615	649	842	704	456	968	978	913	482	302
Median	28.3	27.4	28.5	29.9	29.0	34.5	35.5	36.8	27.7	31.6	27.4	21.4
Female	3 857	6 015	3 265	1 938	2 443	1 951	1 244	3 012	3 960	2 120	1 255	941
Under 5 years	292	478	250	142	138	96	49	167	311	125	69	14
5 to 9 years	320	556	244	110	100	105	52	172	280	94	61	4
10 to 14 years	386	580	232	128	99	120	77	256	319	102	44	10
15 to 19 years	396	604	267	169	253	129	103	244	366	133	106	277
20 to 24 years	329	508	295	209	454	149	95	122	418	253	229	303
25 to 34 years	705	1 172	746	270	362	332	179	412	709	373	203	56
35 to 44 years	578	829	370	168	167	203	154	405	397	154	65	22
45 to 54 years	491	519	270	193	168	212	148	388	315	168	72	29
55 to 64 years	243	339	246	235	241	258	146	423	304	180	92	45
65 to 74 years	80	201	145	177	248	217	133	253	271	228	129	60
75 years and over	37	229	200	137	213	130	108	170	270	310	185	121
3 and 4 years	115	183	99	51	44	35	19	76	114	34	21	4
16 years and over	2 779	4 263	2 479	1 527	2 093	1 608	1 051	2 355	2 977	1 769	1 071	910
18 years and over	2 587	4 021	2 370	1 462	2 060	1 548	1 001	2 243	2 829	1 728	1 050	902
21 years and over	2 408	3 688	2 242	1 358	1 722	1 479	943	2 149	2 599	1 616	915	511
60 years and over	211	567	449	427	585	475	307	620	674	645	358	207
62 years and over	182	507	401	376	532	419	283	546	617	606	345	196
Median	28.1	27.6	29.0	32.1	28.9	37.1	39.1	37.9	28.7	34.3	30.1	21.5
HOUSEHOLD TYPE AND RELATIONSHIP												
Total persons	7 633	11 620	6 406	3 725	4 216	3 731	2 383	5 819	7 563	3 922	2 362	1 727
In households	7 633	11 413	6 245	3 725	3 797	3 731	2 383	5 819	7 525	3 795	2 183	556
Householder	2 567	3 748	2 257	1 462	1 762	1 548	1 016	2 127	2 803	1 829	1 244	376
Family householder	2 096	3 009	1 716	997	1 016	1 064	659	1 760	1 927	938	387	72
Nonfamily householder	471	739	541	465	746	484	357	367	876	891	857	304
Living alone	349	560	387	394	620	390	304	321	769	769	727	269
Spouse	1 903	2 689	1 518	779	834	944	574	1 605	1 490	742	252	47
Other relatives	2 970	4 673	2 237	1 327	1 002	1 104	706	1 996	2 808	1 034	470	70
Nonrelatives	193	303	233	157	199	135	87	91	424	190	217	63
Inmate of institution	–	197	161	–	10	–	–	–	19	117	116	265
Other, in group quarters	–	10	–	–	409	–	–	–	19	10	63	906
Persons per household	2.97	3.05	2.77	2.55	2.15	2.41	2.35	2.74	2.68	2.07	1.75	1.48
Persons per family	3.32	3.45	3.19	3.11	2.81	2.92	2.94	3.05	3.23	2.89	2.87	2.63
Persons 65 years and over	213	634	494	531	716	562	387	743	837	803	437	266
In households	213	454	336	531	662	562	387	743	837	732	365	125
Householder	127	325	216	378	457	389	268	475	588	547	313	99
Nonfamily householder	39	177	89	175	223	178	131	175	289	339	239	80
Living alone	39	173	86	171	212	171	128	165	274	327	234	78
Spouse	58	83	84	115	169	143	95	213	174	144	33	12
Other relatives	28	44	32	32	27	24	20	50	60	32	14	3
Nonrelatives	–	2	4	6	9	6	4	5	15	9	5	11
Inmate of institution	–	178	158	–	10	–	–	–	–	70	72	141
Other, in group quarters	–	2	–	–	44	–	–	–	–	1	–	–
FAMILY TYPE BY PRESENCE OF OWN CHILDREN												
Families	2 096	3 009	1 716	997	1 016	1 064	659	1 760	1 927	938	387	72
With own children under 18 years	1 265	1 947	977	459	417	448	274	799	1 035	417	197	28
Number of own children under 18 years	2 442	3 806	1 804	916	742	818	508	1 522	2 089	779	339	39
Married-couple families	1 903	2 689	1 518	779	834	944	574	1 605	1 490	742	252	47
With own children under 18 years	1 121	1 712	842	354	323	383	236	721	774	297	103	12
Number of own children under 18 years	2 200	3 388	1 583	720	587	712	440	1 387	1 588	585	194	18
Female householder, no husband present	150	263	151	172	149	98	66	128	367	162	110	22
With own children under 18 years	119	205	106	89	82	52	32	66	237	109	80	16
Number of own children under 18 years	206	372	178	165	138	86	58	115	469	177	120	21
MARITAL STATUS												
Male, 15 years and over	2 765	4 040	2 335	1 358	1 430	1 404	906	2 194	2 664	1 434	919	768
Single	704	1 051	580	371	426	345	247	470	851	471	454	561
Now married, except separated	1 916	2 729	1 542	806	847	957	581	1 622	1 523	765	275	96
Separated	19	33	30	23	14	21	10	7	35	18	24	12
Widowed	14	44	34	40	45	27	27	48	55	55	32	31
Divorced	112	183	149	118	98	54	41	49	200	125	134	68
Female, 15 years and over	2 859	4 401	2 539	1 558	2 106	1 630	1 066	2 417	3 050	1 799	1 081	913
Single	638	959	556	319	817	323	242	416	809	505	419	619
Now married, except separated	1 914	2 739	1 544	807	853	952	585	1 622	1 526	769	272	93
Separated	20	46	25	30	21	14	9	16	72	17	28	13
Widowed	105	359	249	227	240	212	149	233	337	327	220	130
Divorced	182	298	165	175	175	129	81	130	306	181	142	58

sizable number of "baby boom" residents, and begins narrowing for the over-35 age groups.

What do table 3 and the two population pyramids tell the comittee about Heritage's neighborhood? First, that in important respects it resembles the population of the U.S. during the 1970s. The number of young adults and elderly grew while the youngest population declined. Second, it makes possible some educated guesses about the near future. In all likelihood the community's age structure will change by 1990. The large number of persons in their prime childbearing years will probably contribute to an "echo effect" as baby boomers begin their own families; by 1990 this community's population profile will probably again broaden at the base. The number of older persons will also grow, although probably no faster than in the past decade. The reason for this is the relatively small number of persons in the 45 to 54 age group. Third, as persons in the 25 to 34 age group age, their incomes will tend to rise as they enter their peak wage-earning years. This could strengthen the neighborhood's economic base.[15]

Tables 4 through 7 view socioeconomic changes between 1970 and 1980. Table 4 shows a rise in the number of college graduates from 8.5 percent of all adults to 14.1 percent. Table 5 deals with labor force participation in three categories: those employed outside the home, those unemployed, and those neither employed nor looking for work. Most notable is the increasing proportion of the employed labor force who are women. In 1970 women represented 36 percent of workers; by 1980 they were 44 percent. The number of women working outside the home grew by 78 percent in the decade.

Tables 6 and 7 examine family income; they include only *family* households and not persons living alone or in "unorthodox" living arrangements. Median family income rose from $11,263 in 1969 (income is reported for the year prior to the census) to $24,414 in 1979, an increase of 117 percent or slightly above the rate of inflation.[16] Much of the increase can no doubt be attributed to a rising number of two-income families.

Table 8 is particularly important as it shows the diversity of household types broken down by major racial-ethnic groups. Looking first at the bottom of the table, 2,235 (21 percent) of the households are classified as "nonfamilies." These include the 1,744 households of one person (from table 8) and 491 households of two or more unrelated individuals. "Family" households are of two types: those containing a married couple and those with related individuals but no spouse present. The neighborhood contains 4,215 married couple households with children; such households represent 40 percent of the total and are the predominant household type. Another 3,089 households contain

married couples without children; they account for 30 percent of the total. Overall, 70 percent of the households contain married couples. The "no spouse present" households are of two types: those headed by men and those headed by women. They are again subdivided into those with and without children present. The table gives the information that 487 of the neighborhoods's households are female-headed single parent households. While the number of minority households is small, the table provides the interesting finding that the vast majority are married couples with children.

Table 9 provides a detailed breakdown of racial groups. Race, for census purposes, is based on self-classification. The census questionnaire listed the groups reported in the table. Spanish origin persons, shown in table 1, can be of any race. Ancestry is also based on self-classification. Persons were asked to write in their ancestry; no response categories were given. Table 10 reports persons who gave a "single ancestry" response (e.g., "Polish," "Irish," etc.); persons of mixed background ("German-English," "Scottish-Irish," etc.) are listed under "multiple ancestry." Nearly half of the residents of this neighborhood reported multiple ancestries. The largest single ancestry group are German (16 percent), English (6 percent) and Irish (5 percent). The vast majority of the community's residents are native Iowans; only one percent were born outside the United States.

Tables 11 through 13 deal with employment patterns. Table 11 examines the industry in which employed persons work. The largest numbers are in manufacturing (32 percent), retail trade (17 percent) and education (7 percent). Table 12 shifts to the kind of work people do. Here there are significant numbers in blue-collar occupations and lower-level white-collar jobs. Table 13 reveals that 69 percent of all families include two or more workers.

The census includes a great deal of information on housing units, some of which is summarized in Tables 14 and 15. The first shows that over three-quarters of the neighborhoods housing units are owner occupied and that these units have a median monthly mortgage of $303. The 21 percent of the units that are rented have a median rent of $309. Only three percent of all housing units were vacant at the time of the census. Table 15 describes different types of neighborhood housing and adds the information that homeowners estimate the value of their homes to be $47,981.

Tables 16 through 18 all deal with population mobility and are helpful to congregations considering membership development programs. The first looks at how long owner and renter-occupied housing units have been occupied by their present residents. It suggests considerable turnover. Overall, 24 percent of the neighborhood's units had been occupied for one year or less, with most of the turnover occurring in rental units. Nearly 65 percent of renters had been in their present unit for less than one year! Table 17 looks at where current residents lived five years earlier. Just over half lived in the same housing unit, 29 percent lived elsewhere in Linn County, and another 9 percent lived somewhere else in Iowa. A scattering of current residents were in another state, mainly in the Middle West. Table 18 takes a third look at mobility, this time at the type of community in which people resided five years ago. Most (74 percent) were in the central city of a Standard Metropolitan Statistical Area (this figure includes those who lived in Cedar Rapids in 1975). Six percent were in a suburb of Cedar Rapids, 11 percent were in another metropolitan area, and 9 percent were in a nonmetropolitan community.

The final tables in the example all deal with poverty. The poverty threshold varies by household type and size of family. For a family of four with two related children under age 18 it was $7,356 in 1979. For an unrelated individual over 65 it was $3,479. Table 19 looks at poverty status of individuals. There were 957 individuals in households whose income was less than 75 percent of the poverty level, whose income is far below that needed to reach the poverty threshold. Approximately the same number had incomes close to the poverty level—just above or just below. Most residents are far above the poverty threshold; 86 percent had incomes two times that of poverty. Table 20 looks at poverty status for racial-ethnic groups. A majority of the Spanish-origin families in the neighborhood are living at below-poverty levels. Table 21 looks at poverty for children and the elderly, and Table 22 at poverty status of families: all families and those headed by women. Most of the neighborhood's elderly residents have incomes above the poverty level. Note that nearly one female-headed family in five is below poverty.

3.3.2 Interpretation

Typically, analysis of a congregation's demographic setting raises questions that merit further research, and that is the case of our statistical tour of south Cedar Rapids. Nonetheless, it has revealed a number of things that would be suggestive to Heritage's community goals committee.

First, what are some of the more salient findings? The community's residents are mainly middle class and living in married-couple households. The neighborhood is growing slowly and is fairly mobile, with residential turnover being especially high in rental

units. In some respects the neighborhood is homogeneous; virtually all residents are white, native-born, and of moderate income; in other respects it is heterogeneous; the neighborhood contains a mixture of age and occupational groups, newcomers and long-term residents, persons in single-family homes and apartments. Comparison of data from the 1970 and 1980 censuses suggests the community is changing; there has been a sizable increase in the number of nonfamily households, both the elderly and baby boom populations are growing and the number of young children will probably also grow in the eighties. Income levels are rising—due in large part to an increase in the number of working women.

The data suggests implications for Heritage's concern for *evangelism and church growth.* It would probably want to look to an evangelism strategy that emphasizes special attention to specific groups who require rather different approaches.

First, the number of persons in their twenties and thirties has been growing very rapidly. This group includes young married couples and singles and will fuel the anticipated rise in the number of young children in the community. The church is wise to look carefully at church-school programs, especially for very young children, and at programs for singles, recognizing that each appeals to a different segment of the baby boom generation. A significant portion of this generation remains at the periphery of congregational life, and programs that build bridges to its members will require considerable sensitivity.

Second, the number of older residents is also rising. Heritage will want to look carefully at this population and at recent migration patterns. Are these persons relocating from other Cedar Rapids neighborhoods and maintaining congregational ties elsewhere or are they true "newcomers." Membership recruitment and social service efforts, such as low-cost housing programs, might be combined in approaching this population.

Third, there has been a rise in the number of nonfamily households (up 196 percent) and a rapid turnover in rental housing (65 percent occupied in 1979-1980). Over 2,500 of the neighborhood's housing units were occupied in the single year prior to the census. This suggests a need for active programs to identify and welcome new community residents. The shape of such programs depends on the willingness of members and staff to visit new residents and families and on available media (local newspapers, radio, and television).

The data also suggests possibilities for *community service and action ministries.* While the data suggests a fairly "comfortable" suburban neighborhood inside the central city, it also points to possible areas of concern.

1980 CENSUS REPORT

<u>NAME:</u>   <u>Number</u>
SE CEDAR RAPIDS   778021

1970-1980 COMMUNITY TRENDS

1. Population and Household Change

	1970	1980	# Change 1970-80	% Change 1970-80
Population	26684	30505	3821	14.3
Households	7398	10532	3134	42.4
Families	6623	8242	1619	24.4
Non-families	775	2290	1515	195.5
In Group Quarters	527	377	-150	-28.5
Average Household Size	3.5	2.9	-0.7	-19.1

2. Racial-Ethnic Change

	1970 Total	Pct.	1980 Total	Pct.	% Change 1970-80
White	26573	99.6	30065	98.6	13.1
Black	52	0.2	218	0.7	319.2
Asian and Pacif/Isl	10	0.0	142	0.5	1320.0
Other	51	0.2	80	0.3	56.9
Hispanic	109	0.4	180	0.6	65.1

3. Age Change

	1970 Total	Pct.	1980 Total	Pct.	% Change 1970-80
Years					
0-4	2823	10.6	2335	7.7	-17.3
5-9	3345	12.5	2540	8.3	-24.1
10-14	3065	11.5	2702	8.9	-11.8
15-19	2275	8.5	2856	9.4	25.5
20-24	1765	6.6	2550	8.4	44.5
25-34	3991	15.0	5970	19.6	49.6
35-44	3264	12.2	3732	12.2	14.3
45-54	2816	10.5	2934	9.6	4.2
55-64	1637	6.1	2480	8.1	51.5
65-74	949	3.6	1360	4.5	43.3
75+	764	2.9	1046	3.4	36.9
Median Age	25.2		28.7		13.9
Average Age	28.2		31.4		11.3

1970 Data Based on Geographic Adjustments by National Planning Data Corp.

1970 POPULATION PYRAMID

	Pct.	Number
Total		26694
Females	50.9	13582
Males	49.1	13112

----Females---

Percent of Total	Number

----Males----

Percent of Total	Number

Female % of Total	Female Number	Age	Male % of Total	Male Number
1.9	515	75	0.9	249
2.1	549	65	1.5	400
3.1	823	55	3.0	814
5.2	1375	45	5.4	1441
6.1	1615	35	6.2	1649
7.8	2069	25	7.2	1922
3.8	1013	20	2.8	752
4.2	1109	15	4.4	1166
5.6	1500	10	5.9	1565
6.1	1639	05	6.4	1706
5.2	1375	00	5.4	1448

```
                          ❀||
                          ❀||
                          ❀||
                          ❀||
                        ❀❀75❀
                          ❀ ||❀
                          ❀ ||❀
                        ❀❀❀65❀❀❀
                          ❀  ||  ❀
                          ❀  ||  ❀
                      ❀❀❀❀❀55❀❀❀❀❀
                        ❀    ||    ❀
                        ❀    ||    ❀
                      ❀❀❀❀❀❀45❀❀❀❀❀❀
                      ❀      ||      ❀
                      ❀      ||      ❀
                    ❀❀❀❀❀❀❀❀35❀❀❀❀❀❀❀
                    ❀        ||        ❀
                    ❀        ||        ❀
                  ❀❀❀❀❀❀❀❀25❀❀❀❀❀❀❀
                    ❀        ||        ❀
                  ❀❀❀❀❀❀❀❀20❀❀❀❀❀❀❀❀
                    ❀          ||          ❀
                ❀❀❀❀❀❀❀❀❀❀15❀❀❀❀❀❀❀❀❀❀❀
                  ❀            ||            ❀
              ❀❀❀❀❀❀❀❀❀❀❀❀10❀❀❀❀❀❀❀❀❀❀❀❀❀
                ❀              ||              ❀
            ❀❀❀❀❀❀❀❀❀❀❀❀❀❀05❀❀❀❀❀❀❀❀❀❀❀❀❀❀
              ❀                ||                ❀
          ❀❀❀❀❀❀❀❀❀❀❀❀❀❀❀❀00❀❀❀❀❀❀❀❀❀❀❀❀❀❀❀❀
   |-|-|-|-|-|-|-|-|-|-|-||-|-|-|-|-|-|-|-|-|-|-|
  10+ 9 8 7 6 5 4 3 2 1 0 0 1 2 3 4 5 6 7 8 9 10+
      <--- Female              Male --->
                    PERCENT
```

1980 POPULATION PYRAMID

	Pct.	Number
Total		30505
Females	51.5	15702
Males	48.5	14803

```
----Females---                                              -----Males----

Percent                                                     Percent
  of                                                          of
 Total    Number                                             Total    Number


                                ❀||
   2.5       762                 ❀||                           0.9       284
                                ❀||
                                ❀||
                            ❀❀❀75❀❀
   2.6       779             ❀  ||  ❀                          1.9       581
                            ❀  ||  ❀
                         ❀❀❀❀❀65❀❀❀❀
   4.1      1244            ❀   ||   ❀                         4.1      1236
                           ❀    ||    ❀
                       ❀❀❀❀❀❀55❀❀❀❀❀
   4.8      1475          ❀     ||     ❀                       4.8      1459
                         ❀      ||      ❀
                      ❀❀❀❀❀❀45❀❀❀❀❀❀
   6.2      1878        ❀       ||       ❀                     6.1      1854
                       ❀        ||        ❀
                  ❀❀❀❀❀❀❀❀❀❀35❀❀❀❀❀❀❀❀❀❀❀
   9.9      3030     ❀          ||          ❀                  9.6      2940
                    ❀           ||           ❀
                 ❀❀❀❀❀❀❀❀❀❀❀25❀❀❀❀❀❀❀❀❀❀❀
   4.3      1305       ❀        ||        ❀                    4.1      1245
                 ❀❀❀❀❀❀❀❀❀❀20❀❀❀❀❀❀❀❀❀
   4.8      1465      ❀          ||          ❀                 4.6      1391
                 ❀❀❀❀❀❀❀❀❀❀15❀❀❀❀❀❀❀❀❀
   4.4      1348       ❀         ||         ❀                  4.4      1354
                 ❀❀❀❀❀❀❀❀❀10❀❀❀❀❀❀❀❀❀
   4.2      1274      ❀          ||          ❀                 4.2      1266
                 ❀❀❀❀❀❀❀❀05❀❀❀❀❀❀❀❀
   3.7      1142       ❀         ||         ❀                  3.9      1193
                 ❀❀❀❀❀❀❀00❀❀❀❀❀❀❀
          |-|-|-|-|-|-|-|-|-|-|-||-|-|-|-|-|-|-|-|-|-|-|
          10+ 9 8 7 6 5 4 3 2 1 00 1 2 3 4 5 6 7 8 9 10+
              <--- Female              Male --->
                         PERCENT
```

4. Education Change (Persons Age 25 and Older)

| | | | ------1970----- | | ------1980----- | | % Change |
			Total	Pct.	Total	Pct.	1970-80
Elementary:	0-8	Yrs.	1933	14.5	1397	8.0	-27.7
High School:	1-3	Yrs.	2107	15.8	1801	10.3	-14.5
	4	Yrs.	6516	48.8	8615	49.4	32.2
College:	1-3	Yrs.	1664	12.5	3177	18.2	90.9
	4+	Yrs.	1134	8.5	2456	14.1	116.6
Median Years Completed			12.4		12.6		1.9
Average Years Completed			11.6		12.2		5.3

5. Employment Status Change (Persons 16 and Older)

| | | ------1970----- | | ------1980----- | | % Change |
		Total	Pct.	Total	Pct.	1970-80
Civilian Labor Force						
Employed						
	Total	10733	100.0	15802	100.0	47.2
	Male	6829	63.6	8839	55.9	29.4
	Female	3904	36.4	6963	44.1	78.4
Unemployed						
	Total	288	100.0	668	100.0	131.9
	Male	114	39.6	367	54.9	221.9
	Female	174	60.4	301	45.1	73.0
Not in Labor Force						
	Total	5889	100.0	5805	100.0	-1.4
	Male	1127	19.1	1377	23.7	22.2
	Female	4762	80.9	4428	76.3	-7.0

6. Family Income Change

| | ------1969----- | | ------1979----- | | % Change |
	Total	Pct.	Total	Pct.	1969-79
Less than $ 5,000	579	8.7	235	2.9	-59.4
$ 5,000 to $ 9,999	1787	27.0	411	5.0	-77.0
$10,000 to $14,999	3014	45.5	739	9.0	-75.5
$15,000 to $24,999	1113	16.8	2923	35.5	162.6
$25,000 to $49,999	114	1.7	3631	44.1	3085.1
$50,000 and Over	16	0.2	289	3.5	1706.2
$50,000 to $74,999	-----	----	233	2.8	----
$75,000 and Over	-----	----	56	0.7	----

7. Income Change Summary

	1969	1979	$ Change 1969-79	% Change 1969-79
Median Family Income	11263	24414	13151	116.8
Average Family Income	12179	25597	13419	110.2

8. Household Type

Family Households:	Total	Pct.	White	Black	Asian Pac/Isl	Spanish Origin
Married Couple:						
With Own Children	4215	40.3	4034	57	21	24
Without Own Children	3089	29.5	3044	11	0	7
No Spouse Present:						
Male Householder:						
With Own Children	123	1.2	110	8	0	0
Without Own Children	94	0.9	79	0	0	0
Female Householder:						
With Own Children	487	4.7	472	0	0	0
Without Own Children	220	2.1	220	0	0	0
Non-family Household	2235	21.4	2108	19	0	0

9. Race

	Number	Pct.		Number	Pct.
White	30065	98.6	Korean	25	0.1
Black	218	0.7	Asian Indian	49	0.2
American Indian	11	0.0	Vietnamese	22	0.1
Eskimo	0	0.0	Hawaiian	5	0.0
Aleut	0	0.0	Guamanian	0	0.0
Japanese	12	0.0	Samoan	0	0.0
Chinese	14	0.0	Other Races	69	0.2
Filipino	15	0.0			

10. Ancestry

	Number	Pct.		Number	Pct.
Dutch	331	1.1	Polish	65	0.2
English	1919	6.3	Portuguese	6	0.0
French	159	0.5	Russian	18	0.1
German	4785	15.6	Scottish	86	0.3
Greek	19	0.1	Swedish	252	0.8
Hungarian	50	0.2	Ukranian	0	0.0
Irish	1489	4.9	Other Ancestry	2417	7.9
Italian	236	0.8	Multiple Ancestry	15081	49.3
Norwegian	524	1.7	Not Specified	3160	10.3

11. Industry (Employed Persons Age 16 and Older)

	Number	Pct.		Number	Pct.
Agric./Mining	100	0.6	Business/Repair	532	3.4
Construction	830	5.2	Recreation	543	3.4
Manufacturing	5018	31.7	Health Services	842	5.3
Transportation	678	4.3	Education	1143	7.2
Public Utilities	587	3.7	Other Professional	485	3.1
Wholesale Trade	837	5.3	Public Admin.	580	3.7
Retail Trade	2646	16.7	Armed Forces	14	0.1
Finance/Insurance	981	6.2			

12. Occupation (Employed Persons Age 16 and Older)

	Number	Pct.		Number	Pct.
Executive/Manager	1482	9.4	Other Services	1462	9.3
Professional	1529	9.7	Farming/Forest	56	0.4
Technical	522	3.3	Craft Worker	2219	14.0
Sales	1771	11.2	Machine Operator	1825	11.5
Clerical	3148	19.9	Transportation	705	4.5
Private Household	37	0.2	Laborers	846	5.4
Protective Service	201	1.3			

13. Workers per Family

	Number	Pct.
No Workers	458	5.6
1 Worker	2109	25.6
2 or More Workers	5661	68.8

14. Housing Units

	Number	Pct.	Median Monthly Mortgage/Rent
Owner Occupied	8229	75.9	303
Renter Occupied	2303	21.2	309
Vacant	306	2.8	

15. Housing Units at Address

	Number	Pct.		Number	Pct.
1	8742	80.7	10 or more	816	7.5
2 to 9	866	8.0	Mobile Home/Trailer	414	3.8

Median Value of Owner Occupied Non-Condominium Units: 47981

16. Length of Occupancy (Housing Units)

	Total	Pct.	Owner	Pct.	Renter	Pct.
1 Year or Less	2541	24.1	1069	12.9	1472	64.7
2- 5 Years	3074	29.1	2463	29.7	611	26.9
6-10 Years	1468	13.9	1349	16.3	119	5.2
11-20 Years	2261	21.4	2221	26.8	40	1.8
21-30 Years	848	8.0	827	10.0	21	0.9
More Than 30 Years	368	3.5	357	4.3	11	0.5

17. Residence in 1975 (Persons Age 5 and Older)

	Number	Pct.		Number	Pct.
Same House	14546	51.6	Different State:		
Different House:			Northeast	154	0.5
Same County	8140	28.9	North Central	1749	6.2
Diff. County:			South	431	1.5
Same State	2649	9.4	West	437	1.5
			Abroad	105	0.4

18. Metropolitan Area Residence in 1975 (Persons Age 5 and Older)

	Number	Pct.
In Metro Area in 1980:		
Same Metro Area as in 1975:		
Central City	20951	74.3
Suburb	1735	6.2
Diff. Metro Area Than in 1975	3126	11.1
Not in Metro Area in 1975	2399	8.5

19. Poverty Status of Persons

	Number	Pct.
Income in 1979:		
Below 75 Percent of Poverty Level	957	3.2
Between 75 and 124 Percent	924	3.1
Between 125 and 149 Percent	603	2.0
Between 150 and 199 Percent	1788	5.9
200 Percent of Poverty Level and Above	25905	85.8

```
    Below  75 %          |**
 75 %  -  124 %          |**
125 %  -  149 %          |*
150 %  -  199 %          |***
200 %   or Greater       |**************************************
                         |----|----|----|----|----|----|----|----|----|----|
                         0   10   20   30   40   50   60   70   80   90  100
```

20. Poverty Status of Racial-Ethnic Groups

	Total	Pct.	White	Black	Asian Pac/Isl	Spanish Origin
Above Poverty Level	28786	95.4	25865	183	0	52
Below Poverty Level	1391	4.6	1280	17	0	108

21. Poverty Status of Children and Persons Age 65 and Older

| | ------Children in Families----- | | | | ----Elderly---- | |
	Under 5 Yrs.		5-17 Yrs.		65+ Yrs.	
	Number	Pct.	Number	Pct.	Number	Pct.
Above Poverty Level	2276	98.0	6703	93.4	1821	93.8
Below Poverty Level	46	2.0	477	6.6	121	6.2

22. Poverty Status of Families

	All Families		Families with Female Head	
	Number	Pct.	Number	Pct.
Above Poverty Level	7940	96.5	583	82.5
Below Poverty Level:				
With Children:				
Under 6 Yrs. and 6-17 Yrs.	42	0.5	19	2.7
Under 6 Yrs. Only	34	0.4	23	3.3
6-17 Yrs. Only	174	2.1	82	11.6
Without Children	38	0.5	0	0.0

The census counted about 1,400 individuals who were below the poverty level in 1979—4.6 percent of the total population. In addition, many individuals and families have incomes only slightly above poverty status. Poverty strikes Hispanics and single parent families headed by women more than other groups (16.5 percent of all female householder families are below poverty). Heritage might begin to explore the services and assistance available to poor residents, perhaps in coalition with churches in other Cedar Rapids neighborhoods.

The fact that over two-thirds of all neighborhood families contain two or more workers and the increase in the number of women working outside the home suggests a possible need for day care and other types of service for children of working parents. This will be especially important if the number of births increases in the 1980s.

There is evidence of need for attention to the elderly. This population is growing rapidly and will probably continue to grow in the 1980s and 1990s. Census data alone cannot tell the committee the extent of the need for elderly housing, but it is certainly an area needing attention.

3.3.3 Using Census Data in Congregations

A small amount of advance planning can take much of the difficulty out of working with demographic data. Experience with churches of different denominations has found the following steps to be particularly helpful:
—Give careful advance thought to the boundaries of the community or neighborhood served by the congregation. The mapping exercises discussed in an earlier session are helpful.
—Some churches find that their "neighborhood" or "parish area" is in two parts: the immediate neighborhood in which the church building is located and a wider area (sometimes covering several townships or counties) from which many members commute. Some churches may therefore find it helpful to divide their community analysis into two parts. Heritage, for example, might want to look at its neighborhood alongside the entire city.
—Many church leaders are unfamiliar or uncomfortable with working with statistical data; others find such work exciting. It is helpful to identify in advance those members who make use of such data in their work and who can help interpret community data. Examples include community or educational planners, market analysts, public officials, bankers, antipoverty workers.
—Assign or delegate someone to familiarize him- or herself with the key concepts and terms used in the presentation of census data. Most suppliers of census data publish study guides and other materials to assist census users.
—Experiment with creative ways of displaying the data itself. Oftentimes a chart or graph can convey information more dramatically than a statistical table.
—Encourage users of the data to "translate" the numbers into terms and experiences with which they are personally familiar. In a discussion of mobility patterns, for example, urge people to think what they went through during a relocation from one community to another. When talking about changes in household patterns, help people visualize the factors associated with such changes.
—One useful way to work with census data is to prepare three sheets of paper (or newsprint for a large group) labelled "Surprises," "Important Findings for Our Church," and "Areas Needing More Exploration." By listing findings on each sheet as it works through the statistics the committee will have the beginnings of a summary.
—Be wary of projecting past trends into the future. While trend data provides clues to the future shape of a community's population (for example, a growing young adult population may be followed by increases in the number of births), one decade's trend often presages the next decade's countertrend!

3.3.4 A Note on Sources of Demographic Data:

The Bureau of the Census, through the Government Printing Office, makes available hundreds of printed reports containing tables from a decennial census. These reports are often available in public libraries or through a network of State Data Centers and affiliates. Most of the State Data Centers are located within state government agencies. The Bureau of the Census (Washington, D.C. 20233) can refer churches to a local source. The Bureau is also the primary resource for information on the census itself. Local, county, regional and state planning offices are valuable sources of data and information on population changes and trends.

A number of public agencies and private companies also make census and other demographic data available to church groups, often in a form that makes the data more accessible to persons without demographic backgrounds. These groups are not listed here because they and their products are continually changing. Several denominations have active programs to make demographic data to churches, usually at low cost, many working through Census Access for Planning in the Church (CAPC), based at Concordia College (River Forest, IL 60305).

Because the census itself is conducted only at

ten-year intervals there are difficulties in obtaining up-to-date population data late in the decade. The Census Bureau and states do conduct occasional "special censuses," and several government agencies and private firms prepare population and income estimates for incorporated places. State Data Centers and local planning groups are good sources of information on these updates.

3.4 Social Interaction

Having examined how demographic trends set conditions for a congregation, it is appropriate now to explore the social fabric of the community and the way the congregation fits within it. The questions are varied and complex, as are the methods for answering them. What are the major groups? Who interacts with whom? Who wields power and influence? What are the sources of unity and of division? Where does the congregation fit into this mosaic of structures and processes? To answer questions such as these requires more than "factual" and "objective" information alone; a more sensitive and searching investigation of the qualitative character of the social context is needed. Put simply, community and congregational analysis requires a healthy "sociological imagination" and a grasp of the interconnectedness of social life.

For the individual or study group concerned to know more about a neighborhood or community, there are various ways of gathering information. Particularly important is information gained from *key informants*: community leaders, pastors, school principals, realtors, business people. *More specific* sources of community data are usually available as well: town histories, church records, business and commercial surveys, information collected by "grass-roots" organizations. And of course there is no substitute for the *direct observation* of individuals and groups in the public arena. Attendance at meetings of a community's board of selectmen or city council; neighborhood planning boards; football games, parades and concerts; church suppers and bazaars; political rallies, wakes, bar mitzvahs and cocktail parties becomes crucial for adding human flesh to statistical bones.

Practically speaking, a church study committee is likely to rely on a variety of methods and will attempt to put together a composite portrait of a community using the information available. Three aspects especially important for congregational analysis are: *social groups*, *community involvement*, and *power and influence*. Let us examine each of these, keeping Heritage United Methodist Church and its neighborhood in mind.

3.4.1 Social Groups

Every neighborhood or community of any size consists of numerous and varied social groups. There are *social classes*, whose members possess roughly equivalent amounts of "the good things of life"—wealth, power and prestige. A person's social class undergirds and affects his or her life-situation in almost limitless ways: personal identity and self-esteem, life-style, mental and physical health, aspirations, values, and beliefs, to name but a few. There are *racial and ethnic groups*, whose members share common origins and a distinctive subculture. Demographic data provides clues to the presence of class and racial and ethnic groups. In most communities there are also *purposeful groups*, whose members share common interests or concerns, which sets them apart from others. Voluntary organizations are the prime examples: churches and synagogues, the PTA, Boy Scouts, political parties, League of Women Voters, NAACP, single-parents' associations, hospice support. In every community there is a wide range of such organizations.

The character of community group life is important to congregations for a number of reasons:
—Congregations tend to remain divided along racial and ethnic, social class, and lifestyle lines. Thus people speak of "black," "white," "high status," and "working class" churches. In socially homogeneous communities this is frequently a reflection of the composition of the community itself; in others it reflects the varying group composition *within* the community. Congregations minister to specialized segments of the community. In either case, group identities give shape to the life of the congregation in its worship style, leadership patterns, definitions of mission, religious beliefs, and ethical norms.
—Congregations in which there is a great deal of overlap in group memberships may serve as especially strong "plausibility structures" for traditional religious interpretations. However, they also affect the congregation's ability to integrate new members or to modifying programs to meet changing circumstances and needs. In the words of one old-timer, "We've been here over two hundred years and we've proved ourselves. If you want us to take you seriously, you'll have to do the same."
—Conflict within congregations is often a reflection of group divisions in the larger community. This is especially true for congregations located in communities of rapid social, ethnic, and economic change or where sharp political divisions pervade community life.
—Members' group involvements help to shape the public identity of the congregation. They "locate" the congregation in the mind of the larger community.

Thus a New England political leader was advised when she moved to a new community, "To be anybody in this town you have to vote Republican and join the Congregational church!"

—The group involvements of members provide important natural linkages between the congregation and community life. These ties are often the source of new members and form the basis for developing alliances around shared concerns.

Since the time of de Tocqueville, visitors from other nations have been struck by Americans' love for organizations. Americans continue to be "joiners." In 1983, the National Opinion Research Corporation surveyed a cross section of 1,599 Americans and asked about the groups or organizations to which they belong. Over 73 percent listed at least one group.[17] The following were most often mentioned:

Group	*% Belonging*
Church-affiliated groups	38
Sports groups	21
Nationality groups	17
Professional or academic societies	16
Labor unions	14
School service groups	14
Youth groups	11
Service clubs	10
Literary, art, discussion or study groups	10
Hobby or garden clubs	10
Fraternal groups	9
Veterans' groups	7
Political clubs	5
School fraternities or sororities	5
Farm organizations	4

A relatively simple exercise for identifying community group patterns is to use the above list as a guide to specific groups represented in the community. The study committee can use a sheet of newsprint for each broad category. For each group represented in the community, note the approximate number of members involved and those with which the congregation has a formal or official relationship. The example looks at service clubs and groups and political groups.

The study of community groups depends in large part on the particular issues facing the congregation. Persons in Heritage Church with evangelism concerns might want to focus on the group involvements of newcomers to their area. One approach would be to bring together persons who have joined the church in recent years to identify the groups or organizations to which they belong. Patterns of new member group involvements are often helpful in identifying friendship networks that represent potential sources of additional

Community Groups

SERVICE CLUBS AND GROUPS

	Number Involved	Ties
Lions Club	10	Two trustees active
Chamber of Commerce	4	None
Elks	3	Marginally important
Kiwanis	9	Pastor on board
Rotary	25	Use grounds for annual picnic
Jaycees	1	Ought to develop a relationship
Cedar Rapids Nutrition Service	5	Active as volunteers
West Side Hospice	2	In the church budget
West Side Housing, Inc.	5	Founded by churches; former pastor active
FISH	10	Meets in parish house
Alcoholics Anonymous	?	Meets in parish house

POLITICAL GROUPS

	Number Involved	Ties
Democratic Town Committee	3	Chaired by church member
Republican Town Committee	4	Two deacons are members
League of Women Voters	15	Close ties through chair of social action committee
Citizens for Housing Justice	1	Supported in budget; church has slot on board
Christians for Peace Action Now	20	Pastor a leader; has been source of six new members
National Organization for Women	8	Meets in parish hall
United Black Voters	0	Becoming important; should have ties
Elders for Action	20	Ladies guild is a contributor

new church members. Those concerned with housing might use a list of key community groups with which the church has strong relationships and which might represent "allies" in the effort to construct new housing for the elderly.

Analyzing the key groups and organizations present within the local community can be a helpful way of identifying the affiliative and friendship patterns of existing members. Perhaps more important, it can also identify segments of the local community with which the congregation has few ties. It is one simple, but effective way of "mapping" the church's relationship to its community.

3.4.2 Community Involvement

The social life of a community is differentiated along many lines: *vertically* as in the case of social class and racial and ethnic group status, and *horizontally* as in the case of voluntary organizations. Another example of horizontal differences important in all communities is the *degree of involvement in local community institutions*. In a highly mobile society where almost one-fifth of the population moves annually, attachments to the local community are highly variable. So tenuous and weak are such bonds that some neighborhoods can be referred to as "communities of limited liability"—that is, settings in which people are cautious about investing too much of their commitment.[18] If people will soon be moving out of the community, typically they begin disengaging themselves from voluntary activities.

An important question to be explored in a community study is the extent of involvement in and commitment to the community itself. Partly this is a matter of length of residence. The longer a person has been in a community the greater the chances he or she will have become anchored in its social life. But also, of course, depth of involvement and attachment are crucial. For many, churches are a natural setting for becoming involved and establishing social contacts. Ties within the congregation serve to bind the individual to the community, its values, and way of life.

In Cedar Rapids, where 24 percent of the neighborhood's housing units had been occupied for one year or less, length of residence is becoming important for congregations. The community is aging, but it is also becoming more diverse with an influx of newcomers. For congregations this raises several key questions:

—Who are the "new" people moving into the community and how is Heritage Church related to them?

—How is the increased diversity along class, race, and ethnic lines reflected in housing patterns? Is there greater housing segregation and if so, how does this affect Heritage's own sense of its "parish?"

—Where do various groups interact—in the neighborhood, in the workplace, in political organizations, in congregations? The "turf" on which groups meet is important in shaping intragroup and intergroup relations and images.

—To what extent is the congregation controlled by "old-timers?"

—Are there differences in religious beliefs and styles of institutional commitment between newcomers and old-timers?

3.4.3 Power and Influence

Like other voluntary organizations, congregations are organized to meet goals. Frequently those goals include attempts to exert influence in the community. This places the congregation into the arena of community power relationships. To "get things done," to bring about change, requires realistic and responsible action in the social and political arena.

To understand how a congregation fits into this larger picture one must look at community power structures. Exactly how power and influence operate in local communities is a matter of some scholarly debate. There are two prevailing models of community power offering quite different scenarios: the "power elite" versus the "pluralist" perspectives.

According to the *power elite model*, power is highly centralized in the political and corporate sectors. The elitist conception of power is that the basic decisions in a community are made by a handful of leaders who occupy high-level positions (e.g., high-status professionals, administrators, and major government officials). Decisions are made at the top and carried out at lower levels. For example, Floyd Hunter found in Atlanta in the 1950s that a relatively small number of decision-makers controlled public policy in the city.[19] The power elite consisted mainly of businessmen, who formed committees to discuss and formulate policies. Their decisions were channeled through a fluid structure of institutional and associational groupings to a lower echelon that executed their decisions.

The major alternative is the *pluralist model*. Pluralists argue that in most communities there are many interest groups competing for influence at any given time. Each group influences all others to some degree; yet each acts independently. At times groups have common interests, but usually they conflict and moderate each other's efforts in exercising power. This perspective emphasizes the role of voluntary organizations in mobilizing influence around specific concerns. For example, Robert Dahl in a study of New Haven, Connecticut, concluded that influence is highly diffused: the economic elite had interest mainly in urban redevelopment, ethnic groups had distinct but limited interests, and few of the social elite were involved in bringing pressure to bear on local government. Community power was held by a majority coalition, and groups making up this coalition shifted periodically, combining and recombining into new controlling constituencies.

Which perspective is correct? Both are, or may be. Communities vary in power structures: some are more closed and oligarchical; others are more open and flexible. Some communities are dominated by a single industry (e.g., a factory town or college community), others are very diverse economically and institutionally. Also, communities change over time in their power structures as a result of leadership changes, emerging new coalitions, and changing issues and concerns. By their nature, power relations are fragile and volatile, vulnerable to forces of conflict and competition. Power abhors a social vacuum, and whenever there is opportunity for leadership to move in on new realms of influence one can expect shifts in the power structure.

Building on social scientific studies of power and influence, George D. Younger has developed four helpful approaches to examining community power structures. He calls these *reputational*, *decisional*, *structural*, and *communications* methods. The choice of method depends in part on the study committee's own assumptions about the exercise of community power and influence and the particular problem or issue it is examining.[20]

Power Worksheets

REPUTATIONAL METHOD

What It Is: A method to find out who people in the community *say* has the power.

1. *How to Do It:* Ask a lot of people who they think the leaders and influential people are.
Sample questions:
   Who really runs things here in town?
   Who is really in charge around here?
   Who really has the power?

2. Keep track of the answers you get to your questions. Those who are mentioned the most times or in the most different places are the ones this method will identify for you.
Example:
   Mayor—mentioned 21 times
   Head of bank—mentioned 13 times
   School superintendent—mentioned 10 times

Department store owner—mentioned 9 times
Factory owner—mentioned 7 times
Heritage Church's pastor—mentioned 4 times

3. If you are able to talk to these people themselves, you can carry your study one step further by asking them who they think the leaders and influential people are, or to whom they turn most often for help.
Sample Questions:
   Who is in charge around here?
   Who do you turn to when you want help on a community project?
   Who really has the power?

COMMUNICATIONS METHOD

What It Is: A method to find out *who communicates with whom* and how messages *get through* to a specified target.

1. *How to Do It:* Choose a given target to whom you want messages, letters or statements of support to get through to.
Example:
   One school board member who could tip a vote in favor of your project is wavering in how she will vote. You want her to support your project.

2. Put out the word to a number of people who you know have some connection with the school board member and who favor your position.
Example:
   Talk with other school board members who are on your side of the issue, groups in the community (including church groups) who are friends or coworkers of the board member. Ask each to speak with her about voting for your proposal and to report back to you with the results of their initiative.

3. Check on what happens as a result of your work and who, specifically, is most effective in obtaining contact with the school board member.
Example:
   Either from those who were asked to report back or the school board member herself (or someone close to her who would have this information) discover who was most effective in getting through to the member with information.

STRUCTURAL METHOD

What It Is: A method to find out *who* in the community is *connected with what organizations*, and how those organizations are *related to each other*.

1. *How to Do It:* Look up information on who in your community is connected with the most influential organizations or those which most affect the issues you are working on.
Possible Resources:
   Who's Who in America
   City directory
   Federal Reserve lists of bank stockholders
   Chamber of Commerce membership lists
   Labor unions
   Lists of public officials
   Lists of political campaign contributors
   Newspaper clipping files

2. List for every organization the persons who are in the most important positions—officials and board members.

3. Trace people who are on more than one board or who work with more than one institution. These are people who hold the structure together.
Example:
   One man, who is a bank president, also sits on the board of a local corporation, heads the United Way organization, is a vestryman at an important church and serves on the mayor's urban redevelopment advisory commission.

DECISIONAL METHOD

What It Is: A method to find out who has the power by checking who actually is *involved in making decisions* on a given issue or situation.

1. *How to Do It:* Pick out an issue that concerns your group which has already been decided (or one you have started to work on and are prepared to keep track of).
Example:
   A church committee wants a traffic light on a busy corner.

2. Trace through with those who worked on the issue (or keep track while you are working on it) all the groups and persons they had to see, wrote letters to, or attended hearings before in order to get action.
Example:
   For a traffic light saw traffic commissioner, who referred us to assistant commissioner, who took us to a traffic engineer. Then we contacted our city councilor and the local newspaper and radio station. After a demonstration at the corner with neighborhood parents we had a response from the traffic

commissioner, the mayor's office and the councilor. This finally got action.

3. Analyze the results of your contact with each person or agency involved in decision making and identify who was most responsible for getting action or blocking it.

Example:
   Analyzing the above case you might conclude that the political officeholders (the mayor, traffic commissioner and councilor), reinforced by media pressure, had more to say about getting the traffic light than the technical group (assistant traffic commissioner, traffic engineer).

Practically speaking, the various methods are likely to be used in combination in a given community. One method may be more useful in one setting than another, or certain methods may lend themselves better to some decision-making issues than other. What is crucial is not the method chosen but what it reveals about the community and its power structure. Alternative methods can help check on the validity and generalizability of your observations.

1. What is the relationship between the congregation and the community power structure? Are community "influentials" present in the congregation? If so, how does their representation affect decision-making in the congregation regarding community issues? In communities with elitist power structures, influence generally flows from the top down and the congregation may be one of the arenas through which it flows; this pattern was documented in Liston Pope's classic studies of "mill churches" in southern textile manufacturing communities.[21] In this circumstance, a church or synagogue often finds itself constrained by dominant ideological interests and limited in its independence. In more pluralist settings, congregations often function more as voluntary associations in the pursuit of one cause or another. Often the expectations in pluralist communities are that congregations will be active in a range of social activities and action-oriented programming.

2. What constitutes a "religious" concern within the community? The boundaries or limits of appropriate "religious" concern vary in different communities and among congregations in the same community. Many factors affect the way concerns are defined: the community's religious heritage, community norms, the social composition of the congregations, the ability of pastors and lay leaders to focus issues and set priorities. In some places, usually those with diverse constituencies, the definition of "what is religious" is up for grabs, and congregations are free to engage themselves in the

full range of community concerns and issues. In others, churches and synagogues have a more clearly defined role.

3. In what ways do congregations exercise power and influence? Churches and synagogues vary in how they respond to the challenges. In a heterogeneous, mobile community the chances are greater that congregations will become centers for discussion and action; community norms of openness and responsiveness to issue-oriented concerns will enter the congregation. In more homogeneous settings, where "grass-roots" causes are fewer, churches are more likely to avoid such "intrusions."

4. What is the pastor's role in the community? Is he or she part of the structures of power and influence? In some settings clergy roles are defined quite specifically, in others less so. Community traditions, the congregation's history and prestige, pastoral tenure and personality all shape the pastor's community role. Often in racial minority or working-class communities the pastor is a major bridge between the congregation and community. This role is frequently critical in defining intergroup relationships and setting the terms on which groups can cooperate. In almost every setting the pastor is a potential power figure and is able to "connect" with diverse agencies, constituencies and interests. Self-critical awareness of existing networks and their opportunities and limitations, is essential to a pastor's

understanding of his or her influence in the community.

3.5 The Church in the Context

To this point the chapter has looked at the social context with relatively little attention to religion's role in it. There are a number of ways to obtain information on a community's religious "climate" and the activities of churches and synagogues. Many are quite simple.

—Assign committee members to attend worship at each of the community's churches and synagogues, giving special attention to what is said about the congregation's role and program in the community. Be alert to the way you are received as an "outsider."

—Visit the local library and check for books and articles that trace the religious history of your community.

—Take a careful look at church buildings and grounds at various times of the day. What intended and unintended messages do the church facilities communicate to the public?

—Convene local pastors for an informal discussion of the neighborhood and the church's role in it.

—Gather a small group of community leaders (town planner, welfare worker, city council representa-

---

RELIGIOUS SURVEY CARD   <u>No Information because:</u> Not at home☐   Refused☐   Type of home: Single☐ Duplex☐

Address: .... Name: ....   Multiple unit☐   Town house☐

1. How many persons live at this address? _____   *(Inquire about family composition, e.g., "Is that a husband, wife and two children?" Make checks in parentheses in column 1 for each. Put an X in front of designation for person being interviewed.)*
2. Could you give me the approximate ages? *(Record in column 2, oldest child at top.)*
3. Is anyone in the home a member of a church, parish, or synagogue anywhere? ...... Where? ..... What denomination? *Record name of church and denomination in column 3. If not local, write denomination and city. If non-member, put dash.*
4. *If membership is out of town, or if persons are not members, ask:* Do you attend a local church? ...Which? ... Do the children attend Sunday School? ... Where? *(Write specific name of church in column 4.)*
5. During the last full twelve months did you attend church more than half the Sundays? More than five times? At least once? How about (the other church members in the home)? *(Record in column 5 making check mark for each person.)*
6. *If not member or attender, ask for denominational preference or background, record in column 6.*

FAMILY COMPOS'N	2. AGE	3. CHURCH MEMBERSHIP What church? Where? Denom.	4. CHURCH ATTENDED Specific church?	5. FREQ. ATTENDANCE None |1-5 |6-25|26-52			6. DENOM. PREFERENCE OR BACKGROUND
Husband ( )								
Wife ( )								
Other adult( )								
			SUNDAY SCH. ATTENDED					
Child ( )								
Child ( )								
Child ( )								
Child ( )								
Child ( )								

7. About how long have you lived at this address? _____ How long in this general area?_____
8. Where did you live before? State _____ City or town: _____
9. If a new Protestant church were to be started, welcoming people of many denominations, would you be interested in participating? *Very interested*☐ *Interested*☐ *Maybe, don't know*☐ *Not interested*☐

tive) for an evening's discussion of the community's problems and future and ways the congregation can help shape it.

—Examine the local news media for stories about congregations and their ministries. What is treated as "religious news"?

—Collect a few months' church advertisements from local newspapers. What are congregations attempting to communicate about their ministry and program? Do the advertisements themselves change or does the same advertisement appear each week?

These are rather informal methods for looking at religion's relationship to community life. There are more formal methods as well.

3.5.1 The Religious Census

Since the U.S. Census does not obtain information on religious affiliation or preference, data on religious background and practice is not readily available. There are a number of ways to fill this void. One is the religious census.

Religious censuses were quite popular in the 1950s, especially in growing neighborhoods and in connection with new church development efforts. Usually conducted ecumenically under the auspices of a council of churches or local clergy group, most censuses relied on volunteers going house-to-house within the neighborhood.

The procedures for a religious census are quite simple. Interviewers are assigned specific streets or buildings and carry cards asking for the name and age of household members and their church membership and Sunday school participation patterns. See the sample survey card on page 74. When all of the interviews are completed, a summary is compiled for participating congregations and the cards of those with a specific denominational preference are shared with the appropriate congregation.

In recent years, religious censuses have fallen out of favor. Many feel the results are not worth the considerable volunteer effort involved. For a "religious profile," however, the religious census remains a valuable tool.

3.5.2 Religion's "Public Presence"

A fairly structured approach to assessing the participation of religious groups in public life was utilized by a team of researchers studying the Hartford, Connecticut metropolitan area. Using volunteer interviewers, the researchers conducted hour-long interviews with a cross section of the region's leaders.[22]

The selection of leaders was made in several stages.

First, twenty religious and secular leaders were each asked to identify five persons in several sectors of public life who they felt were broadly knowledgeable about life in Greater Hartford. The sectors were business and corporate affairs, education, politics, the media, social service and voluntary agencies, minority group concerns, and the professions. To the original list were added the names of persons not listed but holding comparable positions in the community and persons listed by a local television station as part of the Federal Communications Commission's "ascertainment process." From the final list fifty individuals were chosen to be interviewed with attention to gender, racial-ethnic background, and city-suburban background. Interviews were completed with forty-four of the fifty persons selected.

3.5.2.1 Interviewer Guidelines

The researchers were concerned with leadership perceptions of community life and the religious community's role in it. Interviewers worked with a pretested interview instrument. Interviewers were given these guidelines:

— In making the appointment to conduct the interview, explain that the study is being conducted to explore the views of community leaders about community life in Greater Hartford and the religious community's role in public life. Give an idea of the areas to be covered, and explain that you need about one hour to complete the interview.

— Keep the interview itself as informal as possible. The interview guide should be just that—a guide. This means that you should know the questions you want to ask before you begin the interview, and you should know them well enough so you can skip around a bit to follow the flow of the discussion. Study the interview guide beforehand!

— Above all, remember that your task is to draw out the feelings, perceptions, and observations of the person being interviewed. You are not there to defend the church or to argue your own beliefs. You are there to listen and to learn—although you may find that occasionally sharing a bit of yourself will keep the discussion moving.

— Probe for details and specifics. Give the person time to make his or her points and pursue a particular line of thought, but if the discussion wanders too far, bring it back to the point or move on. Not everyone will be able or willing to answer every question. That is OK.

— The anonymity of the interviewee should be guaranteed and honored. In no case should you use the name of the person in discussing the interview with others unless you have explicit permission to do so.

Sample Outline of Topics for Community Leader Interviews

1. American Jewish support for Israel, clergy support of the civil rights and disarmament movements, Catholic prolife efforts, and the Moral Majority bring to mind different images of religious groups' attempts to influence public policy. What are your impressions and feelings about these attempts to influence public policy, their methods, effectiveness, legality, and theological integrity?
2. What would you describe as the major issues facing this community?
3. What is your sense of the impact religious leaders and groups now have on public issues in *local community*? Are there persons or groups that have special impact?
4. Is there an issue or concern in which you have taken an active interest or role? Were there religious groups that have made their voices heard on this issue? If a religious group, church, synagogue, or clergyperson wanted to affect the outcome of decisions regarding this issue, what would be the most effective way for them to proceed?
5. People sometimes speak of churches and synagogues as assets to a community. Can you think of specific ways such organizations make contributions to the life of this community? Are there particular congregations or religious groups that seem to be doing an especially good job in this community? Are there religious leaders whose views and opinions are especially valued by persons in positions of secular leadership in the community?
6. Have there been occasions when you personally have found the input of a religious group or leader important for your own reflection/decision on an issue facing you?
7. Will you tell me something about your own religious beliefs and views?
8. Do you presently attend a church or synagogue? If yes, how would you assess the importance of your congregation or pastor in helping you deal with choices and decisions around public issues and concerns? If no, under what kind of circumstances could you envision yourself becoming involved in a church or synagogue?

3.5.2.2 Analysis

For the study from which this instrument was taken, the researchers taped and transcribed all of the interviews, which were then examined for their content. Each substantive comment was placed on a three-by-five-inch card, similar comments were grouped, and a detailed written report was prepared summarizing the major findings from the study.[22]

Less elaborate procedures for analysis will be adequate for most congregations assessing religion's role in their community. One method is to prepare several sheets of newsprint covering themes such as the following:

— What Is Special About Our Community?
— What Special Problems Does Our Community Face?
— In What Ways Do Congregations Represent Assets to Our Community?
— How Can Our Congregation Be a More Effective Public Presence in Our Community?

3.5.3 Possibilities for Community Mission

One of the main reasons congregations seek to understand their social context is to assess possibilities for community-oriented programming. This is true of Heritage United Methodist Church. Some members see the need for increased efforts in housing for the elderly, while others would have the church begin new work in evangelism and church growth.

The study of a congregation's social context will not, of course, tell a church what it must do. It can document and clarify community needs and suggest strategic options for meeting them, but church leaders must still make choices and set priorities among them.

One simple technique for obtaining a sense of members' community mission priorities is suggested by the "Community Mission Questionnaire" developed by the United Church Board for Homeland Ministries.[23] This simple instrument is designed to elicit responses to a wide variety of local mission possibilities. It can be used in a number of ways. If a congregation is devoting an evening or part of a planning retreat to outreach ministries, it is possible to have each group member complete the questionnaire just before a break. During the break volunteers can tabulate responses and record them on a large sheet of newsprint. When the group reconvenes it has a springboard for a discussion of community mission possibilities.

Tabulating the results is quite simple. Using a sheet of lined paper, list the question numbers from one to 32 on the left of the sheet. At the top, list the five response

Mission Opportunity Questionnaire

This brief questionnaire is designed to elicit response to the data in our census report. It lists a number of projects and activities in which local churches are engaged and that may be possibilities for our church. Check the response that comes closest to your reaction to each possibility. There is room for you to note your own additional suggestions. You do not have to sign your name.

	Not Needed in Our Community	Not Appropriate For Our Church	Low Priority At This Time	Only Moderate Priority At This Time	High Priority/ Needs Immediate Attention
1. Set a goal for membership growth	☐	☐	☐	☐	☐
2. Improve our church's outreach to young adults	☐	☐	☐	☐	☐
3. Develop more effective outreach to members of minority groups	☐	☐	☐	☐	☐
4. Review our church's ministry to families and family members	☐	☐	☐	☐	☐
5. Look for ways we can minister to persons in nontraditional families	☐	☐	☐	☐	☐
6. Broaden our church's appeal to educational and income groups not now represented in our congregation	☐	☐	☐	☐	☐
7. Examine ways our church can address problems of unemployment in our community	☐	☐	☐	☐	☐
8. Consider more effective programs for the elderly and persons living alone	☐	☐	☐	☐	☐
9. Review our congregation's stewardship potential in light of community income data	☐	☐	☐	☐	☐
10. Review church staff salaries in light of community income data	☐	☐	☐	☐	☐
11. Develop new ministries to single persons in our community	☐	☐	☐	☐	☐
12. Consider ways our church can reach out to persons who are divorced and separated	☐	☐	☐	☐	☐
13. Broaden our church's appeal to ethnic groups not now represented in the congregation	☐	☐	☐	☐	☐
14. Do a better job of introducing newcomers in the community to the life and program of our church	☐	☐	☐	☐	☐
15. Develop new ministries to military personnel living in our community	☐	☐	☐	☐	☐
16. Strengthen our ministry to and with college students	☐	☐	☐	☐	☐

	Not Needed in Our Community	Not Appropriate For Our Church	Low Priority At This Time	Only Moderate Priority At This Time	High Priority/ Needs Immediate Attention
17. Do a better job meeting the needs of persons in local nursing homes	☐	☐	☐	☐	☐
18. Consider new ministries with persons living in institutions such as prisons and mental hospitals	☐	☐	☐	☐	☐
19. Improve our church's ministry to persons with disabilities	☐	☐	☐	☐	☐
20. Look at our church building with a view to making it accessible to persons with physical handicaps	☐	☐	☐	☐	☐
21. Find new ways to attract young people and families to our church school or church education program	☐	☐	☐	☐	☐
22. Look for ways to appeal to young people who might be attracted to our church's youth groups	☐	☐	☐	☐	☐
23. Explore the possibility of a vacation church school for neighborhood children	☐	☐	☐	☐	☐
24. Explore the feasibility of a volunteer program to teach English to persons whose primary language is other than English	☐	☐	☐	☐	☐
25. Convene a meeting of churches and other groups to look at problems in our community and ways we could address them together	☐	☐	☐	☐	☐
26. Invite community leaders to meet with our church board to look at ways our church can work to address community concerns	☐	☐	☐	☐	☐
27. Develop a "partnership" relationship with another UCC church or a group of churches facing pressing community needs	☐	☐	☐	☐	☐
28. Consider the possibility of a church-sponsored day care center for children of working parents	☐	☐	☐	☐	☐
29. Examine the feasibility of our church sponsoring a housing project for the elderly or low income families	☐	☐	☐	☐	☐
30. Other _____	☐	☐	☐	☐	☐
31. Other _____	☐	☐	☐	☐	☐
32. Other _____	☐	☐	☐	☐	☐

options ("Not Needed in Our Community," "Not Appropriate for Our Church," etc.) across the page. Draw vertical lines to separate the response options. Using "hash-marks," transfer the responses from the questionnaire onto the tally sheets and total the results. Transfer the results onto a clean sheet of paper and you have a quick and helpful summary of member views.

And what about Heritage United Methodist Church? What should the community goals committee report back to the church board? Should Heritage institute a new evangelism program to attract young families into its membership or should it move ahead with the construction of housing for the elderly? Should it try to undertake both projects? This chapter cannot answer these questions. Analysis of the congregation's social context can bring members to increased awareness of their community setting; it can bring the church into closer contact with its neighbors; it can inform and influence decision making. But it cannot, and should not, tell a church what it must do. That remains, happily, a problem in the hands of the gathered community of God's people.

NOTES _____

1. *Treasure in Earthen Vessels* (New York: Harper and Bros., 1961), p. 112.
2. For an example of this approach, see Jackson W. Carroll, William McKinney, and Wade Clark Roof, "From the Outside In and the Inside Out," in Carl S. Dudley, ed., *Building Effective Ministry* (San Francisco: Harper & Row, 1983).
3. *The Protestant Church As a Social Institution* (New York: Russell and Russell, 1935), p. 237.
4. The question of perspective is an important one. For more on the position represented here see David A. Roozen, William McKinney, and Jackson W. Carroll, *Varieties of Religious Presence* (New York: Pilgrim Press, 1984); and Parker J. Palmer, *The Gathering of Strangers* (New York: Crossroad, 1981). For a more explicitly liberationist perspective see Joe Holland and Peter Henriot, S. J., *Social Analysis* (Maryknoll, N.Y.: Orbis Books, 1984). The orientation of advocates of the "church growth movement" is somewhat different from the one outlined here; for an introduction see Peter J. Wagner, *Your Church Can Grow* (Glendale, Cal.: Regal Books, 1976). It also differs from the position outlined in Lyle Schaller's recent writings; see "A Consultant's Perspective" in Carl S. Dudley, ed., *Building Effective Ministry* (San Francisco: Harper & Row, 1983).
5. David Morris and Karl Hess, *Neighborhood Power* (Boston: Beacon Press, 1975), p. 1.
6. Some congregations find it difficult to think of their community in geographic terms. These include congregations gathered around the special needs of racial or ethnic groups, those whose members have left urban neighborhoods to relocate in suburban communities and congregations that serve highly specialized constituencies (handicapped persons, "liberals" in "conservative" communities—and vice versa). We recognize that some of the methods and exercises presented in this chapter may have less applicability for these specialized constituency congregations. At the same time, we view even congregations whose members are not drawn from the immediate community as having a responsibility for the neighborhood in which they are present.
7. *The Heretical Imperative* (Garden City, N.Y.: Doubleday, 1979).
8. This point cannot be overstated. In 1984, as part of the Congregational Studies Institute, two teams of skeptical church executives and seminary faculty were set loose on the West Side of Manhattan and in the affluent New York suburb of Scarsdale to explore the social worlds of those very different communities. They returned from the two communities, which share a reputation as being cold and suspicious of strangers, amazed at the willingness of people on the street to talk freely and openly about their communities and their personal lives.
9. *The Consciousness Reformation* (Berkeley: University of California Press, 1976), pp. 3-5.
10. In analyzing this survey data, Wuthnow found three additional meaning system groupings. Traditionals are those who combine theistic and individualistic meaning systems, moderns blend social scientific and mystical modes, and transitionals combine elements of both the traditional and the modern. Overall, 15 percent of his sample were classified as theistic, 8 percent as individualistic, 14 percent as social scientific, 13 percent as mystic, 4 percent as traditional, 12 percent as modern, and 25 percent as transitional.
11. See Wade Clark Roof, *Community and Commitment* (New York: The Pilgrim Press, 1983).
12. Some census data is available for smaller units known as blocks and block groups (in urban areas) and enumeration districts (in nonurban areas). Most churches will find the above groupings adequate for church planning purposes.
13. These reports contain more detail than some people need or want. In the discussion that follows we will look at Heritage Church's neighborhood using a report prepared by the United Church Board for Homeland Ministries with church users in mind. This profile report includes detailed data from the 1980 Census and selected supplementary data from 1970 to help congregations look at local-level population changes. The report is in three sections covering trends between 1970 and 1980, detailed characteristics for 1980, and individuals and groups with special needs.
14. While the church is fictitious, the neighborhood is real and all data referred to in this section is taken from the 1980 and 1970 censuses.
15. As discussed in the following chapter, it is often helpful to compare community population pyramids with a similar breakdown of a church's own membership by age and sex.
16. If one makes the assumption that the income of Heritage's families parallels that of its neighborhood, a traditional tithe would total $2,441, a far higher level of giving than found in most United Methodist churches—or churches of other denominations!
17. James A. Davis, *General Social Surveys, 1972-1983: Cumulative Codebook* (Chicago: National Opinion Research Corporation, 1983).
18. See Morris Janowitz, *The Community Press in an Urban Setting* (Glencoe, Ill.: Free Press, 1952).
19. *Community Power Structure* (Chapel Hill, N.C.: University of North Carolina Press, 1953).
20. "Worksheets on Researching Power" (East Orange, N.J.: American Baptist Churches of New Jersey, mimeo, n.d.).
21. *Millhands and Preachers* (New Haven: Yale University Press, 1942).
22. For a full discussion see William McKinney, David A. Roozen and Jackson W. Carroll, *Religion's Public Presence* (Washington, D.C.: Alban Institute, 1982).
23. William McKinney, *Handbook: Census Data for Community Mission* (New York: United Church Board for Homeland Ministries, 1983), pp. 28-29.

For Further Reading on Context _____

Berger, Peter L. *The Heretical Imperative.* Garden City, N.Y.: Doubleday, 1979.

———. *The Sacred Canopy.* Garden City, N.Y.: Doubleday, 1969.

Caplow, Theodore, Howard M. Bahr, and Bruce A. Chadwick. *All Faithful People.* Minneapolis: University of Minnesota Press, 1983.

Cohen, Stephen M. *American Modernity and Jewish Identity.* New York: Tavistock Publications, 1983.

Dahl, Robert. *Who Governs? Democracy and Power in an American City.* New Haven: Yale University Press, 1961.

Douglass, Harlan Paul, and Edmund deS. Brunner. *The Protestant Church as a Social Institution.* New York: Russell and Russell, 1935.

Ducey, Michael H. *Sunday Morning.* New York: Free Press, 1977.

Earle, John R., Dean D. Knudsen, and Donald A. Shriver, Jr. *Spindles and Spires.* Atlanta: John Knox Press, 1976.

Greely, Andrew M. *The American Catholic.* New York: Basic Books, 1977.

Gustafson, James M. *Treasure in Earthen Vessels.* New York: Harper and Brothers, 1961.

Hadaway, C. Kirk. "The Church in the Urban Setting," in Larry L. Rose and C. Kirk Hadaway, eds., *The Urban Challenge.* Nashville: Broadman Press, 1982.

Holland, Joe and Peter Henriot, S. J. *Social Analysis: Linking Faith and Justice.* Washington, D.C.: Center of Concern, 1980.

Hunter, Floyd. *Community Power Structure.* Chapel Hill, N.C. University of North Carolina Press, 1953.

Janowitz, Morris. *The Community Press in an Urban Setting.* Glencose, Ill: Free Press, 1952.

Kohn, Melvin L. *Class and Conformity.* Homewood, Ill: Dorsey Press, 1969.

McKinney, William, David A. Roozen, and Jackson W. Carroll. *Religion's Public Presence.* Washington, D.C.: Alban Institute, 1982.

Pope, Liston. *Millhands and Preachers.* New Haven: Yale University Press, 1942.

Rokeach, Milton. *Understanding Human Values.* New York: Free Press, 1979.

Roof, Wade Clark. *Community and Commitment: Religious Plausibility in a Liberal Protestant Church.* New York: The Pilgrim Press, 1983.

Roozen, David A., William McKinney, and Jackson W. Carroll. *Varieties of Religious Presence.* New York: The Pilgrim Press, 1984.

Vidich, Arthur J., and Joseph Bensman. *Small Town in Mass Society.* Princeton: Princeton University Press, 1968.

Warren, Rachelle B., and Donald I. Warren. *The Neighborhood Organizer's Manual.* South Bend, Ind.: University of Notre Dame Press, 1977.

Warren, Roland L. *Studying Your Community.* New York: Free Press, 1965.

Wuthnow, Robert. *The Consciousness Reformation.* Berkeley: University of California Press, 1976.

CHAPTER 4

Process

4.1 Introduction

In congregational studies, process refers to the dynamic interaction between values and events. Process is not what happens, but *how it happens*. It is the link between the identity, values, and commitment of members, and the specific programs which the members attend and support. We have defined process as the underlying flow and dynamics of a congregation that knit it together in its common life and affect its morale and climate.

In defining process, writers in organizational studies usually differentiate between task, structure and process. Task is the content or the goal that a group is trying to accomplish. For example, James Anderson and Ezra Earl Jones say that

the primary task of the church is faith development. It is to move [the individual member] from a faith dependent upon others through a process of personal search and exploration to a faith that is owned—integral to self identity and freely chosen personal values.[1]

Task has to do with the substance of the organization's life, what it is for, what it does, its purpose. Process has to do with the way the goals are accomplished. In this chapter we will explore several expressions of process, including planning, role clarification, training, support giving, crisis management, and problem solving. In each expression we will be concerned with the formal process, or structure, and with the informal process, which is more hidden and less accessible to review. We begin with an introduction to process and a discussion of data gathering procedures.

Formal processes, or group structures, reflect the overt, agreed upon, and more static elements of the organization:

Written and agreed upon goals.
Approved division of labor and job descriptions.
Authority, responsibility, and accountability at defined levels in the hierarchy.

Edgar Schein says there is another part of organizational life which also must be taken seriously, that which we are calling informal process:

The network of positions and roles which define the formal organizational structure is occupied by people, and those people in varying degrees put their own personalities into getting their job done. The effect of this is not only that each role occupant has a certain style of doing his work, but that he has certain patterns of relating to other people in the organization. These patterns become structured, and out of such patterns arise traditions which govern the way members of the organization relate to each other. . . . To put the issue another way, the roles which people occupy [a part of the structure] partly determine how they will behave. It is important to have the right structure of roles for effective organizational performance, but at the same time, people's personalities, perceptions, and experiences also determine how they will behave in their roles and how they will relate to others.[2]

Understanding the tension between formal and informal process is essential in congregational studies. Formal process, or structure, refers to the formal, agreed upon, and usually written understandings that the members of a congregation have about congregational procedures such as decision making, delegating responsibility, defining authority, and role differentiation. Informal process, as we will use the term in this chapter, has to do with the procedures that people actually follow, which may be different from what they are authorized to do in the congregation. This tension between the approved procedures (or espoused values) and the common practice makes the study of process essential.

Many informal processes in churches and other organizations are not thought out. They just happen. However, they happen with regularity and predictability. Just because a process has not been formally agreed upon does not mean that a congregation or group does not have a regularized way of proceeding. For example, there may be no policy about how meetings are run

(Leading), but each time the group meets the pattern is much the same: the chair opens the meeting (there is no agenda), asks that the minutes be read, and once they are completed the leader asks what the group wants to talk about, and the conversation wanders wherever the members of the group lead it. The minutes in the next meeting may bear little resemblance to the dialogue that occurs naturally, but everyone also takes that for granted.

An informal process may be just as real to the membership as a formal process and often far more pervasive and permanent. It is simply a process about which the members have not made a conscious decision regarding the way it should be or the way they want it to be. Many informal processes are adequate, sometimes ingenious. Changing what is functioning may waste time at best, or replace a functional process with one that is dysfunctional, increasing frustration and perhaps getting in the way of a smooth-running organization. "If it ain't broke, don't fix it."

However, sometimes informal process inhibits the group or subverts the goals of the membership. Because the informal processes are out of view, if they are to be changed, they must first be "surfaced"—that is, made visible—so they can be observed and evaluated. Then they can be modified. If one tries to change or create a formal process without also examining the underlying informal processes already in existence, the organization could put a formal process (structure) on top of usual patterns of behavior that run counter to what is written. When the formal and informal processes challenge one another, the informal is likely to win—because it is the one the members of the organization understand, are familiar with, and intuitively know how to work.

To give an example of warring informal and formal processes, some churches attempt to set goals once a year at a church board retreat without looking at what is already being done. The members of the board ask the question "What else should we be doing?" They set a number of new goals, write them in the minutes, and forget them until next year. The informal goals were entrenched in what the church is currently doing. These are not easily changed. The formal goals will not be actualized until the informal practices have been carefully and consciously amended to provide space for something new to fit in.

Many lay leaders and pastors do not think about the process until something goes wrong. In the constant interaction between social context, congregational identity, and particular programs, process is a key to maintain the health as well as discern the ills of a local church.

4.2 When to Address Process Concerns

Each of the cases in the initial chapter can be viewed as a breakdown in process, the kinds of experiences which pastors and church leaders know all too well. Sometimes the problems are obvious to everyone and are easily confronted. There are times, however, when symptoms of difficulty will not be apparent and when an audit of the congregation's process functioning would be appropriate. Consultants to local churches recommend an annual audit, committee by committee, group by group, to assess whether the informal parts of the system are healthy and sharing in the life of the whole. Usually this can be done by the groups or committees themselves in their regular, program-year-end evaluation.

Sometimes it is appropriate to do a process study in the congregation as a whole, especially when:

—There is an increase in hostile or unfavorable gossip.
—The number of committees in the church is decreasing.
—The number of programs in the church is decreasing.
—Participation at church social functions is decreasing.
—Members seem sour, withdrawn, or simply exhausted.
—There is frequent conflict, the cause of which is difficult to determine or understand.

A similar process audit might be appropriate for committees or groups, especially when particular symptoms persist:

—It is very difficult to find a chairperson.
—Attendance at meetings is spotty.
—When assigned tasks, members forget to do them.
—Meetings are boring, or definitely unpleasant.
—The committee doesn't meet.
—The work of the committee doesn't get done.
—Members complain about many issues not related to the work of the group.

This chapter, and indeed the whole handbook, has been written to address questions such as these. However, we must recognize that some members will not wish to spend time in reviewing process issues. They may believe that process concerns get in the way of the church's real work. Or they may believe that process deals too much with what some call "touchy-feely" activities. These critics must be appreciated, since they often have called attention to some of the pitfalls of inappropriate or self-indulgent concentration on process.

This chapter, and the study of process generally, must be kept in perspective. We need to study process not as an end in itself but as one way to facilitate the mission of the church. The issues of process are not primary, but without addressing process issues from time to time, a congregation's life together may be substantially hindered by the ways it approaches its tasks. Understanding process is appropriate and essential in the interaction of Christian identity and social context, of dynamic process and specific program.

One final introductory note: the elements of process that we consider exist in all parts of every congregation. All committees and groups have informal goals, just as the whole church has informal goals. Subcommittees engage in problem solving just as official boards do. The reader should imagine the application of each dimension in every activity. For example, when discussing planning, we may consider the annual activity of the whole church through its official board. We may fail to note that planning and evaluation are equally important in the choir, for the pastor, and in the nursery school—although each may go about it very differently. Therefore, while we will address ourselves at times to the total organization, at other times to the relation of a particular organizational component or process to a part rather than the whole, the reader should imagine that each of the elements discussed here are relevant *both* to the parts and to the whole.

Before beginning the discussion of specific congregational processes, we will first examine several ways of gathering the kind of information that is especially helpful in understanding process.

4.3 Gathering Information

Numerous ways of gathering information on congregational functions have been discussed in a later chapter on methodology. Here we are concerned with the application of those methods that grant unique insight into church process. In particular we will consider observation, document study, questionnaire, interview, and group discussion. Each of these methods has strengths and weaknesses, and none is "the right way" at all times. Each method must be chosen carefully and applied in a way which is sensitive to the area under study.

The act of collecting data is itself an intervention, which may attract interest, heighten concern, and may even arouse suspicion and distrust. Insofar as possible, the members of the congregation should be apprised of the planning and share in the data collection and interpretation. Especially in the analysis of unexamined and assumed process, the study committee may embarrass and alienate the very persons whose support is essential for the possibilities of change. Congregational study that is open and inclusive builds support for a new vision even in the way it approaches and honors the present "reality."

Let us look briefly at the implications of several methods of gathering information in the study of congregational process.

4.3.1 Direct Observation

By far the most frequently used method of gathering information about organization process is the direct observation and personal experience of participation. Sometimes it is called "sensing," since all of the senses are significant elements of participation: watching, listening, touching, tasting, smelling, feeling. As one participates in the life of a congregation certain effects are noticed that give clues to the functioning of the formal and informal processes in that system.

In particular the thoughtful observer will be aware of:

Flow

What is the pattern of movement in the organization? Through whom do decisions have to pass before they are accepted? How careful are the members about sticking to formal agreed upon means of deciding? Are the patterns stiff and formal, easy and quick?

Incidents

What stimuli create which results? What is the "weight" of the stimuli? For example, in some churches little incidents seem to create excessive response on the part of the leadership; in other churches momentous occurrences generate little or no response.

Success and Failure

Members' perceptions of their church as succeeding or failing will give clues that the process may be working or not. "The meeting was a great success!" may be the only language that a participant has immediately available to describe an effective meeting. Or "It was a waste of time" may be an invitation to review process in the work of that group.

Surprises

Whenever expectations are not fulfilled, there is a disjuncture between prior experience and a particular event. The study committee may explore who is surprised (leaders? members? outsiders?) and why.

Hunches

Hunches are intuitions based on experience. They are similar to hypotheses discussed in the chapter on methodology, except that hunches remain as informal notations. Hunches are only useful when they stimulate and focus further study—and they are most unhelpful when they stand as data in a progress report.

Direct observation in the congregation has the unparalleled advantage of "feeling" for the congregation and contributions of particular members. Because by definition it rests on the feelings of the observers, it has the distinct disadvantage of inviting the imposition of categories and conclusions that are alien to the participants of an activity being "observed." Therefore, while it can provide the most sensitive data, the information can be irrelevant or oppressive. There is no substitute for observing as a participant, but taken alone it is an exceedingly subjective source of information. The disciplines of observation are noted in the chapter on methodology.

4.3.2 Documents

Although more frequently used in the study of congregational identity and program, the documents of the local church can provide valuable insight into the processes of the local church. Creeds exhibit the values that seemed of primary importance at the time of their adoption. Constitutions and bylaws of the congregation provide the clearest expression of formal process, the most official version of the way things are supposed to happen. Newsletters offer insight into the procedures that support the program life of the congregation. Announcements printed in the Sunday bulletin (and spoken in worship) reflect styles of leadership, patterns of communication, and conscious efforts to expand participation.

Annual reports announce the way the congregation sees itself through the eyes of the leadership in the reporting groups and say as much about how things happen as the specifics of events. The budget with its income and expenses, annual expectations, and year-to-date reports is a veritable showcase of decisions, crises, and affirmations. Attendance reports reflect commitments to the church as a whole, and constituent parts. Printed sermons, lenten booklets, and even the mailings for stewardship campaigns reflect the dynamic of process, which holds the church together.

Church documents are the mundane tools of analysis constantly produced to keep the leaders and members in touch with the life of the congregation. They provide a rich resource for those who have "ears to hear and eyes to see." However, like observation, documents are best understood when seen through the eyes of those who have created them.

4.3.3 Questionnaires

Questionnaires are the most popular way to gather information from the participants' point of view. There are many kinds of questionnaires, some homemade for the occasion. Commercial "instruments" or "inventories" are available from denominational offices and numerous consultants. These may be administered and interpreted by a study group in the congregation or by an outside resource person who will work with the study team in interpreting the results.

There are many advantages to using questionnaires. They make it relatively easy to hear from many people. They are much more objective than observation and less time-consuming than interviews. Questionnaires also provide information that is comparable, quantifiable, and anonymous. Some responses come from people who may not be active or who may be reluctant to talk with anyone face-to-face about the issues or problems under consideration. Such anonymity may create problems for interpretation of the data, but it provides important access in process issues that deal with sensitive attitudes and feelings.

But questionnaires also have problems. The information returned can be vague and confusing. For example, in response to the question, "What are the weaknesses of this church?" someone wrote "Fair clergy." Does that refer to one or all of the pastors? To a current or former pastor? Does it mean one or all was mediocre? Does it refer to their complexion or their sense of justice?

In an effort to define the responses, some questionnaires offer more specific alternatives. Even then the information can seem to be precise when, in fact, it is quite vague. One might ask people to respond on a scale:

Rate your enthusiasm for this group:

Low		Medium		High
1	2	3	4	5

The average response might be 3.2. It looks like hard data, but its meaning is not clear. Is enthusiasm important to the work of the group? Does everyone rate "3" on an enthusiasm scale by the same criteria? Does the scale compare to previous enthusiasm in this group, or is it a comparison to other groups? What does it mean to average the responses of individual group members? Without much more information, *including an opportunity to explore its meaning with respondents,* such data provides only one piece of the puzzle.

Further, questionnaires do not reveal much reliable information about what people, in fact, do. They will tell you something about their attitudes, something about what they would like to do perhaps, or the way they think they behave. But their responses may differ radically from their actual behavior.

Some people simply do not respond to questionnaires. The congregation may have been "surveyed to death"; or the results of former questionnaires may have been mismanaged by sins of omission, commission, or both. Responding to questions implies a trust that the information will be handled discreetly and used effectively.

Finally, the questions themselves are inevitably biased. Questionnaires begin by making assumptions about what problem areas might need to be addressed. Whether the instrument is made by a consulting firm, an organization interested in research, or a committee of the congregation, those developing it begin by making some guesses about what the problem areas might be. Frequently this is very helpful, because it gives you ideas about "places" to look. On the other hand, it can introduce a bias by ignoring important areas and highlighting other areas of concern—especially important in sensitive process issues. In the questionnaire there is very little opportunity for the questioner to follow up or the respondent to explain beyond the initial concepts that are built into the instrument.

Despite their limitations, questionnaires can be very useful in unpacking the overt and hidden process in the church. Especially when they are immediately and directly coupled with an opportunity to discuss the results with those who filled them out, they can be provocative and useful foundations for understanding and change within the congregation.

4.3.4 Interviews

Interviews provide the kind of information that is inaccessible from observation, documentation, or questionnaires. The most important advantage of interviews is the opportunity for the interviewer to work with the person giving the information to explore an area of common concern. If the person finds it difficult to express opinions, he or she can be supported and encouraged to do so. If the person has an idea that is not yet fully shaped or finds the discussion of a particular topic new and awkward, the interviewer can help the speaker clarify and amplify her or his thoughts. Interviews provide an opportunity for clarity of expression and an exploration of relationships and complexity of ideas. Once rapport is established with the respondent, she or he is likely to say more and explore more in the safety of a trusting relationship. In process issues, the confidential conversation may provide the basic insight to interpret the relationship between observed behavior and responses to a questionnaire.

Two kinds of interviews are frequently used for process research: unstructured and schedule-structured. An unstructured interview starts with a broad statement of task or common concern and lets the respondent take the discussion wherever seems appropriate. A typical question might be: "We're here to talk about your perceptions of the church; tell me what you see are its strengths and weaknesses." The schedule-structured interview employs a more formal approach, such as:

Are the goals of the church clear to you?
What do you think they are?
How do you make decisions in this group?
Do you have enough information to do your work?

The privacy of the personal interview can provide information that helps the interviewer to understand how the member believes the congregation "really functions." However the very intimacy of such sources sometimes makes the material awkward or unusable in more inclusive social settings. Information from interviews often needs to be verified through other sources before it is useful in the interpretation of congregation processes.

4.3.5 Group Discussion

A combination of several data gathering methods may be employed in group discussion or collective interviews. Although others may find the group interview too "messy" in its combination of disciplines, it seems well-suited for understanding the dynamics of process. The interviewer must be alert and "reading the situation" on several levels at once.

These discussions can be open-ended: "Let's talk about how we get work done around here." They can also be focused around a schedule of questions such as those listed above. Sometimes a group discussion will come directly out of the experience of asking all group members to fill out a brief scaled questionnaire, the answers from which are immediately shared with everyone present. Opportunity is thereby given to amplify and explore what is meant by the numeric responses. A third way to explore group processes is to ask the group to simulate an activity similar to those in which they usually engage. This simulation sometimes makes it possible for the group to be slightly more objective about its experience, by analyzing something less threatening than their regular (or real) task, structure, and process. Typically, simulations are role plays of genuine problems, but not with the specific details of issues currently facing the group. A fourth group discussion method is through the use of a case study. In this method the group lifts up an incident from the life of this church or a similar congregation. Based on their experience but without the passion of urgency, the members explore: What happened, what made it worse, what made it better, and what can we learn from this experience?

In group discussion, the study team can observe the dynamics of congregational life at work, including the leadership styles, communication patterns, norms of behavior and belief, decision-making process, and conflict resolution. Thus the members of the church may both act out and explain the formal processes and the informal processes that are natural to the congregation. With some guidance they may see the distinctions within their own behavior and beliefs, and they may model strategies that could help the congregation move in the desired direction.

Not all issues can be examined in the group context, and some individuals are uncomfortable in such settings. Some group settings exaggerate the issues, and all such procedures are slow and uncertain.

No single method of data gathering is sufficient. Ultimately the congregation is more than can be measured. But taken together, observation, questionnaires, documents, interviews, and group discussion can provide functional insights into the "way we do it around here."

4.4 Organizational Processes

Any list of organizational processes would be inadequate since there are a wide variety of analytical tools that have been used to describe the dynamics that knit the common life together. In this chapter we have gathered a few examples around several basic themes:

1. Planning: approved procedure and hidden process
   1.1 Agreement on task
   1.2 Agreement on role
2. Training and nurture of leadership
3. Support, feedback, and process review

4. Needs, norms, and sanctions
5. Diversity and conflict
6. Problem solving

4.4.1 Planning: Approved Procedure and Hidden Process

"Planning refers to any method of thinking out acts and purposes before hand," says one dictionary. This is a helpful definition for the purposes of this chapter. Congregations, committees, leaders, program groups, and teams all engage in some kind of planning. There is always some kind of informal planning, figuring out what they are going to do. Sometimes there is formal planning, that is, a routinized, agreed on process for determining their needs, adapting to their social context, and affirming their identity in the goals they choose, the programs they support, and the way they go about their common life.

Planning is one arena where task, structure, and informal process all come clearly into focus. Certain questions are basic for our discussion and can be used in the local church as a basis for analysis through observation, reading, documents, interviewing, and questionnaires:

—Does the group have a formal planning procedure?
—What is the informal planning process, and how well does it serve the needs of the group?
—If there is a formal procedure for planning, does it work with or against the informal process?

Is there a formal planning procedure? This can be determined by observation, interviews, and review of the documents. This information is available from leaders, minutes, and other documents. Recent church leaders may be able to describe what steps were taken to carry out the planning procedure and what the results of that process have been. The team can examine the minutes of the official board for the last several years to look for descriptions and results of various planning procedures. Further, the team should ask if the congregation has developed a standard operating procedures manual that describes how planning is supposed to be done in the congregation, including who is to do what by when. In many cases the congregation will invoke procedures developed by a denomination or church-related agency.

If, indeed, there is a formal planning process in place, the team should talk with the clergy, board members, and members of the planning committee, if there is one, to determine:

Whether the planning procedure is fully or partially utilized;

Where people are having troubles with it;
Where it is helpful in clarifying tasks and roles.

A helpful formal procedure is described in the program chapter, which can be a resource for congregational planning.

What is the informal process for planning, and how well does it serve the needs of the group? It is assumed that all congregations have developed a way for agreeing on what they are going to do and who will do what, for defining task and role. However, it is not always easy to see and understand how it works. Planning may not be consciously undertaken. Many congregations plan by an informal process that seems appropriate to them in their situation, as illustrated in the following statements:

"The pastor tells us what to do."
"Only those who have been here many years (or who contribute substantially) can influence what will be done around here."
"We wait until there is no disagreement about our ideas before they are implemented."

This is only a partial list to suggest that informal planning processes have to do with the way people approach the task, who is involved, who is not involved, how decisions are made, and who is informed about those decisions.

The study group must develop appropriate criteria for effectiveness, for example: Are the members satisfied with it? Are the leaders satisfied with it? Is it responsive to the demands of the gospel and to the needs of people in and out of the church? Does it help many participate in leadership, or only a few? Is decision making appropriately and fairly distributed among those who participate in the congregation?

If there is a formal procedure for planning, does it work with or against the informal process? Here the question has to do with what parts of the system are most significant in shaping what the organization actually does. When the formal and informal are "out of sync," people are likely to experience considerable frustration, sometimes for opposite reasons. Some had expected the formal procedure to work, and others had assumed that the informal would prevail naturally. Each can war against the other and interfere with its smooth operation. This kind of tension is seen when an elected board in a church decides to use democratic, open planning procedures, involving the participation of many members in rational planning and task agreements, only to have this agreement sabotaged by certain powerful individuals or groups who have always been influential in the congregation and now disagree with the directions in which the church is moving. Pastors can be such powerful individuals, as can be choir members, trustees, large donors, or volunteers who have given generously for many years of their time and leadership to the congregation.

But the struggle between formal and informal does not have to be around "power;" it can also be within the processes themselves. The formal procedure may rely heavily on rational, planned change models for shaping congregational directions. When tested, the members may find that they are accustomed to, and prefer, more intuitive, "Let change come in God's good time" models.

What is going to be helpful to the pastor and other leaders studying the congregation at this point is the use of investigatory disciplines that will help to describe what is happening formally and informally within the congregation. When the descriptions of what is actually happening and the available alternatives are outlined side-by-side, then the study team or leader will be best able to modify the formal and informal systems to increase compatibility between them.

Two dimensions of planning are frequently process issues in local congregations: agreement on task and agreement on role. We will examine task in this section and role in the next.

4.4.1.1 Agreement on Task

In chapter 1 the case of Heritage United Methodist Church was introduced. It is an illustration of the problems generated and discovered by the clash between formal and informal planning processes. The bishop and the pastor made informal plans, which were translated into extraordinary procedure of a new committee. The bishop wants "both mission and ministry," by which phrase he may mean that the church ought to involve itself in activities that would serve the needs of persons who are not members of the congregation. The Rev. Ms. Jones's goals seem to be compatible with the bishop's goals in that the redevelopment of a building into studio apartments for the elderly would seem to meet his desires for more mission to the community. We are also told that the bishop has hopes that Ms. Jones will "bring life into the congregation"; however, this priority may hinder if not be contradictory to the goal of mission in the community. But the bishop and the pastor have goals that are apparently incompatible with those of some of the leadership in the congregation who want "evangelism of adults for the church and children for our church school." Thus, in this case, the process issue is one of a conflict of goals.

In a typical congregation that has disagreement on task, the process often looks like this: members discuss with each other privately (for example, when they gather at Bob's Big Boy Restaurant) their troubled feelings about the tension they are experiencing. The focus of the conversation is on complaint and on bad feelings. Many may try to influence others to join their side, though there is probably little action being taken to actually call the church or its leadership into a clear decision. The pastor acts much the same as the parishioners—not really knowing "what to do" she will talk with individual members privately, to some people at the denominational headquarters and others, perhaps, at a continuing education conference.

At some church meetings there will be what seems to be progress, but no one is exactly sure what progress means—unless it is the absence of acrimony.

When these symptoms appear, how can the pastor and church leaders get the information they need to move into and through this frustration? How can they make it a learning experience, an opportunity for insight into themselves and the development of skills and resources for facing similar situations when they occur in the future? In a comprehensive way, this handbook is a response to such questions: the congregation can claim its identity and study its context (as suggested in previous chapters) and the congregation can engage in an inclusive and open-planning procedure (as suggested in the chapter on program). Often when the church leadership is involved in direct study and dialogue with the community, the impact of that experience raises consciousness and has a profound, positive effect on the clarity of goals within the congregation.

In this chapter we are primarily concerned with the impact of process on the planning procedures. Several helpful instruments for setting priorities and determining membership commitments are available in bookstores and through denominational offices. For example, Grayson Tucker has developed and documented an instrument called *A Church Planning Questionnaire*[3] (see Appendix 4–1). This questionnaire has several useful features. First, a list of sixteen proposed goals provide the respondents an opportunity to determine the popular program priorities for the congregation. Second, the questionnaire explores how process issues affect program priorities. There are a number of specific questions about the congregational climate that give the leadership quick and direct feedback from parishioners about how they feel about themselves at this point and the level of tension that they are now experiencing. There are questions that measure the following climate categories:

—warmth and support
—morale
—openness to change
—the amount of conflict
—decision participation

These responses, coupled with the data about program goals and social context, can profoundly help the leadership assess *how* people are handling their differences as well as what it is about which they disagree.

Third, this instrument provides data about other congregations and allows the members to compare their levels of warmth and support, their morale, their openness to change, and so on with other congregations. This can be useful to a vestry, council, or session. Usually that board has only itself and no one else with whom to compare. With the comparative scores, board members can see that certain responses in churches tend to get higher scores and other responses lower scores. Thus the leadership has a way to measure climate that is better than an assessment based on the responses of this congregation alone, which leads to statements like "a slightly positive score is as good as one can expect." Perhaps a "slightly positive score" tends to be higher than that of many or most other churches. This would give the study team a different perspective when it discovers "slightly positive" is more positive than anyone else. On another question, what seemed to be a low response, compared to others, may be quite respectable. Of course, it is not possible from Tucker's relatively small sample to draw conclusions, but it helps those in the congregation have something with which to compare their experience.

One church that used the instrument discovered that while there was substantial agreement about goals (what the people wanted to do in the church), and while there was a good deal of warmth and support for one another, morale was low and people felt they were not substantially involved in the congregational decision making. The investigation, then, made it possible for them to see those process areas in which work was needed.

The comparison between planning procedures and process issues cannot be conducted by an elite group or pushed through the congregation. Such sensitive materials take time to explore and digest, and they need to be shared in a way that gives church members an opportunity to respond. Retreat settings are often appropriate arenas for such discussion since these provide the intensity of presentation, the time for reflection and informal discussion, and a continuity of participation. Consultants, even neighboring pastors and trained laity, may help the congregation achieve the combination of objectivity and intimacy essential in these discussions.

The method for using this questionnaire is substantially outlined in Tucker's book. The study team may make its own tabulation of the responses or use the resources provided by Tucker. A similar service is provided when using the Parish Profile Inventory of Hartford Seminary, which contains a section on various organizational processes. (See General Appendix.) Some denominational offices provide similar resources, and denominational officials are often willing to work on an ecumenical or interdenominational basis. A wide variety of these tools is also available through the *Whole Church Catalog*.[4]

4.4.1.2 Agreement on Roles

"A *role* consists of one or more recurrent or patterned activities of the *player*, activities that involve corresponding expectations on the part of others who are related to the player. The term is borrowed from the theater and is used to make clear that the expected behavior relates to the *position* of the focal person and not the *person* who occupies the position," says Donald Smith in *Clergy in the Crossfire*.[5] This is a distinction easier to make with formal role definitions than with those that are informal.

Most recent literature about roles in the church has focused on role conflict with reference to the pastor. It highlights the importance of clarifying the expectations of the pastor by the congregation's leadership, as well as the pastor's expectations (which might be quite different) of what his or her appropriate tasks are, their relative priorities, and the style with which they are carried out. Typical problems of role conflict concerning the pastor are:

Formal
   whether the pastor should attend Christian education meetings.

   whether the pastor should be the person to call on shut-ins.

Informal
   whether the pastor's spouse should work outside the home.

   whether the pastor may be an elected official on the school board.

These are not the only role conflicts, however, that congregations experience. Frequently there is confusion and disagreement about tasks, priorities, and styles related to lay leadership and lay committees. Examples of role conflicts that occur in relation to committees are:

—The church board asks the evangelism committee to find ways for members personally to invite newcomers into the church, and the committee develops a plan to mail three letters to new people who worship there on Sunday morning. The board believes mailing letters is the task of the church secretary, and the committee should find a more personal approach.

—The Christian education committee orders a complete new curriculum for the church school, far exceeding its budget for the year.

—The women's group raises money from church members at a bazaar and doesn't report what it has earned or how it is using the money.

Examples of role conflicts that occur in relation to lay leadership include:

—The head of the building and grounds committee never calls a meeting; however, when he or she notices tasks that need to be done around the church he or she either does them alone or asks someone else to do them.

—The elected lay leader of the church is very bossy in meetings, not allowing others to express their opinions if they differ with his or hers.

—When a person is in the hospital, members of the family don't share that information with the pastor.

These examples relate to two kinds of role conflict, *task* and *authority*. The case of Hope Church in chapter 1 suggests a congregation with much role confusion. The congregation assigned certain program tasks to each pastor, but it is not clear if it granted the authority necessary to achieve those tasks. The congregation retained certain responsibilities in its dialogue with the conference minister, and the issue of authority (the right to ask and the willingness to respond) is being carefully negotiated.

All organizations, including churches, divide *tasks* among roles, giving some responsibilities to this person or group and others to that person or group. Problems arise when there is disagreement or misunderstanding about what those tasks are or should be. When the "evangelism" committee becomes the greeting committee, some of the members of the congregation may be frustrated and disappointed in its behavior. Others may be disappointed by the building and grounds chairperson who they hoped would function as a convener of people to reflect on the property needs of the church, but who actually functions as a dispatcher of maintenance tasks in the congregation.

Disagreements about *authority* have to do with who has the legal or traditional right to make particular decisions within the organization. Many times the legal right to make these decisions is given to a person holding an office or to a committee. For example, in some denominations church membership is authorized by the pastor, in others it is authorized by the church board, and in others by the congregation.

Where authority issues become problematic, the situations are usually not related to authority that is legally established by the denomination, but relate to that which people thought was "understood" but has not been formalized or publically agreed upon. For example, a role problem related to authority has to do with whether the church board has the right to meet without the pastor being present. In some congregations the authority to meet without the pastor is granted under certain conditions and clearly spelled out. Meeting without the pastor becomes an issue when it was assumed that the pastor would be there—but some on the board want to meet without him.

In the life of the congregation, role difficulties concerning task and authority are often related to differences in the levels of "contracts" among individuals and within the group. Bradley, Harper, and Mitchell have distinguished between three levels of contract (that is, promises people make to each other about how they will behave): formal, informal, and tacit contracts.[6]

> *Formal contracts* are public, articulated, often officially witnessed. They can be changed only with effort and a process as public as that in which they were established.

> *Informal contracts* are private, articulated in conversation, easily changed but, until changed, create a sense of obligation.

> *Tacit contracts* are private, unspoken, and sometimes unconscious, revealed through behavior patterns. People behave as *though* they have made certain promises to each other.

An example of a formal contract is a job description, a wedding vow, or a motion made at a meeting. An example of an informal contract is a statement agreed to, such as "Would you mind picking up the kids after school?" or "We usually open our meetings with prayer," or "Let's go to the ice cream shop after the meeting." Tacit contracts are profoundly more subtle, but every bit as powerful as formal and informal

contracts. Though they may not talk about it directly, an unspoken agreement between two young persons falling in love with each other is that they will not "see" anyone else. In a church, tacit contracts often center around such things as frequency of church attendance, deference to the pastor or certain older (or wealthier) members of the church, or whether it is alright to challenge another's theology.

Illustrations of formal contracts that have to do with authority are budget statements stating that this committee is authorized to spend this much money, constitutional provisions stating that the president may name the nominating committee, and so on. Informal contracts regarding authority are verbalized agreements between individuals such as the understanding that "none of us likes to be told what to do," or "Why don't you go ahead and make those decisions for us, Jack, since none of us will have the time to go to the store with you." Tacit authority contracts are illustrated by assumptions that some make about the kind and amount of initiative men may take toward leadership as opposed to the amount and kind of initiative women may take; or they are reflected in the rights that some seem to have that allow them more influence in decisions than others because they are more active, more pious, or larger contributors.

A local church has trouble when members have different understandings of their role contracts with one another—especially when some of the role contracts are tacit, not expressed or openly agreed upon. The tensions in High Ridge Presbyterian Church in chapter 1 are rooted in a conflict of tacit contracts of appropriate behavior for members. Each side apparently believed in the Bible and quoted scripture to the others, but the particular issue of wine at the wedding had never been tested. No formal or informal roles had been established, but the informal authority of the bride's father is clearly at odds with the formal authority of the session to set policy.

To gather information on role, task, and authority, a comparison of formal documents, observation, interview, and questionnaire is useful. For illustration we offer three typical role clarification situations: overall task clarity for clergy, task clarity in a multiple staff, and authority patterns in a group or committee.

4.4.1.3 Overall Task Clarity

When looking at tasks that need to get done within a local church, often the congregation decides that it will examine the committees and what they do, the staff and what they do, *or* individual laity and what they do. Thus, the church loses the big picture of how the parts interact and their total ministry. Rusbuldt, Gladden, and Green[7] have included in their manual on local church planning an instrument for assessing mutual understanding of the roles that a minister takes and those taken by the church members (see Appendix 4–3). This instrument consists of fifty statements describing activities that might be appropriately undertaken by either clergy or laity. The pastor (or pastors) and laity are asked to rate on a scale from 1 to 10 how high a priority each activity has for clergy and how high a priority each has for laity. Once each statement has been rated by all who are participating in this research, they are summarized into ten categories and comparisons can be made between the variety of lay responses and their differences with the clergy responses.

A design for carrying out this research could include sending the questionnaire to all the members of the parish. Unless the congregation is quite small, however, the amount of information might be overwhelming. Usually, this data gathering is best done with the official board or the official board plus ten to fifteen other key church leaders. To maximize the use of church time, it is recommended that those who fill out the questionnaire do so at home and send it to the person who will be collating the information before the meeting, so that summaries can be prepared before those who will be examining the data arrive.

The study committee would want to note the pastor's ratings separately, the degree of agreement among the laity, and the comparison between pastor and membership. Generally the degree of disagreement among the laity is greater than the comparison between pastor and members, thus helping the board and the pastor to appreciate and interpret the pressures that each are feeling.

4.4.1.4 Task Clarity in the Multiple Staff Team

Churches with more than one professional person sometimes experience conflict and confusion about who is supposed to do what—or who is in charge of what. Sometimes work falls through the cracks, sometimes staff members believe their prerogatives have been usurped, sometimes members of the team feel there is much wasted motion because of disagreement, duplication, and inefficiency. Even job descriptions and other official documents may not untangle the tensions that conflict can generate.

One way to investigate these concerns is to look into team task agreement through the use of a structured group interview in a staff team setting. This design for data gathering works best in a one- or two-day retreat setting.[8] First, ask the members of the team who will be at the retreat to answer these questions in writing, before they arrive:

What do you feel the church expects you to do in your job?

What do you actually do in your job?

Identify specific difficulties or concerns you have in working with other persons on this committee, or in this relationship.

What do you need to know about other people's jobs that would help you in your work?

What do you feel others should know about your job that would help them (and you)?

What do you need from others in order to do your job the way you would like?

This list amounts to an interview schedule when every member of the team is asked to share his or her answers with the rest. It puts the data out in front of all, making it possible for all to join in correcting, amplifying, and analyzing those pieces of the whole of which each has given a part. Careful study of all of the information can help the staff team identify what is missing, where help is needed (perhaps more paid or volunteer participation), where some may be duplicating work, or where some may be working in areas that are not appropriate to their job description.

4.4.1.5 Authority Patterns in a Group or Committee

Authority issues continue to be an area of discomfort and, sometimes, conflict in certain congregations. Some older members' groups and committees have been schooled in (and been successful in) more hierarchical structures and ways of relating, whereas some younger members do not believe "hierarchy" and "democracy" are compatible terms. In other cases the congregation has established multiple paths of accountability, which may be confusing to the staff and members of the congregation. These situations and many others have to do with agreement on authority, including who exercises it, to what extent, and how.

A useful instrument for analyzing the authority patterns of church leadership groups and committees has been devised by a Lutheran staff team including Gary Anderson, William Berge, William Behrens, George Keck, and Joseph Wagner, and published in a book entitled, *Strengthening the Multiple Staff.*[9] This instrument (see Appendix 4 –2) explores four kinds of structure. The following is a summary from the book:

4.4.1.6 Four Types of Authority Relationships

Type 1: Dependent. Dependent groups have clearly identified decision-makers. Members share in decision making as advisory participants, but often decisions that are made at one level are subject to the authority of yet higher level decision-makers.

The major goals of dependent groups are not usually established by group action. Group members may contribute to the discussion of such goals, but they are finally fixed by higher authority. The expected behavior of members is to conform.

Dependent groups have some positive features. Often they are efficient. They have the ability to get things done. If the leader is capable and respected, there can be a great sense of purpose and accomplishment. Decisions can be made and carried out quickly.

The major disadvantages for a dependent group are a possible lack of unity and low commitment to goals. Creativity may be stifled, and members, apart from the leader, may have little program ownership or zeal.

Type 2: Independent. In the independent style, the pastor and all group members function quite separately. Each has his or her own sphere of ministry and the interaction between them is minimal. Areas of work are generally clearly defined and significant group meetings are few and far between.

At its best, this style allows for much creativity and freedom. Group members do not work under the sense of constantly being watched or told what to do. If goals coincide and the work of various members meshes well, much good can be accomplished.

On the other hand, this style has potential for trouble. There is the probability of competitive conflict. There is little opportunity for exercising concern among group members. Goals are generally not commonly arrived at. The potential for each group member to build a competitive following in the congregation is greater than in other styles.

Type 3: Interdependent. Interdependent groups are characterized by frequent and intensive interaction between members. Such interaction is prized, not only as a vehicle for conducting business but also as a means for developing a supportive system among group members. Members practice confrontive communication with minimal risk. Differences are viewed as assets for improving the quality of problem solving and decision making. Feelings are considered a natural and legitimate element in human interaction.

Goals in interdependent groups are established by all and cared about by all. Meshing individual and team goals is prized.

Decisions in these teams are typically made by consensus. Participation by all members in this process is encouraged. Leadership rotates among members according to the contribution they make. Members practice mutual accountability. Commitment to the group is high and significant personal investment from members is required.

A possible negative effect is that not all persons are suited for this working style. Some people are more independent, and others are more dependent. Also, some situations call for a different working style. The best working style is the one that works best for the people involved as well as the situations in which they work. A group is working at its best when it gets the job done while caring for the needs of the persons in the group.

Type 4: Collaborative. This is the least common group style of the four. In this kind of team, there are no independent decisions. Every decision is referred to the team. Team goals are established by the team and shared fully by the whole team. There can be no individual failure or success. There is only team failure or success.

Harmony and fully shared responsibilities are highly prized by collaborative teams. The style minimizes differences. The collaborative style shares many characteristics of the independent style. But the independent style fosters interdependence between the members, the collaborative style fosters dependence on the team.

The collaborative style can work well if the balance between meeting personal needs and doing the task is kept. However, this style has the potential for inhibiting individual creativity and initiative as well as taking too much time in decision making.

The Lutheran instrument is specifically designed for analysis of authority styles among multiple staff teams of clergy, but it can be useful for interpreting styles among members of boards and committees throughout the congregation. It does not assume that any group falls completely into one category, but that there is a mixture of structures functioning at once, perhaps changing with different combinations of issues and individuals. It is not assumed that each member will have the same perception of experience. Therefore, each member's perceptions are scored separately so that one can be compared with another.

Use of the instrument should be combined with group discussion of results. Often there is a striking similarity between the pattern of group discussion and the results of the data from the instrument, for which observation and further inquiry seem appropriate. Even if the instrument is not used, the four types of group authority provide a framework for observation in a group, and a basis for interview and discussion with the group concerning their perceptions and practice of group participation.

4.4.1.7 Tacit Authority

By far the most difficult processes to analyze are the tacit contracts that members and staff persons have with one another. These are difficult because they are hidden and often personally threatening. Formal and informal contracts have been expressed and discussed by the people in the relationship. Often tacit contracts have not been discussed and may even be below the conscious awareness even of persons who participate in the tacit contract.

To examine these organizational dynamics, the study team may want to begin by identifying what they already know to be formal and informal contracts in the organization's life. As they begin to understand what formal and informal contracts are operating, they should try to assess which of these contracts are functional, and which are not helpful to the relationship or the group. There may be tacit contracts working in opposition to the formal or informal contracts.

For example, in the case of Hope United Church of Christ described in chapter 1, the search committee clearly has a formal contract with the congregation to find a new minister, and, likely, an informal contract with the conference minister to do what he requests so that he will give them names of potential candidates for the job. Something is not working, however, with the contract with the conference minister. An analysis of the formal and informal contracts with the conference minister could be done by the search committee. They could ask:

What are the terms of our understandings?

What is expected of us by the conference minister?

What has, in fact, happened in relation to those contracts? Have we fulfilled our part of the bargain?

Has the conference minister fulfilled his part?

What do we gain by resisting following through on our agreement?

Is there anything the conference minister gains when we resist our part of the bargain?

These questions are difficult to "get a hold on" and to keep in focus by the group. Sometimes they generate a good deal of discomfort—especially if members begin to realize that, perhaps unintentionally, they have joined in a process to punish the conference minister for past difficulties they have had with their clergy. When groups decide to work at this level without skilled and dispassionate facilitation, they may find the task quite threatening. In these situations they might benefit by including someone who is not on the committee, who could help them sustain their analytical task in ways that can produce learning.

4.4.2 Training and Nurture of Leadership

The word "training" comes from the Latin *trahere*, which means "to draw or to drag along"; in English we find other words that retain the same root meanings: railroad train (pulls railroad cars), mule trains, gear train, the train of a bridal gown, a train or course of thought. Churches have many ways they draw or drag newcomers and old-timers into their life and work. By *training* we mean bringing people into the organization's life and processes by various means so that they can function as leaders with confidence and competence.

There are various ways that training gets done in the church but the major ones are these:

Orientation

Giving people material to read on a subject.

Telling people about what's happening during the week.

Giving newcomers a "walk-through" of the building.

Giving someone new to the board instructions on how to read the budget.

On-the-job training

Giving a person a job and hoping he or she figures out how to do it like everyone else has done.

Standing with the person as he or she goes through the various steps, correcting and helping.

Continuing education

Sending the person to a training session outside the church.

Holding classes in the church.

Formal training can include:

Classes (Bible study)
Opportunity to practice skills (Choir practice)
Films
Discussion groups
Feedback sessions
Orientation
On-the-job, supervised experience
Preaching
Reading a manual

Informal training can include:

On the job, unsupervised experience
Trial and error

One of the most regular and, in some churches, regularized patterns of training (both formal and informal) is done when a new family is drawn into the life of the congregation:

On first arriving Mr. and Mrs. Jones are shown where the toddlers' room is for the two-year-old.

As worshippers they are given a bulletin to guide them through the worship service.

After the service they are directed to the coffee hour.

After they have attended a few times the Jones's receive a letter from the pastor and a brochure describing the various activities in the church.

After participating for a couple of months and attending a social event, the pastor talks with them about how they might officially join the congregation. Part of the procedure would include attendance in a membership or confirmation class.

After joining the church Mrs. Jones is appointed to the missions committee and is given a course on the missions her church is supporting through the congregation and the denomination. Mr. Jones is asked to serve on the annual stewardship campaign. . . .

The point of this outline is to underscore the fact that formal and informal training is occurring throughout the life of the church. Some congregations do these tasks well, others do them poorly, but every church is engaged in the processes of training its members formally (that is in a class or coaching session) and informally (on-the-job experience or comments made by disgruntled parishioners who do not like what has been done).

The resistance to training is high in the church, and with good reason. Much that has passed for formal training has been shoddy, ill-prepared, and delivered poorly. Often volunteers who do not know what they are doing are asked to train other volunteers in the implementation of the tasks of the church. Their lack of experience and knowledge is picked up by the "trainees" who, next time, prefer to muddle through the task rather than "waste their time" on training.

Some of the resistance to certain training for church leadership comes from the fact that it may *seem* esoteric, arcane, and irrelevant. Here we are not talking about the holy mysteries, but relatively simple tasks including

group process and community building. Some church members are not used to talking directly with others about their behavior and feelings in groups, and requesting them to do so may generate perplexity and resistance. Without clarity about the importance and practicality of the task in the church and for her or his everyday life, the parishioner will resist taking what will seem like extra time (add-ons) to an already overcrowded volunteer schedule.

How, then, does one discover whether the formal and informal training processes in the church are adequate? One begins by looking at the way the church is functioning and then builds on the experiences of leaders now in place. The most effective programs of leadership development build from the insights and feelings of those who are doing the job. Even people who are doing poorly can be helpful when they are included in a review of the formal and informal training processes in the congregation.

Formal documents (such as job descriptions and manuals of procedure) may be a place to begin and may be a resource that will eventually be upgraded as a result of the study. But interviews and especially group discussion can be most revealing of training needs done through formal procedure and informal processes. The interview might well include asking people in every part of the church's life what kind of training and guidance they have had to help them participate in the life of the church or carry out their work effectively. They should be encouraged to talk about what experiences they have had to help them "learn the ropes" and gain the skills they need to participate or to carry out their tasks. They can do this by sharing their reactions, new knowledge, skill development, and other results of the training experience. Here is an example of an assessment of the training received by official board members upon being elected to the board.

Each new board person is interviewed one year after taking the position. The interviewer requests one hour for the interview. After establishing the reason for the interview and discussing what will be done with what is learned, the interviewer follows a schedule of questions similar to these:

Tell me about your experiences before the first board meeting. Did anyone talk to you about what they did there, when they met, how they were structured, or what your responsibilities would be outside of the meetings?

Had you heard about what goes on at board meetings from any of your friends at church or had you had experience on other church boards?

Was there an orientation or training session for new board members?

How did you learn what the ground rules were for who could talk at meetings, how decisions were made, what the goals and purposes of the board are?

Had you been given material to read about this church board: the constitution, the book of order, past minutes, or budgets?

What is your reaction to the way you were helped into the board?

What knowledge do you think it would be important to share with others who will have an experience similar to yours?

What skills do you think it would be helpful to have to be an effective board member?

From the responses to these questions, a group discussion can be organized to help members of the board become more aware of their process of mutual training. Note that the adequacy of training and guidance is best learned not by asking people what they need before trying to do it but by talking to those who have been through the experience in order to understand what they are up against. "Experience is the best teacher"—especially if it is carefully reviewed and openly shared.

Any part of the life of the congregation has potential for improving the way people are helped to be involved and to participate well. Here is a partial list of roles, activities, and experiences that could be helped by competent training and guidance:

Teaching a class	Singing
Becoming a member or adherent	Setting goals
Leading a study group	Preparing budgets
Leading a committee	Ushering
Calling on members	Preparing for communion
Worshipping	Preparing for marriage
Praying	Greeting newcomers
Cleaning the building	Pledging
Evaluating the pastor	Listening
Calling a new pastor	Interviewing job applicants
Planning church outings	
Being with a friend in grief	Preparing a meal at church

4.4.3 Support, Feedback, and Process Review

In the chapter on program, assessment and evaluation are discussed as formal processes in the local congregation. The material provides a procedure for regular personnel and program evaluation. But formal evaluation is not the only way members and staff discover "how they are doing." Most of us want to know how we are perceived by others in all our relationships and have developed an informal means to check this out. We note the posture and attentiveness of the persons with whom we are dealing; we note whether most of their responses are negative or positive; we are attentive to what third parties say about how we were received by others not present in the discussion; some are even so bold as to ask others what they thought of their performance or the experience of which they were a part.

Churches and committees also have various ways by which they "check out" the responses of worshipers, committee personnel, volunteers, and participants in all sorts of church activities. Leaders are attentive to the numbers of participants, the frequency of attendance, the comments that are made after the meeting, the amount of enthusiasm expressed for what has happened.

Not always, however, are these informal means of regular assessment of life together accurate or complete indicators of individual or congregational satisfaction. A scowling face may be the result of poor process or an upset stomach. Decreasing attendance may have more to do with contextual factors than the substance of a program. Lack of enthusiasm may come more from poor process than from poor content. The person or group interested in analyzing those systems which help people accurately analyze "how they are doing" will want to explore several levels of process. The annual formal evaluation system is discussed in the next chapter. Here we are concerned with feedback, communication, and disciplined evaluation of process.

Areas to be considered in reviewing feedback and communication would include:

—How the board lets the staff know how they are doing on a regular basis

—How the board lets committees know how they are doing on a regular basis

—How the staff members let each other know how they are doing

—How lay leaders discover whether they are appreciated and are "on target" with their leadership

—How participants in worship and programs let the staff know how they are doing

Knowledge about this informal feedback and communication best comes from direct *observation* and *interviews*. Observers of group life often undertake this assessment of group life with a set of values or assumptions about appropriate informal communication and feedback. Through observations of behavior and questions of the various participants, the observer can assess the quality of the feedback processes. Here are a series of criteria for observation that can be used in staff, committee, or congregational settings:

—People tell one another what they have been doing.

—Information on results is collected and given to those who have carried out the task.

—There are preset and agreed upon goals or objectives concerning the tasks people carry out in the organization.

—Assessment of what people do is not based on their personality.

—Trust is high.

—Excuses, blaming, and low ownership are short-term and atypical.

For example, this evaluation can occur in the official board. The board may want to assess informal feedback to committees and program groups. One way this can be done is to ask one person in a meeting to keep track of all the evaluations that are done of work or behavior of a particular group within the congregation and then review the above criteria assessing the extent to which each is met.

—Have the people who were discussed been told about the discussion, before and after?

—Has the group which was discussed had an opportunity to describe what was done, why, and how?

—Was there any assessment of the quality of what happened by those who experienced it?

—Had the board talked with the people doing the task before it was done to come to an understanding of what its purpose or goal was?

—Does more weight seem to be given to the peculiarities of a group personality than to what was done and how it was done?

A more thoroughgoing assessment would observe not only one meeting, but would observe several meetings of both the board and the group being assessed. Leaders in each would be interviewed to learn their perceptions of what the group was trying to accomplish, the means used in attempting that accomplishment, and what helped or stood in the way of that accomplishment. Each would be asked what they thought was accomplished and the answers between the two compared. The learning that comes from this evaluation of feedback and communication can then be shared with both the board and the group. Problem solving (see below) could then be undertaken to deal with any issues needing attention that might have come to light.

Another method for assessing a group's feedback and communication process is to use a "PMR," that is, a Post Meeting Reaction form. One such device that has been used for many years by group leaders is that developed by Philip Anderson, called Christian Group Life.[10]

Figure 4–A
Post Meeting Reaction Form*

This is a checklist to help you evaluate your meeting and to increase sensitivity to some of the relationships in the life of the Christian community of faith.

Check the number on the rating scale that corresponds to your evaluation of the meeting in each of the following categories.

For example, if you feel that responsible participation was lacking, check 1; if you feel that responsible participation was present, check 7; if you feel that the responsible participation of the group was somewhere in between, check an appropriate number on the scale.

A. RESPONSIBLE PARTICIPATION
was lacking. We served our own needs. We watched from outside the group. We were "grinding our own axes."

1 2 3 4 5 6 7

A. RESPONSIBLE PARTICIPATION
was present. We were sensitive to the needs of the group. Everyone was "on the inside" participating.

B. LEADERSHIP
was dominated by one person.

1 2 3 4 5 6 7

B. LEADERSHIP
was shared among the members according to their abilities and insights.

*From *Church Meetings that Matter* by Philip Anderson
(The United Church Press, 1965), pp. 50-52. Used by permission.

C. COMMUNICATION OF IDEAS
was poor, we did not listen. We
did not understand. Ideas were
ignored.

1 2 3 4 5 6 7

C. COMMUNICATION OF IDEAS
was good. We listened and understood one another's ideas.
Ideas were vigorously presented
and acknowledged.

D. COMMUNICATION OF FEEL-
INGS
was poor. We did not listen and
did not understand feelings. No
one cared about feelings.

1 2 3 4 5 6 7

D. COMMUNICATION OF FEEL-
INGS
was good. We listened and understood and recognized feelings.
Feelings were shared and accepted.

E. AUTHENTICITY
was missing. We were wearing
masks. We were being phony and
acting parts. We were hiding our
real selves.

1 2 3 4 5 6 7

E. AUTHENTICITY
was present. We were revealing
our honest selves. We were engaged in authentic self-revelation.

F. ACCEPTANCE OF PERSONS
was missing. Persons were re-
jected, ignored, or criticized.

1 2 3 4 5 6 7

F. ACCEPTANCE OF PERSONS
was an active part of our give-and-
take. We "received one another in
Christ," recognizing and respect-
ing the uniqueness of each person.

G. FREEDOM OF PERSONS
was stifled. Conformity was explicitly or implicitly fostered. Persons were not free to express their
individuality. They were manipu-
lated.

1 2 3 4 5 6 7

G. FREEDOM OF PERSONS
was enhanced and encouraged.
The creativity and individuality of
persons was respected.

H. CLIMATE OF RELATIONSHIP
was one of hostility or suspicion
or politeness or fear or anxiety or
superficiality.

1 2 3 4 5 6 7

H. CLIMATE OF RELATIONSHIP
was one of mutual trust in which
evidence of love for one another
was apparent. The atmosphere
was friendly and relaxed.

I. PRODUCTIVITY
was low. We were proud, and
happy, just coasting along. Our
meeting was irrelevant; there was
no apparent agreement.

1 2 3 4 5 6 7

I. PRODUCTIVITY
was high. We were digging hard
and were earnestly at work on a
task. We created and achieved
something.

Groups that use this form at the end of every meeting find that the consciousness of the members is raised: they assess themselves and become their own researcher and purveyor of feedback. The system becomes self-evaluating, then, on an almost immediate basis.

4.4.4 Needs, Norms, and Sanctions

Every organization has a needs process that metes out rewards and, in some cases, punishments. In the formal system, there is often a reward procedure by which, after staff is evaluated (formally or informally), salaries are raised or other compensations given. Often there is formal procedure by which a nominating committee decides who is ready for an appointment to the board, or the board names delegates to a denominational convention. Young people's groups decide who can go on trips. Budget committees decide who gets funded.

In chapter 1, the crisis in the High Ridge Presbyterian Church provides a heated example of the challenge between the formal authority of the session and the very real but informal rewards and punishments among the membership. From the case we cannot tell the relative influence of informal processes that guided their decision and subsequent action. Did they really believe that wine was out of place in the church, or had some members of the board been waiting for an opportunity to cut the "giant" down to size? Did the pastor not know that wine was to be served because he had not nourished an informal network, or because his staff avoided him, or because he might have objected, or because he gets upset with such news in advance? Is this event a surprise, or does this congregation really enjoy a toe-to-toe conflict from time to time (such as attempting to withdraw from the denomination or changing the church school curriculum)? We will not know how to proceed with the High Ridge church until we explore the process issues of needs, norms, and sanctions.

Informally members are rewarded for their participation in the church's life as it meets their needs both personally and organizationally. People participate in church life because they want to grow, because they are looking for friends and a support group, because they are looking for opportunities to serve their Lord and their community, because they want to worship with others who approach liturgy as they do, and many, many other reasons. When one is not able to have these needs met (or, at least the important ones), one is not "rewarded" for participation. This will inhibit full and active participation in the life of that congregation. Thus, the study committee will want to investigate whether dwindling participation or growing dissatisfaction in the congregation is the result of an increasing inability of the church to meet the needs of the members. If the board doesn't know what the needs of the members are, then a needs assessment should be undertaken as described in the next chapter. If the board does not know how to meet the needs, resources should be brought in to help train and guide the congregation to better respond to its members. In addition to those concerns, interpersonal needs should also be explored.

A useful instrument for assessing interpersonal needs is the FIRO-B developed by William Shutz.[11] The name, FIRO-B, stands for Fundamental Interpersonal Relations Inventory–Behavior. It has six scales, measuring each individual's need for:

Expressing Inclusion
    The need to be with people.

Wanting Inclusion
    The need to be invited to be with people.

Expressing Control
    The need to take charge with people.

Wanting Control
    The need to let others decide what to do.

Expressing Affection
    The need to have close relationships with others.

Wanting Affection
    The need to have others act close and personal.

These scales can be easily understood by people using the instrument. They offer immediate feedback to the person taking the instrument and to others in the group regarding individual motivations and their effect on group dynamics. Use of this instrument can be limited to as short a period as two hours or can be the beginning of an in-depth exploration taking several days, depending on how deeply the group and the observers wish to explore the ramifications of need levels in group dynamics.

The FIRO-B provides a way to appreciate each individual's different levels of need with regard to human relationships and to understand how these need levels affect participation. As the group becomes more sophisticated about the various levels of need for each person, it can compensate for and enhance the different levels of motivation within each participant. It can thus increase the ability of the group to get work done more easily and help individuals meet their own interpersonal needs within the group.

For some groups the FIRO-B would be perceived as too personal or threatening. The United Church of Christ in its manual on volunteer systems in churches[12] has an instrument that also assesses interpersonal needs, but is not perceived as quite so "psychological." (See figure 4-B.)

Congregational studies on personal needs and interpersonal dynamics provide a special ethical issue for church leaders. These materials should be presented in ways that are sensitive to the participants' willingness to be vulnerable and to learn in group settings. They should be shared in an atmosphere of mutual trust and common cause. Because such information is not generally available, these instruments may be threatening to individuals and groups. The information must be carefully gathered and positively shared for the best interest of the individuals and the group as a whole.

Norms and Sanctions

In addition to processes for providing rewards, organizations also have means by which they bring

Figure 4–B

Personal Preferences

The following chart asks you to express your preferences in relation to two choices. You are asked to mark on the line (a continuum) to indicate which of the two choices is your preference and how strong that preference is.

Example: When asked to become a volunteer in the church or community I prefer:

to be a leader _____ __X__ to be a follower

This person has a relatively strong preference for being a follower and, therefore, probably would prefer being a member of a committee rather than the chairperson of the committee.

If you are attracted to both choices equally, then mark the line in the middle. Please note that not all choices are opposites. You are asked to place only one mark on each line.

When asked to become a volunteer in the church or community I prefer:

to be a leader —— ——	to be a follower
simple, routine tasks —— ——	challenging, new projects
an informal fellowship —— ——	a task group with a clear assignment
to do whatever is needed —— ——	to do a job that is important and respected
to work with people I know well —— ——	an opportunity to meet and get to know new people
much responsibility —— ——	little responsibility
to be known as skillful and intelligent —— ——	to be known as friendly and caring
to be liked by others —— ——	to achieve something significant
a job that doesn't require much preparation —— ——	a job I can prepare for by reading and doing homework
to see concrete results —— ——	to maintain smooth and harmonious relationships
to work on a small task or problem —— ——	to tackle large problems facing the community and world
a job where I can witness to my faith —— ——	a job that will be appreciated by my closest friends
a job that will strengthen the church —— ——	a job that will make my community a better place for the poor and disadvantaged
to know what is expected of me —— ——	to try new things and redesign the job to fit me

sanctions to bear against those who do not conform to their standards of behavior. In churches these tend to be informal but nonetheless real. Usually it is in the arena of norms and standards that sanctions are brought to bear against members. For a group to hold together it must have norms. It is not possible for people in their various organizational environments to agree formally about all the rules by which they will abide and by which they will judge others within the system. Therefore, every organization has a system of "understandings" by which most of the adherents live. As was noted in chapter 3, in the discussion of the "underlife" of a congregation, these norms are related to a congregation's identity.

One usually does not notice an organization's norms until they are broken—for example, when a deviant enters the system. Some unwritten understandings about congregational life lead "outsiders" to frustration

and, sometimes, separation from the parish. Pastors new to a congregation, for example, are sometimes unpleasantly surprised to find that they have offended some members of the congregation or alienated them because they were operating out of a different set of "understandings" about what is appropriate behavior from those that are operative for the parish. One pastor's wife did not wear gloves when she attended a reception for women in the parish. She was shocked the next week to receive, anonymously, a new pair of white cotton gloves in the mail. Another pastor expected to stay in the board meeting when his salary was discussed and was offended when he was later attacked for this "boorish" behavior. Sometimes newcomers find themselves in difficulty when they are "too pushy" in expressing a desire to serve on a church committee. In one church a member was criticized for being an "enthusiast," and in another a newcomer was chastised by a delegation of deacons who thought it inappropriate for him to bring his children to the "adult" worship service.

Gordon Lippit says this about norms:

As it interacts with the environment, an organizational system will develop expected and prescribed ways of acting in relationship to its goals and objectives. These standards of behavior will be influenced by what has happened in the past as well as new experiences and requirements . . . . To act contrary to the norms may bring severe censorship or even total rejection by the group. Some norms are functional in getting the organization's task done; others may be incidental and nonproductive. Standards may rest on tradition as well as on changes produced by new experiences and requirements. Because norms and values sometimes persist beyond the point where they are functional, some groups and organizations find it useful . . . to periodically make their operative norms explicit. They ask, "Is this the way we really want to behave? What purpose is served by this norm?" Norms and values form the culture in which people work, [live and pray].[13]

The difference between norms and simple behavior patterns is that norms have sanctions or punishment connected to them. Behavior patterns do not. If the behavior pattern is that men do not wear suits to church in the summer but attend in their shirt sleeves, no one will "pay attention" to deviance or try to get nonconformers to dress like the rest. However, if proper attire has the status of a norm, some kind of action will be taken to call the deviant person into conformity with the accepted standard:

"Perhaps you'd be more comfortable hanging your coat in the closet."

"Gosh, aren't you uncomfortable in that coat?"

"You seem awfully formal and aloof from the rest of us when you dress like that."

Of course, norms differ in intensity and importance in an organization. Some relate to things that are quite trivial and unimportant. Others relate to behavior that is absolutely taboo. Wearing ties may be trivial, but sexual advances by married persons toward persons who are not their spouses are strongly governed by powerful norms.

Norms also differ in the intensity with which they apply to different persons within the system. Norms related to assertive behavior (still) apply differently to men than they do to women. Cursing norms apply differently to pastors (and women) than they do to lay men. Breaking dress codes is usually treated with more tolerance when a newcomer does it than when it is an "old hand."

The case of St. Augustine's Episcopal Church illustrates the tension that can be experienced when established norms are broken. The norm had been for music in worship to be in the historically white, Anglican tradition. With the introduction of black gospel music into the service the norm was being broken; and attempts were being made by some of the congregation's leaders, including Father Cummings even though he liked the "new" music, to bring the members back into conformity with the previous standards for worship.

The case also illustrates how the punishments come in response to the breaking of traditional ways of being together:

—making rules against certain music;

—protesting in public about the behavior of members;

—and probably, although the case does not say so, talking about and against one another in "private."

Congregations get into trouble in relation to norms not because they have them but because:

—the norms are changing and are not agreed upon;

—the norms are counter-productive to church health;

—norms that are irrelevant to effective church functioning or that are meaningless to positive human interaction are treated as taboo items;

—the members of the church do not know how to bring sanctions to bear in a constructive way.

For the person or group interested in studying how penalty systems operate within a local church, a first task will be to discover what the norms of the system are. Once they are identified it will be possible to evaluate them in terms of whether they are changing, counter-productive, or irrelevant. The other main task will be to assess whether the members of the church know how to bring sanctions to bear in a constructive way. Let us look first at a means of identifying norms. This can be done much like the process discussed above for uncovering informal contracts. Indeed, norms are a tacit contract members have about their behavior together, and tacit contracts are difficult to "surface" and even more difficult to change.

The first task of norms assessment is best done among persons who know each other, who like and appreciate one another, and who anticipate discovering information about their processes that help them be closer and work better together. Groups in conflict are not likely to be successful at this task because of the low levels of trust and, frequently, low levels of optimism.

One effective method for gathering data involves the use of a case study. The working group should consist of people who know the congregation well and have participated in a recent experience in the church where there was some tension (such as the situation at St. Augustine's over the gospel music or conflict in the Presbyterian congregation over the use of champagne at the wedding reception), and it should have a research leader who will help the group stick to its task. The leader explains to the group that the purpose of its meeting is to study the norms of this congregation and how they affect its life. Then the leader describes what norms are and how they shape life in the congregation—sometimes positively and sometimes negatively. The way they will study these norms will be to review the recent events surrounding, for example, the unscheduled debate at the board meeting about the use of champagne at the wedding and the reactions consequent to it. This review is done by asking the group:

—to identify who was involved;
—to describe what happened;
—to describe their feelings and those of others.

Then the leader of the research team asks what were the written and unwritten rules by which the key actors in this situation were operating. The group is encouraged to identify these in a brainstorming fashion, initially without judgment, challenge, or contradiction. This will enable a freer flow of ideas. As the group begins to warm to the task and the list begins to develop, the leader asks for those items to be removed that are not norms. (It is likely that some first thoughts about norms will result in descriptions of behavior patterns or other nonrelevant statements.)

The leader should then direct the group's attention to the task of analyzing the norms the group agrees are now operating in the church.

—Which norms are changing?
—Are any norms counter-productive to the church's health—especially:
   helping direct and open communication;
   supporting shared and participative leadership;
   helping work get done;
   clarifying responsibilities;
   appreciating differences?
—Are any norms irrelevant or meaningless?

This discussion should yield rich and deepened understandings of how the church is currently functioning.

The other task, of course, is to analyze what sanctions have been brought to bear, or have been threatened, in order to keep members in conformity to group norms. Again, the group is likely to be threatened by this discussion, and the leader will want to keep the group focused on the task of identifying, as objectively as possible, what actually happens in the life of this church.

4.4.5 Diversity and Conflict

When it comes to diagnosing a local church in conflict, the key process questions are mostly informal. Usually—indeed, almost always—congregations have formal systems for managing differences. The constitution or the book of order tells them that they must follow *Robert's Rules of Order*, or that the Bishop must be consulted and his or her decision "will be determinative." These formal processes may reach decisions but also may leave angry and dejected congregants. Many times they do not seem to "get at" what has created the tensions in the first place. Therefore, it is important in conflict to examine carefully who cares about what is happening and how these individuals are relating to one another both within and alongside the formal decision-making processes.

To do diagnosis in a church that the leadership perceives to be in conflict can be problematic in itself. If the leadership is uncomfortable and frightened by the tension, they may not want to get too close to it. They may be especially uncomfortable if persons are in the same room together who have differing opinions or bad feelings. Thus, the leadership may take precautions (sometimes elaborate) to keep people away from each other and to restrict the flow of information.

For example, as tension begins to develop in a congregation, the vestry, board, or session may find that its members are reporting to the board that they have talked to "certain individuals" (who remain nameless) who are very upset. Without knowing who these persons are, it is not possible for the board to know how upset they are or what they will do if they do not get their way. Further, it is not possible for the board to assess the numbers they represent—whether they represent "many" or "most," whether they are active participants or inactive, or whether they represent large givers in the congregation. When the messages come in anonymously, the board has no way of assessing the real extent of dissatisfaction in the congregation. The dynamic of rising conflict seems to push board members apart from one another and chokes off their ability to talk openly with one another and with others in the congregation. The board, if it is caught up in this dynamic, may then accept anonymous information, set itself up as a "secret" committee (not sharing what it has discussed or its decisions with others), and take actions based on information that may be partial and slanted.

This dynamic of organizational tension, which squeezes and distorts information, must be dealt with by the board or other persons obtained to study the conflict, to get a picture that is balanced and realistic. Several precautions, therefore, should be considered before attempting to gather information in conflicted churches.

First, those gathering the information should be, and should be perceived to be, impartial by the members of the congregation. If they have something at stake in the conflict, their judgment is likely to be skewed *and* other members are not likely to be candid with them. Second, these persons should be trained, not only in the art of listening, but also in the skills of patiently probing for clarity of detail, depth of meaning, and full description of what has or has not happened that has generated the tension in the organization. Those who are angry, frightened, upset, or have an axe to grind often find it difficult to assess facts and meanings in a balanced fashion, and, sometimes, they become overimpressed with other's anxieties. Data gathering in conflict settings must include information about how people feel. It must include information about what has happened, what the various groups want, and an understanding of the values that shape their desires.

The third precaution to the persons gathering information in conflict is that, if they have any intention of using this information for helping people deal with the conflict, both respondents and researchers should understand that the information gathered is *not* "confidential." A good deal of what is learned will need to be shared with all of the parties involved so that they will know who has what concerns, as well as the depth of those concerns. If those complained against are going to change their behavior, they will need to know what the "charges" are that are being brought against them. Further, the various parties will probably need to speak with one another about whatever is causing the tension. If the data gatherers cannot reveal who feels what and cannot encourage the various persons to talk with each other, the conflict management process will end with the gathering of data.

Finally, those who are gathering information should make substantial efforts to canvass the *active* membership of the congregation in seeking to understand what is going on in this situation. It is not necessary to hear from those who have long since dropped out (though recent dropouts may have useful information). It is important to work with what is affecting the organization *now* (not what affected it once). Further, it is those

who are currently involved who are going to be responsible for "fixing" the situation. To discover the needs and wants of those who have lost their motivation to continue and who may now have commitments elsewhere, may lead the church to develop programs and processes that are not relevant to the current church population.

There are two useful ways to go about getting information in a conflicted church. The data gatherers can be trained to visit in the members' homes or they can invite members to come to the church to small (eight to twelve persons) meetings where the issues will be discussed.

There are some ways that many churches use to gather data in a conflict that are not helpful: mailed questionnaires, large public meetings, hearings. Let's look at each of these methods briefly.

4.4.5.1 *Mailed Questionnaires*

The problem with questionnaires is that they do not give the researcher enough information about what is really going on. They can measure feelings or attitudes, but they do not do a very good job helping people express the complexities of the situation that are likely shaping those feelings and attitudes. To get in-depth data, it is important for interviews to be held where dialogue can help people clarify what they are thinking and feeling. Questionnaires do not allow that to happen. Further, much of the data from mailed questionnaires may be anonymous (even though names were asked for). Also the compilation of the data from mailed questionnaires is sometimes treated as a vote, affecting a decision before the various parties have had full opportunity for discussion and problem solving together. In other words, before the leadership and others are given opportunity to study many alternatives, the decision is made.

4.4.5.2 *Large Public Meetings*

Likely it is obvious to every reader why large public meetings are not good means for gathering information. However, let us reiterate them here. At public meetings people are often not given ample time to speak fully about their perceptions and concerns, and sometimes the atmosphere of the meeting raises rather than lowers the sense of threat that people have. This often leads to exaggeration and distortion, giving meanings that participants would regret under more comfortable circumstances. Further, meetings sometimes turn into decision-making groups prematurely. Getting reliable data and understanding it takes time and a dispassionate environment. This is often not the case in public meetings, especially where feelings are intense.

4.4.5.3 Hearings

Hearings are another poor way to gather data. The way some congregations have done this is to invite members to bring "evidence" to a panel of church leaders who listen to all sides and then attempt to make judgments about who is right or what is to be done. Often these panels are made up of people with good intentions but also with decided points of view: some are on one side, some the other, and some neutral. Hearings put the decision-making power in the same hands as those who are gathering the information. Thus, the people confronting the panel are constantly aiming their remarks to judges who will make our decisions for us.

If the congregation wants to help *manage* conflict (rather than submit it to arbitration), the purpose of data gathering should be to discover who needs to talk with whom and how they will do it in order to work through the conflict. Panels make decisions for others and do not help the people involved to make decisions for themselves. Thus, the way information is collected will strongly affect the results that follow.

4.4.5.4 Visiting in Homes or Small Groups

Two better ways to gather information in conflict settings are to talk with people individually in their homes or in small groups to discover their concerns and the extent of their commitment. Home visits will require finding individuals or teams who are neutral and will have the time to visit as many in the church as will see them. A less time-consuming method[14] is to ask groups of individuals to come to the church in small groups of eight to twelve people to share their perceptions and concerns. This can be done on a Saturday, with groups coming in at designated times. In some large congregations it will be necessary to have groups meet on Sunday as well; in small congregations not as many meetings are required.

It is best for each of these groups to consist of people who are fairly compatible with one another, that is, individuals who would feel comfortable talking in one another's presence. When the groups are highly heterogeneous, the conversation often gets focused on one issue or one part of an issue and does not explore the many other facets of what is happening in the church. Further, some people are intimidated by encounters with "the opposition" and either do not show up or do not say anything. It is very important to hear from everybody as fully as possible.

The usual pattern in these meetings is to begin with an introduction of the person gathering the information to explain his or her understanding of the purpose of the meeting and what will be done with the information that is being gathered, and then to ask for any other questions the people may have. Once these questions have been responded to, a very brief questionnaire can be given to the participants. This questionnaire is a means to double-check what the people have said orally and is a way to count the number of responses and concerns that people have, to provide an opportunity for people to communicate about what is positive as well as what is negative, to have some information that is a little more concrete than just the interviewer's memory and impressions of what was said, and to help people get into thinking about why they are in this meeting and how to best express their positive and negative impressions of the church.

The questionnaire usually asks these questions:

—Name.
—Age.
—Groups, programs, committees, activities in which you are now active.
—Frequency of public worship attendance at this church per month.
—Do you now pledge or regularly contribute financially to the general fund of this congregation?
—Why do you attend this congregation?
—What are the strengths of this congregation?
—What are the weaknesses of this congregation?
—If you could change anything in this congregation at the present time, what would you choose as the most important thing to change?

The respondents are asked to write their name on the paper, again to communicate that the interviewer does not want them to perceive their remarks to be anonymous (or, for that matter, confidential). It also makes it possible for the interviewer to go back to individuals who have written things that are not understood to ask for amplification or clarification of their concerns.

It is a good idea to ask for people to tell their age because there is often a myth in the congregation that older members believe so and so and younger members something else. This may be purely a myth, or it may be a fact. Checking it out may help later on.

Asking about worship attendance and giving will give the interviewer information about the respondent's level of activity in the church.

Asking the participants to tell why they attend this church will give the interviewer and those who are attempting to work on the differences some clues about the "glue" that holds people to the church. In some churches it is strong family ties; in others positive relationships that go back many years; in others the fact that the church is near their home; in others the particular faith stance of that congregation. Some of these motives are not very strong for holding people through intense conflict; others will help the members endure severe and protracted confrontation. Answers to this question should help in the development of strategies to deal with the differences there.

The question about strengths of the congregation will not only help to bring understanding of some of the motives for participation of some of the members, but it will also help to assess how much organization and structure there is for a variety of commitments.

The last two questions generate lists of information about the problems that need to be addressed and help some with the level priority that the members attach to them.

Why is it that the interviewer takes all this time to talk to so many people? Would not this process be less costly and have a lower profile in the congregation, if the interviewer just spoke with a few key individuals and tried to work out things between them? The answer is yes and no. It certainly would cost less in terms of information gathering to talk to just a few. But it is likely to not help people work through their differences. One of the most common problems in addressing problems in the congregation is the assessment of the numbers of people who are "upset," or are "dissenters," or want the pastor to leave. Often board members' analyses of the numbers pro and con and their assessment of the commitment of the various pro-and-con parties tend to be exaggerated or understated. An interviewer can help the board and congregation get better data on the extent of polarization than board members might be able to procure.

The interviewing process, whether it is done by board members or a consultant, provides a good opportunity to ask questions about a variety of issues and carefully explore how deeply each person feels about each issue. It is important to note whether people in the church are completely polarized (that is, all members of each faction or party agree about every issue confronting the church) or are only partially polarized (on some issues members of a faction agree and on other issues they do not). An illustration of a partially polarized church would look like this:

Pro-Sanctuary	Con-Sanctuary	Pro-Inclusive Language	Con-Inclusive Language
Bob	John	Bob	Carol
Carol	Mary	Mary	John
Ted	Bill	Bill	Jane
Alice	Jane	Alice	Ted

An illustration of a completely polarized church would look like this:

Pro-Sanctuary	Con-Sanctuary	Pro-Inclusive Language	Con-Inclusive Language
Bob	John	Bob	John
Carol	Mary	Carol	Mary
Ted	Bill	Ted	Bill
Alice	Jane	Alice	Jane

Sometimes board members are quite concerned as to whether they have input from every body in the church, and they believe they have incomplete or invalid data if not every person has been spoken to. Or some members of the board may believe that they must have a true random sample of the whole membership if they are to have an accurate picture of what the issues are and the level of commitment of various members to each issue. This is not necessary. When one is gathering information in a church about participation and commitment, one is not doing social-science research; rather one is *assessing the current leadership's concerns and points of view*. Therefore, the board should be most concerned that the current leaders and all of the parties or factions of the church are well represented in the sample. Interviewing a random sample gets information from many who have long given up on the church and might well provide information from people who would like to see the church do such and such but are quite unlikely to support it or be a part of its ministries either as a recipient or an actor.

4.4.5.5 Diagnosis

Once the information has been gathered, the following diagnostic questions should be asked by those wishing to understand what is keeping the tension alive.

Who is involved? How many? Is it just one person or the whole congregation? Of those who care about the issues, how central are they to the congregation's decision-making process? Are they marginal? Elected to office? Do they have great influence in the congregation?

What is the arena? Is this a legal battle, one over which the participants are likely to go to court, or is it one that can be dealt with by two individuals privately? Is it a congregational matter, a board matter, or a committee matter? Sometimes the arena is not public and those concerned about the conflict will want to assess where the conflict has been surfacing—in meetings at church, or in private conversations in people's homes.

What is the extent of polarization? Are members highly committed to one side or the other? Is there a large group that has not yet "made up its mind?" Perhaps there are many issues and people that are on different sides on different issues. Though such a church would be highly conflicted, it would not be highly polarized because the same people are not in the same camps on all of the issues.

What kind of issues are the people dealing with?

Role conflict would have to do with lack of agreement on lay or clergy roles. Structural conflict relates to the formal structure of the congregation where organizational components are to be in conflict with one another, perhaps intentionally, perhaps not. The balance of powers in the federal government is an example of intended conflict, or checks and balances. Sometimes congregations find that deacons and trustees function as a check and balance system—and this may not be desirable to the members.

Substantive or issue conflict can occur over goals, processes, questions of fact, or values. Usually there is a significant interpersonal dimension included in these substantive conflicts, but not necessarily so.

Interpersonal conflict has its roots in individual needs for recognition, esteem, feeling adequate in another's eyes, feeling valued, needs that are not being met to the satisfaction of some or many within the church. Those examining the conflict will want to explore as deeply as possible the roots of these feelings, because it could be that they come from a sense of inadequacy on the part of those feeling deprived, or it could also be that the feelings come from conscious or unintended distancing on the part of others in the congregation.

What distortions are occurring in perceptions? In higher levels of conflict it is difficult for participants to be objective. They tend to see themselves as substantially benevolent in their motives and their opponents as essentially malevolent. They tend to see issues dichotomously, as either/or, right or wrong. They tend to believe they know the true motives of the opposition's behavior, and they tend to greatly exaggerate both the level of threat and the consequences of any actions which are taken or might be taken. The higher the distortion, the more difficult and frightening the conflict will be to those experiencing it.

How are members communicating?

Is it one way, "I'll tell you what you need to know, and I will not listen to you"?

Is it public or secretive?

Is it only with those in one camp or with all camps?

Is the communication ample, or spare—leaving much room for speculation?

What are the stakes and how high are they? What will happen if one group loses? What will be the effect on

them? What will be the effect on the church? Is this an emergency? Is it possible to explore at length the concerns that people are raising?

As the groups concerned explore the answers to these questions, and the dimensions and depth of the conflict begin to become clearer, there will be some reduction in tension just because developing understanding takes some of the anxiety out of the situation, which had previously felt even more chaotic and confusing.

Once the data have been collected and analyzed, it will be necessary to bring together those who have a concern about the issues to help them understand the problems, and search together for solutions that will be meaningful and useful to the individuals involved and the church as a community.

4.4.6 Problem Solving

Much of the literature on problem solving says that effective processes are orderly and rational. For example, Don Koberg and Jim Bagnall[15] have listed the steps in a problem-solving process:

—accept the situation
—analyze the situation
—define the problem
—ideate (brainstorm)
—select
—implement
—evaluate

They believe the place to begin in a formal problem-solving process is with acceptance of the problem. Have those who need to do something about the situation accepted the problem? In other words, is there motivation to work on it?

Once the situation is accepted, it should be analyzed. Information must be gathered from various sources to help one understand the dimensions of the problem— from the political to the technical. Therefore, information will need to be gathered from a reasonable sample within the congregation for there to be a broad enough analysis to make it possible to find those "solutions" that are going to be best for the most people.

Defining the problem, says Koberg and Bagnall, has a great deal to do with the kind of approach that will be taken to solving it. If the problem definitions are not clear or agreed on, the group may have to come back to this step in the process in order to make progress toward solutions. Koberg and Bagnall believe that the problem definition is the bridge between the analyzed facts and attributes we have just discovered and the alternatives and decision making that follows:

We can "conceive" the statement or set of guidelines which expresses our new comprehension of the problem now analyzed; a statement which, like the "eye of a needle," will provide alignment for all decisions after the fact. We have reached the point of declaration.

Our definition becomes the filter for future decisions regarding the problem. And our solution, in the end, will become a physical translation of this statement.

Later on, if we discover the situation to mean different or expanded things, we can always change our mind and try it differently the next time around.

We begin each problem with some basic "definition," which is the sum of our experience to that moment; what we think the problem means as we attempt to describe it at that beginning level of understanding. Then as we progress through the process, our understanding of the situation develops into progressively clearer statements until at last we can say the problem is understood. If the situation occurs again, we either apply the same hard-won previous definition to the new situation or we begin anew, with a higher level of understanding, prepared to progress to even greater levels of understanding.[16]

Ideation or brainstorming is the way groups explore the many alternatives and choices open to them for resolving the difficulty. The best process explores many possible solutions to the problem before choosing one.

The final steps in problem solving are choosing one of the possible alternatives available to the group, putting that alternative to work, and then checking back to see how well the group has done.

Areas where the organization is most likely to notice symptoms that may point to difficulties in the problem-solving process are the following:

Decisions are not getting made. At meetings the same issues come up over and over again. People seem stuck without enough information or enough gumption to get on with what needs to be done.
There is little commitment to decisions once they are made. The board (or other group) will vote to do something, but nothing comes of it—or no one shows up to help when it comes time to implement the work.
Decisions are only made by a few. In voluntary systems, morale and involvement in decision making seem to go hand in hand. When the many don't feel they are participating in shaping the decisions, there may be difficulty with conflict, apathy, or other confusion around leadership.

If these symptoms appear, one area worthy of exploration should be the problem-solving processes currently being used by the church, the board, or subunits within the church. There are several ways this can be approached. The case-study method could be used where persons involved in problem solving and decision making in the congregation could be asked to go back over the history of a recent problem-solving process documenting each step, including who was involved, how they operated, and what each did to help or hinder the process.

Another method would be to ask the investigating team to interview persons involved in the problem-solving process as to what they did and those affected by it as to what their reactions were. This will give insight into the process and its effectiveness. A rather complete interview schedule (it is abridged here for the group leader) was developed by Woodcock and Francis in their book *The Unblocked Boss.*[17] The following statements are for exploration into what was done by the leader:

—identifying the causes of problems
—identifying problems quickly
—asking for help when necessary
—involving others in problem solving
—delegating effectively
—selecting appropriate membership
—setting agendas clearly
—making good use of meeting time
—building an open climate
—drawing out contributions from others
—facilitating consensus
—maintaining discipline
—reviewing the performance of the group
—making good use of meeting time
—listening to the ideas of others
—inviting contributions from others
—leading brainstorming sessions
—displaying information clearly
—identifying information gaps
—seeking new information
—identifying options for action
—evaluating options for action
—deciding what has to be done
—allocating tasks
—coordinating plans
—taking time to review
—discussing errors openly
—identifying ideas for improvement
—giving feedback to individuals
—using checklists to assist systematic review
—developing the team's skills
—improving the use of resources

A final way to explore how well this group is doing its job at problem solving would be consciously to observe itself as it moves through a problem-solving process by appointing one of its members as a process consultant. At a couple of times during the meeting and at the end of the meeting the consultant will give "feedback" on what he or she saw happening and direct the group in an analysis of the process.

Edgar Schein, in his book *Process Consultation: Its Role in Organization Development*,[18] illustrates how this is done in his section on decision making. He says that groups make decisions by six methods:

—by lack of response
—by authority rule
—by minority
—by majority rule: voting
—by consensus
—by unanimous consent

Schein describes how this kind of analysis works, as follows:

The process consultant must first make the group aware of decisions which it has made and the methods by which it has made them; then he must try to get the group to assess whether they feel that these methods were appropriate to the situation. For example, the members might well agree that the chairman did railroad the decision, but they feel that this was appropriate because they were short of time, and knew that someone needed to make that decision quickly so that the group could get on with more important things.

On the other hand, the group might decide that a decision such as having each person in turn state his point of view introduces an element of formality and ritual into the group which undermines its ability to build creatively on ideas already advanced. The group might then wish to choose a different method of idea production. The important thing is to legitimize such process discussion and to have some observations available in case the group is finding it difficult to discern what the consultant is talking about.[19]

This method proposed by Schein is research and intervention at the same time. It has been very popular with consultants wishing to focus on process concerns because it helps the group become its own consultant as it quickly becomes more conscious of its problem-solving processes.

In this chapter we have explored the function of process as one of the elements of congregational life. We have not explored all of the possible areas of process concerns, but we have looked at several that are commonly problematic in churches and other voluntary organizations. Taken with identity, context, and program (as dimensions of a system), process concerns help to round out our understanding of the way churches function. The way people encounter and deal with one another defines their life together, just as it affects what it is they are trying to accomplish and become. Being faithful means not only being concerned about ends, but the means as well.

NOTES

1. James D. Anderson and Ezra Earl Jones, *The Management of Ministry* (San Francisco: Harper & Row, 1978), p. 131.
2. Edgar H. Schein, *Process Consultation: Its Role in Organization Development* (Reading: Addison-Wesley, 1969), p. 11.
3. Grayson L. Tucker, Jr., *A Church Planning Questionnaire* (Louisville: Grayson L. Tucker, n.d.).
4. James F. Hopewell, ed., *The Whole Church Catalog, Where to Get Tools for Congregational Study and Intervention* (Washington, D.C.: Alban Institute, 1984).
5. Donald P. Smith, *Clergy in the Cross Fire* (Philadelphia: Westminster Press, 1973), p. 23. Don Smith explores a variety of clergy role conflicts far beyond the scope of this essay.
6. June Bradley, R. S. Harper, and Kenneth Mitchell, *Building the Multiple Staff* (Toronto: Center for Christian Studies, 1975), p. 15.
7. Richard E. Rusbuldt, Richard K. Gladden, and Norman G. Green, Jr., *Local Church Planning Manual* (Valley Forge: Judson Press, 1977), pp. 235-39.
8. William Dyer, *Team Building: Issues and Alternatives* (Reading: Addison-Wesley, 1977), pp. 86-87.
9. Gary Anderson, William Berge, William Behrns, George Keck, and Joseph Wagner, *Strengthening the Multiple Staff* (Minneapolis: The American Lutheran Church, 1982).
10. Philip A. Anderson, *Church Meetings That Matter* (Philadelphia: United Church Press, 1965), pp. 50-52.
11. William Schutz, *FIRO-B*, available from Consulting Psychologists Press, 577 College Ave., Palo Alto, CA 94306.
12. Office of Church Life and Leadership, *The Ministry of Volunteers: A Guidebook for Churches*, in "Volunteers and Volunteer Ministries" (New York: The United Church of Christ), p. 53.
13. Gordon L. Lippit, *Organization Renewal* (New York: Appleton-Century-Crofts, 1969), p. 49.
14. Speed Leas, *Moving Your Church Through Conflict* (Washington, D.C.: Alban Institute, 1985), chaps. 5, 10.
15. Don Koberg and Jim Bagnall, *The Universal Traveler: A Soft-Systems Guide to Creativity, Problem-solving, and the Process of Reaching Goals* (Los Altos: William Kaufmann, 1976), p. 20.
16. Ibid., pp. 59-60.
17. Mike Woodcock and David Frances, *The Unblocked Boss* (San Diego: University Associates, 1981), pp. 31-35.
18. Edgar Schein, *Process Consultation*, pp. 53-57.
19. Ibid., p. 55.

For Further Reading on Process

Dyer, William. *Team Building: Issues and Alternatives*. Reading: Addison-Wesley, 1977.
Hardy, James M. *Corporate Planning for Nonprofit Organizations*. New York: Association Press, 1972.
Hare, A. Paul. *Handbook of Small Group Research*. New York: The Free Press, 1976.
Hopewell, James H., ed. *The Whole Church Catalog, Where to Get Tools for Congregational Study and Intervention*. Washington, D.C.: Alban Institute, 1984.
Janis, Irving, and Leon Mann. *Decision Making: A Psychological Analysis of Conflict, Choice and Commitment*. New York: The Free Press, 1977.
Leas, Speed. *Moving Your Church Through Conflict*. Washington, D.C.: Alban Institute, 1985.
Levinson, Harry. *Organizational Diagnosis*. Cambridge: Harvard University Press, 1972.
Maier, Norman R. F. *Problem-solving Discussion and Conferences: Leadership Methods and Skills*. New York: McGraw-Hill, 1963.
Mintzberg. *The Structuring of Organizations: A Synthesis of the Research*. Englewood Cliffs: Prentice-Hall, 1979.

Napier, Rodney, and Matti Gershenfeld. *Group Theory and Experience.* Boston: Houghton Mifflin, 1973.

Office of Church Life and Leadership, *Church Planning.* New York: The United Church of Christ.

Office of Church Life and Leadership, *The Ministry of Volunteers: A Guidebook for Churches,* in "Volunteers and Volunteer Ministries." New York: The United Church of Christ, n.d.

Pfeiffer, William, and John Jones. *The Annual Handbook for Group Facilitators.* San Diego: University Associates, 1972, 1973, 1974, 1975, 1976, 1977, 1978, 1979, 1980, 1981, 1982, 1983, 1984, 1985.

Rusbuldt, Richard E., Richard K. Gladden, and Norman M. Green. *Local Church Planning Manual.* Valley Forge: Judson Press, 1977.

Schein, Edgar H. *Process Consultation: Its Role in Organization Development.* Reading: Addison-Wesley, 1969.

Smith, Donald P. *Clergy in the Cross Fire.* Philadelphia: Westminster Press, 1973.

Wilson, Charles. *Planning Organization Workbook.* Lebanon: Jethro Publications, 1980.

APPENDIX 4–1

*A Church Planning Questionnaire**
by Grayson Tucker

In this section of the questionnaire, we are interested in your views and beliefs in a variety of areas. You will find statements about how you see things in your parish or congregation and statements about your religious beliefs. Other items deal with the work of your Pastor. Still others seek your views about Christian education.

In each case, YOUR impressions, feelings, and opinions are important for church planning. In some cases, you may feel that your opinions are not well informed. Please go ahead and give your impression as it is now, even though you realize it could change by talking with others. Use the "Don't Know" response only in those rare cases where you have no impression at all.

For those statements which begin, "Our Pastor . . . ," think of the head of staff, if there is more than one. A summary of these items will be given only to your Pastor to use in planning future growth and development.

In the blank by each of the following statements, write the number from the following scale which best expresses your view:

1	2	3	4	5	6	7
Strongly Disagree	Disagree	Tend to Disagree	Tend to Agree	Agree	Strongly Agree	Don't Know

_____ 1. It doesn't matter so much what I believe so long as I lead a moral life.

_____ 2. Our Pastor leads worship skillfully, involving the people in a meaningful way.

_____ 3. There is a disturbing amount of conflict in our church.

_____ 4. Spiritual matters, and not social or political affairs, should be the concern of the church.

_____ 5. My religious beliefs are really the basis of my whole approach to life.

_____ 6. It seems to me that we are just going through the motions of church activity. There isn't much excitement about it all among our members.

_____ 7. Problems between groups in this church are usually resolved through mutual effort and understanding.

_____ 8. Our church changes its program from time to time to meet the changing needs of members.

_____ 9. I experience the presence of God in my life.

_____ 10. The whole spirit in our church makes people want to get as involved as possible.

_____ 11. When conversing with a person, our Pastor listens for feelings, as well as words, and treats feelings as important.

*"A Church Planning Questionnaire," © Grayson L. Tucker.

_____ 12.   The leaders of our church show a genuine concern to know what people are thinking when decisions need to be made.

_____ 13.   Among most of our members there is a healthy tolerance of differing opinions and beliefs.

_____ 14.   The stories in the Bible about Christ healing sick and lame persons by His touch probably have a natural explanation.

_____ 15.   Our church tends to stay very close to established ways of doing things.

_____ 16.   Christian education takes place primarily in church school classes.

_____ 17.   Our Pastor has developed a good plan of visitation to members with special needs.

_____ 18.   On the whole, members have a healthy pride in belonging to our church.

_____ 19.   Our Pastor helps develop opportunities for church leaders to receive training for their tasks.

_____ 20.   The main purpose of Christian education is to help people learn to live as Christians in contemporary society.

_____ 21.   The best Christian education programs are planned by the people who lead them and participate in them, rather than by church publishers.

_____ 22.   A small group of people seem to make most of the important decisions in our church.

_____ 23.   Converting persons to Christ must be the first step in creating a better society.

_____ 24.   Our Pastor is willing to spend extra time and effort to help a committee carry out a job in difficult circumstances.

_____ 25.   A friendly atmosphere prevails among the members of our church.

_____ 26.   Our Pastor shows concern for community problems by working with others to help find solutions.

_____ 27.   Our church tries to adapt its program to changing needs of our community.

_____ 28.   In preaching, our Pastor consistently relates the message of Scripture to the needs of the people and the world.

_____ 29.   The behavior of people is determined primarily by the influences of society.

_____ 30.   Scripture is the inspired Word of God, without error not only in matters of faith, but also in historical, geographical, and other secular matters.

1	2	3	4	5	6	7
Strongly Disagree	Disagree	Tend to Disagree	Tend to Agree	Agree	Strongly Agree	Don't Know

_____ 31. I sense an atmosphere of genuine care and concern among our members in time of personal need.

_____ 32. In important decisions in our church, adequate opportunity for consideration of different approaches is usually provided.

_____ 33. On the whole, our people welcome new patterns or styles of worship.

_____ 34. There is frequently a small group of members that opposes what the majority want to do.

_____ 35. I try hard to carry my religion over into all my other dealings in life.

_____ 36. Strangers are usually made to feel welcome and at home in our church.

_____ 37. Our Pastor preaches with a sense of conviction.

_____ 38. The primary purpose of people in this life is preparation for the next life.

_____ 39. People whose times of illness or special need are known by the members are assured of support in prayer.

_____ 40. On the whole, I am satisfied with how things are in our church.

_____ 41. Persons who serve on our church committees and Board (Council, Vestry, Session, etc.) represent a good cross-section of the membership.

_____ 42. I would rather be in a Christian education group where an informed leader uses most of the time to give a presentation, than in one where members are led to study and share their ideas.

_____ 43. Although I believe in my religion, I feel there are other things more important in my life.

_____ 44. The main purpose of Christian education is to help people know what is in the Bible.

_____ 45. As I see it, Christianity should be clear about separating spiritual and secular realms and putting emphasis on spiritual values.

_____ 46. Our Pastor shows concern for the church's educational program.

_____ 47. Christian education is primarily for children and youth.

_____ 48. Our Pastor does good work in counseling persons with special problems.

APPENDIX 4–2
Multiple Staff Inventory *
from *Strengthening the Multiple Staff*

GROUP 1: Staff Structure

For each statement in this section you are requested to indicate which of four alternative responses most accurately reflects your perception and feelings about your staff. You will have seven points to distribute over the four alternative responses. The higher the number of points assigned to a response, the more completely that response corresponds to your perceptions or feelings.

The following are example combinations:

1. If you think that A corresponds to your perceptions and feelings, then write "7" on the A blank and "0" on the other blanks. Thus: **A** _7_   **B** _0_   **C** _0_   **D** _0_

2. If you think A closely corresponds to your perceptions and feelings but B has only slightly less correspondence, then you would write: **A** _4_   **B** _3_   **C** _0_   **D** _0_

3. If you think A and B are pretty much the same but C has some slight correspondence to your perceptions and feelings, then write: **A** _3_   **B** _3_   **C** _1_   **D** _0_

Distribute the seven points over the four alternative responses in each item of the MSI in the way that best represents your perception and feelings about your staff.

When you have finished Group 1, check each item to insure that the points assigned add up to seven.

(1) Goals for ministry are:
     A. Established by leader
     B. Decided by the whole staff
     C. Established by each individual
     D. Sometimes established by whole staff and sometimes by individuals   **A**____   **B**____   **C**____   **D**____

(2) Meetings are run by:
     A. The leader
     B. A set of traditional rules
     C. Full group agreement
     D. Rotating leadership   **A**____   **B**____   **C**____   **D**____

*By Gary Anderson, William Berge, William Behrens, George Keck, Joe Wagner, and Wilson Egbert (ed.), © the American Lutheran Church (Minneapolis, MN), pp. 2-4 of the Inventory, pp. 12-13.

(3) Authority:
  A. Is primarily a function of rank or position
  B. Is primarily a function of expertise
  C. Is not very important
  D. Is primarily held by the whole group   A____ B____ C____ D____

(4) Meetings are generally used to:
  A. Share information
  B. Receive and clarify orders
  C. Develop staff plans and programs
  D. Insure staff cohesion   A____ B____ C____ D____

(5) Jobs are usually:
  A. Assigned to individuals by leader
  B. Assigned to whole staff by the staff
  C. Assigned to individuals by the staff
  D. Assigned by individuals to themselves   A____ B____ C____ D____

(6) Staff leaders usually serve to:
  A. Coordinate staff activities
  B. Direct staff activities
  C. Develop activities with staff
  D. Don't exist   A____ B____ C____ D____

(7) Agenda of staff meetings:
  A. Are developed by the staff during the meeting
  B. Are usually routine
  C. Are determined and enforced by staff leader
  D. Are easily adjusted by staff members   A____ B____ C____ D____

(8) Staff decisions about ministry are made:
  A. By leader
  B. By voting
  C. By group consensus
  D. By voting and consensus   A____ B____ C____ D____

(9) Responsibility for success and failure of staff:
  A. Is of little concern to members
  B. Is held by leader
  C. Is sometimes held by staff and sometimes by individuals
  D. Is shared fully by all members   A____ B____ C____ D____

(10) Members usually see themselves as:
    A. Sharing a relationship
    B. Protectors of special interests
    C. Advisors to leader
    D. Participants in a common cause   A____ B____ C____ D____

(11) Congregational programming tends to emphasize:
    A. Cooperation between staff members
    B. Individual members goals and responsibilities
    C. The leader's goals and priorities
    D. Search for common goals and shared responsibilities   A____ B____ C____ D____

(12) Members work together:
    A. Because it is a staff expectation
    B. Because cooperation and information exchange are to their best self-interest
    C. Because their collaboration is personally satisfying and challenging
    D. Because they are required to do so by leader   A____ B____ C____ D____

(13) The way the staff functions:
    A. Is considered a responsibility of the leader
    B. Is generally accepted and given little attention
    C. Is examined and discussed by staff
    D. Is less important than staff relationships   A____ B____ C____ D____

(14) Feedback on individual performance:
    A. Is rarely given because the staff holds itself responsible for all performance
    B. Is given by staff members
    C. Is given by leader
    D. Is rarely given because individuals are not responsible to the staff   A____ B____ C____ D____

(15) The staff spends most of its energy:
    A. Trying to be a model Christian community
    B. Trying to help the leader do his/her ministry
    C. Trying to help individuals do their own ministries
    D. Trying to help the whole team do its ministry   A____ B____ C____ D____

APPENDIX 4–3

*Role Expectations Checklist**
by Rusbuldt, Gladden, and Green

"The origin of this form is unknown. I received a shorter version from the Rt. Rev. John R. Wyatt, Episcopal bishop of Spokane, who found it being used in one of his churches. I have expanded and revised it, reworked the questions for easy scoring, and have used it many times."

—Paul Beeman

PURPOSE:

A mutual understanding of the role which a minister takes and the roles taken by the church members can do much to improve the effectiveness of a church. This checklist is designed to help each person look at what he/she expects of lay members and of the pastor. Each answer expresses a personal feeling. There are no right or wrong answers. Sharing answers among church members and the minister can start a fruitful discussion that leads to mutual goals and expectations.

EXPECTATIONS OF THE PASTOR. In your opinion what should demand the greatest amount of time, thought, and preparation? What should have priority over other activities on the pastor's schedule? Enter your priority ratings for **pastors** by *circling* the appropriate number for each item.

EXPECTATIONS OF CHURCH MEMBERS. In your opinion what should demand the greatest amount of time, thought, and preparation? What should have priority over other activities for the members of your church? Enter your priority ratings for church members by *underlining* the appropriate number for each item.

	Priority
	low high
1. Relates to sick, dying, and bereaved persons.	10 9 8 7 6 5 4 3 2 1
2. Maintains a disciplined life of prayer and personal devotion.	10 9 8 7 6 5 4 3 2 1
3. Teaches or works directly with Christian education classes in church school or Bible school.	10 9 8 7 6 5 4 3 2 1
4. Does church office work, typing, mimeographing, record-keeping.	10 9 8 7 6 5 4 3 2 1
5. Understands how groups work well and helps church groups and organizations function efficiently.	10 9 8 7 6 5 4 3 2 1
6. Visits in the homes of church members.	10 9 8 7 6 5 4 3 2 1
7. Participates in denominational activities beyond the local church, district, conference or regional work.	10 9 8 7 6 5 4 3 2 1
8. Seeks to locate needy persons and families in the community.	10 9 8 7 6 5 4 3 2 1

*Adapted from: *The Interpreter*, Program Journal of The United Methodist Church, vol. 18, no. 5 (May, 1974).

	Priority		
	low		high

9. Participates personally in community projects and organizations (such as school board, PTA, United Fund Campaign). 10 9 8 7 6 5 4 3 2 1

10. Seeks to bring about constructive social change and community improvement. 10 9 8 7 6 5 4 3 2 1

11. Leads or assists in public worship. 10 9 8 7 6 5 4 3 2 1

12. Reads and studies the Bible. 10 9 8 7 6 5 4 3 2 1

13. Teaches special courses or adult study groups. 10 9 8 7 6 5 4 3 2 1

14. Works on (or with) church board and committees. 10 9 8 7 6 5 4 3 2 1

15. Tries to identify and resolve conflict among church members and leaders. 10 9 8 7 6 5 4 3 2 1

16. Calls on new residents and prospective members. 10 9 8 7 6 5 4 3 2 1

17. Interprets and implements denominational programs within the local church. 10 9 8 7 6 5 4 3 2 1

18. Personally assists victims of fire, flood, injury, injustice, neglect, or unemployment. 10 9 8 7 6 5 4 3 2 1

19. Represents the church in local organizations (such as Chamber of Commerce, YMCA, Council of Churches). 10 9 8 7 6 5 4 3 2 1

20. Identifies who are victims of social neglect, injustice, discrimination, or prejudice, and helps bring them to public attention. 10 9 8 7 6 5 4 3 2 1

21. Studies for, writes, and preaches sermons. 10 9 8 7 6 5 4 3 2 1

22. Cultivates a personal social life outside of church activities. 10 9 8 7 6 5 4 3 2 1

23. Works with church young people in classes or fellowship groups. 10 9 8 7 6 5 4 3 2 1

24. Works on (or with) church budget, finance drive, and building campaign. 10 9 8 7 6 5 4 3 2 1

25. Leads or helps the church in the process of setting its goals. 10 9 8 7 6 5 4 3 2 1

26. Talks with persons about their spiritual development, religious life, and beliefs. 10 9 8 7 6 5 4 3 2 1

27. Explains home and foreign missionary work and promotes financial support from church members. 10 9 8 7 6 5 4 3 2 1

28. Encourages church members to help persons in need by contributions, counseling, and tutoring. 10 9 8 7 6 5 4 3 2 1

29. Seeks to involve church members in program to help others through organizations (such as

	Priority		
	low		high

YWCA, Indian Center, groups for older persons).

10 9 8 7 6 5 4 3 2 1

30. Testifies before city council or state legislature committees to correct or improve unjust ordinances or laws.

10 9 8 7 6 5 4 3 2 1

31. Counsels people about personal and moral problems and about major decisions of life, such as marriage or vocation.

10 9 8 7 6 5 4 3 2 1

32. Maintains prayer and devotions in the family circle.

10 9 8 7 6 5 4 3 2 1

33. Serves as summer camp counselor.

10 9 8 7 6 5 4 3 2 1

34. Recruits and trains church program and organization leaders.

10 9 8 7 6 5 4 3 2 1

35. Seeks to maintain openness among church leaders and members.

10 9 8 7 6 5 4 3 2 1

36. Finds ways to witness for Christ in daily life contacts with people.

10 9 8 7 6 5 4 3 2 1

37. Serves as an example by generously donating to church benevolences.

10 9 8 7 6 5 4 3 2 1

38. Seeks to understand the special needs of minority groups, such as Indians, Blacks, Asians, migrants.

10 9 8 7 6 5 4 3 2 1

39. Is an active member of a service club (such as Rotary, Lions).

10 9 8 7 6 5 4 3 2 1

40. Speaks before church, community, and civic groups, on radio or TV, regarding problems and needs in the community.

10 9 8 7 6 5 4 3 2 1

41. Provides for baptisms, Communion, weddings, and funerals.

10 9 8 7 6 5 4 3 2 1

42. Serves as an example of higher than average moral and ethical character.

10 9 8 7 6 5 4 3 2 1

43. Conducts or assists in church membership or confirmation classes for youth and adults.

10 9 8 7 6 5 4 3 2 1

44. Supplies main ideas and sets directions for the church.

10 9 8 7 6 5 4 3 2 1

45. Leads or helps in evaluating the past year's programs.

10 9 8 7 6 5 4 3 2 1

46. Seeks the commitment of persons to the Christian life and to church activities.

10 9 8 7 6 5 4 3 2 1

47. Promotes interchurch cooperation in the community.

10 9 8 7 6 5 4 3 2 1

48. Organizes church programs to assist persons in need.

10 9 8 7 6 5 4 3 2 1

	Priority	
	low	high

49. Serves on the board of a social agency (such as Goodwill Industries, Salvation Army, Rescue Mission, YMCA).   10 9 8 7 6 5 4 3 2 1

50. Works personally for the election of good candidates for public office.   10 9 8 7 6 5 4 3 2 1

OTHER THINGS I EXPECT OF THE PASTOR:

OTHER THINGS I EXPECT OF THE CONGREGATION:

SCORE SHEETS

The questions in the Checklist are divided into ten categories of five questions each, dealing with different aspects of the life and work of church members and ministers. To compare scores among members or between members and the minister by various categories, simply write in the priority number you *circled* for Question I on the line beside Question I under the "Pastor" column on the next page.

Write the priority number you *underlined* on Question 1 under the "Lay" column for Question 1 below. All questions ending in "1" deal with the priestly aspects of the ministry. You may add each column to show how highly you rate priestly functions for your pastor and how highly you rate them for the laypersons of your church. Do the same for the other functional areas.

1 Priestly Ministry		2 Spiritual Life		3 Christian Education		4 Church Leadership		5 Group Process	
Pastor	Lay	Pastor	Lay	Pastor	Lay	Pastor	Lay	Pastor	Lay
1. ___	___	2. ___	___	3. ___	___	4. ___	___	5. ___	___
11. ___	___	12. ___	___	13. ___	___	14. ___	___	15. ___	___
21. ___	___	22. ___	___	23. ___	___	24. ___	___	25. ___	___
31. ___	___	32. ___	___	33. ___	___	34. ___	___	35. ___	___
41. ___	___	42. ___	___	43. ___	___	44. ___	___	45. ___	___
Totals		Totals		Totals		Totals		Totals	
___	___	___	___	___	___	___	___	___	___

6 Evangelism and Witnessing		7 Work Beyond Local Church		8 Service to Needy Persons		9 Work Through Social Agencies		10 Personal Agent of Social Change	
Pastor	Lay	Pastor	Lay	Pastor	Lay	Pastor	Lay	Pastor	Lay
6. ___	___	7. ___	___	8. ___	___	9. ___	___	10. ___	___
16. ___	___	17. ___	___	18. ___	___	19. ___	___	20. ___	___
26. ___	___	27. ___	___	28. ___	___	29. ___	___	30. ___	___
36. ___	___	37. ___	___	38. ___	___	39. ___	___	40. ___	___
46. ___	___	47. ___	___	48. ___	___	49. ___	___	50. ___	___
Totals		Totals		Totals		Totals		Totals	
___	___	___	___	___	___	___	___	___	___

WHAT NEXT?

Now go back to the questionnaire. Discover those questions which influenced the scores in special ways. In small groups, with the pastor present, try to develop an understanding and even a consensus as to what the pastor and the members reasonably ought to expect of themselves and of each other.

CHAPTER 5

Program

5.1 Introduction

The purpose of this chapter is to examine the relationship between program and the other dimensions of congregational life and to describe specific methods for studying and evaluating the program of a congregation.

Program, as defined earlier in this handbook, consists of those organizational structures, plans, and activities through which a congregation expresses its mission and ministry both to itself—its own members—and to those outside. Program gives concrete expression to beliefs and norms held by members, present and past; it carries the values to which members commit financial resources and energies. Program is the plan of action, what a congregation does.

This chapter is deliberately placed near the end of the handbook for two reasons: (1) to emphasize the relationship of program—be that positive or negative—to other dimensions of congregational life and (2) to alert persons engaged in congregational studies to the tendency for program issues to dominate the study process to the exclusion of other dimensions.

Congregations generally provide more visible clues about program than they do about their identity or process. This explains why, from a research perspective, program is often the most accessible dimension of congregational life. Program descriptions are usually what local churches set forth in their official communications with both members and persons in surrounding communities. For instance, churches' advertisements in newspapers characteristically describe their most prominent programs such as services of worship, special speakers, and seasonal events. They seldom mention contextual features or relational qualities although these have been shown to be important criteria for persons considering membership in a particular congregation.[1] The activity aspect of program is also what a congregation may most prominently display through posters in foyers, hallways, and assembly rooms. These seem more likely to capture the attention of members and visitors than the visual representations of identity found in the furnishings and sacramental objects of sanctuaries.

Program provides the terms for description, in part, because it is the dimension around which church members are most likely to organize both corporate activities and individual participation. Traditionally, congregations have structured their activities around a combination of the liturgical calendar and the *program calendar*. For example, education and stewardship emphases are scheduled in the fall; mission programs in late winter or early spring, and observances of Advent and Christmas claim appropriate blocks of time. Many congregations across the country, regardless of denomination, are engaged in the same kinds of activities at the same time of year.

The organization of the congregation's schedule and resources around program is reflected in most annual reports. A year's worth of investment, interaction, caring, and, in some cases, conflict is reduced to summaries of *activities* and associated costs.

These highly visible program activities can provide the researcher with important data about less visible dimensions of congregational life. However, in isolation from other dimensions, study of program can lead to inappropriate conclusions and premature closure of the research endeavor. The researcher must ask the question, "What is the relationship between the program and other dimensions of congregational life?" Program activities *may not* be a direct extension of values expressed in statements about identity.

Why study program as program? Primarily, to help the congregation and its leaders make decisions about what the church does: use of resources and energy, starting new things, ending old ones, and facing new possibilities. Persons in leadership positions face such decisions constantly. Sometimes the choices are clear and decisions are easily made. Often, insufficient information is available to make decisions between alternatives, or there is a desire to know whether one particular course of action may be better than another.

Among the questions that program studies of congregations ask are:

+ How are resources used? How are finances and human energy allocated among the various activities?
+ What is the "fit" between existing programs and the needs of members?
+ How do the goals of members correspond to current programs and use of resources?
+ What is the "fit" between existing programs and the need of members to minister to persons beyond the congregation?
+ How well do existing programs accomplish what they were initially intended to do?
+ Do programs have effects other than those for which they were intended?
+ Given more resources, would the congregation (1) expand existing programs, (2) create new programs?
+ If a congregation senses a need to change some program, should it (1) stop doing the activity entirely, (2) modify the way it is currently done?
+ How do participants feel about particular programs? Do they help them realize their potential as persons, whether as providers of ministries or recipients of ministries?

The programs of congregations can be studied in a variety of ways. This chapter will describe two basic types, *needs assessment* and *program evaluation*.

5.2 Getting Started with a Program Study: Basic Decisions

Both needs assessment and evaluation can be effective regardless of a congregation's size or the nature of existing program. Both are usually used in the context of a planning process, but that process need not be elaborate or even encompass every aspect of a congregation's program. An evaluation may be limited to only one program and a needs assessment to only one aspect of program activity.

5.2.1 Qualitative or Quantitative Data?

Needs assessment and program evaluation each employ the standard methods of social science described later in chapter 6. Neither is a methodology in itself; therefore, in either type, the researcher or study team will need to decide on the type(s) of methods to be used in data collection.

Quantitative measurements offer the advantage of results that can be aggregated for analysis and compared between groups (such as relative learning achievement of two classes using different curricula) or within a group (such as differences in opinion along age lines within a group engaged in the same activity). These measures are systematic, standardized, and easily presented.

Qualitative measures gather another kind of data. The findings are usually more detailed and variable in content. This methodology provides more depth, expresses what people say in their own words, and is deliberately open-ended in order to discover how people attach meaning to their lives, experiences, and interactions.[2] Qualitative measures represent an inductive approach, a methodology that asks questions without imposing set categories of responses. They do not allow researchers to manipulate the setting and allow for evaluation of program in its own context.

But qualitative techniques have disadvantages. This type of research is labor intensive and often costly. Furthermore, not all situations for data collection lend themselves to qualitative methods. Qualitative methods presume that activities can be observed and that respondents can articulate their experiences. This is not always the case.

If the leadership of the congregation does not, or cannot, retain a consultant to assist with a program study, the method of data collection may depend upon the amount of time the volunteer study team members can give. This is not the ideal criterion for determining the research method. The more professional the study, the greater flexibility in methodology and the more information the leadership will have for interpretation.

Since no perfect methodology exists, any choice involves trade-offs in time, accuracy, detail, or rapport with respondents.[3] These trade-offs need to be weighed by the researcher/study team in designing a program study as is the case with other types of congregational study efforts.

Users of this handbook will find that quantitative data collection techniques are emphasized in the part of this chapter on needs assessment. This is the case because such approaches are more common in needs assessments of congregations and, consequently, more instruments utilizing quantitative measures are available. Furthermore, needs assessment often aims at gathering information from as many persons as possible within a congregation's service area, a process that generally requires a quantitative approach to data collection.

Quantitative measures are typically used when evaluation has as its goal the measurement of outcomes against some prespecified standard, such as with educational testing. But this will not be the interest in many congregations undertaking program evaluation or needs assessment. Therefore, in order to ascertain the context for program and the relationship of a program's effectiveness to other dimensions of congregational life, qualitative approaches to data collection are often required.

5.2.2 Timing

The timing of a program study process is related to the type of study undertaken. The type, in turn, is determined by the information needs at the time. Evaluation and needs assessment are naturally related, but each is useful at different times in the planning cycle of a congregation. A needs assessment is usually done only periodically, perhaps every three to five years, because changes in the characteristics of persons/ groups with specified needs are generally not measurable over shorter time frames. (Exceptions to this rule would be found in places undergoing significant social or economic upheaval.) The timing of evaluations is related to the needs of congregations to make decisions about the effectiveness of specific programs, thus evaluation would probably occur with greater frequency than needs assessments.

Needs assessments are conducted at times when congregations are unsure about the directions they should be taking programmatically or when they sense that existing programs do not address existing needs. Vacancies in the pulpit or in program staff positions are among the natural points in the life of a congregation when such openness to new directions may occur. Such transitions give the congregation unique opportunities to reexamine program activities in light of membership needs and community context rather than in terms of the skills or personalities of specific individuals, including professional personnel.

Another point at which needs assessment is appropriate is when a congregation is experiencing lethargy or stagnation. Congregations can give reasons for a lack of vitality or growth. These reasons include aging membership, membership loss, the entry of women into the work force with a concomitant decline in volunteerism, and competition for members' time by other institutions. In attempting to regain vitality, some congregations adopt strategies that sound good but may not correspond to the actual need or the realistic potential. For example, a church with an aging or declining membership may decide that its renewal depends on a new youth ministry. That may prove to be the case, but it may also be true that the congregation has a paucity of young people simply because the immediate community has few adolescents. A youth ministry may not be in order because it is impossible. A

needs assessment would provide the kind of information necessary for this sample congregation to understand its context and select program strategies that fit possibility.

5.2.3 Who Should Be Involved?

This is a two-part question: (1) who will be involved in formulating the research design, and (2) who will be the audience(s) for the research? Put another way, who will pose the questions and who will answer them?

1. The issue here is not whether to use a consultant in the study process. Rather, the decision concerns the choices of persons beyond the congregation's leadership and the study team who could be helpful in shaping the study and formulating research questions. Some possibilities to be considered by the team include:

The *expert* who has a specialized understanding of the program or problem being studied and who can contribute to the study by sharpening questions, suggesting additional lines of inquiry, and providing information about standardized measures of user need or program effectiveness.

Friendly critics—outsiders who have the trust and respect of the study team and a knowledge of the congregation. Such persons may be able to look more objectively at programs than can those who have a role and an investment in the existing activities. The study team might invite friendly critics to comment on either the proposed study process or on specific programs being studied.

Nonparticipating members (sometimes called hostile critics) who bring a perspective that may illuminate the unsatisfactory aspects of existing programs or pinpoint the needs of members that have not been successfully addressed.

Of course, program leaders, both professional and volunteer, should be consulted about the research design and the questions. Especially helpful might be persons who had a role in developing a general program direction or a specific activity. If a particular program is to be evaluated, program leadership in other areas whose work could be affected by a new initiative should be involved. For example, suppose a congregation is considering the possibility of a day care program. This should not even be investigated without extensive consultation with staff or volunteers responsible for the Sunday or church school program, because the shared use of facilities and equipment would likely be necessary.

2. From whom should data be collected in a congregational program study? A survey strategy for an evaluation would normally be selective while one for needs assessment would strive toward inclusiveness,

especially in the early stages of program planning. In needs assessment, a major part of the goal is to measure the breadth of a congregation's concept of "service area," that is, potential participants in its program. A needs-assessment design may include the gathering of data on the community beyond the congregation, and some of this can be obtained by consulting census and other secondary data already available. The study team may also want to interview representatives of community groups that might want to take advantage of programs. This will provide qualitative measures of experiences, attitudes, and interest in church programs.

In needs assessment, the collection of information from as many potential users as possible is important to ensure that the data represents the diversity found within the membership and the surrounding community. One inherent value of this approach is in giving a voice to the voiceless. It affirms a belief in fairness and equal access to resources and in decision making. Questioning everyone gives those who feel powerless or disenfranchised the same opportunity to affect change as those in power positions. Once the study team has narrowed its focus and identified specific program possibilities, additional information may be in order from a smaller group that appears to be the target audience for a program.

5.3 Program Research Strategies: Needs Assessment

5.3.1 *Definition and Purpose*

The term *needs assessment* has become a catch-all encompassing many usages and meanings. The former U.S. Department of Health, Education, and Welfare defined needs assessment as a process for identifying needs, setting objectives, setting priorities, and relating them to programs on a continuing basis.[4] This is a useful definition because it describes a process in which data collection is only one stage. While data collection for its own sake, or for replicating findings from other studies, is common in academic and other research settings, we assume that the gathering of information by a congregation is a means to some specified end. The research is linked to a broader planning process in which identified needs are addressed through strategic activities.

The purpose of a congregational program needs assessment is to identify the following:

+ the needs of the congregation to be considered from the perspective of what is understood to be fidelity to the gospel;

+ the needs of persons to be ministered to within the congregation;
+ the needs of persons to be ministered to beyond the congregation;
+ the needs of members to fulfill their own unique understandings of ministry;
+ the resources, both human and financial, available to address the needs identified.

In addition, needs assessment is a means of making the congregation more sensitive to persons and groups about whom God cares but who may not be readily visible to members.

Some church people object to the idea of a congregation engaging in needs assessment because they equate the process to that of a consumer demand analysis. To such persons, needs assessment suggests a reactive response, the lack of a sense of the church's purposes in all times and places, a "knee-jerk" approach to ministry and mission. This negative response is not confined to religion. Critics of needs assessment say that needs are socially or contextually defined, representing a limited view of what individuals or groups see as a need at a given moment in time.

Such criticism should not be taken lightly. It is a warning about the limitations of any social research; however, many congregations, along with other organizations providing human services, have found needs assessment helpful in clarifying future directions for ministry and for affirming the validity of existing programs or making improvements in them.

A definition of *need* that can be usefully applied to the concerns of the church is "any identifiable condition which limits particular individuals or communities from realizing their full potential."[5] The unfulfilled needs of a congregation as a group or as individuals limit potential for realizing personhood as creations of God and inhibit abilities to fulfill unique ministries. In addition, some congregations are in a position to address other basic human needs related to social or economic conditions or to health. For example, food or shelter programs are well within any definition of ministry.

A congregation usually does not have the resources to respond to all the needs of its members, let alone of persons in the surrounding community. Nevertheless, an awareness of needs allows the congregation to focus the use of resources where the most good can be done. Needs assessment also helps in applying program resources to levels of need.

An open attitude to what constitutes a "legitimate" need is important in seeking to identify the needs of church members and other persons for whom the congregation has concern. At least, openness should be attempted. Otherwise, a patronizing attitude will be communicated to those from whom the researchers are seeking information, and respondents will not be inclined to answer honestly.

The needs assessment process involves the following general steps or stages:

1. *Identify the area of research (scope of the study).* What types of information will be collected? Who will be surveyed: members, persons in the community, denominational officials, others?

2. *Identify roles, functions, or responsibilities.* Who is involved in carrying out the process and what are their assignments? Who does what?

3. *Collect data.* This means finding out about needs and resources through various data collection methods.

4. *Measure and rank.* This involves decisions about the assignment of values to needs.

5. *Set priorities.* This task rates needs in relation to other factors of the congregation's context, identity, beliefs, norms, and values; identifies the cost of meeting needs and making comparisons with resources; and determines the order in which needs might be addressed given the resources.

6. *Translate needs into program.*[6] Some of these steps, such as the identification of the audience, have been addressed above, and some will be discussed in greater detail below.

5.3.2 Scope

Needs assessment has the potential for being a *change-oriented process.* Determining the scope of the study begins with the researchers identifying its purpose and mandate from the congregation and answering the questions, "What are we willing to change?" and "What are we able to change?" The first relates to the theological context in which decisions are being considered, to the congregation's relationship to a parent denomination and to the world views of members who might be affected by change. The second has to do with some of the same issues but also with external limitations and with available resources.

The study team should bear in mind that while information may be interesting, it is not useful in and of itself. The purpose of data collection is to assist the congregation in making better decisions: to either affirm what it is doing or to create something more appropriate. The scope must be determined by the decisions to be considered and made. Naturally, the research method should leave room for persons to tell the researchers things the design team may not have thought to question about programs.

The remainder of this section will focus on decisions related to data collection procedures. The final stages of a needs-assessment process have less to do with the model of research and more to do with how information is used. Those final stages will be touched on briefly but are not the main focus here.

5.3.3 Data Collection

Membership characteristics and facilities are two areas of information about the internal context from which it is possible to deduce much about the program needs and potential of a congregation. Data collection instruments used in congregational needs assessment often focus on these areas.

5.3.3.1 Membership Characteristics.

The two aspects of membership characteristics that are most frequently examined in needs assessments are (1) factual, descriptive information about respondents' backgrounds (age, sex, educational level) and (2) opinions about subjects related to the matters under consideration in the future. Quantitative measures are often used to obtain information about backgrounds to develop a congregational profile. The range of responses is predetermined by the researcher so that the data can be easily aggregated and comparisons made within or across subgroups of the total membership. Certain opinions, experiences, and feelings can also be examined by means of quantitative measures.

A considerable literature has developed on congregational studies carried out in different denominational contexts. A review of instruments used (some of which are found in the appendix to this chapter and in the General Appendix) indicates the most frequently examined background variables. These are:

+ gender
+ age
+ race and ethnicity
+ marital status
+ educational attainment
+ occupation
+ employment status (retired, part-time, and so forth)
+ income
+ number and ages of children (when applicable)
+ number of years in current residence or community
+ distance from residence to church
+ home ownership
+ household living arrangement
+ likelihood of moving in the near future
+ number of times moved since age 18

+ hobbies
+ special skills or expertise
+ involvement in other voluntary organizations

Typical background factors about members' religious upbringing and current involvement in the church include:

+ length of membership in the congregation
+ frequency of attendance at worship
+ extent of involvement in activities beyond worship
+ leadership roles held in congregation
+ number of hours spent in church-related activities in a typical month
+ amount of financial support
+ whether level of involvement has changed in last few years and reasons for change
+ number of close friends who also belong to the congregation
+ whether the member has invited others to visit or join congregation
+ previous denominational affiliation, if any
+ denomination in which respondent was raised
+ importance of church activities to respondent
+ importance of religious beliefs
+ frequency of Bible reading and prayer

How is such data on membership characteristics used in a congregational program study process? Several realities pertinent to church program and to its decisions about the future are informed by this data. Key among such realities are (1) membership age profile, (2) family organization and related life-style matters, and (3) occupational and socioeconomic patterns.

Age. Basic questions here concern the age profile and the relation of current programs to the needs of differing age groups. What are the trends in the age profile? Are these trends likely to change in the foreseeable future?

Trends in the age structure of the United States are well known and need not be treated in depth, especially since they do not necessarily translate directly to the specific membership characteristics of any particular congregation. Generally, congregations of the older, mainline Protestant denominations are comprised of a growing number of adults in the middle and later stages of the family life cycle. Other congregations, including some mainline Protestant churches, are not experiencing the phenomenon of an aging membership.

Congregations have tended historically to direct their resources and orient their facilities around age-specified needs of young children, adolescents, and families in the child-rearing stage of the family cycle. A fundamental question in any program study is, "How well do current program activities fit the needs of the current age profile." Program strategies that work for a congregation with one age profile will not necessarily be appropriate for another.

Curiously, members are often unconscious of the age-profile dimension of a congregation's characteristics, although visually it is one of the most obvious realities. For example, members often fail to notice that the large youth program functioning ten years earlier has virtually vanished. This may result in part from the fact that so many church programs are conducted along age lines and persons taking part in separate activities do not often have an opportunity to observe the spectrum of ages and their distribution in the congregation as a whole.

Patterns of family organization and related data. Historically, congregations have been structured around the values and norms of that pattern of family organization we call the "nuclear family," that is, the household unit comprised of a mother, a father, and their children living together. This concept of family is deeply embedded in most church programs, both in the way age-specified activities have been undertaken and in the functional logic of the congregation's thinking.

The nuclear family is still assumed in most church programs despite all that has been written about changes in patterns of family organization in the United States. As is well known, the country has greater numbers of persons living together without marriage, later age at first marriage, soaring rates of divorce and remarriage, numerous single-parent households, and a generally aging society. Congregations have been slow to respond to these changes, in part because those persons who have quietly departed are often precisely those whose family circumstances mirror the new patterns. They no longer feel comfortable or welcome in churches set up for nuclear families. A recent study shows that the profile of persons outside the church is more likely to be one that does not fit the traditional family pattern.[7]

Norms and values assuming a nuclear family are not articulated within congregations so much as they are built into the program structures. Changes in the domestic life of members unavoidably have an impact on their feelings of acceptance. (As a research topic, the experience and feeling of members concerning family patterns would be best approached by the use of qualitative measures.)

Without arguing for the intrinsic value of any particular form of the family, we need to recognize that many programs should be reinterpreted to relate to the needs of persons in living arrangements radically different from the norm of even two decades ago. The availability of volunteers for churches has been dramatically affected by changing family patterns. Increased single-parent households means fewer adults who can leave the children with a spouse to take part in church meetings or activities. And the very nature of "single" within the congregation has changed. Today "single" includes not only older, widowed persons but persons who have not married, young and old, or who are divorced or separated.

Proposals that congregational programming should take account of changes in family life cause controversy in some communions, especially in those with a theology placing a high value on traditional male-female and parent-child relationships. Such orientations are even skeptical of church-provided child care, since any option that does not conform to the nuclear pattern is seen as a threat to the inherited morality. Changing family patterns are not likely to weigh heavily in the program decisions of congregations adhering to strict sex-role definitions.

Occupational and socioeconomic characteristics. Certain quantitative questions included in a needs-assessment survey will help us to understand more about the work lives of members, their resources, and their capacities in ministry. Such factors are not always easy to ascertain from observing members at worship on Sunday morning.

Census and other secondary sources can supply information about the kind of work available in the community where the church is located. These same sources can tell the study team about the general educational levels of people in the area. In many cases, general occupational information on members is well known or self-evident and need not be studied. It may be necessary to gather other, more personal and specific information from members in order to learn how economic and occupational circumstances affect daily lives. For example, how many households in the congregation have more than one adult in the work force? Are local industries organized around shift work? How many families have parents working different shifts? What arrangements, if any, must be made for child care while parents work? How much free time do adults in the congregation have? How many teenagers work while also going to school? Is unemployment a problem in any age or occupational group?

Researchers may assume that a major change in the occupational profile of the congregation will be the increased number of women in the work force outside the home. This trend may be associated with new needs of families, including access to child care. The increase of women in the work force is sometimes regarded as having a negative impact on the congregation by decreasing the availability of volunteers and also

putting church participation in competition with limited time for family activities. At the same time, an increase of salaried members could have a positive impact on stewardship programs and could challenge a congregation to look for another kind of volunteer—the retired, perhaps—and thereby expand the base of participation. A membership survey should determine how many retired persons are in the congregation and what kinds of programs they want for themselves and programs for others in which they might work.

5.3.3.2 How to Ask Questions

Any question can be asked in a variety of ways. The research team will need to determine the style it wants to use. Sensitivity is especially important in making inquiries about personal matters, such as marital status or income.

Here are some examples of how to ask about marital status:

Are you currently—married, widowed, divorced, separated, or have you never been married?
1____married
2____widowed
3____divorced
4____separated
5____never married
(From the General Social Surveys, 1972–1983.)

Or,

What is your present marital status?
1____single, never previously married
2____single, married previously
3____married once, living with spouse
4____married once, separated from spouse
5____married more than once, living with spouse
6____married more than once, separated from spouse
7____widowed, not remarried
8____divorced, not remarried
(From the LCA Nurture Study. See Appendix 5–1.)

But another, simpler, and perhaps more sensitive way to put the question is:

Are you married or single?
1____single 2____married
If currently single, have you ever been married?
1____yes   2____no

Many people are uncomfortable when asked if they are divorced or separated, especially in a religious context. The research team should decide on the degree of specificity with regard to such personal issues and not ask more than is pertinent to the study.

Age and income can also be matters of sensitivity. Each can be handled by providing range options, such as this sample question on income:

What is your (or your family's) income range?
1____under $7,500 annually
2____$7,500–14,999 annually
3____$15,000–24,999 annually
4____$25,000–34,999 annually
5____$35,000–49,999 annually
6____$50,000–74,999 annually
7____$75,000 or more annually

Or, you could simply ask,

What is your (or your family's) gross annual income?
$_____

Questions about personal beliefs, social and political attitudes, and opinions about congregational life are also usually included in needs-assessment questionnaires. The following subsections discuss these topics.

Personal beliefs. Information on how members interpret Scripture and describe their own religious faith is helpful in a needs assessment as well as in studies of a corporation's identity, as was noted in chapter 2. A variety of instruments can be used. Here are three samples in addition to those in chapter 2:

Which of the following best expresses your belief about God?
1____I do not believe in God.
2____I really don't know what to believe about God.
3____I do not believe in a creating and saving God, but I believe in a higher power of some kind.
4____God is the creator of an orderly world but does not now guide it or intervene in its course of affairs or the lives of individuals.
5____Although God has acted and can act in history and can communicate with persons directly, it is not something that happens very often.
6____God is constantly at work in the world from "above" directing people, nations, and events.
7____God is in the world and in every person, thing, and event.
(From the Parish Profile Inventory. See General Appendix.)

In the next example, respondents were asked to indicate whether they "agree strongly," "agree somewhat," "both agree and disagree," "disagree some-what," "disagree strongly," or "have no opinion" on the individual statements.

In terms of my personal situation or viewpoint:
____I believe my relationship to God has importance for my life after death.
____I believe my relationship to God has importance for my life here on earth.
____I imagine God to be mostly like a caring friend.
____Much of my daily life with my family or work is different because of my faith in God.
____I would be disappointed if my children changed to a non-Lutheran denomination.
____Because of the pressures of the world, what I need from God is comfort and consolation.
____Experiences in church are the most important sources of my sense of trust in God.
____My experiences in church have helped me accept the fact that other people are considerably different from myself.
(From the LCA Nurture Study. See Appendix 5–1.)

The same Lutheran study contains this question:

Which of the following statements comes closest to expressing your view of life after death?
1____I don't believe there is life after death.
2____I am unsure whether or not there is life after death.
3____I believe that there must be something beyond death, but I have no idea what it may be like.
4____There is life after death but no punishment.
5____There is life after death, with rewards for some people and punishment for others.
6____None of the above expresses my views.

Other examples of such questions can be found in the Parish Profile Inventory, Section III, "Personal Beliefs" and are also scattered throughout that portion of the Lutheran Nurture Study called "In Terms of My Personal Situation and Viewpoint." Certain of these approaches to the identification of beliefs are applicable to congregations of virtually any denomination. On the other hand, questions about beliefs must often be custom-tailored to the theological context of the specific congregation in which they are asked. More than any others dealing with membership characteristics, questions about beliefs involve a value-laden process of interpretation. A pivotal consideration in formulating the questions is that of how the information will be used.

Social and political attitudes. This category of membership characteristics is helpful because of the relationship between religious profiles and other areas of behavior and belief. Most such questions that have been used in congregational studies focus on issues that tend to divide persons on the "liberal" to "conservative" political spectrum. They examine attitudes on topics of personal freedom, such as abortion, use of marijuana, and sexuality, as well as social and political issues such as disarmament, nuclear weapons, racial integration in schools, equal employment, and the like. One national survey that included questions on social and political awareness was a 1978 study of "unchurched" Americans. Findings from that study have contributed greatly to an understanding of differences between churched and unchurched individuals.[8] The use of some questions on social and political attitudes in a congregational needs-assessment study might identify differences in the perspective of groups frequently in conflict over program directions and use of resources.

Examples of this type of question are:

Do you Strongly Agree, Agree, Disagree, or Strongly Disagree with the following statements?
_____The United States should freeze production of nuclear weapons regardless of what Russia does.
_____The use of marijuana should be made legal.
_____The law should allow doctors to perform an abortion for any woman who wants one.
_____It is wrong for a person to have sexual relations before marriage.
_____We are spending too little money on welfare programs in this country.
(From the Parish Profile Inventory. See General Appendix.)

Or,

How would you feel about a program that requires all young women to give one year of service to the nation—either in the military forces or in non-military work such as in hospitals or with elderly people. Would you strongly favor it, probably favor it, probably oppose it, or strongly oppose it?

Some people think that the government in Washington is trying to do too many things that should be left to individuals and private businesses. Others disagree and think that the government should do even more to solve our country's problems. Still others have opinions in between. How do you feel about this?
(From the General Social Surveys, 1972–1983.)

More examples may be found in the "Social Attitudes" section of the Parish Profile Inventory (General Appendix). Questions on social and political attitudes are not as common in congregational studies as the other types discussed here. This may be the case because the average person may have difficulty in seeing how they relate to local church concerns. At the same time, these are questions at the very heart of a congregation's identity.

Opinions about congregational life. This area of research explores process issues as well as matters relating to congregational identity. One subgroup of questions deals with leadership, another with goals.

Questions on leadership probe the thinking of members on expectations of the pastor, preferences regarding leadership style, views on access to leaders and whether leadership is seen as representative of the membership. A more detailed discussion is contained in the sections on "Tasks of the Pastor" and "Style of Ministry" in the Parish Profile Inventory (General Appendix). Styles of ministry and leadership issues in the church are the focus of Donald Smith in his book, *Congregations Alive*[9], a summary of the author's study of Presbyterian congregations. Smith's questionnaire (see Appendix 5–2) is an example of a finely focused examination of program concerns.

Opinions on goals cover the members' familiarity with stated purposes, perceptions about the appropriateness of the goals, agreement or disagreement with them, personal objectives and the relation of those to congregational goals. Robert Worley provides an example of a series of questions centered around goals in his book, *A Gathering of Strangers*.[10]

This instrument is designed to help you indicate your perceptions about the goals of a congregation. There are no right or wrong answers. Check the appropriate space that best expresses your perception about the goals.

1. The goals of this congregation are clear to me.
   Agree _ _ _ _ _ _ _ Disagree
        1 2 3 4 5 6 7

2. The goals of this congregation are not clear.
   Agree _ _ _ _ _ _ _ Disagree
        1 2 3 4 5 6 7

3. Someone else has established the goals of this congregation.
   Agree _ _ _ _ _ _ _ Disagree
        1 2 3 4 5 6 7

4. My personal goals are consistent with the goals of this congregation.
   Agree _ _ _ _ _ _ _ Disagree
        1 2 3 4 5 6 7

5. I have been involved in establishing the goals of this congregation.

Agree _ _ _ _ _ _ _ Disagree
1 2 3 4 5 6 7

6. The goals of the congregation are unexamined.

Agree _ _ _ _ _ _ _ Disagree
1 2 3 4 5 6 7

Goals are intrinsically related to the manner in which congregations arrive at decisions about program, especially levels of support and degrees of "ownership" among the members.

A number of items in the appendix to this chapter and in the General Appendix can help study groups explore feelings about goals. Others appear in *Congregations Alive* and in the *Smaller Church Study Guide*.[11]

Questions about specific programs or ministries gauge perceived relevance to the needs of members and non-members and degrees of satisfaction with programs provided. Highly relevant in a congregational study is the fact that members may be both *users* and *purveyors* of certain programs; in other cases they may be only users. When persons surveyed are primarily users, needs-assessment instruments may focus on the perceived effectiveness among members, that is, whether the level of service being offered is sufficient to the need. Questions along these lines often stray into the area of evaluation research, but, as we have already seen, these processes are not neatly separated. Interestingly, relatively few questions in church self-study guides focus on church members as providers of ministries. The questionnaire (Appendix 5–2) used in the book, *Congregations Alive*, is a notable exception. It contains a far more focused examination of one area of experience and opinion about leadership—as shared ministry—than is typical of needs-assessment materials.

Information about the characteristics of members and persons in the larger community enables church planners to better comprehend the context into which a program or service would be introduced and to measure likelihood of its acceptance or use. The types and extent of information about potential users needed by planners depends on the scope of the program decision to be made. If the congregation is contemplating extensive program development or redevelopment, a broader range of information is required than if the purpose is to evaluate a particular program or program area.

The types of information discussed so far in this chapter, especially membership characteristics, are often used by program planners to *infer* needs. The availability of program resources, notably people resources, can also be estimated from such data. For example, a combination of data on age, occupation, and family organizational patterns would allow planners to estimate the potential need for child day care services, or adult recreational and support groups, and to project the availability of volunteers for these programs.

Most church planners would not want to proceed with the actual development of programs or services without further verification of the need for and interest in them among potential users. More direct measures would be employed in determining realistic expectations for uses, attendance, or participation.

In order to get the most reliable assessment of interest and potential use, specific details about the program under consideration should be provided to the respondents. When will the program be offered—time of week and time of day? Will there be associated costs? Will transportation be available for persons who could not otherwise participate? Any relevant information that planners can offer will increase the reliability of responses and help to establish the extent to which a program will be used.

When program planners are not at the point of focusing on the audience for a specific program, questions must be relatively open-ended. Lacking program specifics, an unstructured approach gives respondents the opportunity to describe their needs and interests without limiting responses to predetermined alternatives. Ideally, the data collection approach at this stage would encourage respondents to think about two basic kinds of needs: (1) those that might be addressed by the congregation (the need to be ministered unto) and (2) those that they would like to address through participation in the congregation (the need to minister to others).

5.3.3.3 Facilities

Facilities are an important contextual factor in the congregation's program and should be considered in a program study. Typically, buildings and other facilities are not thought of as program resources. Most often maintenance costs and other expenditures associated with property are seen as competing with the program budget.

Systematic observation of the congregation's use of facilities and of the conditions of facilities should be part of the church's needs assessment. This part of the study might begin with these questions:

+ How appropriate are the facilities to current program emphases?
+ Are there problems of access for any age group or for persons with special limiting conditions?

+ Does the space available represent an untapped, potential program resource?
+ Is the space a program liability?
+ If the congregation lacks financial or human resources to carry out a needed and desired program, do existing facilities represent an asset in the achieving of this goal?

A recent study of congregational child day-care centers conducted by the National Council of Churches concluded that the property holdings and historical construction patterns of many parish churches make them well equipped to provide such services.[12] Furthermore, the location of many churches in their communities, and, even their tax-exempt status, recommend them for child day-care programs. It is not always requisite that a congregation fully fund or staff a program that might fit both within its theological understanding of ministry and be responsive to the needs of the surrounding community.

The research team will overlook an important feature of the program context if it fails to consider the potential use of the existing facilities. At the same time, the availability of facilities that might be suited for a particular type of program must be weighed against other factors and the ministry goals of the congregation. The scheduling of space must be carefully considered. A congregation that has a single auditorium with basketball facilities could not give *carte blanche* use to a community team whose practice hours may conflict with the established hours of the Girl Scout troop or the weekly meeting of the "golden age club."

5.3.4 Relating Program Decisions to Identity, Context, and Process

What are the next steps for the study team once the data collection is completed? An underlying assumption in some needs-assessment literature seems to be that the gathering of information will automatically lead to decisions and program change. That is no more true for churches than it is for individuals. As persons, we may be informed that we are overweight, or that our blood pressure is dangerously high, or that we smoke too many cigarettes. Knowing this does not automatically lead us to change eating habits, introduce exercise, or stop smoking. Purposeful change requires intentional efforts and a desire to do it. The information gathering stage of the needs assessment process is only a means to an end.

Change, in fact, is only one possible outcome of a needs assessment. Another is affirmation of the existing program as the most viable course toward the congregation's goals. And if the need for change is indicated by study findings, any implementation will depend on the desire of leadership and membership to follow through, given available resources.

The decision-making phase of the needs-assessment process comes when the study team decides what the information means, when it *interprets* the findings in light of the congregation's context, identity, and processes. If the study reveals needs that are not being met through existing programs and there is a will for change, the next step is that of *assigning values* to the needs that have been identified. This involves grappling with such questions as:

+ Can the newly identified needs be addressed within this congregation's understanding of its faithfulness to the gospel, other contextual factors and present or potential resources?
+ Considering all of the needs identified, which seem to be most critical?
+ Which should be taken up first; what ideas can be deferred?

Answering such questions begins the process of determining priorities, that is, rating the needs that have emerged. Few congregations are ever able to address all needs discovered in a program study, and often doing more of one thing means doing less of another. Income and expenditures figure heavily in program decisions. Newly identified needs and resulting program costs must be compared with those of beneficial existing programs. An exercise from the *Smaller Church Mission Guide* (see Appendix 5–3) may be helpful to some congregations in illustrating how the prioritizing of a list of new activities also entails decisions on whether the church can do more or less in existing programs. Another option, of course, is to find new sources of income and personnel for new or expanded programs.

In considering expressed needs for basic human services, such as food pantries or clothing ministries for street people, relevant inquiry goes beyond asking how the specific congregation can meet the need. Thinking can be broad:

+ Is providing the service directly the best form of stewardship and ministry? Would an advocacy program be more effective?
+ Should the congregation attempt the program alone or in cooperation with another church or coalition of churches?
+ Should the program be physically lodged in the church or should the congregation's resources be used to fund the effort at another site?

+ If facilities are the major resource of the church, how does it obtain the dollars and the people required by the program?
+ Is it necessary to start something entirely new? Could an existing program be expanded or modified to fit the need?
+ How do existing programs interrelate in terms of needs that have been identified? Can a third program be created out of two existing ones with little or no increased cost? (An example of this might be day-care programs operated in conjunction with activities for senior citizens. The ministry goal of each might combine to accomplish a third, say the fostering of intergenerational relations and learning experiences.)

Study teams should be aware that strong proposals for new programs may be interpreted within the congregation as challenges to activities that appear to be structurally requisite and, therefore, may encounter resistance even if the idea is generally favored. Many church programs become entrenched over time for a variety of reasons having to do with theological tradition, local history, and denominational factors. Such programs can develop lives of their own, sometimes in isolation from changes taking place in other areas of church life. If this is the case, the issue for the study team may not be whether the congregation is going to continue these programs but, rather, how they can be done better, or somewhat differently in order to respond to more needs. How can they be made more responsible to the current membership? Can the congregation fulfill the specific needs of its people though activities that were originally begun to carry out an organizational goal? The study team will want to ask several questions about these institutionalized activities in attempting to translate the findings of the needs assessment into programs:

+ Are changes needed in the times of day or the seasons when certain programs are undertaken? How does scheduling relate to the characteristics of members' work and family obligations?
+ Who is involved? Have members expressed a desire to be more involved in the planning of whatever the program is? Do they want more or less direction from the clergy and elected lay leadership?
+ How relevant is the content to a majority of the users or potential users?
+ Should age group activities be expanded to include others? Or, are more age-graded activities needed? Would it be helpful to increase the diversity of participants, or is there need for more careful division along the lines of special interest?
+ Are the facilities appropriate for the current form? Do they fit the size of the group for which the program is intended? Does the space pose problems for any particular age group or for disabled persons?

The needs-assessment approach outlined in this chapter tends to be *person-oriented* rather than *content-oriented*. This is deliberate in order to demonstrate that, in most cases, the same types of needs articulated in different contexts can be addressed in a variety of ways. Many different programs can fulfill an expressed need, and the program that is ultimately adopted should be tailored to the context in which it will be conducted.

The final stage of needs assessment is the translation of needs into programs. It is not in the scope of this handbook to elaborate on how that is done. However, the topic of the concluding section of the chapter discusses, among other things, means by which the congregation can study the early stages of program implementation. Evaluation research can assist in developing and maintaining relevant, effective congregational programs.

5.4 Program Evaluation: Research Strategies

5.4.1 Definition, Purpose, and Scope

Informal evaluation goes on all the time in the congregation. Church members in casual conversation evaluate the pastor's sermons, the choir's anthems and the food at the Sunday school picnic. Such informal evaluations entail a process of judging the merits of persons, activities and things. Formal definitions of evaluation also use the language of value and worth. Formal evaluation appraises, judges effectiveness, and, commonly, seeks to determine the extent to which goals have been achieved. Whether formal or informal, evaluation involves subjective judgments.

Evaluation research, however, is the process of collecting the information upon which evaluative judgments can be based. It is characterized by: (1) intentional, planned data collection, (2) systematic, uniform instruments and processes for that collection, and (3) the use of objective criteria in measuring effectiveness, efficiency, or excellence.

Types of evaluation approaches. As noted earlier, evaluation research employs the standard social science methodologies for data collection. The type of methodology used is determined by the evaluation context, the questions to be answered and the audience or reference group for the research.

Ernest House identifies four major models in his taxonomy of evaluation approaches[13]:

+ Systems
+ Behavioral objectives
+ Decision making
+ Goal free

The first two models are goal-oriented and raise such questions as: Were the expected effects (goals) achieved? Can they be achieved more economically? What are the most efficient methods of achieving certain outcomes? Is the program producing?

Evaluation contexts in which these questions are typically asked include business, industry, government, and, in some cases, education. Those contexts are assumed to be characterized by programs with pre-specified goals and objectives with quantifiable outcomes. The audiences or reference groups for the evaluative data are managers, economists, psychologists and educators. Measurements of effectiveness may include the use of standardized tests to compare achievements to national averages or cost-benefit analyses.

As contexts for evaluation, congregations are usually quite different from government or educational institutions. Goals, if stated, are usually general, and their attainment difficult to measure because church goals rarely lend themselves to quantification. The audience or reference groups for evaluative data may be decision makers—congregational leadership—but members of that audience may be as concerned about intangible human outcomes, such as faith development, as about cost efficiency.

The decision-making and goal-free evaluation approaches cited by House are better suited to the congregational context. The goal-free model, for example, is concerned for *all* effects of a program, not only with those set forth in a statement of goals.

All of House's evaluation models utilize standard social science methodologies. The questions asked determine what method is selected. Quantitative measures and experimental design would be more common in a systems or behavioral-objectives context. Surveys and questionnaires are more frequently used in decision-making and goal-free evaluation, but interviews and unobtrusive measures are also likely to be regarded as essential components to data collection when evaluators are interested in how persons feel about programs.

A variety of questions are pertinent in a congregational program evaluation:

+ How effective is the program in achieving what it set out to do?
+ Should it be continued as is?
+ Is it possible to improve it?
+ How has the program context changed, if at all?
+ How should funds be allocated among several competing programs?
+ Is the underlying purpose or method of the program acceptable to the program planners and participants?
+ Are the relational aspects of the program in keeping with the congregation's values?
+ How does the program affect how participants feel about themselves?
+ How do participants feel about the program?
+ What needs does this program address?

Formative and summative evaluation. A major distinction is made in evaluation literature between formative and summative evaluation. Formative is conducted for the purpose of improving ongoing programs; summative is done for the purpose of making basic decisions about whether a program should be continued or discontinued.[14]

Situations in which a congregation must decide whether to continue or terminate a program are far less common than those in which the concern is to improve an existing program. Yet the summative study process is the one that most often comes to mind when persons think of evaluation research.

Increased understanding of the benefits of formative evaluation is needed in the church study process. Knowledge of a variety of methods that can be used for formative evaluation should lead congregations to see the value of year-round evaluation that both affirms and builds upon that which already exists. An example of what is meant is in order.

A United Methodist congregation decided to start a meals program for what it perceived as a growing number of elderly persons in the congregation and the surrounding community. The decision was made to provide dinner, the evening meal, since it was assumed that those volunteers preparing the food would be working or caring for children during earlier hours.

The congregation's needs assessment indicated that at least one hundred persons within walking distance of the church would benefit from the program. Most of those elderly persons lived alone, had low incomes, and were unable to prepare nutritional meals for themselves. Many were also without any means of transportation for grocery shopping. The meals program seemed to its planners to be an excellent service project for the congregation. Yet during the first few weeks of the program's operation, the number of persons coming for dinner was only about one-third of that projected on the basis of information from the census and a survey.

The program developers were frustrated by the low response until they interviewed several participants. They discovered a flaw in the program design. Many of the elderly persons who would have liked to come for a free meal were afraid to go out after a certain time of the day because they did not want to walk home after dark. The dinner hour was the problem. With this new information, the program was modified to offer the meal at lunch. But along with this change went the need for an alternative source of volunteers. Planners found a partial answer in retired persons who were not only willing to help with meal preparation and serving but could also provide transportation to elderly participants of limited mobility.

This example of a formative evaluation shows how information obtained early in a program's life-cycle can be used to enhance its effectiveness and ultimately determine its success. If the program organizers at the church had not collected additional information in trying to figure out why the meals program was underused, they probably would have made an inaccurate judgment; namely, that there was not a sufficiently large elderly population in need of the service to warrant its continuation.

Relationship of evaluation and needs-assessment studies. It should be apparent that considerable overlap occurs between needs-assessment and evaluation processes. Both tell the congregation something about the quality, accessibility, or suitability of existing programs. An important distinction between the two is the *focus of the data-collection process.* In needs assessment, the focus is on persons, whereas in evaluation it centers on specific programs. Needs assessment uses the information gathered about the needs of persons and available resources to inform decisions. Evaluation uses the information gathered about programs, projects, or activities to inform decisions. Both are geared toward decision making, which is not the case with certain other types of research which use the same data-collection methodologies. (This should signal a caution to church study groups that may use an outside specialist in setting up an evaluation process. The questions asked should be those of the persons who will be making the decisions, not those of a person who may want to formulate them in keeping with independent research interests.)

The findings of both needs assessment and evaluation are for use in decision making. Both have potential as agents of change in the congregation and neither should be initiated for its own sake. Each is time-consuming and usually not proposed unless there is some idea that change is in order or could help a church better achieve its goals. As with the old adage, "If it ain't broke, don't fix it," so with needs assessment and program evaluation: "If you don't intend to change it, don't ask people what they think of it." The result of asking questions, of studying a program, may be to affirm it but that is not an outcome that can be assumed in advance.

5.4.2 *Process Issues in Evaluation in Congregational Contexts*

The primary issue to keep in mind is that the research strategies used must relate to the different motivations for participation among church members. It is not really important in business or government whether the people who are required to do planning and evaluation want to do it; the goals of the organization—from the perspective of those responsible for production—are not necessarily related to the personal goals of the staff. The overriding reality is the "system" to which the personnel are accountable.

The church is a voluntary organization and the continued existence of any voluntary group depends in part on the rewards gained from participation.[15] In a congregation, those rewards include faith fulfillment, pleasure in performance, sociability, ideological symbolism, and accomplishment of tasks. That the structure of rewards continues must be of concern to the leadership and to the congregation as a whole. The factors of voluntarism and rewards make evaluation research in a congregation different from that in many organizations that engage in program study.

Evaluators of congregational program must recognize the investment and commitment of persons involved and share the genuine desire of most such persons to assure that the programs are effective. The people of the congregation, particularly the leadership and those who designed and operate current programs, should have a sense of ownership of the evaluation process. Relational factors are highly significant and evaluation approaches predicated on hierarchial models may have to be modified before they can be used in a congregation.

The relational aspects of church programs should be kept in mind at every stage in the evaluation including initial assessment of goals. Church program goals, when these have been articulated, may not state that a particular activity was intended to build shared leadership or to increase dialogue between certain groups within the membership. Evaluation processes that are heavily goal-oriented may overlook these unstated but essential relational qualities of programs and their outcomes. Evaluators need to discover how people have felt about the program. Perhaps a program that seems to be lacking in terms of quantity or quality really was successful in other ways. Or perhaps some program that looked wonderful on paper actually failed in relational aspects. For example, a service project dependent on volunteers accomplished its task but set a negative precedent for such future efforts; the persons supervising the effort were so critical of volunteers who failed to follow instructions perfectly that the participants had no joy in the activity. In a congregation, the goals of individuals are important and should be taken into account in program evaluations. Personal satisfaction cannot be overstressed as motivation in voluntary organizations.

5.4.3 Getting Started

5.4.3.1 Who Should Be Involved?

Getting started with an evaluation entails many of the same early steps involved in a needs assessment. Initially, persons who will provide leadership for the evaluation must be identified and recruited. In some cases, the pastor and the governing unit of the congregation might comprise the evaluation team, with or without an outside consultant. In other cases, a task force made up of key leaders and program personnel (staff or volunteer) might be designated. Pivotal leaders and program staff should automatically be included in the evaluation process. If, for example, the evaluation is to focus on the Christian education program of the congregation, some members of the study team should be familiar with the literature of this content area, the local organization, the efforts of other churches or denominations and issues currently under debate in the discipline of Christian education. The team needs to be able not only to look at the existing program but to be able to take account of alternatives.

The team will want to determine the degree of emphasis it wants to place on measurements of the effectiveness or success coming from outside the particular congregational context. Depending on that degree, several approaches can be used to receive input from beyond the program context and to expand the horizons of the program planners. "Blue ribbon panels" or "accreditation" approaches feature outside experts who are invited in to examine the program and make judgments based on agreed upon standards considered appropriate for the program under study.[16] Some congregations may even contain such experts or they may be in neighboring congregations, on regional denominational staffs, or in nearby seminaries or colleges. Quantitative and qualitative data may be collected by these persons in the course of their examination, but this is not usual.

The advantages of using such experts are threefold: (1) the congregation gets a fresher look at program than may be possible from persons who have vested interests as participants, (2) information on how others provide program may suggest new approaches, and (3) negative criticism is sometimes more palatable from outsiders, if they are perceived as genuinely objective.

Recourse to outside experts also has potentially negative implications. Patton notes that the approach is essentially deductive, applying criteria from outside the program context to determine whether it meets certain standards. In many cases, the experts do not report data but make judgments, a stage of the evaluation process more appropriately done by the congregation's leadership; listening to the opinions of experts may short-circuit a thorough research effort. Patton also observes:

The connoisseur [expert critic] has no commitment to produce a descriptive, holistic analysis that brings the decision maker into the program experience so that informed judgments can be made by those decision makers; the connoisseur's criticism and metaphors are both the data and the judgment.[17]

Use of a "friendly critic" may be a more appropriate technique. Knowing the program context is important, as is knowing general standards.

Another evaluation method, called the "adversary approach," transforms members of the study team into outside experts. This approach sets up two groups to discover and present data exclusively on negative aspects and positive outcomes of a program. Each group is expected rigorously to defend its conclusions on effectiveness or ineffectiveness with data gathered from observation. The danger of this method is that it precludes a unified (holistic) approach to data collection. It may also pose ethical problems for persons involved since it sets up the possibility of the manipulation of data to support negative or positive conclusions.[18]

"The adversary approach" is probably most appropriate in testing new program *ideas* within the congregation. Persons from the target audience of a proposed program might be asked to list anonymously positive and negative arguments they can imagine. The rationales could then be debated.

5.4.3.2 The Issue of Goals

A lack of stated program goals often hampers evaluation efforts in a congregation. When that is discovered, one typical response is to embark on a goals-writing binge, the leadership listing all the programs and preparing objective statements for each.

This dubious exercise often results in the translation of existing programs into standard planning and budget language, even if that is not the way in which the congregation does its planning and budgeting. This turns a process into an end in itself rather than a means to an end, and it will frustrate people.

Goals and objectives in a congregational context are vehicles for helping people think about what they want to accomplish with a program and what steps they need to take. The language of *measurement criteria* used in goals statements is there to indicate how the evaluators would know whether a program is a success in its own terms. If First Church is committed to liturgical dance and starts a program to increase its use in regular services of worship, planners should attempt to be specific about what they mean by the word "increase." From one to six times per year? From one to ten times? Every other Sunday? Clarity at the outset makes later evaluation much easier. But program goals and related statements need not be quantitative if the activity does not lend itself to such language. No objective standards are available for the measuring of goals such as "the deepening of faith" or "making members more aware of their neighbors on a day-to-day basis." The tools in evaluation research must be appropriate to the context and topic.

Not infrequently, a congregation finds itself wanting, or needing, to evaluate a program for which no written goals exist. How does it proceed? One approach is a process of *goals clarification* that may involve the research team or a broader spectrum of the members. This process could begin with an examination of current expectations of the program as well as the intentions of the original designers, insofar as the history can be reconstructed. Interviews with the original planners might uncover the roots. A questionnaire can be used to determine the current expectations and views on how the program should function. This research would allow the evaluation team to write a simple set of *assumed goals* and, perhaps, specific statements on how components of the program should be operated.

The phase of evaluation research that looks at goals should not be overly complicated or time consuming. Initial exercises, such as determining assumed goals, are for the purpose of providing rudimentary standards with which to compare current program characteristics and outcomes—all means to ends. The objective is to evaluate the program, not to write a goals statement. If no consensus about the intended purpose exists at the end of a goals clarification process, the various perspectives expressed should be recorded as plausible goals to be tested in the course of the ensuing evaluation. After all, it is possible for a program to fulfill

several, sometimes disparate, goals of both developers and users.

Programs often stray or are guided away from their original courses. Program plans are modified by a host of contextual factors. Real goals are not always the official goals, and a failure to observe that fact can frustrate evaluation research and cause it to be disregarded. Evaluation is most likely to affect decisions in the congregation when it accepts the values, assumptions, and objectives of the leadership and the members who make program decisions.

Goal-free evaluation liberates the evaluators from the problem of constructing or reconstructing goal and objective statements. The distinctiveness of this approach influences both the data collection and interpretation components of the research. It proceeds from the assumption that program has many *unintended* outcomes, some of which may be negative but many of which may be more valued by the group than those originally intended. A goal-free approach avoids the incorporation into data-collection instruments of a bias favoring only outcomes projected in a statement of program purpose. It permits questions that provide information on all effects of the program. House uses the example of a goal-free approach in a consumer survey asking people how they used a particular product and how they viewed its utility. The manufacturer's intended use would not be particularly pertinent.[19]

An example will suggest the relevance of goal-free evaluation to congregational program. Take an annual stewardship drive. As part of its program, the local stewardship committee organized teams to visit the home of every member, to talk about pledging and explain the church program. A deliberate part of the plan was to match callers with certain characteristics of the persons they were to visit: women called on women, senior adults on other seniors, youths on youths.

Subsequent evaluation of the program focused almost exclusively on the increase of pledges and on the average amount of the contribution. The report showed only a three-percent increase in giving, and the stewardship committee was discouraged. Planners felt that the amount of effort that went into the visitation program did not justify the results and decided to drop the plan for the next year. The committee did not notice the unintended positive outcomes because it was only looking at money results.

The committee failed to observe that attendance at Sunday worship increased after the campaign and remained at a higher level than at any time in the previous five years. The fact was that many members who had felt ignored by the church's leadership came back when visited, and some got involved in other activities in addition to worship. The image of the congregation as a "cold" place was changed for some. These outcomes of the visitation program were highly visible and valued within the congregation but not by the stewardship committee which had a single standard for measuring success.

5.4.4 Data Collection

The evaluation team must decide what types of data collection techniques will be used and, if surveys are to be conducted, who will be interviewed or asked to complete a questionnaire. Unlike the ideal in a needs assessment, everyone in the congregation is not approached in the course of program evaluation unless the program, such as worship, is one in which all members are potential participants. (Even then, equal weight would not be given to the opinions of persons who attend worship on only Christmas and Easter, unless the concern is to find out why certain persons are present so rarely.) Program evaluation looks primarily to the views of a fair representation of users and leadership.

A list of program participants may be available. If not, research options are available short of a mailing to all members. Select a typical day to distribute questionnaires—when the program is operating and normal attendance is expected, or set up interviews. Respondents should be assured of anonymity and encouraged to be honest in their comments or responses. Be mindful that church programs are closely identified with personalities and members may be reluctant to say anything critical.

If a questionnaire is used, a minimal number of questions about the respondent's background should be included in order to identify characteristics of the program users. This will, among other things, help the congregation to know whether the program is serving the persons for whom it was designed. Helpful background information might include:

+ age
+ sex
+ economic status, if relevant to program
+ race/ethnicity
+ length of residence in the community
+ member or nonmember of congregation
+ other programs in which persons participate

The amount of background information requested would vary with the focus of the evaluation.

The central concern in program evaluation is a respondent's opinion based on experience. The survey might ask about:

+ frequency or length of time in the program
+ participation by other family members/friends
+ reasons for participation
+ expectation for and from the program
+ actual experience in the program

The last question opens to investigation a range of program components, such as schedule, facilities, leadership and quality of service. A sample of a variety of questions that might be asked of participants is included in the evaluation guide for workshops, conferences, or seminars in Appendix 5–4.

The nature of the responses will depend on the nature of the program. For example, if a meals program is being evaluated, *quantity* may be a major issue: is sufficient food served? If the program is educational reactions to the material will be significant: are there too few resources provided? Too many? Are they appealing? Does the program leadership feel the resources provided by the church are adequate? Readily available? Is it bothersome to share a slide projector with another program?

Quality of service may be relevant. It can be expected that responses on quality will vary considerably since this is an area of acute subjectivity. The evaluation team may find it necessary to define its concept of quality in regard to the specific program.

The team may have concerns about the *organizational* characteristics of the program: the decision making involved in developing and conducting the activity on an everyday basis, communication, working relations among leaders, resource usage, and costs. Information on some of these components can be obtained only by examination of secondary sources—reports, budgets, attendance records. Comparison of budgets with actual expenditures will help the team when it discusses priorities, or the lack thereof, and might reveal a need for more consensus on what the congregation ought to be doing.

Issues of *performance* are even more difficult to quantify or evaluate than are organizational components. Users and leaders should be asked about *the way* a service is provided or a program conducted rather than *what* was provided or done. In the church, the "why" is frequently more important than the "what." Questions about why deal with style, faithfulness to the congregation's understanding of the gospel, and sensitivity to identity issues.

Some program aspects allow a fairly limited range of responses; some anticipate complex, nuanced expressions. Matters such as scheduling, resources, frequencies, and quantities, perhaps even quality, can be explored by using a *closed-ended* question:

Was the amount of time scheduled for orientation to the program:

1__too much?   2__about right?   3__too little?

If this event were held against next year, what would be the best month for you?

__January	__May	__September
__February	__June	__October
__March	__July	__November
__April	__August	__December

Questions can also be phrased to provide opportunity for deviation from anticipated responses without using an entirely open-ended approach. For example:

How did you learn about this program?

__from a friend who is a member of the congregation
__from a newspaper advertisement
__from a flyer distributed door-to-door
__from a sign on the church lawn
__from some other source _____
                                        (please specify)

What portion of the program did you find most useful?

__small group discussion
__workshop experience
__special presentation by guest speaker
__opportunities to exchange information during coffee
  break
__other _____
                                        (please specify)

Open-ended questions are quite common in evaluation and are used when the researcher does not know or is not sure what responses are possible. They are especially appropriate for use in formative evaluation efforts where unobtrusive measures such as observation are best for getting a feeling for how a program is working. Open-ended questions were necessary when members of the United Methodist congregation, noted above, were trying to find out why the meals program was less popular than had been projected:

+ What would you suggest could be done to improve this program?
+ What are ways in which you have personally benefited from this program?
+ Do you have any suggestions about how the

program could be organized to provide for more involvement of participants in the leadership?

Close-ended and open-ended questions are sometimes used in conjunction:

a. How would you describe the facilities chosen for the retreat?

1 __ more than adequate 3 __ somewhat inadequate
2 __ adequate   4 __ totally inadequate

b. If you found the facilities *inadequate* in some respect, please tell us why this was the case.

An evaluation instrument may also include a question that measures a respondent's overall reaction to a program:

Overall, how would you evaluate the effectiveness of this program?

1__ very effective   3__ ineffective
2 __ effective   4__very ineffective

Or,

How would you describe your feelings about the curriculum approach used in the class?

1__ very satisfied   3__ dissatisfied
2__ satisfied   4__very dissatisfied

Respondents may have many minor criticisms of individual components of a program and still feel that overall it was rewarding. If some overall measure is not used, the evaluators may not be able to tell whether the criticism of components should be read as commentary on the whole and whether they cumulatively add up to a negative evaluation.

Finally, a good survey instrument should most often conclude with an opportunity for persons to express feelings about issues on which no questions were provided. This gives people a chance to say what it means to them to be involved in a program and, perhaps, to give clues to unintended outcomes.

5.4.5 *Interpretation*

The interpretation phase is the most difficult in any evaluation process. As with needs assessment, the information gathered in an evaluation, even when the data collection is extensive, does not answer the question of *what to do*. The data may show that a program is not working as intended; it will seldom indicate a clear direction for solving the problem.

Interpretation of the data requires value judgments on the part of the study team. Evaluators must own and take responsibility for making the judgments or seeing that they are made within the congregational structure. This is a hard point to drive home: decisions are made by people, not data. There may be no right or wrong conclusion; a conclusion about effectiveness or success reached in one context may not be appropriate in another. To make a decision, the study team must go back to the purpose of the program, to the means set forth for doing it, and ask whether it has been done—to what degree given the time, place, and resources.

If answers are negative, the team will want to examine the possibility that something was done which may be valuable, although that was not what was intended. Should that be the case, the study team may still need to consider how the congregation can do that which it started out to accomplish and also affirm what it did without deliberate intention. If a congregation cannot do both, decisions must be made on which is more valuable.

The study team should also examine the fit between characteristics of participants and what the program provides or does. Are adjustments needed? Have people changed over the years while the program remained the same? Where are the people for whom the program was originally designed?

Program evaluation as discussed in this chapter points out strengths and weaknesses, but where weaknesses show up it offers the barest hints for solutions.[20] Carol Weiss has observed:

There is a gap between data and action that will have to be filled in with intuition, experience, gleanings from the research literature, assumptions based on theory, ideology, and a certain amount of plain guessing. Moving through this gap to new program experimentation requires a commitment by decision makers to the belief that a new trail is better than continuation of a proven error.[21]

The purpose of this chapter has been to suggest methods and tools to help a congregational study team to make decisions about choices that work for its church, and to allow persons a fuller expression of ministry. The content of those decisions—the actual program—cannot be considered outside the living context of the congregation itself. The content of the decisions remains, appropriately, in the hands of the congregation itself.

NOTES _____

1. Edward A. Rauff, *Why People Join the Church* (New York: The Pilgrim Press, 1979).
2. Michael Q. Patton, *Qualitative Evaluation Methods* (Beverly Hills, Cal.: Sage, 1980), p. 22.
3. Ibid., pp. 95-98.
4. *Needs Assessment: An Exploratory Critique*. Office of the Assistant Secretary for Planning and Evaluation (HEW), Washington, D.C., U.S. Department of Commerce, 1977, p. 21.
5. Ibid., p. 29.
6. Ibid., p. 22.
7. Princeton Religion Research Center, *The Unchurched American* (Princeton, N.J., 1978).
8. Ibid.
9. Donald P. Smith, *Congregations Alive* (Philadelphia: The Westminster Press, 1981).
10. From *A Gathering of Strangers: Understanding the Life of Your Church* (Revised and Updated Edition), by Robert C. Worley, p. 44. Copyright © 1976 The Westminster Press; © 1983 Robert C. Worley. Reprinted and used by permission.

11. Henry A. Blunk, *Smaller Church Mission Study Guide* (Philadelphia: The Geneva Press, 1978).
12. Eileen Lindner, Mary Mattis, and June Rogers, *When Churches Mind the Children: A Study of Day Care in Local Parishes.* (Ypsilanti, Mich.: The High/Scope Press, 1983).
13. Ernest R. House, *Evaluating with Validity.* (Beverly Hills, Cal.: Sage, 1980), p. 23.
14. Patton, *Qualitative Evaluation Methods*, p. 71.
15. Aida K. Tomeh, "Formal Voluntary Organizations: Participation, Correlates, and Interrelationships," in *New Perspectives on the American Community.* Roland L. Warren, ed. (Chicago, Ill.: Rand McNally, 1977).
16. Patton, *Qualitative Evaluation Methods*, pp. 50-53.
17. Ibid., p. 52.
18. Ibid., p. 53.
19. House, pp. 30-31.
20. Carol H. Weiss, *Evaluation Research: Methods of Assessing Program Effectiveness* (Englewood Cliffs, N.J.: Prentice-Hall, 1972).
21. Ibid., p. 125.

For Further Reading on Program _____

Carini, Patricia F. *Observations and Description: An Alternative Methodology for the Investigation of Human Phenomena.* North Dakota Study Group on Evaluation Monograph Series. Grand Forks: University of North Dakota, 1975.
Edwards, Ward, Marcia Guttentag, and Kurt Snapper. *Handbook of Evaluation Research, Vol. 1.* Beverly Hills, Cal.: Sage, 1975.

House, Ernest R. *Evaluating with Validity.* Beverly Hills, Cal.: Sage, 1980.
McCall, George J., and J. L. Simmons. *Issues in Participant Observation: A Text and Reader*, Reading, Mass.: Addison-Wesley, 1969.
Morris, Lynn Lyons and Carol Taylor Fitz-Gibbon. *Evaluators Handbook.* Beverly Hills, Cal.: Sage, 1978.

Needs Assessment: An Exploratory Critique. Office of the Assistant Secretary for Planning and Evaluaton (HEW). Washington, D.C., U.S. Department of Commerce, 1977.

Patton, Michael Q. *Qualitative Evaluation Methods*. Beverly Hills, Cal.: Sage, 1980.

———. *Utilization-focused Evaluation*. Beverly Hills, Cal.: Sage, 1978.

Rutman, Leonard, *Planning Useful Evaluations: Evaluability Assessment*. Beverly Hills, Cal.: Sage, 1980.

Schaller, Lyle E. *Looking in the Mirror: Self-Appraisal in the Local Church*. Nashville: Abingdon Press, 1984.

Schatzman, Leonard, and Anselm L. Strauss. *Field Research: Strategies for a Natural Sociology*. Englewood Cliffs, N.J.: Prentice-Hall, 1973.

Walrath, Douglas A. *Planning for Your Church*. Philadelphia: The Westminster Press, 1984.

Wax, Rosalie H. *Doing Fieldwork: Warnings and Advice*. Chicago: University of Chicago Press, 1971.

Weiss, Carol H. *Evaluation Research: Methods of Assessing Program Effectiveness*. Englewood Cliffs, N.J.: Prentice-Hall, 1972.

APPENDIX 5–1
*Lutheran Church in America**
Nurture Study

<u>CONGREGATIONAL QUESTIONNAIRE</u>

_____
Your Congregation's Name and Location

By answering the questions on this form, you will help us gain a better understanding of your congregation and you as an individual member. Would you please check here to indicate that you have read the enclosed explanation of the LCA's use of this questionnaire? _____

I. *First, a series of questions about you and your religious background. Read each question carefully, then CIRCLE the number of the answer which is best for you. For example:*

Is your church located within one mile of your residence?   1. Yes   2. No

---

1. a. *On the average, how often do you attend Sunday worship services?*
   1. *Every Week*   3. *About 3 times a month*   5. *About once a month*   7. *Once or twice a year*
   2. *Nearly every week*   4. *About twice a month*   6. *About every 6 weeks*   8. *Less than once a year*

   b. *If you are married, how often does your spouse attend?*   1   2   3   4   5   6   7   8   *(as defined in 1 a.)*

2. *In addition to Sunday morning services, approximately how many hours per month do you spend in church activities?*
   1. *1 hour or less*   3. *5- 7 hours*   5. *11-13 hours*   7. *17-19 hours*   9. *None*
   2. *2-4 hours*   4. *8-10 hours*   6. *14-16 hours*   8. *20 hours or more*

3. *Do you presently hold or have you held an elected position in your congregation in the past three years?*
   1. *Yes*   2. *No*

4. *Are you presently serving or in the last three years have you served in any volunteer leadership position in your congregation (such as Sunday School teacher, woman's group, etc.)?*
   1. *Yes*   2. *No*   *If yes, how many?*   1   2   3   4   5   6   7   8   9

5. *Within the last three years, have you held an elected office in a voluntary association other than the church (e.g. a civic, professional, social, or community organization)?*

   1. *Yes*   2. *No*   *If yes, how many?*   1   2   3   4   5   6   7   8   9

6. *In how many different church organizations (such as choir, educational group, church committee) have you participated during this past year?*   0   1   2   3   4   5   6   7   8   9

7. *How long have you been a member of your congregation?*   1. *1 year or less*   2. *1 to 2 years*
   3. *3 to 4 years*   4. *5 to 7 years*   6. *More than 10 years, but less than all your life* 7. *All your life*

8. *What is the approximate distance from your home to church?*
   1. *1 mile or less*   2. *2 miles*   3. *3 miles*   4. *4 miles*   5. *5 to 6 miles*
   6. *7 to 9 miles*   7. *10 to 12 miles*   8. *13 miles or more*

9. *If you were not a member of this congregation all your life, indicate the denomination(s) of all prior congregations of which you have been a member. Circle as many as applicable.*

   1. *Lutheran Church in America (or its predecessors)*   7. *Methodist*
   2. *American Lutheran Church (or its predecessors)*   8. *Presbyterian*
   3. *Lutheran Church - Missouri Synod*   9. *Roman Catholic*
   4. *Other Lutheran church bodies*   10. *United Church of Christ (or its predecessors)*
   5. *Baptist*   11. *None*
   6. *Episcopalian*   12. *Other* _____
                                                              (Please Specify)

10. *What is your present marital status? (Circle ONE please.)*

   1. *Single, never previously married*   5. *Married more than once, living with spouse*
   2. *Single, married previously*   6. *Married more than once, separated from spouse*
   3. *Married once, living with spouse*   7. *Widowed, not remarried*
   4. *Married once, separated from spouse*   8. *Divorced, not remarried*

11. *If married, is your spouse also a member of your congregation?*

   1. *Yes*   2. *No*

12. *Do you have children now living at home with you?*

   0. *No, none*   2. *2 children*   4. *4 children*

   1. *1 child*   3. *3 children*   5. *5 or more children*

---

*From *Congregations as Nurturing Communities*, by Roger A. Johnson. Published by the Division for Parish Services, Lutheran Church in America.

13. Were your grandparents, or the grandparents of your spouse, members of your congregation or a former congregation that either merged into or sponsored your present congregation?   1. Yes   2. No

14. How many of your grandparents, and/or the grandparents of your spouse, were ever members of any Lutheran congregation?   0   1   2   3   4   5   6   7   8   9

15. In addition to those members of your household who live with you, how many other relatives are also members of your congregation?
    0. None   1. 1 or 2   2. 3 or 4   3. 5 or 6   4. 7 or 8   5. 9 or 10   6. 11 or 12   7. More than 12

16. Of your closest friends, who live within 10 miles of your home, how many are also members of your congregation?
              0   1   2   3   4   5   6   7   8   9

17. Of your closest friends, who live within 10 miles of your home, how many are <u>not</u> members of your congregation?
              0   1   2   3   4   5   6   7   8   9

18. When you get together with acquaintances for social or recreational activities, how often are some other members of your congregation likely to be present?
    1. Almost always   2. Frequently   3. About half the time   4. Occasionally   5. Almost never

19. How long have you lived in your present town or city?

    1. 1 year or less   3. 3 to 4 years   5. 8 to 10 years   7. All your life

    2. 1 to 2 years   4. 5 to 7 years   6. More than 10 years, but less than all your life

20. How many times have you moved to a different city or town since you were 18?

    1. Once   3. Three times   5. Five times   7. Eight or nine times   9. Never
    2. Twice   4. Four times   6. Six or seven times   8. Ten or more times

---

II.   Second, here are a number of statements offering an opinion about a congregation, or an individual's experience in that congregation. There are no right or wrong answers. You will probably disagree with some items and agree with others. First impressions are usually best in such matters. After reading each statement, decide if you agree or disagree and the strength of your opinion, and then circle the appropriate number or circle "N" if you have no opinion.

	If you agree strongly, circle 1.
	If you agree somewhat, circle 2.
Read each statement carefully. Then indicate the extent to which you agree or disagree by circling the number or letter following each statement. The meaning of the numbers and letter is indicated to the right.	If you both agree and disagree, circle 3.
	If you disagree somewhat, circle 4
	If you disagree strongly, circle 5
	If you have no opinion, circle N.

IN OUR CONGREGATION:

	1	2	3	4	5	N
1. people are friendly to strangers and newcomers.	1	2	3	4	5	N
2. people help each other out in times of trouble.	1	2	3	4	5	N
3. the members have a voice in making the important decisions.	1	2	3	4	5	N
4. people do differ in their beliefs about Christianity.	1	2	3	4	5	N
5. people feel free to disagree openly with each other on matters of policy.	1	2	3	4	5	N
6. specific Lutheran doctrines play an important and prominent role.	1	2	3	4	5	N
7. people share God's love in what they do for and with each other.	1	2	3	4	5	N
8. there are cliques or exclusive groups which make one feel unwelcome.	1	2	3	4	5	N
9. people feel free to disagree openly with the pastor.	1	2	3	4	5	N
10. people are open to new experiences and ideas.	1	2	3	4	5	N
11. people care for one another in a way that is qualitatively better than what I have experienced in other groups.	1	2	3	4	5	N
12. the pastor dominates our congregational decisions.	1	2	3	4	5	N
13. people are relaxed and comfortable with each other.	1	2	3	4	5	N
14. people speak about experiences of the continuing action or presence of God.	1	2	3	4	5	N
15. people laugh and joke and have a good time, even when engaged in serious business matters.	1	2	3	4	5	N
16. to reach out to unchurched people is a high priority.	1	2	3	4	5	N
17. the people who have joined have done so primarily because it is Lutheran.	1	2	3	4	5	N

18. the pastor is available whenever members need him.   1   2   3   4   5   N

19. helping people in need who are <u>not</u> members of the congregation
    is a high priority.   1   2   3   4   5   N

20. our Christian beliefs and practices are typical of the majority
    of people in our community.   1   2   3   4   5   N

21. the educational program for children is a program of high priority.   1   2   3   4   N

22. members turn to each other for help as often as they turn to the
    pastor.   1   2   3   4   5   N

AS FAR AS MY EXPERIENCE IN MY CONGREGATION GOES:

23. I feel I have had some influence on the direction of congregational
    decisions.   1   2   3   4   5   N

24. I find myself accepted and included in the life of the congregation.   1   2   3   4   5   N

25. I feel I am well informed about the activities of the congregation.   1   2   3   4   5   N

26. I find my experience at church to be a source of personal strength
    for meeting the challenges of daily life.   1   2   3   4   5   N

27. if I had to leave my present congregation, I would want to find
    a new congregation like the present one.   1   2   3   4   5   N

28. I discover and express some of my deepest and truest feelings in
    church groups.   1   2   3   4   5   N

29. I am likely to sense God's presence mainly in fellowship with
    other Chrstians.   1   2   3   4   5   N

30. I am likely to sense God's presence mainly when I am alone.   1   2   3   4   5   N

31. if I had to leave my congregation, I think it would be easy
    to find another one like this one.   1   2   3   4   5   N

32. I find my experience at church to be out of touch with the
    realities of everyday life.   1   2   3   4   5   N

33. my experiences in church have helped me to accept myself,
    including my faults and shortcomings.   1   2   3   4   5   N

34. I think my congregation is special and unique.   1   2   3   4   5   N

IN TERMS OF MY PERSONAL SITUATION OR VIEWPOINT:

35. I believe my relationship to God has importance for my life
    after death.   1   2   3   4   5   N

36. I believe my relationship to God has importance for my life
    here on earth.   1   2   3   4   5   N

37. I imagine God to be mostly like a caring friend.   1   2   3   4   5   N

38. much of my daily life with my family or work is different
    because of my faith in God.   1   2   3   4   5   N

39. I would be disappointed if my children changed to a non-
    Lutheran denomination.   1   2   3   4   5   N

40. because of the pressures of the world, what I need from God
    is comfort and consolation.   1   2   3   4   5   N

41. experiences in church are the most important source for my
    sense of trust in God.   1   2   3   4   5   N

42. my experiences in church have helped me accept other people
    who are considerably different from myself.   1   2   3   4   5   N

III.   Thirdly, here are a number of statements which make a comparison. Each statement is followed by several
        items. From these suggested items, choose the three which you rate highest and number them 1, 2 and 3.
        Thus, mark 1 before your highest choice, 2 before your next highest, and 3 before your next highest.
        Also, choose the item for each statement that you rate lowest, and mark that 9. Note that in each case
        the lines before several choices will be left blank.

---

1. Of the many spheres of my life in which I gain personal satisfaction, the <u>three</u> <u>most</u> <u>important</u> are (1, 2 and 3).
   The <u>least</u> <u>important</u> is (9).

   _____ Group Recreational Activities   _____ Work*   _____ Friendships   _____ Family Life

   _____ Clubs or Community Organizations   _____ Hobbies   _____ Church   _____ Relatives

2. *Of the many groups of people from whom I might seek help in times of personal trouble, the* three *most* likely *are (1, 2 and 3). The* least likely *is (9).*

_____ Persons I know at work*   _____ Members of my church

_____ Persons I know through recreational activities   _____ A professional counselor

_____ Persons I know through community organizations   _____ Friends

_____ The pastor of my church   _____ Immediate family   _____ Relatives

3. *Of all the people who know me, the* three groups *that know me* best *are (1, 2 and 3). The* group *that knows me* least *is (9).*

_____ People I know at work*   _____ Members of my immediate family

_____ People I know through recreational activities   _____ Friends

_____ People I know through clubs or community organizations   _____ People at church

4. *Of all the pastor's many responsibilities, the* three most important *are (1, 2 and 3). The* least important *is (9).*

_____ Preaching   _____ Assisting laity in carrying out the work of the congregation

_____ Conducting public worship   _____ Administering the church office   _____ Teaching the young

_____ Pastoral care for members   _____ Serving the needs of the larger community   _____ Teaching adults

_____ Serving as a personal example of spiritual life for others.

5. *Of all the activities of my congregation, the* three most important *for me are (1, 2 and 3). The* least important *is (9).*

_____ Sunday morning worship   _____ Retreats or camping programs   _____ Projects to meet local social concerns

_____ Communion or Eucharist   _____ Church sponsored recreational activities

_____ Bible study   _____ Weekday prayer or worship services

_____ Fellowship occasions   _____ Small groups for sharing personal insights and concerns

6. *When the different spheres of my life create conflicting demands on me, I most often tend to resolve such matters by assigning* highest priority *to (1, 2 and 3). I most often give* lowest priority *to (9).*

_____ Clubs or community organizations   _____ Work*   _____ Church   _____ Relatives

_____ Solitary activities   _____ Recreation   _____ Friends   _____ Immediate family

7. *For me the* three most important *characteristics of a good sermon are (1, 2 and 3). The* least important *characteristic is (9).*

_____ That it is easy to understand and down to earth   _____ That it is a Christ-centered message

_____ That it is expressive of a strong form of religious authority   _____ That it is illustrated from the local community where I live

_____ That it has a pleasing style of delivery   _____ That it is biblically based

_____ That it is consistent with Lutheran doctrine   _____ That it is applicable to my life

8. *If I had to move and look for a new congregation, the* three most important *considerations would be (1, 2 and 3). The* least important *consideration would be (9).*

_____ The quality of pastoral care for members   _____ Other congregational programs (in addition to those listed)

_____ The preaching and teaching of Lutheran doctrine   _____ The fellowship of members with each other

_____ The style of pastoral leadership   _____ The location of the congregation in relation to my home

_____ The role of lay leadership in the congregation   _____ The number of members in the congregation

_____ The Sunday Church School program   _____ The youth program

9. *Of all the considerations which contributred to my decision to join this congregation, the* three most important *were (1, 2 and 3). The* least important *was (9).*

_____ The church location   _____ The preaching

_____ The friendliness of members   _____ A relative who was already a member

_____ A sense of Lutheran loyalty   _____ The youth program

_____ The style of worship   _____ Other church programs

_____ The quality of pastoral care   _____ The similarity of othr members to myself

_____ The personality of the pastor   _____ The style of leadership

*Any reference to work should include homemaking and for students the work associated with being a student

IV.   *Fourth, here are some additional questions about yourself. Remember all information is anonymous. Your answers to these questions will help us understand the makeup of your congregation. Please circle the number immediately in front of the appropriate answer.*

1. *What is your sex?*   1. Male   2. Female

2. *What is your age?*

   1. 15 or younger   3. 19 - 24   5. 35 - 44   7. 55 - 64   9. 75 or older

   2. 16 - 18   4. 25 - 34   6. 45 - 54   8. 65 - 74

3. *What is the highest level of schooling you have completed?*

   1. Some grade school   6. Trade school, business school, junior college degree
                                              or certificate

   2. Finished grade school (8th grade)   7. College graduate (4 year degree)

   3. Some high school   8. Some graduate school or professional school after college

   4. High school graduate   9. Completed graduate or professional school after college

   5. Some college

4. *How do you identify yourself in terms of racial or ethnic origins?*

   1. No single racial or ethnic origins   4. Swedish   7. Black or Afro-American
      with which I identify

   2. Norwegian   5. Danish   8. Hispanic

   3. Finnish   6. German   9. Other _____

5. *Are there a significant number of persons whose racial or ethnic origins are the same as yours and who are members of your congregation?*

   1. Yes   2. No   3. Inapplicable because I answered 1 in Question #4

6. *If yes, how important is the presence of persons of the same racial or ethnic origin for you?*

   1. Very important   4. Not important at all

   2. Important   5. Not a relevant question since I answered 1 on Question #4

   3. Somewhat important

7. *What is your total family income before taxes? Estimate as best you can.*

   1. $ 4,999 or less   4. $15,000 - $19,000   7. $30,000 - $39,000

   2. $ 5,000 - $ 9,999   5. $20,000 - $24,000   8. $40,000 - $49,000

   3. $10,000 - $14,000   6. $25,000 - $29,000   9. $50,000 or more

8. *How many other members of your household are also completing this questionnaire? CIRCLE the appropriate number.*

   Spouse   0 1   brothers/sisters   0 1 2 3 4 5 or more

   children   0 1 2 3 4 5 or more   grandchildren   0 1 2 3 4 5 or more

   parents   0 1 2 3 4   grandparents   0 1 2 3 4
      (including in-laws)   other relatives   _____

Finally, we have asked a variety of questions about you and your religious life. We may have missed some areas that you find very important. If so, please complete the following sentences. (You do not have to complete either of these sentences if you have already expressed your own sense of faith and congregational life in an adequate way).

1. For me, the most important aspect of my personal faith is_____

   _____

   _____

2. For me, the most important characteristic of my congregation is _____

   _____

   _____

-- *THANK YOU VERY MUCH FOR YOUR COOPERATION* --

Please put your completed questionnaire in the enclosed envelope NO POSTAGE is needed.

APPENDIX 5–2
Presbyterian Panel
April, 1979, Questionnaire

The Vocation Agency of the General Assembly is making a study of the ministries within our United Presbyterian Church. This Panel, which is part of a larger study, seeks to learn how people in our denomination understand and carry out those ministries. From this study, the Vocation Agency hopes to recommend ways in which pastors and sessions can exercise the kind of creative leadership that will enable their membership more faithfully to fulfill Christ's mission within the congregation and in the world.

1. The word "ministry" is used with different meanings. Please circle the number opposite each of the following statements which best represents the extent of your agreement with that statement.

	Strongly agree	Agree	Agree & disagree	Disagree	Strongly disagree	No opinion
Ministry is the special work of the pastor which serves the spiritual needs of the congregation (preaching, Bible teaching, pastoral calling, etc.)	1	2	3	4	5	6
Ministry is the work shared in by pastors and elders which serves members of the congregation and their spiritual needs	1	2	3	4	5	6
Ministry is the work shared in by the whole congregation which serves the people of the congregation	1	2	3	4	5	6
Ministry includes serving people of the community outside the congregation such as visiting prisoners, volunteering for community service projects, or serving on the boards of community organizations	1	2	3	4	5	6
Ministry includes corporate action by the church to change unjust economic or political conditions of life (such as a task force to deal with issues related to the disparity between rich and poor nations)	1	2	3	4	5	6
Ministry includes the ways a member lives out his/her faith in relation to family, friends and neighborhood	1	2	3	4	5	6
Ministry includes the ways a member lives out his/her faith in his/her occupation	1	2	3	4	5	6

2. To what extent do each of the following statements accurately describe your congregation? (*Circle one response for each.*)

	Very much like my congregation	Somewhat like my congregation	Only a little like my congregation	Not at all like my congregation	Don't know
Members have a clear sense of the congregation's purpose	1	2	3	4	5
Pastors and lay leaders share leadership as genuine partners	1	2	3	4	5
Members know that the church has high expectations for their commitment to and accountability for service	1	2	3	4	5
Members actively serve in the community	1	2	3	4	5
Members actively participate in evangelistic activities	1	2	3	4	5
Members pray together in many different times and places about common concerns	1	2	3	4	5
Members are involved in the work of the church as soon as they unite with the church, if not before	1	2	3	4	5
Members may choose many different ways to serve	1	2	3	4	5
Members are challenged in specific ways to participate in community activities or organizations	1	2	3	4	5
Pastor(s) invite the sharing of joys and concerns before offering the pastoral prayer during Sunday worship	1	2	3	4	5
Members frequently minister to one another's needs	1	2	3	4	5
There are many small groups or other face to face opportunities for study, prayer, and mutual ministry	1	2	3	4	5

| Members feel the congregation is like a warm, caring family | 1 | 2 | 3 | 4 | 5 |
| Members take initiative in identifying needs and proposing ways to serve | 1 | 2 | 3 | 4 | 5 |

3. When you think of the terms "vocation," or "Christian calling," which of the following comes to your mind MOST READILY? *(Please check only one response.)*

(Col 31)   1____I am not familiar with these terms

2____terms which have to do with the ordained ministry

3____terms which might apply to anyone who feels called by God to enter some specific occupation like a doctor, teacher, mechanic

4____terms which mean that God wants us to live a responsible Christian life in whatever we do

5____terms which mean that God wants a person to enter some form of full-time Christian work

6____terms which mean the same as occupation

7____other *(please describe)*_____

4. Who suggests most of the ideas for new programs in your congregation? *(Check one response only.)*

1____pastor   3____elders   5____other church members

2____other church staff   5____church officers other than elders   6____don't know

5. How does most planning for the work of your congregation take place? *(Check one response only.)*

1____The pastor plans the programs and informs the session

2____The pastor (and staff if any) plans the programs and gets session approval

3____A few strong lay leaders make the plans

4____The session plans the programs

5____Session committees plan the programs and secure session approval

6____There is broad participation and input from church membership through expanded session committees followed by session approval

7____I am not sure how plans are made

8____Other _____
                        (Please specify)

6. How often have you observed the following types of relationships between pastors and lay persons? *(Circle one response for each.)*

	Frequently	Occasionally	Seldom	Never	No opinion
Pastors are forced to assume complete control of their congregations because of the failure or poor performance of lay persons in exercising leadership	1	2	3	4	5
Lay persons feel they should not attempt to perform those functions for which the minister has been specifically trained	1	2	3	4	5
Pastors are reluctant to invest the time required to develop effective lay leadership	1	2	3	4	5
Pastors do not know how to encourage members to take leadership	1	2	3	4	5
Active exercise of leadership by members appears to be threatening to the status and self-understanding of pastors	1	2	3	4	5
Church members want to see their pastor as a very human person like themselves but with access to special resources	1	2	3	4	5
Pastors and lay persons seek a relationship in which there is freedom to complement each others' knowledge and skills	1	2	3	4	5
My experience has been that these relationships are too diverse to categorize	1	2	3	4	5

7. From what source(s) do church members receive the most adequate training for the leadership positions in your congregation? (*Check one response only.*)

1____Presbytery events or programs
2____Synod events or programs
3____Leadership programs developed in your own congregation
4____Teaching, preaching guidance by the pastor

5____Reading and individual study
6____Interdenominational events
7____Other_____
                    (*Please specify*)

8. There are many ways in which pastors carry on their work. At different times they may give more or less emphasis to different aspects of ministry. Please indicate your opinion as to the relative priority which the pastor of your congregation has been giving to each of the following ways of working with the congregation. (*Circle one response for each.*)

	Very high priority	High priority	Low priority	Very low priority	No opinion/ don't know
(Col 43) Focuses attention on issues outside of the congregation	1	2	3	4	5
Inspires and motivates members to be involved in service in the community	1	2	3	4	5
Frequently communicates the importance and the possibilities of ministry by church members	1	2	3	4	5
Identifies and encourages the use of members' gifts and talents	1	2	3	4	5
Interprets biblical and theological perspectives on current issues	1	2	3	4	5
Listens to people and responds to their needs with caring love	1	2	3	4	5
Serves as a facilitator and provides resources to members in their ministries	1	2	3	4	5
Shares his/her humanity in specific ways	1	2	3	4	5
Develops confidence and feelings of self worth in church members	1	2	3	4	5
Asks people to do only what he/she would do	1	2	3	4	5
Clearly articulates a dream or goal for the congregation	1	2	3	4	5
Has a clear sense of his/her own appropriate roles in relation to the roles of church officers and members	1	2	3	4	5
Provides strong leadership in developing the program of the church	1	2	3	4	5
Responds to the program ideas of others and helps them to implement them	1	2	3	4	5

9. How much help in living a life of service to others (at home, at work, in the community or in the church) do you now receive: (*Circle one response for each.*)

	Very much	Quite a lot	Some	Little	None	Not sure
from Sunday worship services and sermons?	1	2	3	4	5	6
from fellowship with other church members?	1	2	3	4	5	6
from small study groups and prayer?	1	2	3	4	5	6
from personal Bible study and prayer?	1	2	3	4	5	6
from the way other church members love and accept me as I am?	1	2	3	4	5	6
from the way my pastor loves and accepts me as I am?	1	2	3	4	5	6
from the inspiration of my pastor as a model of Christian service?	1	2	3	4	5	6
from the way others in my congregation express their belief in my ability to serve?	1	2	3	4	5	6
from the work of the Holy Spirit in our congregation?	1	2	3	4	5	6
from appreciation I receive when I have served?	1	2	3	4	5	6

10. How often do you think of yourself as a "minister" to the people around you at home and/or at work? (*Check one response.*)

1___daily   4___2 or 3 times a month   7___once a year or less

2___several times a week   5___about once a month   8___never

3___about once a week   6___several times a year

11. If a program in your congregation seemed to be in jeopardy because the members in charge were not carrying through on their commitments, what do you think your pastor would be most likely to do? (Pastors answer in terms of what you would be most likely to do.) (*Check one response only.*)

(Col 68) 1___allow the program to fail without attempting to intervene

2___step in and take control in order to save the program

3___encourage the persons involved by providing additional resources

4___assign responsibility for the program to another person or group

5___other_____
                          (*Please specify*)

12. To what extent do you agree with the following statement: The terminology used by most pastors and lay persons is so different that they frequently do not really understand each other. (*Check one response.*)

1___Strongly agree   3___Agree & disagree   5___Strongly disagree

2___Agree   4___Disagree   6___No opinion

13. Do you feel that you have a vocation or Christian calling? (*Check one response.*)

1___yes   2___no   3___not sure   4___I don't feel I understand these terms

If "yes," when do you feel your Christian calling began? (*Check one response.*)

1___when I decided what kind of occupation I would prepare myself for

2___when I started work in a job I thought I would spend much of my life at

3___when I was baptized

4___when I became a member of the church

5___when I recognized injustice or social need

6___when I committed my life to Christ

7___when I began to think seriously about the kind of person I want to be

8___at some other point in my life, namely:_____
                                                    (*Please specify*)

APPENDIX 5-3

*An Exercise in Determining Mission Emphases**
Henry A. Blunk

During Meeting 6, you will be making some decisions about the mission emphases of your congregation for the months ahead. The following weighting exercise will prepare you for that. It deals with your personal life, but in the meeting you will be deciding what you as a group think the emphases of your congregation should be.

■ Pretend it is now 1 P.M. on a weekday. Considering your own personal circumstances, decide among the following areas of your life the activities that you think you need to be doing from 3 P.M. to 9 P.M. this evening. Check one appropriate choice for each activity. What activities would you emphasize? To which would you give minimal attention?

■ Participate in your favorite recreation, like playing cards or watching TV.

_____ Do more (than you would normally do).

_____ Do some.

_____ Do less (than you would normally do).

_____ Do none.

■ Take care of personal hygiene, like taking a bath, getting a haircut, seeing a physician.

_____ Do more (than you would normally do).

_____ Do some.

_____ Do less (than you would normally do).

_____ Do none.

■ Attend to a church responsibility.

_____ Do more (than you would normally do).

_____ Do some.

_____ Do less (than you would normally do).

_____ Do none.

■ Engage in a family activity.

_____ Do more (than you would normally do).

_____ Do some.

_____ Do less (than you would normally do).

_____ Do none.

■ Prepare and/or receive nourishment by eating at home, snacking, or going out.

_____ Do more (than you would normally do).

_____ Do some.

_____ Do less (than you would normally do).

_____ Do none.

■ Do some household task you've been intending to do.

_____ Do more (than you would normally do).

_____ Do some.

_____ Do less (than you would normally do).

_____ Do none.

■ Visit a friend or neighbor.

_____ Do more (than you would normally do).

_____ Do some.

_____ Do less (than you would normally do).

_____ Do none.

■ Do something for personal enrichment, like reading a book, or listening to music.

_____ Do more (than you would normally do).

_____ Do some.

_____ Do less (than you would normally do).

_____ Do none.

■ Complete a job started earlier at your place of employment.

_____ Do more (than you would normally do).

_____ Do some.

_____ Do less (than you would normally do).

_____ Do none.

Probably you would not spend the entire six hours doing only one thing. You would plan to do several things and to leave others undone. That is the way it will be with your congregation's mission. The leader will be prepared to help the group decide what should be emphasized in your congregation's mission.

*From SMALLER CHURCH MISSION STUDY GUIDE, by Henry A. Blunk. Philadelphia: The Geneva Press, 1978. Reprinted and used by permission.

APPENDIX 5-4

Questions for Use in Evaluations of Congregation-Sponsored Workshop, Conference or Seminar-Type Events

The purpose of this instrument is to provide a sampling of questions that might be used in evaluating certain types of events sponsored by congregations. The order in which the questions are presented is not a suggested order, since it is assumed that not all of the items would be used. The numbering of the questions, therefore, is simply for ease of reference. The questions are designed to be used as models of questions which congregations might use *after modifying them to suit their particular needs/circumstances.*

Background Questions (About Participants in the Event)

The following questions about your background will help us to understand possible differences among respondents in their evaluations of this event.

1. What is your age? ____   2. Your sex? ____male ____female

3. What is the number of years you have been a member of or a regular participant in this congregation? ____

4. Did you have a planning and/or leadership role in this event?

    1 ____ yes   2 ____ no

5. How would you evaluate the following aspects of the event? (Select ONE response for each item listed.)

	Very Good	Good	Average	Poor	Very Poor
Leadership	____	____	____	____	____
Meeting design	____	____	____	____	____
Materials used	____	____	____	____	____
Group process	____	____	____	____	____
Overall content	____	____	____	____	____

6. As a result of attending this event, did you increase your knowledge (skills, understanding, whatever was the intended goal of the event) in . . . financial stewardship (strategies for evangelism, teaching adolescents, etc.)?

    1 ____yes, to a great extent   3 ____no, not really
    2 ____yes, somewhat   4 ____not sure

    If "no," what would help you in this area?

7. Do you think the amount of time allocated to various components of this event (retreat, workshop, seminar, etc.) was:

	Too Little	About Right	Too Much
Devotions/worship...............................			
Fellowship opportunities.......................			
Personal time.......................................			
Study time...			
Formal presentations............................			
Small group discussion..........................			
Panel discussion...................................			
Other_____..............			

8. Please check the one response that best represents your evaluation of the following aspects of this event.

	Strongly Agree	Agree	Disagree	Strongly Disagree
I felt free to be open and honest in small group sessions......................................				
I know more about this subject than I did before I attended this event..............				
The accommodations provided for this meeting were adequate............................				
Participants were friendly and made everyone feel included in the group				

(List other items and goals of the event that you would like evaluated.)

9. How well would you say you understood the purpose of this meeting?
   1 ____very well   2 ____fairly well   3 ____not very well   4 ____not at all

10. If another workshop of this type were offered would you attend?
    1 ____yes, definitely   3 ____no, probably not
    2 ____yes, probably   4 ____no, definitely not

    If "no," why is this the case?

11. What topics (and speakers) would you suggest for future events of this type?

12. What topic would you particularly like to see included in a future workshop event?

13. Please rate the resources used during the course of the workshop.

	Very Useful	Useful	Not Useful
Resource A...			
Resource B...			

(continue listing resources to be evaluated)

14. a. What do you feel are the most important concerns in the area of ____(whatever was the topic of the event)?
    b. Were there concerns addressed adequately during the course of this workshop (seminar)?
       1 ____most were   2 ____some were   3 ____some were not   4 ____most were not

15. Were any points of view expressed during this event with which you are not comfortable? 1____yes   2____no
    If "yes," what were they?

16. What would you say was the most outstanding new experience/information you gained at this event?

17. a. What did you understand to be the goal(s) of this event?
    b. To what extent would you say that this goal was realized?

    1 ＿＿fully realized
    　　　　　　　　　　2 ＿＿to a great extent   3＿＿somewhat
    4＿＿only minimally   5＿＿not at all

18. What do you wish would have happened at this event that didn't happen, if anything?

19. What about the timing of this event? Was it a good time for you?
    1 ＿＿very good   2 ＿＿not good, but manageable   3 ＿＿somewhat difficult   4 ＿＿very bad

20. What month of the year (time of the week, time of the day) would you recommend for scheduling of future events of this kind?

21. What about the cost of attending this event (where applicable)? Did you find it was reasonable or too high?
    1 ＿＿reasonable   2 ＿＿too high

22. Please give us any suggestions you might have about how future events of this type could be improved.

23. Is there anything else that you would like to say to the planning committee or leadership of this event? If so, please use the space remaining to do so.

CHAPTER 6

Methods for Congregational Studies

The primary purpose of research is to solve a problem or answer an important question. This is the purpose of *any* research and not just congregational studies. The questions posed and the problems which can be solved are numerous, and there are almost as many possible research procedures as there are subjects of study. In this book, we limit our subject matter somewhat to the congregation, and also assume that the questions we ask and the problems we hope to solve are of a practical nature. In other words, we hope actually to *use* the results of our research to help further the goals of the church.

Research is another name for inquiry. As mentioned in a previous chapter, "In the broadest sense, everyone does research. That is, everyone gathers information, tests it against experience, and acts in a way which seems appropriate." We all seek to understand our surroundings and to do so we constantly gather, process and analyze information, eventually drawing conclusions. This process, which occurs consciously and unconsciously may result in accurate "findings," but it can also lead to faulty conclusions because of its typically *casual* nature. Casual inquiry is prone to many mistakes, which is the reason we have stressed social scientific techniques of research in this book. This is not to say that social scientific techniques remove the possibility for error. They do not. Yet they do guard against many sources of error through the use of logic, systematic inquiry, objectivity, sampling techniques, the replication of results, by being open to new (even negative) input, and through the use of hypothesis testing.

Pastors, denominational leaders, laypersons and others with little research background may suspect that social scientific research is always heavily statistical and as such is beyond their ability. There also may be the preconception that the results of such "numbers oriented" research will have little to say to them. After all, their problems involve *people*, not numbers, and are too complex to be reduced to some statistical formula. Perhaps some of the stereotypes of social research have

been dispelled in the previous chapters and observing how varied research can be. Throughout the book we have seen emphasis on participant observation, interviews, oral histories, and other "soft" or subjective research techniques as well as the "hard" or numerically oriented procedures involving questionnaires, census data, church statistics and the like. It also should be clear that a complete investigation of any question or problem will normally require a *variety* of complementary research techniques.

This methodological chapter is designed to be a brief overview of methods and procedures anyone can use in conducting research on the congregation. It is an overview in that thorough coverage of this subject would require at least two books, one on research methods and another on statistics. Obviously, we cannot include full treatment of every topic. Our purpose here is to provide simple usable tools. We should add that our emphasis is on *social scientific research methods*, particularly sociological methods. If further help is needed the reader can refer to the previous chapters, which offer practical suggestions in techniques appropriate for investigating context, identity, program and process. The identity chapter, for instance, includes considerable methodological detail on anthropological/ethnographic research which we have chosen not to repeat here. More technical assistance is available in many statistics and methods texts published by social scientists.[1]

6.1 The Cyclical Research Process

Research is not simply a matter of collecting and analyzing data. It is a process that should proceed through a series of well defined steps, which usually end in a set of recommendations for action and often in the need for further research. The tendency of research to create new questions has led us to diagram the process in a circular fashion, as seen in chart 1.

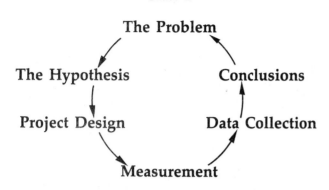

Chart 1

6.1.1 *The Problem*

The starting point for any research project is the statement of the problem or the research question. No one does research for the sake of doing research; there is always something that the researcher wants to discover. Usually the problem can be posed as a question which begins with why, what or how. Why is our church not growing? Why did the church council turn down the proposal for an elderly housing project? How can our church reach blacks in the community? What kind of worship format should this Episcopal church use?

Often the need for research surfaces in awareness of a problem or a "mess," a term used in an earlier chapter. The need to do or change something must be translated into a question to be answered before meaningful research can begin. Without a clearly stated question to be answered, research may deteriorate into aimless data-gathering. This is an essential first step. For example, Hope United Church of Christ, which has a history of brief pastorates, might pose the difficult research question, "What factors led to the resignations of our last three pastors?" Unfortunately, such a direct question might be too explosive in Hope Church, which blames the former pastors for its problems. So the study committee might want to ask the question, "How can our programs be more effective?" and then incorporate the role of pastoral leadership and conflict over programs into the project design.

6.1.2 *The Hypothesis*

What do you expect to find through your research? An hypothesis is essentially an informed hunch or expectation which helps to focus research on an issue or a series of issues which are central to the research question. In some cases a research project will include a very structured test of a hypothesis. For instance, the hypothesis might be that an evangelistic outreach campaign would lead to a significant increase in Sunday school enrollment. In many other cases, however, the

hypothesis and the research itself will not be so structured. It may be hypothesized that a negative vote on a particular program proposal was due to the conflict between a church's identity and the new program. No real test can be performed to totally confirm or deny this informed hunch, yet stating it beforehand can help focus the direction of the research.

In many cases a study committee or an outside consultant may not be able to develop any expectations prior to beginning the research project. Their knowledge may be so limited or the problem may be so difficult that preliminary research is necessary to develop a plausible theory which might answer the research question. Close observation and interviews should be employed in that case, out of which hypotheses would probably emerge.

6.1.3 *Project Design*

Many different kinds of research projects can be designed to answer a particular research question. Essentially, the committee must look at its methodological "workbench" and select the proper tools. The selections made will be based on the type of research question being addressed, the type and number of subjects, the resources available (both time and money), the skill of the researchers and the kind of answer needed to the question. There are several basic *research designs*: needs analysis, case study, experiment and correlational (these will be discussed in depth at a later point). Within these overall designs various *research procedures* are available. A case study (or ethnography)[2] of a congregation may include participant observation along with unstructured interviews. A correlational design, on the other hand, might include a questionnaire or a schedule-structured interview. In some instances two or more research designs, such as the case study and the experiment, may be combined in a research project along with appropriate research procedures which accompany each. The study committee must choose which designs and procedures are to be employed.

6.1.4 *Measurement*

The study team may decide in the project design phase to use a questionnaire, an interview form or another type of data collection instrument. These instruments are constructed in the measurement stage. Questions are formulated, scales are developed, and experimental procedures are designed. Social scientists call much of this "operationalization." For instance, the team may want to measure the level of religious commitment among church members. To do so through a survey, one must first define the concept and then design questions which actually measure religious commitment as you have defined it. If you want to interview older members rather than having them fill out a questionnaire, an interview guide must be drawn up, complete with probing, open-ended questions.

6.1.5 Data Collection

Once a problem has been identified, the hypotheses stated, a research project designed and data collection instruments produced, it is time to collect the data. Data is simply another word for information or facts, of course, so the data can be in the form of numbers, or at the other extreme, it can be in the form of elaborate answers to interview questions. In either case, the data must be collected, not haphazardly, but in accordance with systematic procedures decided by the study team and outlined in the project design.

6.1.6 Data Analysis

The data collected must be analyzed in order to answer the research question. This by itself is a good reason not to collect too much data. Only so much data can be meaningfully analyzed, digested and understood by a pastor or a study team. Statistics may be used in this stage, depending on the type of data collected.

6.1.7 Conclusions

The final stage is to draw conclusions from the research. What has been discovered? Can the original research question be answered? Have the hypotheses been supported or shown to be false? Usually the conclusions are more complex than originally expected and the hypotheses are partially confirmed and partially disconfirmed. But if the research has been well designed some conclusions can be made which can assist the pastor, committee, board, denominational worker, or layperson in dealing with the original problem. At the same time the results of the study may call for additional research to answer new questions which emerged along the way.

6.2 Key Concepts

In the main body of this chapter we will describe various research designs, procedures and techniques in detail. To do so, however, requires the use of certain terms, some of which may not be familiar. We define these terms and concepts below so there will be no confusion.

6.2.1 The Variable

1. *Attribute*. An attribute is a character or quality that can be used to describe something. "Small" is an attribute that some churches have. "Conflicted" might be another attribute, as would "evangelistic."

2. *Variable*. A variable is a logical *set* of attributes. Thus, church size can be seen as a variable which is composed of the attributes, large, medium, small, tiny, etc. Church harmony would be another variable (composed of a set of attributes ranging from idyllic harmony to murderous conflict). Denomination would be another variable, as would the type of "myth" under which a congregation operates.

3. *Independent Variable*. This is a variable which is presumed to cause or influence a change in another variable. For instance, if we hypothesize that the demographic variable of population change is related to church membership change, such that we expect a growing population to foster church membership growth, then the independent variable in this case is population change. We presume that it "causes" or at least influences churches to either grow or decline.

4. *Dependent Variable*. The dependent variable is the variable which has been caused or influenced. In the above case, the dependent variable was church membership change. Normally, the dependent variable is the key variable in a research design. You are generally seeking to identify those factors (independent variables) which influence a particular dependent variable.

5. *Control Variable*. A control variable is used to see if a relationship between two other variables remains the same under different conditions or among several different groups. Thus, we might ask if the relationship between population growth and church growth holds among both regional and neighborhood-oriented congregations. Membership dispersion would be our control variable in this case. Similarly, it might be expected that a relationship between two variables is stronger among Baptist churches than among Episcopal churches. The control variable here is denomination. In *many* instances a relationship will be stronger among certain groups than among others.

6.2.2 Association

1. *Relationship Between Variables*. An association or relationship between variables exists when one variable changes in value and there tends to be a corresponding change in another variable. We might hypothesize, for instance, a relationship between congregational liberalism on theological issues and support for social issues. As congregational liberalism increases (independent variable) we expect support for social issues to

also increase (dependent variable). If this were true, we could say that an association or a relationship existed between the two variables.

2. *Causation.* Causation implies that one variable actually causes, determines, or produces the change in another variable. It is impossible to actually prove causation using statistical procedures. You can only infer causation, because something else, which is unknown to you, may actually be producing the change. Rule of thumb: do not use the word "cause" in your research reports, use relationship or association.

3. *Strength of Association.* Relationships between variables can range from weak to strong, and measures exist which indicate the strength of an association. For instance, if all churches in areas growing in population are growing in membership, and all churches in declining areas are declining, the relationship would be very strong (in this case a perfect association). If *most* churches in growing areas are growing, the relationship is strong, but not perfect; and if there is only a slight tendency for areas which are growing in population to have growing churches, then the association is weak.

4. *Statistical Significance.* This refers to a measurement of the likelihood that a relationship occurred by chance. It does not necessarily mean that the finding is substantively important, only that it is trustworthy in terms of probability. Any time one draws a sample (see the description of sampling below), even using the best procedures, there is a chance that the sample does not truly represent the population. To say a finding is "statistically significant" means that there is an acceptably low probability that the relationship was produced by an odd sample rather than by a true relationship between variables. Typical levels of significance are 5 chances in 100 (or the .05 level of significance) or 1 chance in 100 (the .01 level of significance) that the finding resulted from chance alone. In general, stronger relationships and larger samples are more likely to produce "significant" findings.

In practical terms the researcher will do a test of significance to see if the finding can be trusted. If it can, the researcher must then turn to the strength of the relationship or the degree of difference between groups in order to draw conclusions about how important or meaningful are the findings.

5. *Direction of Association.* Relationships can be either "positive" or "negative." A positive relationship occurs when an increase in the independent variable tends to produce a corresponding increase in the dependent variable (or when one decreases, the other tends to decrease). A negative or inverse relationship occurs when an *increase* in the independent variable tends to

produce a *decrease* in the dependent variable (or vice versa).

6.2.3 Sampling

1. *Population.* This refers to a complete set of individuals, groups, objects, etc. All of the components (elements) which make up the set have something in common which allow them to be identified as part of the population. All churches in the United States would be a population. All United Church of Christ congregations would be another, smaller population. The members of one church would be yet another population.

2. *Sample.* A sample is a subset or a part of a population. One samples a pot of stew with the assumption that a spoonful will be representative of the entire pot. Similarly, one draws a sample of church members for study with the assumption that results obtained within the sample will hold for the larger congregation.

3. *Element.* An element is a single unit of a population. If the population is all UCC churches, each congregation would be an element.

4. *Random Sample.* A sample is random when it has been chosen in such a manner that all elements in a population had an equal chance of being selected. A computer, a calculator (only certain models) or a table of random numbers is normally used to draw such a sample.

5. *Systematic Sample.* A systematic sample is drawn by selecting every "nth" person from the population. In other words, to choose a sample of forty persons from a membership list of four hundred names one could select every tenth person on the list. A systematic sample approximates a random sample if the first element on the list is selected randomly. This can be done by using a calculator which can generate random numbers or by using a table of random numbers which the researcher can find in the back of most statistics texts. Such tables are simply lists of numbers randomly generated by a computer.

6. *Accidental Sample.* This is the worst type of sample because it is drawn haphazardly rather than randomly or systematically. One cannot be sure that such a sample actually represents the population. Handing questionnaires to fifteen people after a worship service who happen to stay late talking would be an accidental sample of the worshippers. The fact that these persons stayed late while others left may mean that they rely on the church more heavily for social interaction or that they are all of a particular clique within the church. In any event, there exists the possibility that the persons

chosen in an accidental sample differ systematically from those who were not chosen.

7. *Stratified Sample.* In a stratified sample elements of the population are divided into subgroups (or strata) and then elements to be included in the sample are selected randomly from each of the *strata* rather than from the entire population. This insures that certain groups within the population are adequately represented in the sample. For instance, in a study dealing with age and satisfaction with worship, to ensure that enough elderly persons are included in a sample researchers might divide the congregation into five age strata and then sample the appropriate number of members from each strata. This would ensure that the proportion of elderly persons included in the sample is the same proportion that is in the total congregation.

8. *Statistic.* A statistic is a number which describes some characteristic of a sample. Samples have various characteristics: range, dispersion, medians, average values, etc. Measures of these characteristics are called statistics.

6.2.4 Measures of Central Tendency

1. *Mean.* The average score or value. To calculate, add all scores and divide by the total number of scores. The mean is affected by extreme scores, and as such is of limited utility when dealing with income, housing values and other demographic measures which may have extreme values. For instance, if among five people, two earn $8,000 per year, one earns $9,000, one earns $10,000 and one earns $500,000, the mean income of this group is $107,000. This is the average income, but it is ten times the income of all except one person.

2. *Median.* The middle score or value. Half fall above the median, half fall below it. The median is not affected by extreme scores. Census data normally reports income and housing values in terms of the median. In the illustration given above, the median income is $9,000. Two people earn more and two people earn less.

3. *Mode.* The score or value which occurs most frequently. Again referring to our illustration, the mode among the five persons would be $8,000. If all five persons earned the same amount, the mean, median and mode would all be the same.

6.3 Designing a Research Project

6.3.1 Developing a Research Question

The translation of a problem into a researchable question is often not easy. Still, one should resist the temptation to begin research on a problem without a clear statement of the research question. When the question is relatively clear, such as how can an Anglo church begin to reach Hispanics, formulating the research question is a matter of translating the raw question into one that is specific and measurable, and that will not be too expensive to investigate. For instance, a research question might deal with barriers which keep Hispanics out of the church or it might be concerned with the relative usefulness of several programs designed to help the church reach this population. We might phrase a research question in this manner: "Will a Spanish language department increase Hispanic attendance at Little Hope Baptist Church?" Alternatively, one could ask, "Why do Hispanics who attend the services of Little Hope Baptist Church rarely return?" These questions may seem overly specific, but at the local church level a problem should be translated into a very specific question.

In many other cases, when the problem is more of a mess, the development of a research question is not easy. Such is the situation in several of the case studies presented in chapter one. In fact, in each case a number of questions could be addressed. The key in such situations is to first develop an *objective.* How would you like to see the situation resolved? In the case of Heritage United Methodist, the objective might be to gain a better understanding of the congregation so a similar aborted ministry could be avoided. On the other hand, the minister may want to know the types of ministries the church would accept, or how can she move the church toward acceptance of the elderly housing project. Because the objective is different in each case, the research question will also be different. Begin with the problem, state how you would like to see it resolved, and formulate a question or series of questions, that when answered will help move the church toward the objective.

6.3.2 Choosing an Appropriate Research Design

There are many research techniques or procedures, but only a few major types of research design. We will deal with four here. The reader will note that certain "types" of research are not dealt with as unique research designs. Evaluation research and action research are two which may be familiar. They are not considered separately because they are distinct from other research procedures only in their goals. Similarly, the ethnographic interview and participant observation are considered research procedures rather than research designs.[3]

1. *Needs Analysis.* In a previous chapter needs assessment assumes a major emphasis. A research design for needs assessment involves the use of good

research procedures to look at the needs in a church or in a community. There is no stated problem, nor a true research question, other than, "What are our needs?" Questionnaires, interviews, panels, and other sound research procedures may be employed, but only to point to needs, not to answer any particular question. The most frequent use of this type of research design is in strategy planning. A church or denominational judicatory (association, synod, conference, etc.) may study its constituency, context, programs, processes, structure, and identity in order to determine needs. It then formulates a series of broad objectives designed to address the needs, sets specific goals so success or failure can be measured, and outlines action plans through which the goals can be accomplished.

2. *Case Study.* The case study is a legitimate research design and is one that may involve a variety of research procedures. A case study is an intensive study of a single subject or a group and includes no control. It is used most often to illustrate a classic example of some form of behavior or some type of group. Other uses are to provide a detailed description of a particularly unusual phenomenon or to provide evidence that a widely held belief is not true. An ethnographic study would fall under this type of research design. It may or may not include research procedures which differ from other types of case studies.

3. *The Experiment.* An experiment tests a specific hypothesis through the manipulation of an independent variable. The researcher is trying to change the attitudes or behavior of his or her subjects through some kind of treatment or experimental stimulus. This can be anything from a series of sermons, a film, a training event, even a series of electric shocks under the seats of a sample of members. The research question is whether or not the stimulus will produce the desired change among the subjects. Measurements determine the extent of the change and indicate whether the hypothesis has been supported or shown to be false.

4. *Correlational Designs.* The aim of a correlational design is to discover and measure the relationship between two or more variables. No attempt is made actually to manipulate one of the variables, as is done in an experiment; rather the purpose is to identify relationships which already exist in the social world. Efforts to discover factors related to church growth are often correlational, especially those which look at the impact of demographic influences. Are longer pastorates associated with church growth? Are regional churches less affected by their demographic environments? Is the proportion of elderly members in a church related to the likelihood of starting new ministries? Is the social class of laity associated with hymn prefer-

ence? These and many other questions can be answered through correlational designs.

6.3.3 *Customizing the Research Design*

The research question chosen will not totally determine which research design is selected, but it will influence the decision. Certain questions are more easily researched using correlational designs, while others are best addressed using experimental procedures. Still others will practically defy the development of an appropriate design. In all cases considerable effort must be made to customize a given project design. Each problem is unique and calls for a unique solution.

Often in congregational studies it is necessary to combine two different research designs in order really to understand the problem. For instance, correlational designs can be combined with case studies when a close look is needed at exceptions to the rule or at prototypical examples. Case study data is particularly useful to have when writing a report of findings for an audience not familiar with research. Case examples provide life and understanding to a statistical report and can make the difference in whether it is believed or doubted.

In all cases, the focus of a research project should be on producing useful findings. As long as the techniques are used appropriately, the study team should feel free to customize as much as possible. Above all, a question should not be chosen on the basis of how easy it will be to investigate. This often happens in Doctor of Ministry projects, and it is unfortunate. Also, it should not be assumed that only one type of research design is legitimate. This is a flaw of some Doctor of Ministry programs which require all students to use experimental designs.

6.4 Needs Analysis: The Simplest Design

The aim of needs analysis is to assess needs so that priorities can be established and a program developed to address the needs. In congregational studies, this research results in a ministry or in an improvement in an area of ministry rather than in an evaluation of a present ministry. Although it calls for research at a very basic level, needs analysis can perform a critical role for the church, both by surfacing hidden needs and by creating a sense of ownership of the program suggestions which may emerge from the process.

For instance, it is possible to imagine that had Heritage United Methodist Church conducted strategy planning and an in depth analysis of church and community needs, the need for an elderly housing project could have emerged from the laity of the church as a priority. If such were the case, there may have been little difficulty in gaining approval. Such an exercise may also have been especially informative to the new pastor in showing her what the members saw as their most pressing needs. Their perceived needs may have been far different from what she may have expected.

Techniques of Data Collection

1. *One-Shot Social Survey (Questionnaire)*. A survey is often conducted in a church in order to gather information about felt needs and to collect data for a church profile. "One-shot" means that the survey is only done once, unlike the experiment where it may be administered two or more times (in order to detect change). The questionnaire is normally distributed at a worship service or mailed to members. It will be composed of a series of questions, most of which can be answered by checking a box. A few questions will be "open-ended," requiring the respondent to write out a response in his or her own words.

When collecting information about needs or when building a church profile there is no reason for complex data analysis. In fact, all that is required is the creation of a *frequency distribution*. An example of this is seen in chart 2.

Obviously, an actual survey would have many more questions than the one in chart 2. Still, the method of tabulation would be the same. Background questions could be used to develop a profile of members and their social characteristics compared to those of community residents. Need oriented questions show which needs in the church and in the community are deemed more important by church members. Analysis is simple. A list of the most critical needs can be made by simply circling the questions to which the largest numbers of people selected as having, "High Priority/Needs Immediate Attention."

Another, more specific, example of needs analysis is the case of a pastor who wanted to better address the needs of church members during sermons.[4] Over several weeks the pastor developed a questionnaire that was designed to identify needs that members had that might be dealt with in preaching. The results of this survey, which was taken over several consecutive Sundays, revealed the congregation's major felt needs, the specific needs which could be addressed in sermons and whether or not the pastor had dealt with any of the needs during that Sunday's message. In this case, the needs that surfaced primarily dealt with preaching, rather than the many needs which might surface in a complete self-study. Many other areas of ministry can

also be considered by using a very specific survey and conducting the simple analysis employed in chart 2.

2. *Analysis of Census Data*. As shown in the chapter on context, and in other chapters as well, data from the United States Census can be of great value to a church. Such data is used in a variety of ways, but its most frequent use by the congregation is in some form of needs analysis. By obtaining census maps from a large public library, a college library, a state data center or from the Superintendent of Documents in Washington, D.C., it is possible to locate a church within its census tract, minor civil division, or some other unit of census geography (see the earlier chapter on context). Armed with this location, very detailed data can be obtained on that geographical area from Census Bureau documents, private data suppliers, or from a denominational research office (in most cases).

Raw data from the census may not mean much at first glance. Does, for instance, the fact that 50 percent of the housing near a church is renter occupied mean anything? Is this level high or low and does it call for any special type of ministry or outreach on the part of the church? A consultant can be of great help here, but the pastor, a staff member, or layperson can begin to draw inferences when data for the tracts surrounding their church is compared to other tracts around the city or county. If they know the area well, it should be relatively easy to develop some real insights from the data. From such insights, needs in the community should also begin to emerge. What are the blind spots of the church? Who in the community is not being reached or ministered to? These questions can be answered with an adequate knowledge of the church and the community.

3. *Interviews*. Interviews also have an important place in needs analysis research. Often the true needs of a church are only revealed through much probing. A questionnaire may be sufficient to collect "hard facts" when the issues are clear and salient to the respondents. However, if deep-seated problems in the church need to be surfaced, if long answers are required, and if trust must be developed in order to receive a meaningful response, then an interview is appropriate.

One way to conduct an interview is with an interview guide (or schedule, as they are often termed). This guide is half outline and half questionnaire. Questions, many purposefully general, are included to get the subject(s) talking. The guide keeps the interview on track and also prevents the interviewer from forgetting the questions he or she needed to ask. If done well, rapport can be developed and the respondent encouraged to "open up." Some people resist candor, but experience shows that most people are eager to have someone really listen to their opinions. They may only give brief answers on a questionnaire, but in an interview they may be willing to talk for hours.

6.5 The Case Study: Magnifying an Example

The purpose of the case study is to draw inferences from the intensive study of a single group, chosen either because it is a prototypical example of some phenomena, because it is rare, unusual or unfamiliar, or because it represents a disconfirmation of conventional wisdom in an area. In some projects more than one case study is used and comparisons are made, but in each situation the cases are studied individually. An effort is made to describe the group, organization or subculture in great detail with the aim of gaining an intuitive understanding which can be communicated to others.

Examples are the best method of teaching. Case studies provide very detailed examples so that a phenomenon can be understood not only in abstract, but as it really operates. A good case study should allow readers mentally to put themselves "into" the group or organization being studied and to feel they know "what makes it tick." This is especially critical when studying complex organizations like churches which do not function primarily through the operation of rational bureaucratic procedures. There is such subtlety and rampant use of informal rules, that the reading of minutes, studying of bylaws and hearing of sermons cannot hope to give a complete picture of a church and its true operation.

In some situations case studies are used simply to represent many other similar examples. Even though there are differences, to completely understand one gives more knowledge than a superficial understanding of many. In other instances the case study is used to describe something that is rarely seen (or simply has not been described before). It may be a disconfirmation in the sense that it can show that an example that exists obviously disconfirms a theory which states that the phenomenon *cannot* exist. More frequently, however, a case study is needed to describe the rare or unusual. It may be well known that such examples exist, but because they are so unfamiliar, complete understanding of them is often lacking.

The case study should be conducted with a clear purpose in mind. This should go beyond a mere desire to understand an interesting case. What questions can the case answer? There should be a clear research question which is to be addressed. If a goal is to determine the congregation's "myth," can this knowledge help the church change?

6.5.1 Techniques of Data Collection

1. *Personal interview.* In the personal interview the researcher asks respondents a series of questions designed to obtain answers pertinent to the research problem. In most cases only one person will be interviewed at a time, but occasionally group interviews can be a useful variation on this method. This is especially true when the interviewer is as interested in group dynamics as in the answers to questions being posed. One major way interviews vary is in the degree of structure.

Schedule-Structured Interview. In the most structured form of an interview the respondent is asked a series of standard questions and must answer by selecting from a set of fixed response categories. The questions, their wording and their sequence is fixed and identical for each respondent. In a real sense this form of interview is virtually identical to the questionnaire, with the only difference being that the interviewer checks responses on the form rather than the respondent. This type of interview is easy to quantify and analyze with statistical techniques, and since the interviewer is in control of the situation, all of the questions will be answered and the meaning of unclear questions can be explained. The schedule-structured interview is normally used when mail questionnaires, phone interviews, or other procedures for administering questionnaires are not likely to produce a high enough return rate or if there is some doubt that respondents will answer all of the questions. It is expensive and time-consuming, but worthwhile in many situations. Virtually all of the high quality national public opinion polls use this method.

Despite its good points, the schedule-structured interview is not often used in the case study. The reason for this is in the closed-ended nature of responses. Rather than gaining detailed insights about a congregation, this procedure only gives yes-no, high-medium-low, agree-disagree type responses.

Structured Open-Ended Interview. This type of interview is often used in case study designs. Questions are designed to be answered in more than one word and explanations for particular responses by subjects are welcome. An interview which deals with conflict in the church might ask, "What are the issues which cause the most serious arguments during deacon meetings?" A project concerned with redeveloping the image of a church might ask members, "When was the greatest ministry era of this church?" Each question would be asked in the same order and the interviewer would write down responses on the schedule. If possible,

Chart 2

Summary of Responses to Membership Survey

I. **Social Background Characteristics**

			Number	%
1.	Sex	Male	56	41.5
		Female	79	58.5
			135	100.0
2.	Age	10-15	19	14.1
		16-21	12	8.9
		22-35	13	9.6
		36-55	40	29.6
		56-65	32	23.7
		66 & up	19	14.1
			135	100.0

II. **Mission Opportunity Responses**

1. Need to set a goal for membership growth?

	Number	%
Not needed in community	17	12.6
Not appropriate for our church	31	23.0
Low priority at this time	12	8.9
Only moderate priority at this time	28	20.7
High priority/Needs immediate attention	47	34.8
	135	100.0

2. Consider new ministries with persons living in institutions such as prisons and mental hospitals?

	Number	%
Not needed in community	27	20.0
Not appropriate for our church	21	15.5
Low priority at this time	46	34.1
Only moderate priority at this time	32	23.7
High priority/Needs immediate attention	9	6.7
	135	100.0

3. Explore the possibility of a vacation Bible school for neighborhood children.

	Number	%
Not needed in community	7	5.2
Not appropriate for our church	2	1.5
Low priority at this time	27	20.0
Only moderate priority at this time	43	31.8
High priority/Needs immediate attention	56	41.5
	135	100.0

interviews should also be tape recorded. Key information can easily be lost if the researcher cannot write fast enough or has a poor memory. Some will not want to be recorded, of course, but if the interviewer says, "I want to record this so I won't miss anything" and then turns on a tape recorder, very few people will ask that it be turned off. Experience also shows that people forget about the recorder very quickly and make comments that an interviewer would not want to lose.

In many cases a researcher will combine this type of interview with the schedule-structured interview. It is useful to obtain factual information, such as the background characteristics of respondents, the number of pastors over the last ten years and other data which calls for fixed rather than open response categories.

This type of interview is difficult to translate into numbers. With much work, long responses can be categorized and subjected to statistical analysis, but this may not always be worth the effort. The key purpose of this method is to obtain detailed, subjective information about a complex phenomenon. It is up to the researcher to draw his or her insights from the data and the quality of the analysis which results is greatly dependent on that ability.

The Unstructured Interview. In this form of interview no prespecified set of questions is used, nor are questions asked in any specific order. Respondents are simply encouraged to tell about their experiences, to describe events which they deem important to the issue being considered, and to reveal their attitudes and opinions as they see fit. The interviewer probes from time to time and brings the respondent back to the subject when he or she begins to stray too far. If the issue being considered is the decision-making process in the church, a respondent might be asked to describe "how things get done in this church." Such a question may cause some people to launch into a two-hour long discourse about decision making, formal and informal leaders, norms, processes and examples of how the system operates. Another person may simply say, "the pastor, board, and church committees do everything here" and assume he had told all. With such a person, considerable probing is necessary in order to get a complete picture of the situation.

Unstructured interviews may also be used to obtain oral histories of a church if such are needed in a case study. Older members are normally used for this purpose, but in order to get a balanced perspective of later years, some newer members are also needed. Like the previous form of interview, the unstructured interview yields data that is hard to analyze. Often a researcher is confronted with a pile of notes and a box of tapes and must then try to turn these into a coherent report. To do so requires considerable skill and much effort.

The Ethnographic Interview. Interviews differ not only in their structure, but in their goals. The ethnographic interview is directed at developing an ethnography—a descriptive study of a society, subculture, or institution. It is combined with observation (often participant observation) so that key informants and others in the group are continually being informally interviewed about recent events, the meaning of frequently used terms, goals, motives and so forth. An interview schedule is not usually constructed; the researcher simply adopts the role of interviewer when he or she needs information or explanation. The primary goal of ethnography is more descriptive than analytical. For this reason, an ethnographic report does not generally answer a research question, but it gives an understanding of a culture, a people and the way they view their social world.[5] Such diffuse goals are rarely sufficient for a church study committee, however. Rather than producing an ethnography of their church the team may use the tools of ethnographic research in order to help answer their research question.

2. *Participant Observation.* In participant observation the researcher becomes a part of the group being studied. Proponents of this method hold that the only way to understand a social group, particularly one which is unfamiliar, is to immerse oneself in it so that the perspective of the members becomes the observer's own for a time.

Good participant observation is not easy and requires considerable skill on the part of the researcher. We all have our blind spots as well as our areas of strength, and these tend to show up in what we observe (and in what we miss). American women tend to notice color and variations in dress better than men[6]; people from the city miss a great deal when asked to observe rural life. Some people are simply better observers than others. Researchers using this technique had best know their observational strengths and weaknesses before beginning participant observation and take great pains to adjust for these weaknesses.

If done poorly, participant observation is not really scientific research; it is just looking around. In fact, a better term might be participant *investigation* rather than observation, because the researcher is not a passive observer. While actively participating in a congregation or other object of study, the participant observer is constantly asking questions, probing and finding "experts" who are willing to teach informal lessons. Theories are developed along the way and are tested whenever possible. In order to test a theory about conflict management in the church, members might be asked, "What would happen in a business meeting if you proposed that the church ordain women deacons?" Alternatively, the researcher might consciously violate minor behavioral norms in order to discover how members discourage such behavior.

In some cases the period of participant observation is a prologue to a questionnaire or some other quantitative procedure. This is in order to make the research more objective and less open to criticism.[7] The observation tells the researcher what questions should be asked in such a survey.

It is up to the researcher whether or not to tell the members of the group being studied that he or she is conducting a research project. Most social scientists would hold, however, that not to inform one's subjects is highly unethical; others are not quite so adamant. From a purely practical standpoint, it is generally best to inform the group of your purpose. In this way the researcher has an explanation for why he or she is asking so many questions. Also, group members will often show more interest in the researcher if intentions are known.

Good notes are essential in the process and provide another reason to let the group know what you are doing. A researcher should take detailed, concrete notes that accurately describe the situation. Instead of "A showed hostility toward B," the researcher should note, "A scowled and spoke harshly to B, saying several negative things, including, 'I wish you had never joined this church' and 'If you open your mouth again in that meeting, I'll put my fist in it.' He then spit in B's direction and walked out of the room."[8]

3. *Social Survey—Analysis of a Frequency Distribution.* As in a needs analysis, it is often useful in a case study to conduct a social survey. In most situations the purpose of this exercise is to construct a profile of members, their beliefs and attitudes. Often this is done after participant observation or key informant interviewing. The researcher develops a mental profile of the average member and a set of generalizations concerning the degree of diversity in the group, the range of opinions, and the proportion who may deviate from the norm. A survey allows the researcher to objectively test these "theories" and rethink his or her perception of the congregation accordingly. The reader should refer to the previous section on needs analysis for a more complete discussion of this procedure.

6.5.2 *Example: A Study of a Racially Integrated Church*

A recent study of Southern Baptist churches in racially changing communities discovered only a handful of integrated congregations. Because of their rarity, a case study of one or more of these congregations would be of great value. The primary research question might be, "How did this church integrate?" or perhaps, "How is this church able to maintain stable proportions of blacks and whites in its membership?" From these questions a series of hypotheses could be developed, such as "integration is fostered by the fact that socioeconomic differences between whites and blacks are negligible" or "this church was able to achieve stable integration by transforming its identity from a dying white congregation to that of a progressive integrated church." Other hypotheses could also be developed.

To conduct a high quality case study of an integrated congregation, a variety of research procedures could be used. Interviews with the pastor, key laypersons, area denominational leaders, local community residents and others would be a first step. Above all, the researcher would want to seek out the first blacks to join the church and some of the whites who were members at the time. Why did the blacks join this church, and why did the whites either stay or leave? Beyond interviews, the researcher might want to use participant observation, especially if one purpose is to discover why the church remains integrated. The researcher could observe how blacks and whites treat one another, the patterns of interaction before and after worship and whether black and white members socialize during the week. Informal conversations with members could explore surface issues such as whether members really believe that the church can remain integrated, and also expose underlying concerns such as attitudes concerning interracial dating. Finally, a survey could be conducted in order to find out if black and white members differ greatly in income and educational levels, attitudes and so forth. Is race the major cleavage between the groups, or do they differ in other areas?

A case study which used the combination of procedures described above would be of great value to the many churches in racially changing communities. By employing a variety of techniques, better data are collected than if only one research method was employed.

6.6 Experimental Designs: Tests, Comparisons, and Evaluation

In all experiments the researcher tests the effect of a treatment. The treatment may be something simple and direct like a film series or it may be something quite complex and costly like a denomination-wide mass evangelism campaign. When the goal is to evaluate a program, we often call this *evaluation research.* The treatment or program becomes the independent variable in such research and one is trying to detect whether or not the presence of the program actually made a measurable difference on the individuals or groups being studied. There is a dependent variable of interest, and a test is made to see if there is a change in this variable as a result of having had the treatment or used the program. For instance, a denominational mass evangelism campaign is designed to increase baptisms in the cities where it occurs. Having the campaign is the treatment. The dependent variable is the number of baptisms recorded among Baptist churches in the city.

Experimental designs are very widely used in Doctor of Ministry projects. A rather tired example of a D.Min. project is the series of lectures designed to increase biblical knowledge. The pastor selects an experimental group and a control group, with the experimental group hearing the lectures and the control group hearing something else. A pretest confirms that the groups are similar in their knowledge before the experiment and a posttest shows that the experimental group increased slightly in biblical knowledge, while the control group had no such increase.

6.6.1 The Quasi-Experiment

The simplest types of experiments are called "quasi-experiments." They are often used in congregational studies.

The most basic form of quasi-experiment might be termed a *single group panel* study. Here only one group is studied, often an entire church. A measurement is taken on the dependent variable before the treatment, then a treatment is administered and finally a second measurement is taken. For instance, a pastor may want to test the effectiveness of a class designed to train members in personal evangelism. Only a small number volunteer for the program and the pastor would be foolish to use half of these willing recruits as a control group. An interview determines each person's current involvement in evangelistic witnessing and their effectiveness as a witness. The training program (treatment) then proceeds and at its conclusion a second test is made of the participant's evangelistic efforts and effectiveness.

Single group panels can yield very helpful information to a study group and in some cases they may be the only type of experiment possible. Their results, however, are somewhat suspect and the study group should try to include a control or comparison group if it is feasible. Without a control it is not possible to know if the treatment caused the change in one's members or if the change resulted from some other influence. For instance, in the previous illustration, it may have been the *pastor's example* as a witness which was effective rather than the *content* of what he was teaching. Thus,

this experiment was not an adequate test for judging whether this evangelistic training program should be used by other churches or even by this church after the present pastor leaves.

A more sophisticated example of a quasi-experiment uses pre-existing groups for analysis rather than creating new ones using sampling procedures. Richard E. Davies in his book *Handbook for Doctor of Ministry Projects* reported on a project that used school classes as experimental and control groups.[9] Two classes were selected in two different schools, so the researcher had two experimental groups and two control groups. The experiment was designed to decrease feelings of anxiety about death among the students. The experimental groups received a treatment, in this case a series of lectures, but unfortunately the research showed that their fear of death *increased* rather than decreased after the treatment. It seems that high school students do not normally think much about death, but the treatment made them think about it a great deal—resulting in greater anxiety.

In another example reported by Davies,[10] pre-existing groups were again used, but in this case there was no control group. The experiment was designed to test the effectiveness of two settings for learning—a twelve-week class where students met once a week in a small group setting and a one-day retreat. Posttest results showed that the twelve-week class was more effective as a setting for learning than the one day retreat. In this case there were essentially two treatments, with each group being a "control" for the other. A preferable design would have included a third group as a true control, but the example illustrates a fairly acceptable design which has no control.

The quasi-experiment is not as powerful a research technique as is the true controlled experiment. Yet this drawback should not dissuade the pastor or other church professional from using such procedures. They are generally *more* powerful than correlational designs and may be the only option in some church situations. Care must be taken, however, to make sure pre-existing groups studied in a quasi-experiment are as similar as possible. Do not use a Sunday school class of elderly persons as a treatment group and a class of youth as a control. Use groups which represent the same basic age range, sex ratio, racial composition and so forth. In this way the experiment will approximate the procedures used in a true controlled experiment.

6.6.2 The Controlled Experiment

The true controlled experiment is simply a more rigorous form of the experiment than the quasi-experiment. Its rationale and most of the research procedures are the same. There are several types of controlled experiments, all of which use *control groups* and either *random assignment* into groups or some procedure of *matching*. A control group is one which does not receive the treatment or take part in the program being studied. This group is necessary for comparative purposes—to determine if the change which was detected in the treatment group resulted from the actual treatment or from some outside factor. If, for instance, the control group's score on the dependent variable rose just as much as the experimental group, then it would be difficult to explain the change as resulting from the treatment (since the control group did not receive the treatment).

It is important that the experimental group and control group be as similar as possible. If they are not, there exists the possibility that changes in scores on the dependent variable resulted from these pre-existing differences. The experimental group might be older, for instance, and something could happen in society to change the attitudes of older persons quite apart from the treatment. If this were the case, a researcher might incorrectly conclude that the change was due to the treatment. Similarity between the groups is attained by either matching the characteristics of persons in the control and experimental groups, so that there is a similar average age, sex ratio, and so forth, or by *randomly* assigning persons to the two groups. If random assignment is done correctly, the two groups would not only be similar in age and sex, but on many other background variables as well.

1. *Types of Controlled Experiments*. Chart 3 shows three types of experimental designs, ranging from simple to more complex.

Static Group Comparison. This type of experimental design has a control group and an experimental group. The experimental group receives the treatment (X on the chart), while the control group receives no treatment. A post-test is used to determine whether the treatment had any effect on the experimental group. Average scores for the two groups are compared, and if significantly different, it is assumed that the difference was caused by the treatment (independent variable).

The matching or randomization procedures are intended to insure that the groups would score similarly on the dependent variable prior to the treatment, but the flaw of the design is that there is no way of knowing this to be true. In fact, the difference found in the posttest could have existed *before* the treatment. If such were the case, a faulty conclusion would have been made. For this reason, the static group comparison produces dubious results.

Pretest-Posttest Controlled Experiment. This design is similar to the static group comparison, but with the

obvious difference that a pretest is conducted among both control and experimental groups. This insures that the groups are initially similar in their scores on the dependent variable, or at least that the magnitude of any pre-existing difference is known. Posttest scores are compared to pretest scores in order to detect how much change occurred over time for both experimental and control groups. Then, posttest scores for both groups are compared. If the treatment has had some influence, the change between the pretest and posttest should be greater for the experimental group than for the control group.

It is expected that the control group will show some change, even though it did not receive a treatment. This is due to testing interaction. Subjects may be influenced by the pretest and change their views even without the treatment. This often happens in the church situation when respondents may "reward" their pastor by artificially changing their attitudes on the posttest.

This form of experimental design is frequently used. It deals effectively with the problems of the static group comparison and is fairly simple.

Four Group Design. The four-group design essentially combines the static-group comparison and the pretest-posttest design. As such, it is able to deal with the need for a pretest and also gives an estimate of the amount of testing interaction. Its drawback is primarily in its expense and in the necessity of selecting four groups rather than two.

2. *Sampling in an Experimental Design*. The key to sampling in the experimental design is to insure that the control and experimental groups are very similar. Random assignment of individuals from the population into the two groups using a table of random numbers is an effective way of doing this. However, it should be noted that randomness is not as essential for experimental designs as it is for correlational designs. It is acceptable to use matching procedures instead, which insure that the two groups are similar with respect to age, sex, race, etc.

3. *Scale or Index Construction*. In experimental research an index that measures the dependent variable is often constructed. If the variable to be influenced by a program or treatment is racism, for instance, then a series of questions is included in the survey which tap various aspects of racism. In chart 4 we see an example of 5 questions that were part of an anti-Semitism scale.[11] Each of the questions deals with different aspects of prejudice against Jews and they also vary in intensity. A respondent answers each question by circling one of five possible responses in the Likert format (strongly agree to strongly disagree). To compute the respondent's score on this index, the responses are summed. In this index the total score indicating the highest level

Chart 3

THREE TYPES OF EXPERIMENTAL DESIGNS

1. <u>Static Group Comparison</u>

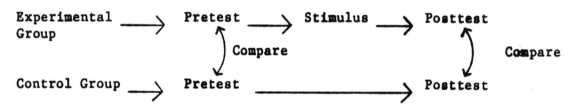

   Comments: Avoids testing interaction, but no assurance groups were
             the same before test.

2. <u>Two Group Pretest-Posttest Design</u>

   Experimental ———→ Pretest ——→ Stimulus ——→ Posttest
   Group   ↕   ↕
                        Compare   Compare
   Control Group ——→ Pretest ————————————————→ Posttest

   Comments: Assures that groups were similar before treatment, does not
             avoid testing interaction (having been pretested, the subject
             figures out what you are doing).

3. <u>Four Group Design</u>

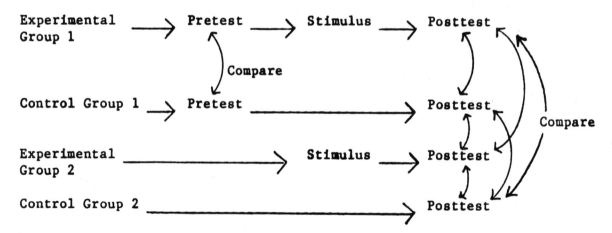

   Comments: Avoids all problems, except complexity.

Chart 4

INDEX CONSTRUCTION AND SUMMATION *

(1) International banking is pretty much controlled by Jews.

5   1. Strongly Agree 2. Agree 3. Uncertain 4. Disagree (5. Strongly Disagree)

(2) Jews are just as honest as other business men.

2   1. Strongly Agree (2. Agree) 3. Uncertain 4. Disagree 5. Strongly Disagree
―
4

(3) You can usually tell whether or not a person is Jewish by the way he looks.

2   1. Strongly Agree (2. Agree) 3. Uncertain 4. Disagree 5. Strongly Disagree

(4) Jews should stop complaining about what happened to them in Nazi Germany.

5   1. Strongly Agree 2. Agree 3. Uncertain 4. Disagree (5. Strongly Disagree)

(5) Jewish employers go out of their way to hire other Jews.

3   1. Strongly Agree 2. Agree (3. Uncertain) 4. Disagree 5. Strongly Disagree

Score = 19   Score indicating highest level of anti-semitism = 5

Score indicating lowest level of anti-semitism = 25

Instructions: Compute scores for all respondents in each group, sum their scores and compute an average (mean) score.

_____

*From The Tenacity of Prejudice: Anti-Semitism in Contemporary America, by Gertrude J. Selznick and Stephen Steinberg, pub. by the Anti-Defamation League of B'nai B'rith as volume 4 in its Patterns of American Prejudice Series. The series is based on the University of California five-year study of anti-Semitism in the United States conducted under an ADL grant.

of prejudice is a 5. To receive this score a respondent would answer all questions by circling the most extreme prejudiced responses. Persons who are the least prejudiced would score a 25.

Scales in which the most extreme scores are all the same are the easiest to sum, because all one must do is add the number value of each response. Usually, however, it is best to vary questions so that, for instance, a highly prejudiced response is a "5" on some questions and a "1" on others. In this way you can make sure that people read the questions and do not simply check the same number for each question. To sum such a scale it is necessary to reverse the scores for items that are worded in a manner opposite to the other questions. Looking at chart 4, we can see that the response to question two is reversed, in order to make its scoring consistent with the other items. The response of a "2" has been crossed out and changed from a "2" to a "4" because the "2" response is similar to the "4" responses on other questions. Once scores are reversed on the necessary items the scale is summed. The hypothetical responses to the example in chart 4 have been summed to produce a score of 19 for this respondent. Each person receives a score and for each group the scores are totalled and an average (mean) is computed. If the aim of the experiment in this case were to reduce anti-Semitism, then we would expect the mean scores on the index to increase (indicating lower prejudice) after the treatment.

4. *Analysis of Experimental Designs.* Analyzing the results of a controlled experiment is normally quite simple. If an index has been used and the hypothesis was that scores on this index should change after the treatment, then analysis only involves comparing pretest and posttest scores. Chart 5 shows some hypothetical results to a controlled experiment designed to reduce anti-Semitism.

In the static group comparison the researcher compares scores on the posttest, which takes place after the treatment. It is assumed that scores for the two groups were the same prior to the treatment, so any difference is due to treatment effects.

In the two group pretest-posttest design the analysis procedure is to compare pretest and posttest scores for the two groups and then to compare the amount of change in each. As seen in the example, the experimental group's mean score increased 8.5 points on the index, while the control group only increased 1.9 points. The fact that the change in the average score was far greater for the experimental group indicates that the treatment had a measurable impact on prejudice.

Analysis of the four-group design is similar to the two group pretest-posttest, with the exception that it is also possible to estimate testing interaction. The posttest scores for the two experimental groups are compared with the difference reflecting the effect of having given a pretest to experimental group 1. Likewise, the posttest scores for the control groups are also compared. In this table the effect of testing interaction is somewhere between 1.9 and 2.3 points. This would indicate a small effect, but one which should be noted in a report of findings.

6.7 Correlational Designs

Many independent variables do not lend themselves to manipulation, thus ruling out the use of experimental designs. There is no way to change the age, birth order, sex, race, etc. of one's subjects, nor would it be possible to alter the size or location of churches as part of an experiment. On the other hand, some manipulation may be possible but is not ethical. For instance, there are ethical problems involved in creating conflict in a church by spreading rumors or in producing many other changes which might be interesting to study.

Correlational designs are often used by researchers who study the congregation. They deal adequately with the issues outlined above and are relatively low in cost. In such designs researchers do not manipulate their subjects in order to measure the effect of a treatment on a dependent variable. Instead, the purpose is to identify relationships which already exist in the social world, but have simply not been described or fully investigated. Rather than creating conflict or moving white churches to black ghettos, the researcher uses the fact that churches can be found in samples which have experienced conflict and that white churches already exist in the black ghettos of our major cities. The effort is then to see if having conflict or being located in a black community is related to a dependent variable of interest.

Two variables that might well co-vary (another way of saying that they are related) are church size and having gymnasiums. We would presume that larger churches would be more likely to have gyms than would smaller churches. Large churches and small churches exist in the church world, as do churches with gyms; we do not need to create one or the other. We simply select a sample of churches and within this sample, we determine whether or not larger churches are more likely to have gyms than are smaller churches.

The major problem with correlational designs is that finding a correlation or an association does not necessarily mean that one has answered the research

Chart 5

ANALYSIS OF EXPERIMENTAL DESIGNS

1. Static Group Comparison

<u>Mean Score on Prejudice Scale</u>

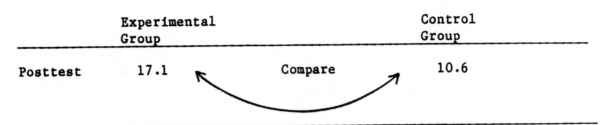

	Experimental Group		Control Group
Posttest	17.1	Compare	10.6

2. Two Group Pretest-Posttest Design

<u>Mean Score on Prejudice Scale</u>

	Experimental Group		Control Group	
Pretest	11.2	Compare	10.6	Compare
Posttest	19.5		12.5	

Compare amount of change *

3. Four Group Design

<u>Mean Score on Prejudice Scale</u>

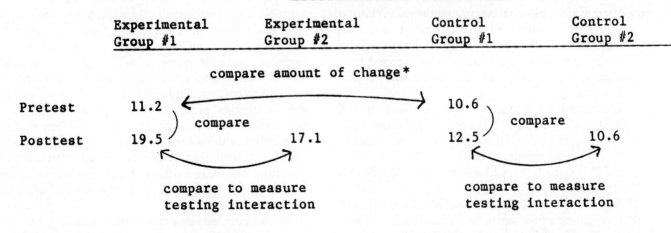

	Experimental Group #1	Experimental Group #2	Control Group #1	Control Group #2
	compare amount of change*			
Pretest	11.2		10.6	
	compare		compare	
Posttest	19.5	17.1	12.5	10.6

compare to measure testing interaction   compare to measure testing interaction

---

* Compute the amount of change between pretest and posttest scores for both groups. Then compare these results to each other.

question. It is often said that "correlation does not imply causation." Church size does not *cause* a church to build gymnasiums any more than smoking directly causes cancer. The variables in both cases are simply correlated. Large churches are *more likely* to have gyms and smokers are *more likely* to contract lung cancer. To really explain the relationship in causal terms requires more research and involves additional variables which help specify the relationship. Often, of course, it is not necessary (or even possible) to truly establish causation. In the case of smoking, the knowledge that it is strongly correlated with cancer and heart disease is enough to justify sanctions which encourage people not to smoke.

Another problem with correlational designs is in determining the *direction of influence*. Which variable is independent and which is dependent? In most cases the question is fairly easy to answer. Gyms are not generally held to produce large churches and cancer does not compel people to smoke. But what about the relationship between ratings of pastoral performance and church growth? Do highly rated pastors influence churches to grow or does church growth lead to a positive image of one's pastor? In most cases both would be true, a situation which makes it difficult to identify the independent variable.

6.7.1 The Social Survey

The most frequently used method of data collection in correlational designs is the social survey. A social survey is a type of a poll, similar to those used to measure public opinion and voting preferences prior to elections. Unlike their use in needs analysis and in case studies, however, they are employed in correlational designs to discover relationships between variables rather than to create a simple frequency distribution. For instance, the Episcopal pastor mentioned in chapter 1 might want to know which age groups are least satisfied with the style of worship in his church. If certain age groups are more likely to be satisfied than others, these two variables (age and satisfaction) can be said to co-vary.

1. *Questionnaire Construction.* The social survey will involve a questionnaire (if filled out by the subjects) or an interview schedule (if filled out by the researcher). Creating such an instrument is an art and before one is finished it is usually best to solicit some help from a research professional.

The questionnaire will be composed of a number of individual questions or items, as they are often termed. Great care should be taken in the wording of each question so they will not be misunderstood or lead to biased results. Above all, the items should include only one question apiece, not two, and should not be worded as to solicit a particular response. An example of a question which makes both mistakes is as follows:

Don't you agree that we should not allow homosexuals to teach in our public schools and corrupt the morals of our children?

Yes _____   No _____

Questions as bad as this are not uncommon, especially if the purpose of the survey is to insure results which confirm one's theory. If, however, the purpose is to measure objectively attitudes and relationships, then such items should not be used. Instead, they can be reworded to ask, "Do you believe that avowed homosexuals should be allowed to teach in public schools?"

Often it is not necessary to construct new survey questions, since there are few which have not been previously asked by social scientists. Tested questions can be borrowed from the National Opinion Research Center's *General Social Survey, The Gallup Poll,* the University of Michigan's *National Election Study,* and from a host of other sources. The reference library or a survey research institute at a college or university are good places to start looking for questions.

Most of the questions included on a survey to be used in a correlational design should be "closed-ended" rather than "open-ended." Closed-ended questions offer a set of fixed responses, from which the respondent chooses one that most closely represents his or her views. Response categories can be Yes/No, Strongly Agree to Strongly Disagree, a set of discrete responses as in a question dealing with marital status (such as, are you: (1) never married, (2) married, (3) separated, (4) divorced, (5) widowed?), a continuum with end points labeled (conservative—(1)—(2)—(3)—(4)—(5)—liberal) or a variety of other formats. If at all possible the researcher should avoid what can be called "list questions." Here the survey asks the respondent to check one or more responses from a long list of possibilities. For instance, a pastor might ask "which of the following influenced you to join this church" and then list twenty or thirty possibilities. List questions like this generally produce poor results because the respondent thinks about each response for about as long as it took the researcher to write the question. They are also difficult to analyze because such a list is not one question, but many, which means that each response category must be treated as a separate variable in an analysis.

Researchers are normally able to think of many more questions to ask on a survey than can be included. A concerted effort should be made to make the instrument as *brief as possible*. Include a few social background variables of interest (age, sex, race, income, etc.), the key independent and dependent variables, an index if one is needed and as few other variables as possible. If the questionnaire is more than a few pages long many people will not fill it out, especially if they receive it by mail. Try for one or two pages, and not more than four at the most. If necessary, have the pages reduced, so that more questions fit on each page. The questionnaire may not be short, but it will at least look short. It is also effective to have a questionnaire professionally printed, rather than typed. This gives the instrument a greater sense of importance and allows more questions to a page than does a typed copy.

Mailing questionnaires to church members is more difficult than it would seem and may lead to dubious results. In congregational studies the questionnaires can normally be handed to members and returned while the study group waits. Mailing may reduce the response rate from 100 percent to well under 50 percent, especially if the questionnaire is long and the subjects are not highly motivated. In some situations mailing may be appropriate (as when trying to reach inactive members), but the researcher should remember that a response rate of less than 50 percent is generally seen as problematic. The research group may find it necessary to use a preparatory mailing, a secondary mailing, follow-up cards, phone calls, small amounts of money included with the questionnaire, and other inducements in order to get the response rate up to 50 percent.

Finally, a questionnaire should always be pretested. This can be done first among one's family, friends and coworkers. Make sure everyone understands the meaning of every question. Do not assume that what is obvious to you is obvious to everyone. A second step is to pretest the questionnaire among a small sample of your members. See if they comprehend the questions and review your preliminary results to insure that the right questions are being asked. If your effort is to measure prejudice and Ku Klux Klan members are scoring as moderates on your scale, then some new items may be needed. Similarly, if you are trying to measure degrees of satisfaction with a congregation, and a pretest shows very little variation in levels of satisfaction, then more sensitive measures may be needed. Pretesting is a critical step, yet one which is often skipped because of deadlines or because of unfortunate presumption on the part of the researcher. Do not make this mistake!

2. *Drawing a Sample*. It is rarely possible in survey research to have every member of the population being studied fill out your questionnaire. This is especially true when the population is very large, like the United States population. In such situations, a sample is drawn and the results are then *generalized* to the larger population. National samples are carefully drawn, usually including 1500 to 2500 persons, and the responses of these persons are taken to represent the entire American public. It may surpise some to know that even the 1980 census made extensive use of sampling. Questions on income, housing, and many other areas were only included on a "long form" which was sent to only twenty percent of U.S. households.

In the church situation the researcher is likely to be dealing with relatively small populations. And the first step in drawing a sample is to identify just what is the appropriate population. Are you interested in generalizing your results to all members of your denomination? If this is the case, then all of these persons would constitute your population. If, however, you are only interested in generalizing your results to the members of your congregation, then the population will be considerably smaller.

In some cases it is not even necessary to draw a sample. The population may include only fifty churches in a city or the members of a single church. In such cases a sample is unnecessary because a researcher can include the entire population in his or her study. Do not draw a sample only because it seems more like "real research." Interview or give a questionnaire to everyone if it is physically possible (and if you have a good probability of receiving a response).

Once a population has been realistically defined (do not, for instance define babies and preliterate children as part of a population which must fill out questionnaires), and you have decided that a sample is necessary, several more questions must be answered. How large will be the sample? Methodology texts may say, "the larger, the better," but be realistic. A typical rule of thumb is to try for at least 100. A sample of less than 100, perhaps as few as 60, is acceptable, but may cause analysis problems if the variables of interest are not well divided or if they contain more than two response categories each. By "not well divided," we mean that if out of two response categories, nearly everyone selects only one of the choices. Thus, investigating the correlates of hard drug use in a church would require a very large sample, because very few persons are likely to be found who actually use hard drugs in most churches. This means that when conducting research in a church with an adult membership of less than 100, it will be necessary to use the entire population, rather than a sample.

A table of random numbers is one of the best ways to draw a random sample. Suppose we want to draw a sample of 120 persons from a population of 500 adult church members. To do this we first assign each of our 500 persons a number from 001 to 500. We then turn to a table of random numbers (see table M in the Appendix to *Fundamentals of Social Statistics* by Kirk Elifson, Richard Runyon and Audrey Haber or most other statistics texts for such a table). The table will have many rows and columns of digits which have been randomly generated by a computer. Start with any row or column to begin sampling from the list of 500 people. If we begin with the first column in the Elifson text and choose the first three digits from each row of this column we obtain the following numbers: 100, 375, 084, 990, 128, 660, 310 and so forth. Any number over 500 (the highest number assigned to any church member) or any repeated number is discarded, and we continue until we have chosen 120 usable numbers. Each of these numbers represents someone from the original list of 500 in the population. Each would be part of our sample and would receive a questionnaire.[12]

There are many ways to draw a sample. In some cases a researcher may, for instance, want to draw a *stratified random sample*. In such cases a population is divided into parts (perhaps into racial or age groups) and random sampling takes place within these parts rather than among the whole population. Random sampling can also be done by computer programs written for this purpose and through the use of some calculators which generate random digits.

3. *Analysis: The Contingency Table*. The contingency table or cross-tabulation table is used to analyze the relationship between two variables. It shows the joint distribution of the variables in tabular form. Chart 6 illustrates a very simple cross-tabulation.

As illustrated in the table, we essentially place "people" into cells of a table. In this case the data are *not* real. The top left cell contains the three persons in the sample who are both blue-eyed and prejudiced, as measured by their responses to a questionnaire. Similarly, the upper right cell contains those who are both brown-eyed and prejudiced. We analyze this table by computing percentages down the columns and comparing them across the rows. Thirty percent of the blue-eyed people are prejudiced and seventy percent are nonprejudiced, for a total of one hundred percent. The column of brown-eyed persons is percentaged in the same manner. To draw conclusions we compare the percentages across rows to see if they differ greatly in magnitude. In this example ninety percent of brown-eyed people are prejudiced as compared to only 30 percent of blue-eyed persons. Thus, we can conclude that brown-eyed people are more likely to be prejudiced. A definite relationship exists, but even if this data were real we could not assume causation.

Obviously, the twenty people depicted in chart 6 represent a very small sample and the findings of this survey were somewhat more dramatic than what one would really find in an investigation of eye color and prejudice. Nevertheless, the chart illustrates how a table should be set up.

We refer next to chart 7, where some guidelines are introduced for summing tables. Rather than using stick people, we now see N-25, for instance. "N" refers to the number of persons (or churches) which fall into that cell, row or column. The first rule in table analysis is to put the independent variable at the top of the table. This naturally means that the dependent variable goes on the side. The order could be reversed, but to avoid confusing oneself and others, it is best to stick to this procedure. As mentioned earlier, we percentage down columns and then compare the values of these percentages across rows. The raw numbers are relatively unimportant and can lead to misinterpretation if considered improperly. Avoid mistakes by dealing with the percentages.

In this table we see that the independent variable has three values, instead of the two seen in chart 6. To interpret it we still compare across rows. Looking at the top row, we see that the percentage value steadily increases as we move from left to right. As an illustration, we can assume that the independent variable was age and it included the following three values: (1) 18-35; (2) 36-50; and (3) 51 and older. The dependent variable might be satisfaction with worship services (1-satisfied and 2-dissatisfied). If this were the case, we could say that a relationship existed between age and satisfaction with worship. As age increased the percent of persons satisfied with the worship services also increased. In other words, if this were real data (which it is not) we could conclude that older persons are more likely to be satisfied with the worship services than are younger age groups.

As indicated earlier, relationships vary according to their strength. When we compare the row percentages in chart 7 we can note a very large percentage difference between the first column and the third column. This indicates a strong relationship or association. If, however, the row percentages had been 27 percent, 31 percent, 35 percent across the top of table 7, such small differences would indicate a weak relationship. Many statistics exist which measure the strength of association. The statistic of "gamma" is one of these. The reader should refer to a statistics or research methodology text for help in computing one of these statistics. There also exist measures of statistical significance, which indicate the likelihood that the relationship may have resulted from chance factors alone. Chi-square is often used for this purpose.

Chart 6

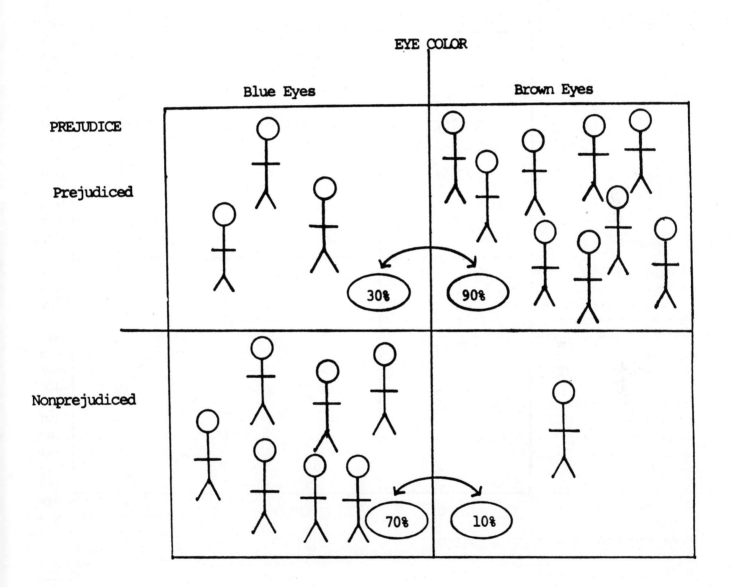

Chart 7

SUMMING TABLES

Independent or
"Causal" Variable

		(1)	(2)	(3)
Dependent or "Caused" Variable	(1)	(n=25) 27.8%	(n=55) 57.9%	(n=70) 73.7%
	(2)	(n=65) 72.2%	(n=40) 42.1%	(n=25) 26.3%
		(n=90) 100%	(n=95) 100%	(n=95) 100%

Rules

1. Place independent variable at the top of table

2. Place dependent variable at the side of table

3. Percentage down columns

4. Compare percentages across rows

Chart 8

CHURCH GROWTH BY URBAN LOCATION

	(1) Midtown (N=0)	(2) Inner City (N=2)	(3) Inner-Urban Neighborhood (N=15)	(4) Outer-Urban Neighborhood (N=24)	(5) City Suburb (N=17)	(6) Metropolitan Suburb (N=19)	(7) Fringe Suburb (N=15)	(8) Fringe Village (N=6)	(9) Fringe Settlement (N=6)	(10) Independent City (N=5)	(11) Rural Village (N=5)	(12) Rural Settlement (N=4)
Growing	0.0%	50.0%	0.0%	12.5%	11.8%	42.1%	73.3%	83.3%	50.0%	40.0%	40.0%	25.0%
Plateau	0.0	0.0	13.3	45.8	52.9	21.1	26.7	16.7	16.7	40.0	60.0	75.0
Declining	0.0	50.0	86.7	41.7	35.3	36.8	0.0	0.0	33.3	20.0	0.0	0.0
	100.0%	100.0%	100.0%	100.0%	100.0%	100.0%	100.0%	100.0%	100.0%	100.0%	100.0%	100.0%

Gamma = -.52, p .001. If only types 1-8 are included, Gamma = -.64.

6.7.2 *Using Contextual Data and Church Records: An Example*

Correlational designs use many types of data other than from questionnaires and interviews. In analyzing congregations researchers will often use church records as a source for key variables. If they are interested in measuring the various sources of church growth or in baptisms, church school or many other programs, the dependent variable will be derived from church records. Similarly, when investigating the effects of context on a church it is generally more effective to find objective measures of that context, rather than relying on survey responses.

The variables created from church records, the census and from other sources can be treated as continuous variables (with many possible values) and analyzed using appropriate measures of correlation, such as Pearson's r, or they can be categorized and analyzed using contingency tables. In most cases the church researcher will use contingency tables and conduct the type of analysis described in the previous section.

An example of how to use church records and contextual data is provided by a fairly recent study of church growth and decline in Memphis, Tennessee.[13] In this study the dependent variable of interest was church membership change over a ten-year period. All Southern Baptist churches were categorized as being either growing, on a plateau, or declining according to the overall trend in their membership records over the period of study. The independent variable was the contextual variable of urban location. The city had been previously divided into regions according to a community typology developed by Douglas Walrath[14] and it was hypothesized that the great differences in contextual characteristics among these regions would necessarily impact the ability of white Protestant churches to grow.

Churches were plotted into the various regions of the city and their membership trends categorized. Next, a contingency table was constructed which revealed a fairly strong relationship between church growth and urban location. This table is shown in chart 8.

The table shows that few Southern Baptist churches are left in or near the center of Memphis. Most have long since moved or died in response to commercialization, population decline, and racial transition. Moving farther out to neighborhood areas and suburban territory, a trend becomes very clear. The percentage of churches growing steadily increases and the percentage of churches declining steadily drops as one moves farther out. The trend is so strong that in inner urban neighborhoods none of the Southern Baptist churches manage to grow, and in the fringe suburbs and the

fringe villages none of the churches are in decline. Once past the growing fringe of the city, a new set of factors impinge upon the church and the trend observed in areas 3 through 8 weakens considerably.

The overall relationship seen in chart 8 is a strong one, and its strength can be measured by a statistic: gamma. A gamma of -.52 indicates the strength of this relation (gammas, like other measures of association range from 0.0 (or no relationship) to +1.0 or -1.0, which indicates a perfect relationship). Note also that leaving off categories 9-12 increases the size of the gamma, indicating that the relationship is stronger when only the first eight categories are used. This was no surprise because the relationship between the two variables is most visible in this part of the table.

The contingency table can also be presented in graphic form, which makes it much easier to comprehend.

In chart 9 we see data from five denominations in Memphis categorized in a manner similar to that shown in the previous chart.[15] The size of the bars represent the percentage of churches in a given area of the city which are growing, plateaued or declining. The solid black bar, which indicates growth, can be seen to steadily increase in size as we move from downtown to the newer suburbs. Similarly, the striped bar, which indicates decline steadily shrinks from its huge size in the downtown category to the newer suburbs. Presenting data in this format or in another graphic form is a very effective way of communicating. Use contingency tables to conduct your analysis, but consider graphics for your report.

6.7.3 *When Research Is Complete*

When final results are obtained from a correlational design or any other design we have considered in this chapter, this does not mean that research on the congregation should end. Just because one question is answered does not imply that *all* have been answered. Research will almost always uncover additional areas which need investigation and this is especially true in institutions as complex as the local church. Of course, a research project must end at some point with a report and its presentation to those who need the information. But we hope those on the study team, the pastor, church staff members or other church leaders will see the value in research and the need to study their church (or churches), the members and the community or context in which the church exists. Churches and their settings are constantly changing and to know how to act and react we must be students in a never-ending process of social research.

Chart 9

CHURCH GROWTH BY URBAN LOCATION*

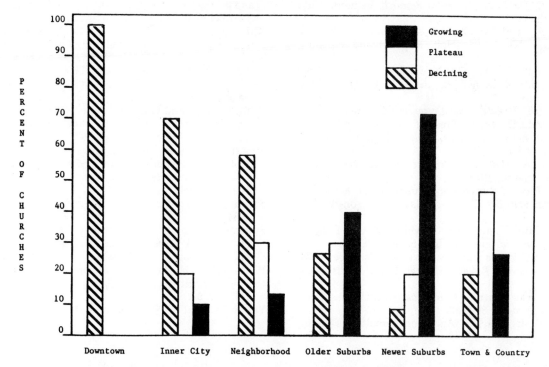

*1970-1980 membership change among all churches of 5 mainline denominations in Shelby County, Tennessee (Memphis). Denominations included Southern Baptist, United Methodist, Presbyterian Church in the United States, and Lutheran Church—Missouri Synod.

NOTES

1. See, for instance, *Fundamentals of Social Statistics* by Kirk Elifson, Richard Runyon and Audrey Haber (Reading, Mass.: Addison-Wesley, 1982) and *The Practice of Social Research* by Earl Babbie (Belmont, Cal.: Wadsworth, 1982).
2. An ethnography is essentially a description of a single group (or culture) which uses certain research procedures common to anthropology (although used by other disciplines as well). Even though some would hold that an ethnographic study is a research design in its own right, the fact that it involves the intensive description of a single case leads us to categorize the ethnographic study as a special type of case study.
3. An ethnographic study, which may result from the ethnographic interview and (or) participant observation, is considered here as a subtype of the case study.
4. Richard Davies, *Handbook for Doctor of Ministries Projects* (Lanham, Md.: University Press of America, 1984), pp. 124-28.
5. See James P. Spradley, *The Ethnographic Interview* (New York: Holt, Rinehart and Winston, 1979). Also see *Participant Observation* (New York: Holt, Rinehart and Winston, 1980) by the same author.
6. Pertti Pelto, *Anthropological Research: The Structure of Inquiry* (New York: Harper & Row, 1970), p. 92.
7. There is a debate in anthropology over the need for objective research procedures to either supplement or supplant traditional, more subjective techniques such as participant observation. Some would hold that anthropologists have conducted enough ethnographies and that the science had best move to analysis and theory development if it is to be accepted as a mature discipline by the larger scientific community. For a number of decades this has been the direction in which anthropology has moved, as evidenced by the increasing emphasis on correlational designs and statistics in methodological texts. Other anthropologists, on the other hand, have begun to reemphasize the ethnography and the validity of simply trying to understand "who" a people are.

   Most anthropologists would take a centrist position, whereby traditional ethnographic techniques are supplemented by questionnaires, formal interviews and inferential statistics. See John A. Brim and David H. Spain, *Research Design in Anthropology* (New York: Holt, Rinehart and Winston, 1974). Also see Pertti J. Pelto and Gretel H. Pelto, *Anthropological Research: The Structure of Inquiry*, second edition (Cambridge: Cambridge University Press, 1978).
8. This illustration was loosely adapted from Pelto, 1970, p. 93.
9. Davies, 1984, pp. 12-13.
10. Ibid., pp. 14-17.
11. The five questions were part of a scale used in a National Opinion Research Center poll. The full text of the interview schedule was reproduced in the appendix to Gertrude Selznick and Stephen Steinberg, *The Tenacity of Prejudice* (New York: Harper & Row, 1969).
12. This description was adapted from Elifson, 1982, p. 273.
13. Kirk Hadaway, "Church Growth (and Decline) in a Southern City," *Review of Religious Research* 23 (1982): 372-86.
14. Douglas Walrath, "Social Change and Local Churches: 1951-1975" in Dean Hoge and David Roozen (eds.), *Understanding Church Growth and Decline* (New York: The Pilgrim Press, 1979), pp. 252-56.
15. This chart is reproduced from "The Church in the Urban Setting" by C. Kirk Hadaway, in Larry Rose and C. Kirk Hadaway (eds.), *The Urban Challenge.* © Copyright 1982 Broadman Press. All rights reserved. Used by permission.

For Further Reading on Methods for Congregational Studies _____

Babbie, Earl R. *The Practice of Social Research*. Belmont, Cal.: Wadsworth, 1982.

Brim, John A., and David H. Spain. *Research Design in Anthropology*. New York: Holt, Rinehart and Winston, 1974.

Campbell, Donald T., and Julian N. Stanley. *Experimental and Quasi-experimental Designs for Research*. Chicago: Rand McNally, 1963.

Davies, Richard. *Handbook for Doctor of Ministries Projects*. Lanham, Md.: University Press of America, 1984.

Davis, James A. *Elementary Survey Analysis*. Englewood Cliffs, N.J.: Prentice Hall, 1971.

Dillman, Don A. *Mail and Telephone Surveys*. New York: Wiley-Interscience, 1978.

Elifson, Kirk, Richard Runyon, and Audry Haber. *Fundamentals of Social Statistics*. Reading, Mass.: Addison-Wesley, 1982.

Fitz-Gibbon, Carol T., and Lynn L. Morris. *How to Design a Program Evaluation*. Beverly Hills: Sage, 1978.

———. *How to Calculate Statistics*. Beverly Hills: Sage, 1978.

Fowler, Floyd J. *Survey Research Methods*. Beverly Hills: Sage, 1984.

Hadaway, C. Kirk. "Learning from Urban Church Research." *Review and Expositor* 80 (Fall, 1983), pp. 543-52.

Hair, Joseph F., Jr., Rolph E. Anderson, Ronald L. Tatham, and Bernie J. Grablowsky. *Multivariate Data Analysis*. Tulsa: Petroleum Publishing Company, 1979.

Kirk, Roger E. *Experimental Design: Procedures for the Behavioral Sciences*, second edition. Belmont, Cal.: Brooks/Cole, 1982.

Morris, Lynn L., and Carol T. Fitz-Gibbon. *Evaluator's Handbook*. Beverly Hills: Sage, 1978.

———. *How to Deal with Goals and Objectives*. Beverly Hills: Sage, 1978.

Pelto, Pertti J., and Gretel H. Pelto. *Anthropological Research: The Structure of Inquiry*, second edition. Cambridge: Cambridge University Press, 1978.

Spradley, James P. *The Ethnographic Interview*. New York: Holt, Rinehart and Winston, 1979.

———. *Participant Observation*. New York: Holt, Rinehart and Winston, 1980.

Stewart, David W. *Secondary Research*. Beverly Hills: Sage, 1984.

Sudman, Seymour, and Norman M. Bradburn. *Asking Questions: A Practical Guide to Questionnaire Design*. San Francisco: Jossey-Bass, 1982.

Weiss, Carol H. *Evaluation Research: Methods of Assessing Program Effectiveness*. Englewood Cliffs, N.J.: Prentice-Hall, 1972.

Yin, Robert K. *Case Study Research*. Beverly Hills: Sage, 1984.

CHAPTER 7

Afterword: The Double Challenge

7.1 Dealing with "Messes"

Oftentimes the motivation for congregational studies is an immediate problem: How is this church going to deal with changes in its community? What can be done about the breakdown in communication between the members and the pastor? Who is going to raise the money needed for the programs the church needs? The motivation is what chapter 1 called a "mess." One of the goals of this handbook is to provide concrete assistance to people who want and need to deal with questions such as these—with "messes."

A challenge of congregational studies, in other words, is to help people solve problems. In doing so it understands problems as entry points for deepened understanding of the congregation's character and mission. This is the point of the framework for thinking about the congregation that was presented in chapter 1 and that has informed the structure and content of the subsequent chapters. How people think about congregations makes a difference in the ways they work with them. Thus, if Hope United Church of Christ is to find a pastor who will stay around long enough to rebuild the congregation's fading self-image, or if High Ridge Presbyterian Church is to deal with its conflict over champagne at a wedding reception, these churches need to be helped to see their immediate problems in relationship to the fullness of their lives as a people of God. In the language of the framework of this handbook, they need to see the relationship between the current "mess" and their *identity* as a people, their location in a particular *social context*, their *program*, and the *processes* that help shape their life.

7.2 Beyond Problem Solving

The promise of congregational studies does not end, however, with its usefulness in solving problems. Part of the excitement of congregational studies, and its potential, lies also in congregations' wrestling with the immediate, concrete problems of their lives—their "messes"—in the light of God's intentions for them. St. Augustine's internal conflict over the appropriateness of black liberation spirituals in the Sunday service, and Heritage United Methodist Church's argument over the relative merits of a new housing program for the elderly and new efforts to reach young families, for example, are more than problems to be solved. They are also opportunities to engage in the most creative form of practical theology. It is as church people address immediate problems in a disciplined way that they discover their essence. As Don S. Browning has put it:

Your job [as students of congregational life] is more than just studying the congregation; you must study, interpret, and understand with an end toward action, prescription, decision. You have the task of relating more or less theoretical and scientific frameworks of interpretation toward the end of *praxis*. You furthermore have the task of relating and using perspectives that are clearly partial, that thematize certain aspects of the total situation but neglect others and, for that reason alone, are inevitably reductive. And you do all this in order to take faithful Christian thought and action.[1]

In the linking of research and action, of inquiry and decision making, of disciplined and prayerful analysis of what now is and what a congregation is called to become lies one of the special and never-finished tasks of church leaders. It is a peculiar calling for which there are few road maps and manuals; it is the special challenge of congregational studies.

7.3 Putting It Together in the Congregation: The Unwritten Section

This handbook has presented a large number of techniques and tools for examining individual dimensions of congregational life. No congregation is likely to use them all! Pastors, those who work with congregations, and local church study teams will pick and choose based on an assessment of the needs of their congregation. Many will want to modify or reshape these tools to meet the needs of a particular congregation in a particular setting. This is not only recognized by the authors; it is encouraged.

The handbook has not presented a step-by-step outline for congregational analysis. There are books available that do this, some of them very well. Intentionally not including such an outline reflects a bias on the authors' part: that the day when a single set of procedures or a single set of materials can be expected to meet the needs of all congregations has passed (if, indeed, it ever existed!). There is simply no one best way for studying congregations.

At the same time, individual chapters (especially chapters 1 and 6) provide guidance to study committees in deciding which specific tools and methods are most appropriate for illuminating the specific questions they bring to the quest for congregational self-understanding. Included are concrete suggestions for "getting started" and for project design. Some readers may find the absence of a "How to Study the Congregation" checklist a problem; more, we think, will find it an appropriate lodging of responsibility where it belongs: with those who know the congregation best and care most about it—its own leaders and members.

The decision to avoid the appearance of seeming to have "all the answers" or to present a standardized technique for congregational analysis grows in part from an appreciation of the work of Donald A. Schoen[2] who has studied ways that "professionals" approach problems. He refers to it as the "knowledge in action" of "reflective practitioners." Reflective practice involves bringing to the "messes" that professionals confront one's values, past experience, analysis of what is going on, and openness to the "talk-back" from the situation. This makes reflective practice much more a transactional conversation with the situation than an objective, detached relationship implied by technical rationality.[3]

The promise of congregational studies depends on a discovery of a new relationship between the religious professional and the congregation itself, one which relies far less on applying pre-existing solutions to problems than on an ability, as reflection practitioners, to analyze the ministerial context, its opportunities and constraints, and to frame responses appropriate to one's convictions about the church *and* the particularities of the situation. That's a tall order for Fr. Cummings of St. Augustine's, for the Rev. Deborah

Jones of Heritage Methodist, for the conference minister working with Hope United Church, for the pastor of High Ridge Presbyterian Church, and for those who work with congregations like them. There are tools and approaches that can help, and this handbook contains many of them; but the tools themselves are not the answer. That answer lies as much in the life and heart of the congregation itself as in anything brought to it from the outside.

7.4 A Second Invitation

This handbook began with an invitation to congregational studies. It closes with another invitation: to use the materials that are presented in the various chapters—and to improve on them! The handbook is in no sense a final word, but one among many and what its authors hope will be many more. There are concrete ways that new ideas and approaches to congregational studies can be shared.

The simplest, but the most important way persons concerned about congregations can contribute to a deepened understanding of congregational life and mission is to become more self-conscious about the ways they share information about their own congregations. Experience, when accompanied by disciplined reflection on experience, is an extraordinary teacher. The authors of this handbook invite readers to share with colleagues in ministry—and with the wider community of persons committed to congregational studies as an instrument of local church life and mission—what they are learning as they use the methods contained here and as they develop new approaches to understanding the congregation.[4]

The Rollins Center for Church Ministries[5] maintains and periodically updates a *Directory* of individuals and groups engaged in the study of the congregation. Readers are invited to submit their names and specific areas of interest in congregational studies for inclusion in subsequent editions. The Rollins Center also collects descriptions of tools for congregational study and intervention for publication in future editions of *The Whole Church Catalog*. The other institutions represented in the Project Team for Congregational Study (listed in the Preface) also welcome readers' interest in their ongoing education and service programs aimed at strengthening local church life and mission.

NOTES

1. Don S. Browning, "Integrating the Perspectives," in Carl S. Dudley, ed., *Building Effective Ministry* (San Francisco: Harper & Row, 1983), p. 221.
2. Donald A. Schoen, *The Reflective Practitioner: How Professionals Think in Action*, (New York: Basic Books, 1982).
3. For an extended discussion, see Jackson W. Carroll, "The Pro-

fessional Model of Ministry—Is It Worth Saving," *Theological Education* Vol. 21 (Spring, 1985), pp. 7-48.
4. One vehicle for doing this is *Alban Institute Action Information*, a newsletter published six times a year "for people who care about congregations" by the Alban Institute (Mount Saint Alban, Washington, D.C. 20016).
5. Candler School of Theology, Emory University, Atlanta, GA 30322.

GENERAL APPENDIX

The following questionnaire, The Parish Profile Inventory (PPI), is placed at the end of the entire book rather than after a specific chapter, since it is referred to in several chapters. The PPI was developed by Hartford Seminary for use as a general study instrument for congregations and, at the time of this writing, has been used in some 200 congregations for a variety of purposes, including program evaluation, needs assessment, planning and, especially, pastoral search consultants.

Two recently developed, shorter versions of the PPI, more tailored for particular uses, are available, one specifically designed for pastoral search processes, the other for planning. The longer, general instrument is included here because of its relevance to the four dimensions of the congregation discussed in this handbook.*

*Further information about the PPI is available from the Center for Social and Religious Research, Hartford Seminary, 77 Sherman Street, Hartford, Conn. 06105.

Parish Profile Inventory

The purpose of this questionnaire is to help your church think about its present life and plan for the future.

Simply check the appropriate box or supply the required information as indicated. When answering questions with a limited number of choices, please choose the answer that comes *closest* to the right answer for you, even if it does not fit perfectly. Unanswered items reduce the usefulness of the inventory.

Please, do not sign your name on the questionnaire. We want to guarantee that your individual answers will be held in strictest confidence.

In some cases, more than one person in a household will receive an inventory. That is the way it is supposed to be, and it is important for each person to work independently and complete separate questionnaires. You will receive instructions from your church on how to return your inventory. If you misplace these instructions, you may use the address printed on the back cover.

Feel free to share any comments or concerns you have about the inventory. Space is provided on the back for that purpose, and for sharing any additional information about your church that you think would be helpful.

Thank you for your cooperation. We hope you enjoy filling out the questionnaire, and that in addition to assisting your church, you may find it a helpful means of reflecting on your faith and the meaning of your church experience.

Parish Profile Inventory

I. TASKS OF THE CHURCH

Listed below are a number of tasks that a local congregation is likely to perform as it seeks to give expression to its unique understanding of Christian ministry. Please respond to each task in two ways:

    (1) In your judgement, how *important should* the task be in your congregation?

    (2) How *satisfied* are *you* with your congregation's *current* performance of the task?

	Importance				Satisfaction			
Worship and Sacraments	Very Much	Much	Some	Little Or None	Very Much	Much	Some	Little Or None
1. Providing worship that deepens members' understanding of the sources and meaning of the Bible, the Church, and the Christian tradition.	☐	☐	☐	☐	☐	☐	☐	☐
2. Providing worship that nurtures, uplifts and strengthens individuals to carry on their daily lives.	☐	☐	☐	☐	☐	☐	☐	☐
3. Providing worship that challenges members to relate the Gospel to the issues and situations that confront them in the world.	☐	☐	☐	☐	☐	☐	☐	☐
4. Providing worship that helps members share each other's faith, doubt, joy and sorrow.	☐	☐	☐	☐	☐	☐	☐	☐
5. Providing worship that reaffirms the familiar traditions of *your* religious heritage, e.g., hymns, liturgy, sacraments, etc.	☐	☐	☐	☐	☐	☐	☐	☐
6. Providing worship that expresses the Gospel in contemporary language and forms.	☐	☐	☐	☐	☐	☐	☐	☐
7. Providing worship that helps members express their joy and thanks giving for God's gifts to them.	☐	☐	☐	☐	☐	☐	☐	☐
Mission and Outreach								
1. Encouraging members to view their daily life and work as a place for ministry.	☐	☐	☐	☐	☐	☐	☐	☐
2. Carrying out acts of charity to needy persons.	☐	☐	☐	☐	☐	☐	☐	☐
3. Involvement in community issues.	☐	☐	☐	☐	☐	☐	☐	☐
4. Supporting the world mission of the church through study and giving.	☐	☐	☐	☐	☐	☐	☐	☐
5. Encouraging members to understand and act on the relationship of the Christian faith to social, political and economic issues.	☐	☐	☐	☐	☐	☐	☐	☐
6. Sharing the Good News of the Gospel with the unchurched.	☐	☐	☐	☐	☐	☐	☐	☐
Spiritual Development								
1. Providing for the guidance and growth of members' spiritual life.	☐	☐	☐	☐	☐	☐	☐	☐
2. Helping members develop practices of prayer and meditation.	☐	☐	☐	☐	☐	☐	☐	☐
3. Helping members develop a stronger personal relationship with God.	☐	☐	☐	☐	☐	☐	☐	☐
4. Helping members to encounter God in serving persons.	☐	☐	☐	☐	☐	☐	☐	☐

	Importance				Satisfaction			
Caring and Community	Very Much	Much	Some	Little Or None	Very Much	Much	Some	Little Or None
1. Developing fellowship opportunities in which members can be with and get to know one another.	☐	☐	☐	☐	☐	☐	☐	☐
2. Encouraging members to care for and support one another.	☐	☐	☐	☐	☐	☐	☐	☐
3. Providing pastoral care and counseling to help members deal with their problems.	☐	☐	☐	☐	☐	☐	☐	☐
4. Providing a caring ministry to sick and shut-in persons.	☐	☐	☐	☐	☐	☐	☐	☐
Stewardship								
1. Educating and challenging members to support the work of the church.	☐	☐	☐	☐	☐	☐	☐	☐
2. Helping members understand and view their use of money, time and talents *in all areas of their life* as expressions of Christian stewardship.	☐	☐	☐	☐	☐	☐	☐	☐
3. Helping members understand their Christian responsibility for the care, development and conservation of the earth's natural resources.	☐	☐	☐	☐	☐	☐	☐	☐
Education								
1. Teaching children and youth about the Bible, the church and the Christian Tradition.	☐	☐	☐	☐	☐	☐	☐	☐
2. Providing education for children and youth that encourages an open search for a faith that makes sense of their lives.	☐	☐	☐	☐	☐	☐	☐	☐
3. Providing fellowship opportunities for youth to be together in a Christian context.	☐	☐	☐	☐	☐	☐	☐	☐
4. Providing educational events that allow children, youth *and adults* to share with each other.	☐	☐	☐	☐	☐	☐	☐	☐
5. Providing adult education that teaches about the Bible, church and Christian Tradition.	☐	☐	☐	☐	☐	☐	☐	☐
6. Providing adult education that deals with contemporary issues, topics and problems.	☐	☐	☐	☐	☐	☐	☐	☐

II. ORGANIZATIONAL CHARACTERISTICS:

In order to carry out its tasks effectively, every church must deal with certain organizational issues, such as making decisions and sharing information. Listed below are a number of statements describing how a variety of such issues might be handled. To what extent do you agree or disagree that each statement describes your congregation? A "don't know" response is provided, *but please use it only when absolutely necessary.*

Communication	Strongly Agree	Moderately Agree	Slightly Agree	Disagree	Don't Know
1. There is ample opportunity for members to make known their concerns and hopes for the congregation to leaders and other members.	☐	☐	☐	☐	☐
2. Members are well informed about the activities taking place in the congregation.	☐	☐	☐	☐	☐
3. Members are well informed about what the various committees and groups in the congregation are doing.	☐	☐	☐	☐	☐

	Strongly Agree	Moderately Agree	Slightly Agree	Disagree	Don't Know
4. The community around the church is well informed about the activities taking place in the congregation.	☐	☐	☐	☐	☐
5. Members are well informed about the concerns, needs and activities of the neighborhood/community around the church	☐	☐	☐	☐	☐

Assessment and Planning

1. The congregation has a clear statement of goals *and* a plan for meeting them.	☐	☐	☐	☐	☐
2. Study of the needs of the congregation and the community is regularly undertaken as the basis for church planning.	☐	☐	☐	☐	☐
3. Committee and group chairpersons regularly attempt to discover how members feel about the way their committee or group is functioning.	☐	☐	☐	☐	☐
4. There is a regular process for laypersons to give feedback to the pastor about his/her performance.	☐	☐	☐	☐	☐

Decision Making

1. Those who make important decisions about the life of our church consistently represent the thinking of the majority of members.	☐	☐	☐	☐	☐
2. Important decisions about the life of the church are rarely made without being openly discussed and debated by a broad spectrum of church leaders and members.	☐	☐	☐	☐	☐
3. The theological and biblical implications of important decisions are always thoroughly and explicitly discussed.	☐	☐	☐	☐	☐
4. It can*not* be said of our church that "some members seem to have a lot more influence over policy than others."	☐	☐	☐	☐	☐

Resource Development

1. The congregation has an effective stewardship program.	☐	☐	☐	☐	☐
2. The congregation has an effective program of new member recruitment.	☐	☐	☐	☐	☐
3. Lay leaders are provided the training they need for their committee and task assignments.	☐	☐	☐	☐	☐
4. Members are encouraged to discover their particular gifts for ministry and services to the church *and* provided the necessary training and resources to develop them.	☐	☐	☐	☐	☐
5. It is important in our congregation for the pastor(s) to participate regularly in continuing education.	☐	☐	☐	☐	☐

	Strongly Agree	Moderately Agree	Slightly Agree	Disagree	Don't Know

Church Identity

1. It is easy to summarize for visitors and non-members how our congregation differs from other congregations in the area. ☐ ☐ ☐ ☐ ☐
2. There is common agreement among members as to what our congregation stands for. ☐ ☐ ☐ ☐ ☐
3. There are clear expectations for being a member of this church (for example, belief, participation, giving, etc.) ☐ ☐ ☐ ☐ ☐
4. When I think of this congregation, I usually think of *"we"* rather than *"they."* ☐ ☐ ☐ ☐ ☐

Church 'Climate'

1. Disagreements and conflicts are dealt with openly rather than hushed up or hidden behind closed doors. ☐ ☐ ☐ ☐ ☐
2. The predominant attitude of the membership is that conflict and disagreement can be a positive force toward growth rather than something to be avoided or suppressed. ☐ ☐ ☐ ☐ ☐
3. There is considerable acceptance *and* appreciation of differing opinions and beliefs among members. ☐ ☐ ☐ ☐ ☐
4. All things considered — worship, programs, policies, people — our church appears much the same today as it did ten years ago. ☐ ☐ ☐ ☐ ☐
5. Most members view change in policies and programs as a necessary *and* desirable dynamic in our church's life. ☐ ☐ ☐ ☐ ☐
6. There would be little negative reaction among members to experimenting with the style or order of Sunday worship. ☐ ☐ ☐ ☐ ☐
7. Members place considerable importance on doing things in the church in traditional ways. ☐ ☐ ☐ ☐ ☐
8. The current morale of our church members is high. ☐ ☐ ☐ ☐ ☐
9. There is a sense of excitement among members about our church's future. ☐ ☐ ☐ ☐ ☐
10. The church leadership (clergy and lay) has the full confidence and support of the membership. ☐ ☐ ☐ ☐ ☐

III. PERSONAL BELIEFS

1. Which of the following best expresses your belief about *God*?

(1) ☐ I do not believe in God.

(2) ☐ I really don't know what to believe about God.

(3) ☐ I do *not* believe in a creating and saving God, but I do believe in a higher power of some kind.

(4) ☐ God is the creator of an orderly world, but does not now guide it or intervene in its course of affairs or the lives of individuals.

(5) ☐ Although God has and can act in history and communicate with persons directly, it is not something that happens very often.

(6) ☐ God is constantly at work in the world from "above" directing people, nations and events.

(7) ☐ God is the world and is in every person, thing and event.

2. Which one of the following best expresses your view of the *Bible*?

(1) ☐ The Bible was written by men who lived so long ago that it is of little value today.

(2) ☐ The Bible is a valuable book because it was written by wise and good persons, but I do not believe it is really God's Word.

(3) ☐ The Bible is the record of many different persons' response to God and because of this persons and churches today are often times forced to interpret for themselves the Bible's basic moral and religious teachings.

(4) ☐ The Bible is the inspired Word of God and its basic moral and religious teachings are clear and true, even if it does contain some human error.

(5) ☐ The Bible is the actual Word of God and is to be taken literally.

3. Which of the following best expresses your belief about *sin* and *salvation*?

(1) ☐ Sin and salvation really don't have much meaning to me personally.

(2) ☐ Sin is a helpful way of talking about people's capacity to harm themselves and others, and salvation is a helpful way of talking about hope for a better future.

(3) ☐ I believe all people are inherently good, and to the extent sin and salvation have meaning to all, it has to do with people realizing or not realizing their human potential for good.

(4) ☐ Although people are sinful, all people participate in God's salvation regardless of how they live their life, even if they do not believe in God.

(5) ☐ All people are sinful but need only to believe in and ask for God's forgiveness to be saved.

(6) ☐ All people are sinful and if they are to be saved must earn it through living a good life, devoted to God.

IV. BIBLE IMAGES

The Bible presents a variety of images of faith in action. How descriptive of your current faith journey is each of the following passages?

	Very	Somewhat	A Little	Not At All
1. Oh that I knew where I might find God. (Job 23)	☐	☐	☐	☐
2. Love your Lord with all your heart . . . and your neighbor as yourself. (Mat . 22)	☐	☐	☐	☐
3. Go therefore and make disciples of all peoples. (Matt . 28)	☐	☐	☐	☐
4. Come unto me all you who are heavy laden and I will give you rest. (Matt . 11)	☐	☐	☐	☐
5. Do not love the world or the things in the world . . . all that is in the world is not of the Father . . . and passes away. (John 2)	☐	☐	☐	☐
6. What does the Lord require of me, but to do justice. (Micah 6)	☐	☐	☐	☐

	Very	Somewhat	A Little	Not At All
7. Day and night you punished me, Lord; then I confessed my sins to you . . . The wicked will have to suffer, but those who trust in the Lord are protected by God's constant love. (Psalm 32)	☐	☐	☐	☐
8. As long as you have done it to one of these the least of my people, you have done it unto me. (Matt . 25)	☐	☐	☐	☐
9. The best thing people can do is eat and drink and enjoy what they have earned. Even this comes from God who gives happiness to those who please him. (Ecclesiastes 2)	☐	☐	☐	☐
10. The Lord is my shepherd, I shall not want . . . I fear no evil for thou art with me . . . (Psalm 23)	☐	☐	☐	☐

V. SOCIAL ATTITUDES

Would you say you strongly agree, agree, disagree or strongly disagree with each of the following statements:

	Strongly Agree	Agree	Disagree	Strongly Disagree
1. The United States should freeze production of nuclear weapons regardless of what Russia does.	☐	☐	☐	☐
2. The use of marijuana should be made legal.	☐	☐	☐	☐
3. The law should allow doctors to perform an abortion for any woman who wants one.	☐	☐	☐	☐
4. It is wrong for a person to have sexual relations *before* marriage.	☐	☐	☐	☐
5. We are spending *too little* money on welfare programs in this country.	☐	☐	☐	☐
6. Women, if they work at all, should take feminine positions such as nursing, secretarial work, or child care.	☐	☐	☐	☐
7. Although Blacks may have achieved legal equality, I believe affirmative action should be used to help them achieve actual equality.	☐	☐	☐	☐
8. Because of their wealth and power, large corporations have a clear moral obligation to help the poor and needy in our country.	☐	☐	☐	☐
9. In a country based on religious freedom such as ours, it is *in*appropriate for Christians to try to impose their beliefs and moral values on others.	☐	☐	☐	☐

VI. TASKS OF THE PASTOR

In your judgement how high or low a priority would you like each of the following tasks to be for the pastor of this church. Remember, not every task can be highest priority.

	Very High	High	Moderate	Low
1. Handling administrative tasks effectively and efficiently.	☐	☐	☐	☐
2. Stewardship development.	☐	☐	☐	☐
3. Involving laity in planning, participating in, and leading church events.	☐	☐	☐	☐
4. Bringing new members into the fellowship of the church.	☐	☐	☐	☐
5. Involvement in local community activities, issues and problems.	☐	☐	☐	☐

	Very High	High	Moderate	Low
6. Planning and leading worship sensitive to the needs of the worshipping community.	☐	☐	☐	☐
7. Preaching the Word of God with urgency and conviction.	☐	☐	☐	☐
8. Attending to the spiritual development of members.	☐	☐	☐	☐
9. Visiting the sick and bereaved.	☐	☐	☐	☐
10. Being a caring and enabling counselor.	☐	☐	☐	☐
11. Developing a strong sense of community among members.	☐	☐	☐	☐
12. Supporting the world mission of the church.	☐	☐	☐	☐
13. Development and support of Christian education for all ages.	☐	☐	☐	☐
14. Holding before members critical issues of social justice and concern.	☐	☐	☐	☐

VIII. STYLE OF MINISTRY

Listed below are 7 pairs of characteristics of a good pastor. You will probably agree that both traits in each pair is desirable. *But if you had to choose*, which characteristic in each pair would you prefer in your pastor. Would you prefer the trait on the right, or would you prefer the trait on the left. Check one answer for each pair.

	Strongly Prefer	Slightly Prefer	or	Slightly Prefer	Strongly Prefer	
1. Expertise in Biblical and theological matters.	☐	☐		☐	☐	High degree of spirituality.
2. Good standing with your denominational officials.	☐	☐		☐	☐	A warm, outgoing, engaging personality.
3. Works hard to accomplish tasks.	☐	☐		☐	☐	Places feelings of others ahead of achieving goals.
4. Tends to be provoking and challenging.	☐	☐		☐	☐	Tends to be comforting and assuring.
5. In preaching and teaching usually emphasizes the Bible.	☐	☐		☐	☐	Usually emphasizes contemporary issues and ideas.
6. Helps people figure things out for themselves.	☐	☐		☐	☐	Advises people what to to do.
7. Is a strong administrator.	☐	☐		☐	☐	Is a strong preacher.

VIII. YOUR CHURCH PARTICIPATION

1. **What is the name of the local church for which you are filling out this questionnaire? (It is particularly important that you answer this.)**

_____

2. **How long have you been a member of this local church?** _____ Years

_____ I am not a member

3. **How far do you live from this church?** _____

4. **On the average, about how many times did you attend church worship during the past year?**
   - (1) ☐ None
   - (2) ☐ About once or twice a year
   - (3) ☐ About once or twice every three months
   - (4) ☐ About once a month
   - (5) ☐ About two or three times a month
   - (6) ☐ Four times a month or more

5. **In how many church organizations, committees, and groups do you hold membership (not counting congregational membership itself?)**
   - (1) ☐ None
   - (2) ☐ One
   - (3) ☐ Two
   - (4) ☐ Three
   - (5) ☐ Four or more

6. **How many leadership positions, if any, do you hold in these church groups?**
   - (1) ☐ None
   - (2) ☐ One
   - (3) ☐ Two
   - (4) ☐ Three
   - (5) ☐ Four or more

7. **How much time would you say you spend during the course of an average month in church affairs? (Including time for meetings, committee work, travel, study, worship, etc.)?**
   - (1) ☐ Less than one hour
   - (2) ☐ 1 - 5 hours
   - (3) ☐ 6 - 10 hours
   - (4) ☐ 11 - 15 hours
   - (5) ☐ 16 - 20 hours
   - (6) ☐ Over 20 hours

8. **Has your involvement in the congregation increased, decreased, or remained about the same in the last few years?**
   - (1) ☐ Increased
   - (2) ☐ Remained the same
   - (3) ☐ Decreased

8a. *If your participation has increased,* **which one of the following is the most important reason for that:**
   - (1) ☐ More time available
   - (2) ☐ Because of children
   - (3) ☐ Accepted office or other responsibility in the church
   - (4) ☐ More positive attitude toward the church.
   - (5) ☐ Better health
   - (6) ☐ Stronger faith

8b. *If your participation has decreased,* **which one of the following is the most important reason for that:**
   - (1) ☐ Less time available
   - (2) ☐ Children are less involved
   - (3) ☐ Given up office or other responsibility in the church
   - (4) ☐ More negative attitude toward the church
   - (5) ☐ Health problems
   - (6) ☐ Decreased faith

9. **Think for a moment of your five closest friends (individuals or couples) with whom you have social and recreational life. Do not include close relatives. How many are members of your congregation?**
   - (1) ☐ None
   - (2) ☐ One
   - (3) ☐ Two
   - (4) ☐ Three
   - (5) ☐ Four
   - (6) ☐ Five or more

10. **Suppose your congregation were in real danger of closing because of financial problems. How much would you be willing to increase your giving to the church in order to prevent this from happening?**
   - (1) ☐ None
   - (2) ☐ A little
   - (3) ☐ A moderate amount
   - (4) ☐ A good bit
   - (5) ☐ A great deal
   - (6) ☐ A very great deal

11. **Approximately how much does your family household contribute to your church per year? (If single or widowed, you as an individual?)**
   - (1) Under $100
   - (2) $100 - 199
   - (3) $200 - 299
   - (4) $300 - 449
   - (5) $450 - 599
   - (6) $600 - 749
   - (7) $750 - 999
   - (8) $1,000 - 1,249
   - (9) Over $1,250

12. **How many persons or families have you invited to visit or join your church in the past year?**
   - (1) None
   - (2) One
   - (3) Two or Four
   - (4) Five or more

IX. FINALLY, WE NEED A FEW ITEMS OF BACKGROUND INFORMATION ABOUT YOURSELF

1. **Gender?**
   - (1) Male
   - (2) Female

2. **Age?**
   - _____

3. **Race?**
   - (1) White
   - (2) Black
   - (3) Other _____

4. **Marital status?**
   - (1) Single
   - (2) Separated or divorced
   - (3) Widowed
   - (4) Married

   4a. *If married*, is your spouse a member of this church? (1) Yes (2) No
   4b. *If married*, is your spouse employed? (1) Yes, full time (2) Yes, part time (3) No

5. **How many children do you have in each of the following age groups?**
   - _____0 - 4 years   _____5 - 12 years   _____13 - 17 years

6. **What is your highest level of formal education?**
   - (1) Less than high school
   - (2) Some high school
   - (3) High school graduate
   - (4) Trade or vocational school
   - (5) Some college
   - (6) College degree
   - (7) Post graduate work
   - (8) Graduate or professional degree

7. **Are you (check one)?**
   - (1) Retired
   - (2) Full-time "houseperson"
   - (3) Employed part time
   - (4) Employed full time

   7a. If *employed*, what is your occupation? _____

8. **What is your family income range?**
   - (1) Under $7,500
   - (2) $7,500 - 14,999
   - (3) $15,000 - 24,999
   - (4) $25,000 - 34,999
   - (5) $35,000 - 49,999
   - (6) $50,000 - 74,999
   - (7) $75,000 or more

9. **How many years have you lived in this general area?** _____

10. **How likely is it that you might move out of this general area within the next three years?**
   - (1) Definitely will move
   - (2) Probably will move
   - (3) Might move (50/50 chance)
   - (4) Probably will not move
   - (5) Very unlikely to move

11. **In how many community clubs or organizations (social, political, civic, service, recreational, etc.) do you hold membership?**
   - (1) None
   - (2) One
   - (3) Two
   - (4) Three
   - (5) Four or more

INDEX

Analysis: categories of, 36-37; of parish history, 25
Anderson, Gary, 91
Anderson, James, 81
Anderson, Phillip, 96
Assumed goals, 135
Authority, 90, 91; and contracts, 96; and process, 81; tacit, 93

Bagnall, Jim, 105
Behrens, William, 91
Berge, William, 91
Berger, Peter, 52
Bradley, June, 90
Browning, Don S., 179
Building Effective Ministry (Dudley, ed.), 26

Calvin, John, 26
Carroll, Jackson, 29
Case study, 160, 163; as research design, 158
Causation, 172; and variables, 156
Census, 59, 123, 126; religious, 15, 75
Census Access for Planning in the Church, 68
Census Bureau, 68, 69
Census data, 16, 55; analysis of, 159; use of, 56, 68
Census geography, 55-56
Center for Social and Religious Research, 181
Character, 21, 22, 23, 45; analysis of, 44; definition of, 43; group, 23; and story, 46; and world view, 43
Chi-square, 172
Christ and Culture (Niebuhr), 31
Church Planning Questionnaire, A, 88
Church records: as data, 176
Clergy in the Crossfire (Smith), 89
Communication, 15; among members of congregation, 21, 33; informal, 96
Community groups: identification and study of, 70
Community mission: possibilities for, 76. *See also* Mission
Comparison: static group, 168
Conflict: in a church, 69, 168; and diversity, 101; management of, 12, 15

Congregational studies: aspects of, 13; in different denominational contexts, 124; planning for, 17; and program issues, 120; starting, 15-17; and theology, 18
Congregations Alive, 129
Consultants, 88, 96, 159
Content analysis: of written materials, 27
Context, 14, 15, 18, 23, 41, 107, 129, 159, 176; investigation of, 153; and program decisions, 130. *See also* Social context
Contingency tables, 176; and analysis, 172
Contracts: tacit, 100
Conrol groups, 164
Controlled experiment, 163-67
Correlational designs, 158, 167-75

Dahl, Robert, 71
Data analysis, 155
Data collection, 136, 155; in correlational designs, 170; and focus of process, 133; qualitative approaches to, 122; techniques of, 159, 160-62
Data gathering: in conflict settings, 102
Davies, Richard E., 164
Decision making, 15, 86; and formal process, 81; patterns of, 9; Demographic data, 56, 69; sources of, 68
Demographic picture, 41; of a group, 23; uses of, 43
Demographic setting: analysis of, 60
Demography, 13, 15, 23, 41
deS. Brunner, Edmund, 48
De Tocqueville, Alexis, 70
Direct observation, 83, 84, 95. *See also* Participant observation
Documents, 86, 90; and process, 84; study of, 83
Douglass, H. Paul, 48
Dulles, Avery, 31

Elifson, Kirk, 172
Ethnographic techniques, 15, 17
Evaluation: goal-free, 135
Evaluation process: people involved in, 134

Experimental research designs, 158, 163-65, 168

Family organization: pattern of, 125-26
Feedback, 95, 96
FIRO-B, 98
Formative evaluation, 132, 133
Frances, David, 106
Frequency distribution, 159
Frye, Northrup, 32
Fundamentals of Social Statistics (Elifson, Runyon, Haber), 172

Gamma, 172, 176
Gathering of Strangers, A. (Worley), 128
Geertz, Clifford, 22, 43
General Social Survey, 128, 170
Gladden, Richard K., 91
Goffman, Erving, 39, 40
Great tradition, 19, 27, 29, 31, 38; definition of, 26; and ritual, 37, 41; and symbols, 36
Green, Norman M., 91
Grierson, Denham, 17, 24, 27
Group discussion, 85-86; and congregational process, 83; and training, 94
Gustafson, James, 48

Haber, Audrey, 172
Handbook for Doctor of Ministry Projects (Davies), 164
Harper, R. S., 90
Hauerwas, Stanley, 43
Hearings, for gathering information, 103
Heritage, 21, 22, 23, 25, 27, 28, 32; and ritual, 41
Hess, Karl, 50
Hillman, James, 45
History, 22, 23; local, 26; parish, 24, 25
Holmes, Urban, 36
Hough, Joseph, 27, 31
House, Ernest, 132, 135
Hunter, Floyd, 71
Hypothesis, 168; in research, 154

Ideation, 106
Identity, 16, 29, 30, 31, 32, 38, 44, 82, 99, 120, 127, 128, 179; as aspect of congregation, 13; Christian, 83; collective, 22; components of, 14; of a congregation, 12, 21, 37; definition of, 12; demography and, 41; as

dimension of a system, 107; elements of, 22-23; and expectations, 40; and heritage, 25-26; investigation of, 153; and process, 81, 84; and program decisions, 130; rituals important to, 39; and social class, 42; and story, 46; and symbols, 35, 36; synonymous with character, 43; theological, 27
Index: construction of, 165, 168
Inductive approach: and qualitative measures, 121
Inductive exploration: techniques for, 27
Information: diagnosis of, 104; gathering of, 83; planning for use of, 17
Ingram, Larry, 40
Interpersonal conflict, 105
Interview, 86, 90, 95, 136, 153, 154, 159, 171, 176; collective, 85; and congregational process, 83; guided, 34-35, 44, 75-76; and oral history, 24; and problem solving, 106; and program evaluation, 135; structured group, 91; and study of character, 43; and training, 94; types of, 160-62; unstructured, 27

Jones, Ezra Earl, 81
Justice: congregation's sense of, 37

Keck, George, 91
Key informants, 69
Koberg, Don, 105

Leadership: questions about, 128; training and nurture of, 93
Likkert format, 165
Lippit, Gordon, 100
Little tradition, 19, 26, 27, 29, 31, 38; and ritual, 37, 39, 41
Local church, 22; diagnosing conflict in, 101; and penalty systems, 100; theological understandings of, 21
Local community: as context, 49
Luther, Martin, 26
Lutheran Nurture Study, 127

McKinney, William, 29
Marty, Martin, 7

Marx, Karl, 42
Mean, 157
Measurement criteria: in evaluation, 135
Measures: types of, 157
Median, 157
Membership characteristics: and program study, 125; used to infer needs, 129
Membership survey, 126
Method in Ministry (Whitehead, Whitehead), 31
Mission, 11; of the congregation, 30, 31; and context, 13. *See also* Community mission
Mitchell, Kenneth, 90
Mode, 157
Models of the Church (Dulles), 31
Morris, David, 50

National Council of Churches, 130
Needs, 97; process issue of, 98
Needs analysis, 159, 170; in research design, 157-58
Needs assessment, 122, 129, 131, 132, 133, 136, 137; of congregations, 121; definition of, 123; process of, 124; of programs, 121
Niebuhr, H. Richard, 31
Norms, 97, 100, 101; assessment, 100; process issue of, 98

Observation, 86, 90. *See also* Participant observation
Open system: congregation as, 48, 49
Operational beliefs: of congregation, 27
Oral history, 24, 153; and unstructured interviews, 162
Organizational development, 9, 12
Outside assistance: in congregational studies, 16

Parish Profile Inventory, 27, 42, 89, 127, 128, 181

Participant observation, 17, 27, 30, 44, 153, 162-63; and case study, 154; to reveal ritual, 40; and study of character, 43; and world view, 34. *See also* Observation
Patterns: dynamics of, 86; revealed in congregational studies, 8
Perrin, Norman, 24
Planning, 81; definition of, 86
Planning procedures, 88
Pluralist model, 71
Pluralization: of social worlds, 52
Pope, Liston, 73
Population pyramids, 15, 56, 59
Post Meeting Reaction Form, 96
Power elite model, 71
Privitization, 52
Problem definition, 15, 154
Problem solving, 81, 105-6; and subcommittees, 83
Process, 11, 12, 13, 14, 15, 82, 87, 106, 126; of conflict management, 102; definition of, 81; formal and informal, 81, 86; investigation of, 153; and planning procedures, 88; and problem solving, 105, 106, 107; and story, 46; study of, 83
Process Consultation: Its Role in Organization Development (Schein), 107
Program, 11, 14, 30, 41, 122, 129, 135, 179; and congregation, 13; definition of, 120; evolution of, 121; interaction with process, 83; investigation of, 153; planning, 12, 15; and story, 21
Program evaluation, 131, 132, 133, 136, 138; timing of, 122
Program goals, 88; lack of, 134
Project design, 154
Public meetings: for gathering information, 102

Qualitative data, 134
Qualitative measure, 121, 123, 125

Quantitative data, 121, 134
Quantitative measures, 121, 124, 132
Questionnaire, 85, 86, 90, 103, 136, 153, 160, 163, 172, 176; about community mission, 76; and congregational design, 154; construction of, 28, 170-71; and demography, 17; mailed, 102; and process, 84; and program evaluation, 132, 135; in research design, 158; and social survey, 159

Random sample, 171
Redfield, Robert, 26
Research design, 157; experimental, 158, 163-65, 168
Rites of intensification, 37, 38, 39
Rites of passage, 37, 38, 39
Ritual, 22, 36, 38, 41; analysis of, 40; group, 23; and identity, 37, 39
Role, 90; clarification, 81; conflict, 89, 105
Roozer, Robert, 29
Runyon, Richard, 172
Rusbuldt, Richard E., 90

Samples: types of, 156-57
Sanctions, 97, 98, 101
Schein, Edgar, 81, 107
Schoen, Donald A., 180
Shutz, William, 98
Single group panel, 164
Smaller Church Mission Guide, 130
Smaller Church Study Guide (Blunk), 129
Smith, Donald, 89, 128
Social context, 12, 13, 49, 51, 69, 82, 83, 88, 179; analysis of, 79; aspects of, 13; definition of, 12, 48; religion's role and, 74-75. *See also* Context
Social research: stereotypes of, 153
Social survey, 163; in correlational designs, 170-72
Stratified random sample, 172
Strengthening the Multiple Staff

(Anderson, Berge, Behrns, Keck, Wagner), 91
Study of the Unchurched American, 128
Summative evaluation, 132
Support giving, 81
Symbols, 21, 23, 35, 40; cross as, 36; and ritual, 37

Task, 90; agreement on, 87; clarity of, 90
Theological identity, 27, 28, 29, 31
Theology, 9
Time line, 24, 25
Training, 81; definition of, 93; formal and informal, 94
Transcendance: and the congregation, 36
Transforming Bible Study (Wink), 31
Tucker, Grayson, 88, 89
Turner, Victor, 36

Unblocked Boss, The (Woodcock, Frances), 106

van Gennep, Arnold, 37, 38
Variables: types of, 155-56
Visiting: for gathering information, 103

Wagner, Joseph, 91
Walrath, Douglas, 176
Weber, Max, 22
Weiss, Carol, 138
Wesley, John, 26
Whitehead, Evelyn Eaton, 31
Whitehead, James D., 31
Whole Church Catalog (Hopewell, ed.), 89, 180
Wink, Walter, 31
Woodcock, Mike, 106
World view, 22, 23, 32, 33, 34, 35; analysis of, 29; and ritual, 38, 39
Worley, Robert, 128
Wuthrow, Robert, 53

Yearbook of American and Canadian Churches, 7
Younger, George D., 72